Gridded Worlds: An Urban Anthology

Reuben Rose-Redwood • Liora Bigon
Editors

Gridded Worlds: An Urban Anthology

 Springer

Editors
Reuben Rose-Redwood
University of Victoria
Victoria, BC, Canada

Liora Bigon
Holon Institute of Technology
Holon, Israel

ISBN 978-3-319-76489-4   ISBN 978-3-319-76490-0   (eBook)
https://doi.org/10.1007/978-3-319-76490-0

Library of Congress Control Number: 2018938091

Printed on acid-free paper

This Springer imprint is published by the registered company Springer International Publishing AG part of Springer Nature.
The registered company address is: Gewerbestrasse 11, 6330 Cham, Switzerland

Reuben dedicates this book to his grandmothers Lillian and Jewel, and his mother Amber.
Liora dedicates this book to Guy and Itush, be-ahava.

Acknowledgments

We thank the editorial team at Springer for their support in publishing this anthology of key works on the urban grid. We are particularly grateful to our primary editor Margaret Deignan as well as editorial assistant Catalina Sava, project coordinator Karthika Menon, and project manager Sindhuja Gajendran. We also acknowledge Julian Bakker for assisting with the transcription of several chapters included in the present volume. Given the nature of this edited collection as an anthology, many of the chapters have been previously published in different scholarly outlets, which have required the securing of copyright permissions to reprint them in the current volume. We therefore acknowledge all the authors whose works are included in this anthology, particularly those who have revised their original publications specifically for the present book. The permission fees for the republication of these studies were paid for with funds from a Book Subvention Grant awarded to the lead editor by the University of Victoria, and we therefore thank the University of Victoria for its financial support.

Chapter 2 was originally published as Stanislawski, D. (1946). "The Origin and Spread of the Grid-Pattern Town." *Geographical Review*, 36(1): 105–120 (Copyright © 1946 by the American Geographical Society of New York, reproduced with permission of John Wiley & Sons, Inc.). Chapter 3 was originally published as Rose-Redwood, R. (2008). "Genealogies of the Grid: Revisiting Stanislawski's Search for the Origin of the Grid-Pattern Town." *Geographical Review*, 98(1): 42–58 (Copyright © 2008 by the American Geographical Society of New York, reproduced with permission of John Wiley & Sons, Inc.). Chapter 4 is an abridged version of Kostof, S. (1991). "The Grid." In S. Kostof, *The City Shaped: Urban Patterns and Meanings through History* (pp. 95–157). London: Little, Brown, and Co. (Copyright © 1991 by Thames and Hudson Ltd., reproduced with permission of Thames and Hudson Ltd.). Chapter 5 is a revised version of Grant, J. (2001). "The Dark Side of the Grid: Power and Urban Design." *Planning Perspectives*, 16(3): 219–241 (Copyright © 2001 by Taylor & Francis Ltd., reproduced with permission of Taylor & Francis Ltd.). Chapter 6 was originally published as Mazza, L. (2009). "Plan and Constitution: Aristotle's Hippodamus: Toward an 'Ostensive' Definition of Spatial Planning." *Town Planning Review*, 80(2): 113–141 (Copyright © 2009 by Liverpool

University Press, reproduced with permission of Liverpool University Press). Chapter 7 is a revised version of Zhu, J. (2004). "City Plan as Ideology." In J. Zhu, *Chinese Spatial Strategies: Imperial Beijing, 1420–1911* (pp. 28–44). London: RoutledgeCurzon (Copyright © 2004 by Jianfei Zhu, reproduced with permission of Taylor & Francis Group).

Chapter 8 was originally published as Stelter, G. (1993). "Military Considerations and Colonial Town Planning: France and New France in the Seventeenth Century." In R. Bennett (Ed.), *Settlements in the Americas: Cross-Cultural Perspectives* (pp. 210–237) (Copyright © 1993 by the Associated University Presses, reproduced with permission of Associated University Presses). Chapter 9 is an abridged version of Low, S. (1995). "Indigenous Architecture and the Spanish American Plaza in Mesoamerica and the Caribbean." *American Anthropologist*, 97(4): 748–762 (Copyright © 1995 by the American Anthropological Association, reproduced with permission of American Anthropological Association). Chapter 10 will be published as Bigon, L. and Hart, T. (2018). "Beneath the City's Grid: Vernacular and (Post)colonial Planning Interactions in Dakar, Senegal." *Journal of Historical Geography*, 59: 52–67 (Copyright © 2018 by Elsevier. Reproduced with permission of Elsevier). Chapter 11 was originally published as Sennett, R. (1990). "American Grids: The Grid Plan and the Protestant Ethic." *International Social Science Journal*, 42(3): 269–285 (Copyright © 1990 by Blackwell Publishing Ltd., reproduced with permission of Blackwell Publishing Ltd.). Chapter 12 was originally published as Rose-Redwood, R. (2011). "Mythologies of the Grid in the Empire City, 1811–2011." *Geographical Review*, 101(3): 396–413 (Copyright © 2011 by the American Geographical Society of New York, reproduced with permission of John Wiley & Sons, Inc.). Chapter 13 is an abridged version of Brown, K. (2001). "Gridded Lives: Why Kazakhstan and Montana are Nearly the Same Place." *American Historical Review*, 106(1): 17-48. (Copyright © 2001 by Oxford University Press, reproduced with permission of Oxford University Press). Chapter 14 is an abridged version of Geyh, P. (2009). "Urban Grids and Urban Imaginary: City to Cyberspace, Cyberspace to City." In P. Geyh, *Cities, Citizens, and Technologies: Urban Life and Postmodernity* (pp. 63–91). New York: Routledge (Copyright © 2009 by Taylor & Francis, reproduced with permission of Taylor & Francis).

Contents

List of Contributors

Liora Bigon is a Senior Lecturer in the General Studies Department at Holon Institute of Technology (HIT) and a Research Fellow at the Truman Research Institute for the Advancement of Peace at the Hebrew University of Jerusalem. Her research interests include urban and planning histories of Europe and Africa, and she regularly pursues fieldwork in Sub-Saharan African countries and has published over seventy peer-reviewed articles, encyclopedic entries, and books, including: *A History of Urban Planning in Two West African Colonial Capitals: Residential Segregation in British Lagos and French Dakar, 1850–1930* (2009), *Garden Cities and Colonial Planning: Transnationality and Urban Ideas in Africa and Palestine* (2014, with Yossi Katz), and *French Colonial Dakar: The Morphogenesis of an African Regional Capital* (2016).

Kate Brown is a Professor of History at the University of Maryland, Baltimore County. Her research interests include ethnic borderlands, atomic cities, and dystopias. She is the recipient of numerous awards, including a Guggenheim Fellowship, and is the author of *A Biography of No Place: From Ethnic Borderland to Soviet Heartland* (2004), *Plutopia: Nuclear Families in Atomic Cities and the Great Soviet and American Plutonium Disasters* (2013), and *Dispatches from Dystopia: Histories of Places Not Yet Forgotten* (2015).

Paula Geyh is an Associate Professor of English at Yeshiva University. Her research interests include twentieth-century American literature, postmodern American and European fiction, cultural theory, and film studies. She is the author and editor of several books, including: *Postmodern American Fiction: A Norton Anthology* (1998, with Fred Leebron and Andrew Levy); *Cities, Citizens, and Technologies: Urban Life and Postmodernity* (2009); and *The Cambridge Companion to Postmodern American Fiction* (2015).

Jill L. Grant is a Professor Emeritus in the Faculty of Architecture and Planning at Dalhousie University. Her research interests include planning theory and practice, new urbanism, sustainable cities, and creative cities. She is the author and editor of numerous books, including: *The Drama of Democracy: Contention and Dispute in Community Planning* (1994); *Towards Sustainable Cities: East Asian, North American and European Perspectives on Managing Urban Regions* (2004, with André Sorensen and Peter Marcotullio); *Planning the Good Community: New Urbanism in Theory and Practice* (2006); *A Reader in Canadian Planning: Linking Theory and Practice* (2008); and *Seeking Talent for Creative Cities: The Social Dynamics of Innovation* (2014).

Thomas Hart is a retired American diplomat and has pursued a second career in heritage preservation, working as Executive Director of the Historic Fredericksburg Foundation in Virginia and on conservation of the historic rooms of the Old Executive Office Building next to the White House. He has published several articles on heritage conservation topics in the US, Kenya, Suriname, and Senegal. Hart was educated at Princeton, Columbia, and Oxford, and has an MA in Historic Preservation from Goucher College. He currently lives in Paris.

Spiro Kostof (1936–1991) was a Professor of Architectural History at the University of California, Berkeley. He is the author of various books that have become classics in the field of architectural history and the history of urban planning, including: *Architect: Chapters in the History of the Profession* (1978), *A History of Architecture: Settings and Rituals* (1985), *The City Shaped: Urban Patterns and Meanings Though History* (1991), and *The City Assembled: The Elements of Urban Form Through History* (1992).

Setha M. Low is a Professor of Anthropology at the Graduate Center of the City University of New York. She has written extensively on the politics of public space, gated communities, and urban parks. Her books include: *On the Plaza: The Politics of Public Space and Culture* (2000); *The Anthropology of Space and Place: Locating Culture* (2003, with Denise Lawrence-Zuniga); *Behind the Gates: Life, Security and the Pursuit of Happiness in Fortress America* (2004); *Rethinking Urban Parks: Public Space and Cultural Diversity* (2005, with Dana Taplin and Suzanne Scheld); *The Politics of Public Space* (2006, with Neil Smith); and *The People, Place and Space Reader* (2014, with Jen Jack Gieseking, William Mangold, Cindi Katz, and Susan Saegert).

Luigi Mazza is a Professor Emeritus of Planning in the Dipartimento di Architettura e Pianificazione, Politecnico di Milano. He is the author of numerous journal articles and book chapters on Italian cities, modern urbanism in Europe, and the ethics of urban planning.

Reuben Rose-Redwood is an Associate Professor of Geography and Chair of the Committee for Urban Studies at the University of Victoria in British Columbia, Canada. His research focuses on the cultural politics of place, the spatial organization of cities, and the historical geographies of the geo-coded world. He is the co-editor of *Performativity, Politics, and the Production of Social Space* (2014, with

Michael Glass) and *The Political Life of Urban Streetscapes: Naming, Politics, and Place* (2018, with Derek Alderman and Maoz Azaryahu), and has published in a broad range of scholarly journals, including *Progress in Human Geography*, *Social & Cultural Geography*, *Urban History*, and the *Annals of the American Association of Geographers*. His work on the historical geography of New York's grid street plan has also been featured in various popular media outlets, such as the Discovery Channel, History Channel, and *New York Times*.

Richard Sennett is a Professor of the Humanities at New York University and a Professor of Sociology at the London School of Economics. His research explores the intersections of culture, social life, and the history of urbanism. He is the author of numerous influential books, including: *The Fall of Public Man* (1977), *The Conscience of the Eye: The Design and Social Life of Cities* (1991), *Flesh and Stone: The Body and the City in Western Civilization* (1994), *The Culture of the New Capitalism* (2006), and *Together: The Rituals, Pleasure, and Politics of Cooperation* (2012), among others.

Dan Stanislawski (1903–1997) was a Professor of Geography at several universities over the course of his career, including the University of Texas and the University of Arizona. His research interests focused on the historical geography of Portugal and Latin America as well as the origin and diffusion of the grid-pattern town.

Gilbert A. Stelter is a Professor Emeritus of History at the University of Guelph. His research interests focus on the history of town planning and architecture in Canada. He is the author and editor of a number of books on Canadian urban development, including: *Shaping the Urban Landscape: Aspects of the Canadian City-Building Process* (1984), *Power and Place: Canadian Urban Development in the North American Context* (1986), *Guelph and Wellington County: An Annotated Bibliography* (1988), and *Cities and Urbanization: Canadian Historical Perspectives* (1990).

Jianfei Zhu is a Professor in the Faculty of Architecture, Building, and Planning at the University of Melbourne. His research examines the political dimensions of architecture and the urban built environment in China. He is the author of *Chinese Spatial Strategies: Imperial Beijing* (2004) and *Architecture of Modern China: A Historical Critique* (2009) as well as the editor of *Sixty Years of Chinese Architecture (1949–2009): History, Theory and Criticism* (2009).

List of Figures

List of Tables

Chapter 1
Gridded Spaces, Gridded Worlds

Reuben Rose-Redwood and Liora Bigon

> *... the grid is the dominant mythological form of modern life....*
> *The grid, however, has a history that long predates modernity.*
>
> (Higgins 2009, 6)

Abstract This introductory chapter provides an overview of interdisciplinary scholarship on the urban grid from a comparative historical perspective. Its general aim is to situate the current edited collection within broader discussions of the grid in urban history from antiquity to the present. In doing so, the chapter explores the political and economic rationalities that have informed the diverse uses of the grid as a mode of urban spatial ordering as well as the wide range of theoretical perspectives that have been brought to bear on interpreting the significance of the grid. In particular, we examine the relationship between the grid plan and political ideology; its role as a political technology of imperialism, colonialism, and the formation of the modern territorial state; and the various ways in which the production of "gridded worlds" has shaped the spatial imaginaries and everyday lives of urban inhabitants around the world. By examining the entangled histories of the grid, this chapter considers the variegated associations of gridded urban space with different political ideologies, economic systems, and cosmological orientations, and outlines the rationale for the present anthology of key writings on the urban grid as a way of taking stock of the existing literature in order to inspire new avenues of research on the past, present, and future of the gridded worlds of urban life.

Keywords Grid plan · Political technology · Spatial imaginaries · Urban design · History of urban planning

R. Rose-Redwood (✉)
University of Victoria, Victoria, BC, Canada
e-mail: redwood@uvic.ca

L. Bigon
Holon Institute of Technology, Holon, Israel
e-mail: liorab@hit.ac.il

© Springer International Publishing AG, part of Springer Nature 2018
R. Rose-Redwood, L. Bigon (eds.), *Gridded Worlds: An Urban Anthology*,
https://doi.org/10.1007/978-3-319-76490-0_1

1

Introduction

On February 28, 2003, the New Museum of Contemporary Art opened an exhibit entitled, *Living Inside the Grid*, which explored the diverse ways in which the "grid" had shaped popular culture and everyday life at the dawn of the twenty-first century. In the accompanying catalogue, the exhibit's curator Dan Cameron maintains that "the imposition of the grid upon all aspects of human existence was an inescapable fact" (2003, 36). As a result, he argues, "the inhabited grid has become the irreducible sign of the world we live in today" (2003, 12). Cameron is not alone in framing the grid as the quintessential symbol of the "modern." Art historian Rosalind Krauss, for instance, maintains that "the grid is an emblem of modernity" (1979, 52). Yet, as Hannah Higgins observes, the grid has served as a technology of spatial ordering for millennia in many different historical and geographical contexts and thus "long predates modernity" (2009, 6). However, while the grid is not unique to the modern era, the prevalence and scale of gridded spaces since the sixteenth century has led many commentators to view the grid as the quintessential symbol of modernity.

Given its ubiquity in multiple fields of human endeavor—from modern art, graphic design, and architecture to mathematics, cartography, and urban planning—the grid has acquired something of a "mythological" status in the modern spatial imaginary. On the one hand, the modern grid is commonly portrayed as marking a spatial and temporal break with the past. Yet, on the other hand, it is also seen as a universal spatial form with a continuous history dating back to antiquity. The "mythology" of the grid—both academic and popular—has generally been framed around conceptual oppositions between modernity and tradition, order and disorder, the planned and the unplanned. In such accounts, which have been repetitiously invoked time and again, the grid plays a leading role in the perennial narrative of civilization imposing "order" upon the chaos of the world. These narratives alternately cast the grid as a symbol of civilized benevolence, heroic monumentalism, economic rationality, or social control. Although the content and emphasis of such narratives vary, they share a common goal of searching for the *essential meaning* of the grid.

The search for the essence of the grid is nowhere more evident than in historical studies of the urban grid plan. As one of the most prevalent forms of urban spatial organization in world history, the urban grid has been viewed as a signifier of everything from imperial rule and authoritarian control to Enlightenment rationalism and democratic egalitarianism. In urban historical scholarship, the grid's essence has typically been sought after by attempting to reveal the intentions and motivations underpinning its design or by determining its primary function. However, the architectural historian Spiro Kostof observed over two and a half decades ago that the motivations and functions of the urban grid have varied considerably. He maintains, therefore, that any effort to reduce the grid to a single political ideology is futile, since political ideologies, economic doctrines, and cultural ideals are "no more natural to gridded patterns than to any other urban form" (Kostof 1991, 100). Similarly, urban planning theorist Jill Grant argues that the historical "record offers no simple correlation between a particular physical form and social patterns or aspirations" (2001, 221). Yet this has not stopped countless urban commentators from seeking to draw precisely such spurious correlations by making claims that the grid represents *this* political ideology or signifies *that* economic system.

The problem with these reductionistic arguments is not their reductionism alone but also that they are wedded to a representationalist conception of spatial form, which reduces the grid to a representation of something else that defines its meaning. Far more than a representation or signifier, the grid is a *world-making device* that literally brings new worlds into being through the partitioning of space-times. By moving beyond the endless debate over what the grid represents, we can develop a better understanding of how "gridded worlds" are performatively enacted through a wide variety of spatial practices. If much of the literature has subscribed to what we might call a hermeneutics of the grid—which poses the question, *what does the grid mean?*—viewing the grid as a political technology of world-making calls our attention to the pragmatics of the grid, thereby shifting the focus from the meaning of the grid-as-representation to the spatial practice of *gridding* and the worlds it both produces and destroys. Such a theoretical reorientation has significant implications for how we narrate the spatial history of gridded worlds, but, before we can fully understand its significance for future research, it is first necessary to come to terms with the different ways in which the history of the urban grid has been narrated over the past century.

Scholars from a wide range of fields have studied the grid, yet much of this work remains scattered in inaccessible academic journals and scholarly monographs. The aim of this book is to bring together key writings on the urban grid in a single volume to serve as an interdisciplinary anthology that explores the histories of the grid from multiple perspectives in a variety of urban contexts. In doing so, this collection seeks to challenge monolithic portrayals of the grid as a fixed spatial form aligned with a singular ideology by demonstrating the diversity of uses to which it has been put in indigenous, colonial, and postcolonial traditions of urbanism. By examining the entangled histories of the grid, this edited volume considers the variegated associations of gridded urban space with different political regimes, economic systems, and cosmological orientations in comparative historical perspective. This anthology therefore seeks to provide one of the first accessible collections of classic and contemporary writings on the urban grid as a way of taking stock of the existing literature in order to inspire new avenues of research on the past, present, and future of the gridded worlds of urban life.

Contrasting Perspectives on the Urban Grid

From the Search for Authentic Origins to Anti-Essentialist Critiques of the Grid

The use of the grid as a mode of urban spatial organization has long fascinated scholars from across the social sciences and humanities, who have drawn upon a variety of theoretical perspectives and methodological approaches to examine the place of the grid in urban history. Early studies of the grid plan took as their point of departure the assumption that "the straight line and the right angle" were features that distinguished "civilization from barbarism" (Haverfield 1913, 14). Such approaches often imbued the grid with moral qualities of civilized refinement and contrasted its geometric rectitude with the supposedly crooked immorality of the "primitive" Other. For instance, in his study, *Ancient Town-Planning*, published in 1913, British historian Francis Haverfield claims that "[t]he savage, inconsistent in his moral life, is equally inconsistent, equally unable to 'keep straight', in his house-building and his road-making" (1913, 14). The conflation of spatial form with moral order was one of the hallmarks of civilizational discourses on the grid, which served as a justification of imperial conquest and colonial settlement.

Much of the early scholarship on the grid adopted a diffusionist approach and sought to trace a continuous lineage of the grid plan back to its foundational "origin," although some scholars at the time acknowledged that the grid was developed independently in different regions throughout the world (for a review of the literature on the origins of the grid in antiquity, see Castagnoli 1971 [1956]). One of the most paradigmatic examples of the diffusionist approach to tracing the origin of the grid plan is geographer Dan Stanislawski's "The Origin and Spread of the Grid Pattern Town" (1946; see Chap. 2, this volume). Like most diffusionist approaches to cultural innovation, Stanislawski's study presents the grid as "a one-time invention which has spread from its source region until at present it encompasses the globe" (1946, 105). The key question for the diffusionist is: *what are the immediate and distant antecedents of the grid in any particular case?* The ultimate goal of the diffusionist approach is therefore to search for the grid's "origin" and reconstruct its lines of descent. Stanislawski provides precisely such an account by explaining the grid plan in Spain's American colonies as a direct descendant of Greek and Roman planning techniques, which he suggests were adaptations of prior grid-based planning that can ultimately be traced back to the Indus Valley settlement of Mohenjo-Daro.

Although the Greco-Roman influence on Spanish colonization is well-established, the linkage that Stanislawski draws between the Greco-Roman grid and the earlier use of the grid in the Indus Valley is based on pure speculation. Yet this chain of equivalence—however speculative—is required for the "one-time invention" thesis to be sustained. The diffusionist argument also depends upon a denial of any evidence suggesting that the grid plan existed in places without a single line of descent from a common origin. It is for this reason that Stanislawski dismisses evidence that the grid pre-dates European colonialism in the Americas, arguing in a related study that "there is no convincing evidence of any grid-pattern town in the New World before Cortes rebuilt Mexico City" (Stanislawski 1947, 97). This claim has been challenged by a number of subsequent scholars (Gasparini and Margolies 1980; Gasparini 1993; Low 1995; Smith 2007), while others have called into question the endless search for the "origin" of the grid (Pattison 1957; Johnson 1976; Butzer 1992; Rose-Redwood 2008). Some have gone so far as to argue that the "privileging of the 'origin' should be rejected as symptomatic of a metaphysics of essentialism" and instead call for a genealogical approach that is "concerned with the discontinuities, contingencies, reversals, contradictions, failures, and reformulations that have accompanied the use of the grid" (Rose-Redwood 2008, 43 and 54; see Chap. 3, this volume). This anti-essentialist, genealogical perspective suggests that the search for the essential meaning of the grid is ultimately fruitless, because "the 'essential secret' of the grid is that it has no essence" (Rose-Redwood 2008, 56).

The diffusionist quest for the "authentic origin" of the grid may have largely been abandoned, but scholars from different disciplines have developed a broad spectrum of approaches to studying the spatial histories of the grid. Many studies of the grid have embraced a formalist approach, which examines the spatial patterns of cities and the evolution of urban forms over time (e.g., Morris 1972; Vance 1990). Kostof's *The City Shaped: Urban Patterns and Meanings Through History* (1991) is a classic illustration of the formalist paradigm, which combines a visually descriptivist empiricism with a hermeneutics of meaning—hence Kostof's emphasis on both the "patterns" and "meanings" of urban form (see Chap. 4, this volume). Like many commentators, Kostof (1991) contrasts the grid with other urban forms such as the radial system of Baroque monumentality, the curvilinear forms of the "planned picturesque," and the irregularly-shaped layouts of the so-called "organic" pattern of urban settlement. However, what distinguishes Kostof's account of the grid is that it offers a particularly forceful critique of essentialist interpretations of the grid's meaning. Whereas many scholars have attributed a singular meaning to the grid, Kostof argues that such arguments are "fundamentally misleading" because the "motivation for the grid" has been multiple (1991, 99 and 102).

Kostof is especially critical of studies claiming that the grid represents democracy and egalitarianism, arguing instead that "the grid, far from being a democratic device employed to assure an equitable allotment of property to all citizens, was the means of perpetuating the privileges of the property-owning class descendent from the original settlers, and bolstering a territorial aristocracy" (1991, 99). He insists, therefore, that "the political innocence of the grid in the West is a fiction" (Kostof 1991, 99) and emphasizes the various ways in which absolutist political regimes—from China and Japan to Spain and France—have used the grid as a political technology of spatial ordering. However, Kostof does not claim that the essence of the grid is absolutist, or anything else for that matter. Rather, he emphasizes the *plurality* of motivations and uses for which the grid has been employed and calls attention to the "versatility of program within what it is possible to see as a simple-minded, uninspiring, unvarying formula" (Kostof 1991, 102). Kostof is thus quite dismissive of those scholars who "blame the grid for the shallowness and callousness of urban experience" and follows geographer James Vance in proclaiming that the grid is "one of the great inventions of the human mind" (Vance 1977, 44–5, as quoted in Kostof 1991, 103).

From the Grid as an Instrument of Social Control to the "Cosmo-Magical" Pivot of the World

If Kostof ultimately presents himself as a champion of the urban grid, planning theorist Jill Grant (2001) offers a more cautionary tale of the "dark side of the grid" (see Chap. 5, this volume). Similar to Kostof, Grant is skeptical of claims that the grid is essentially "democratic" and "non-hierarchical" (2001, 220). Responding to the revival of the grid among New Urbanist planners during the 1990s, Grant contends that the grid is "more frequently associated with the concentration of military power and wealth rather than with egalitarian traditions" (2001, 220; for an overview of the New Urbanist reclamation of the grid, see Cozens and Hillier 2008). To support this claim, she examines the uses of the grid in societies where different forms of power prevail, which she defines as diffusing, centralizing, and globalizing modes of authority. While Grant acknowledges that the grid has occasionally been employed for egalitarian purposes, she observes that in such cases "what began as an egalitarian grid may well become hierarchical" as property ownership is monopolized into fewer and fewer hands over time (2001, 234). By focusing on the uses of the grid under different political regimes, Grant is concerned less with what the grid *represents* than with what *use* it serves as a spatial technique of power. One of the primary functions of the grid is its capacity to render urban space "legible" to a centralizing power (Grant 2001, 237; also, see Foucault 1995 [1977]; Scott 1998; Brown 2001). It is for this reason, Grant argues, that the grid has commonly been utilized as a spatial strategy of political control over colonized populations and occupied territories. Whereas some scholars have interpreted the use of the grid as an aid to colonialism in benevolent terms (Stanislawski 1946; Malverti and Picard 1991; Pinol 2003), Grant contends that the grid has more often than not been employed as a political technology of repressive power. "Thus, when we examine societies using the grid," she maintains, "we cannot help but conclude that the grid has a dark side in as much as it has served so frequently as a tool of dominance and repression" (Grant 2001, 237).

The repressive potential of the grid as a mechanism of social and political control has been widely recognized by numerous scholars and other commentators, leading some to raise the prospect of "a growing totalitarianism of the grid" (Siegert 2015, 98). Even proponents of the grid plan have argued that "a tortuous street facilitates defense by individuals and a straight street lends itself to control from without" (Stanislawski 1946, 107; for further discussion of the use of the grid as a technology of state control and a tortuous street system as part of anti-colonial struggles, see Robinson 1990; Çelik 1997). This argument is generally attributed to Aristotle's

Politics, in which he observes that the grid system of laying out dwellings in "straight rows is considered pleasanter and more useful for general purposes. But, when it comes to security in wartime, the opposite plan, which prevailed in ancient times, is thought to be better. For it makes it difficult for foreign troops to enter and for attackers to find their way around" (1998, 209–10, section 1330b/22–26). Aristotle therefore recommends a combination whereby "certain parts and areas are laid out in straight rows, but not the city-state as a whole," so that "both safety and beauty will be well served" (1998, 210, section1330b/28–30). In this account, the grid is simultaneously understood as a model of aesthetic beauty yet also a security risk.

Aristotle refers to the grid plan as the "Hippodamean scheme" (1998, 209, section 1330b/22), in reference to Hippodamus of Miletus, who is often erroneously portrayed as the "inventor" of the grid plan. In his study of Hippodamus, urban planning theorist Luigi Mazza re-examines Aristotle's commentary on the grid and argues that Hippodamus's primary contribution was to highlight "the association between grid and constitition, and to identify the political nature of planning practices" (2009, 114; see Chap. 6, this volume). More specifically, Mazza argues that although Hippodamus did not invent the grid plan, he appears to have popularized its use among the Greeks and his primary contribution to the early development of planning was to have developed "a zoning plan in which there is a *partial match* between the political organisation of the city (division into classes) and spatial plan (division into zones)" (2009, 123, italics in original). The Hippodamean plan, in other words, was an attempt to devise a system for the division of cities based upon the co-constitution of social and spatial order. Through his commentary on "Aristotle's Hippodamus," Mazza maintains that the socio-spatial partitioning of cities has played a crucial role in the constitution of political communities, where planning has served as an "instrument of social control through spatial control" (2009, 114). Kostof (1991) similarly suggests that the spatial layouts of military, refugee, and prison camps are prime examples of how the grid has been used as a form of social control.

However, this emphasis on the grid plan as a technique of social control is not without its critics. For example, Paul Carter argues that "the grid plan has not only been imposed from without: it has also been accepted from within. It has not only been a tool of authority: it has itself been accepted as authoritative" (1988, 210, italics omitted). In a similar vein, Michel Foucault maintains that the grid—and power more generally—is not only repressive but also a productive force, since it "produces domains of objects and rituals of truth" (1995 [1977], 194). As a technology of power, the grid operates by producing a field of "visibility" (Foucault 1995 [1977], 171), which has the effect of rendering space legible to facilitate governance at a distance. Yet it can also have the effect of producing new social and political subjectivities for which the "inhabited grid" is experienced as the taken-for-granted order of the world (Cameron 2003). The adoption of the grid as a spatial plan may occur through a combination of force and consent, which complicates reductionistic interpretations that conceive of the grid as a repressive force alone.

Scholarship on the grid is often prone to making broad generalizations about its representational and functional significance. However, the specificities of time and place clearly matter because the grid is a historico-geographical formation, not a timeless Platonic form (Carter 1988; Rose-Redwood 2008). Moreover, the grid is not a singular spatial object; rather, there are multiple gridded spaces in diverse locales and "the same form can be produced by quite different interests" (Marcuse 1987, 289). While it is tempting to view all grids as contributing to the repetition of the same spatial form, the grids of ancient Chinese imperial capitals are by no means identical to the military camps of the Roman Empire, the grid-plaza complexes in Latin America, or the gridded cities of the United States. If grids vary across space from one city to the next, they also differ temporally since a given city's grid is not a fixed and static object but rather an assemblage of patterns and processes that change over time. In other words, there is always difference even within what appears to be a repetition of the same (Lefebvre 2004).

One of the primary distinctions that the neo-Marxian urbanist Peter Marcuse highlights is that between *open* and *closed* grids. As Marcuse explains, "the classic grid is laid out for a clearly limited area defined by city walls, fortifications, major outer termini for central streets, greenbelts, etc., whereas the open grid is laid out with a view towards expansion and reduplication, in one or more directions, theoretically without limit" (1987, 290–1). While the closed grid is clearly "bounded," open grids are expansionary, "plotting an unknown and perhaps unlimited area capable of indefinite expansion" (Marcuse 1987, 291; also, see Pope 1996). Drawing upon Krauss's (1979) terminology, closed grids can be understood as centripetal (inward-oriented) and are often directed toward a central focal point, while open grids are centrifugal (outward-oriented) offering the potential for limitless growth. Marcuse maintains that the urban grid has served different functions throughout history. In particular, he argues that the transition from the pre-capitalist to the capitalist era resulted in a general shift from closed to open grids, although as capitalist cities matured there were often competing economic interests at play in the implementation of the grid plan.

Following Marcuse, Kostof likewise asserts that "[t]he open grid is predicated on a capitalist economy, and the conversion of land to a commodity to be bought and sold on the market" (1991, 121). Some scholars, however, have questioned the universality of these claims. For instance, Grant challenges Marcuse's argument that pre-capitalist grids are closed and capitalist grids are open, noting that there are "closed grids in contemporary gated communities within capitalist societies, while pre-capitalist communities like Teotihuacan feature open grids" (2001, 239). Complications also arise in other geographical contexts, such as the rapidly expanding open grids in the urban centers of the Sufi Mouride brotherhood in Senegal, which are integrated into the global capitalist economy through export-oriented, commercial agriculture yet are composed of gridded configurations based upon pre-capitalist Islamic spiritual practices (Guèye 2002; Ross 2006). However, even if the historical uses of open and closed grids are not as straightforward as Marcuse suggests, the very distinction between the two underscores the point that the gridding of space is a differentiated process and thus the urban grid is not reducible to a monolithic and unchanging spatial form.

If Marcuse (1987) is primarily concerned with the political economy of the grid, others have focused more on the grid's symbolic power and its use by political rulers who have attempted to align their own worldly sovereignty with the cosmological forces of the universe at large. In his landmark study on the history of Chinese urbanism, *Pivot of the Four Quarters* (1971), historical geographer Paul Wheatley explores the "cosmo-magical" symbolism of ancient Chinese cities, where the centripetal, closed grid was designed as a microcosm of the heavens. More recent scholarship has also documented how the symbolic uses of the grid in ancient Chinese cities were of paramount importance. Architectural historian Jianfei Zhu (2004), for example, provides a detailed historical analysis of the "spatial strategies" employed in the making of imperial Beijing (see Chap. 7, this volume). He argues that Beijing's grid plan produced a space in which imperial ideologies were inscribed, symbolically articulating Confucian ideals of the sacred emperor residing at a "pivotal point that mediates and unifies the cosmos and the human world" (Zhu 2004, 34). Through an in-depth interpretation of ancient Confucian texts, Zhu seeks to demonstrate that the spatial plan of Beijing was an ideological representation that produced both a symbolic and functional space where cosmological principles and ideals of rulership could be translated into physical form. Framed in these terms, the grid is conceived as both a "symbolic representation" and a "functional practice" of ordering space at the very center of empire (Zhu 2004, 44). Similarly, prominent early Islamic cities such as Basra, Kûfa, and Al-Fustât/Al-Qāhirah were based on a closed grid plan, which contrasts with the popular Eurocentric perception of Muslim cities as "organic" and "chaotic." These classical cities, initially established as encampments, were configured as gridded residential quarters organized around a vast rectangular public square, symbolically comprising the Friday Mosque and the ruler's palace (Hakim 1986; AlSayyad 1991; Denoix 1992).

From Eurocentric Narratives of Urban Form to the Entangled Spatial Histories of the Grid

The use of the grid as a spatial strategy of imperialism and colonial expansion has been extensively studied. Much of the literature is Eurocentric in the sense that narratives of the grid often portray European colonizers as the active agents of history imposing grids upon passive colonized landscapes. The primary focus has been on the influence of the Greco-Roman grid as a precursor to the colonial grids that the European powers embraced as part of their efforts to colonize the world. To be sure, it is indeed the case that long before the age of European colonial expansion, the grid plan had served as a spatial template for Roman imperial settlement in Europe itself. Yet following the collapse of the Roman Empire, the "old gridded Greco-Roman cities [lost] their physical integrity or disappear[ed] altogether" (Kostof

1991, 108). Then, during the twelfth century, a new set of grid-plan settlements known as *bastides*, or new towns, were constructed across Europe and had increasingly become the norm, particularly in southern France, by the thirteenth century (Beresford 1967; Morris 1972; Kostof 1991; Stelter 1993). Much like the later fortified towns of the Renaissance, the *bastide* was generally composed of a grid enclosed by a wall for military defense, and the French adopted similar town plans for their early colonial settlements in West Africa and North America during the seventeenth century, where "military considerations" also played a significant role in town planning (Stelter 1993; see Chap. 8, this volume; also, see Sinou 1993; Pinon 1996). Historian Gilbert Stelter thus concludes that "the way in which these towns were used as agencies of territorial occupation and settlement in the New World was largely derived from the practice that European states such as France developed in securing and expanding their homelands" (1993, 210). Similar arguments have been made regarding the strictly European derivation of the grid in other regions of European colonization as well, such as East Asia and Sub-Saharan Africa (Culot and Thiveaud 1992; Soulillou 1993; Goerg and de Lemps 2003).

The general assumption underpinning Eurocentric narratives of the grid is that European colonizers imposed grids on previously ungridded spaces, transforming the landscape into a *tabula rasa* upon which European colonial power was inscribed. The problem with this narrative is that indigenous communities—from the Americas to Sub-Saharan Africa—often had their own traditions of urbanism, settlement, and land use that long pre-dated European colonialism, and the entanglement between indigenous and colonial settlement practices generally resulted in the production of hybrid urban spaces. This was especially the case in South and Central America, where, as anthropologist Setha Low notes, there is considerable "archaeological and ethnohistorical evidence that many, if not most, Spanish American towns were built directly on top of or otherwise utilized the existing [indigenous] settlement patterns and buildings" (1995, 750). In her study of grid-plaza urban design in Meso-America and the Carribean, Low challenges Eurocentric interpretations of the grid-plaza complex and contends that "the correspondence between the indigenous plaza forms and Spanish reconstruction is so well documented that the denial of its significance is startling" (1995, 750; see Chap. 9, this volume). Viewing the gridded spaces of South and Central America as solely a product of Spanish colonial rule obscures the indigenous influence on the spatial formations of Spanish colonialism in the Americas and thus perpetuates a colonialist reading of the grid (Low 2000).

Low's (1995) critique of Eurocentric-colonialist interpretations of the grid has inspired other scholars to re-examine the spatial entanglements between indigenous and colonial planning traditions in different world regions as well. In their study of the planning history of Senegal's capital city, Dakar, Liora Bigon and Thomas Hart (2018) highlight the limits of such Eurocentric narratives by demonstrating how the settlement patterns of the Lebou, a community indigenous to the Cap Vert peninsula in West Africa, became intertwined with the gridded spaces of French urbanism in colonial Dakar (also, see Chap. 10, this volume). Their work illustrates how the colonial grid did not simply erase indigenous landscapes and conceptions of place but rather resulted in a "multiplicity of hybrid forms of urban space." In the case of

Dakar, central meeting places, or *péncs*, were an integral feature of indigenous settlements prior to colonial contact, and many *péncs* are still evident in the gridded spatial structure of postcolonial Dakar today. As Bigon and Hart explain, "the obstinate and vivid persistence of traditional Lebou settlement forms and toponyms beneath the orthogonal lines of the colonial system is remarkable, and the initial tension between the exogamous and endogenous planning cultures gradually turned into absorption and coexistence." Geographers have long recognized that the cultural landscape is comparable to a *palimpsest* with different layers of material and symbolic culture intermixed in the morphologies of the city. Yet Eurocentric narratives nevertheless persist in much of the interdisciplinary literature on the urban spatial histories of the grid. Given the hybridity of spatial formations in postcolonial cities, it is crucial to move beyond reductionistic explanations of the grid that reaffirm colonialist discourses of European power while ignoring the myriad ways in which indigenous modifications of the land have literally been "woven into the grid" of the colonial and postcolonial urban landscape (Bigon and Hart, this volume; Ross and Bigon forthcoming).

One common trope in Eurocentric narratives of the grid in North America is portraying the pre-grid landscape as an untamed "wilderness" (Trachtenberg 1964; Sennett 1990; Cohen and Augustyn 1997). The grid is commonly viewed as an instrument to facilitate the mastery of nature, which is either understood as a sign of reason and progress or as the irrational imposition of uniformity by an arbitrary power. In his essay, "American Cities: The Grid Plan and the Protestant Ethic," the urbanist Richard Sennett argues that the North American grid plan transformed the American "wilderness" into a neutralized space through the obliteration of the "natural landscape" in order to create a space of social control (1990, 272 and 274; see Chap. 11, this volume). Drawing upon Max Weber's Protestant ethic thesis, Sennett contends that the use of the grid as a city plan resulted in the "denial of difference" through the act of "geometric repression" (1990, 278 and 284). Sennett likens the grid plan to the Protestant ethic, because both played a central role in "a story in which men create the very conditions and circumstances which they then feel to be cold and empty" (1990, 284). As a neutralizing and repressive force, he argues, the grid has radically transformed the North American landscape, sweeping away the last vestiges of the "wild" to make way for the impersonal, cold, and alienating spaces of modernity. In Sennett's words, "[t]he American grid plans were the first sign of a peculiarly modern form of repression, one which denies value to other people and specific places by building neutrality" (1990, 284). Yet, as discussed above, the grid has not only been a force of repression but has also produced new taken-for-granted spaces of everyday life for urban inhabitants across North America and beyond.

The gridded spaces of North America have by no means obliterated everything in their path, even if that may very well have been one of the desired goals of such plans. For instance, New York's grid plan of 1811—which Sennett views as an exemplary case of spatial repression—was indeed mapped onto the Manhattan landscape without regard for the existing topography. Yet, during its implementation, topographical concerns could not be avoided, especially in northern Manhattan, which resulted in subsequent changes to the plan during the 1870s (Marcuse 1987; Scobey 2002; Ballon 2012). Moreover, although hills were leveled and wetlands filled, the topographical variation underlying Manhattan's gridded streetscape remains much the same today as it was before the grid was imposed upon the island (Rose-Redwood and Li 2011). Additionally, the indigenous pathway of Wickquasgeck—which would later come to be known by the settler society as Broadway—was also incorporated into New York's street grid and is just as much a part of the city's contemporary streetscape as Fifth Avenue or Martin Luther King Jr. Boulevard (Young 2015).

Viewing the grid plan as a spatial manifestation of the Protestant ethic, or any other mode of thought, reduces the multiplicity of spatial formations to a singular meaning, privileging the authorial intentionality of the grid's origins over its entanglements with prior indigenous landscape modifications or subsequent uses. While the designers of New York's grid plan sought to employ its Cartesian order as a means of instilling the discipline of economic rationality into urban life—not to mention establishing a standardized real estate market—the grid is not reducible to the intentions of its original designers alone (Rose-Redwood 2011; see Chap. 12, this volume). In his genealogical critique of scholarship on the grid, Rose-Redwood (2011) contends that this form of "morphological essentialism" has produced a historical mythology that repetitiously and uncritically invokes the "official" meaning of New York's grid plan based upon the designers' publicly-stated intentions. By contrast, he argues that the original designers of a city plan do not hold a monopoly on its symbolic significance, since it is through the everyday uses of urban space that the material and symbolic power of the grid come to "life" (Rose-Redwood 2011, 412; also, see Higgins 2009).

Throughout the course of history, the grid has been embraced by those espousing a diverse range of political ideologies, economic doctrines, and religious cosmologies as a means of re-ordering the world in their own image. Yet, as historian Kate Brown reminds us, one of the things that most adaptations of the grid have in common is the utopian dream of constructing the "perfectly-governed city" (Foucault 1995 [1977], 198, as cited in Brown 2001, 47). This dream of the sovereign grid in the governable city is utopian, because its vision of perfection can never be fulfilled. However, different political regimes have nevertheless continuously attempted to transform their utopian visions into reality through the spatial form of the grid. For instance, while the ideologies of the Soviet Union and the United States were diametrically opposed during the Cold War, both political-economic systems produced similar gridded spaces. From the prison city of Karaganda in Kazakhstan to the railroad town of Billings, Montana, the grid provided a common template for the spatial organization of the modern city (Brown 2001; see Chap. 13, this volume). Despite their differences, Brown argues that the gridded worlds of American capitalism and Soviet communism both "made a lasting stamp on the nature of the lives that took up residence on the plains and steppe" (2001, 46). These "gridded lives" were not merely passive recipients of the grid's spatial order. This is true even in the case of Karaganda, where the grid was literally constructed as a carceral space of control by the very prisoners who came to inhabit it. Over time, "the prisoners were gradually given amnesty, the prison barracks were dismantled, the barbed wire was lifted, and, curiously, what remains is a neatly ordered city of broad avenues and shady sidewalks, monumental squares and symmetrically plotted parks, ample and verdant" (Brown 2001, 17). This example underscores the importance of considering the *temporalities* of the grid, rather than viewing gridded space solely through the lens of spatial fixity.

The temporalities of the grid are multiple. On the one hand, the grid has a history that dates back millennia; on the other hand, it has also come to be seen as "one of the hallmarks of modernity" (Geyh 2009, 69; Chap. 14, this volume). Literary theorist Paula Geyh suggests that the grid's association with the "modern" is largely a result of the influence of René Descartes's philosophy—especially "his most famous invention, the coordinate 'grid'" (2009, 69)—on the rise of modern thought generally and modern science in particular. The Cartesian grid has been used as a technology of visibility and legibility in multiple domains of modern life. Although critics of modernity have sought to move beyond Cartesian modes of thought and practice, the coordinate grid remains "one of the primary modern conceptual structures found in the postmodern city" (Geyh 2009, 72–3). In other words, the modern grid does not disappear in the age of postmodernity; rather, as Geyh notes, it is reconfigured in both the "real" and "imagined" spaces of postmodern urbanism and the digital worlds of cyberspace. Drawing upon Gilles Deleuze's (1997) theorization of the "societies of control," Geyh argues that the grid is simultaneously a striated space of control and the very terrain within which resistance unfolds. Instead of abandoning the grid altogether, she insists that the making of smooth, nomadic spaces must necessarily also entail the creation of "more productive striations and grids" that reject the totality of the modern grid in favor of a more "open-ended order" (Geyh 2009, 84).

Gridded Worlds: The Need for a Critical Anthology on the Urban Grid

The literature on the urban grid is extensive and scholars from different fields of study have approached the grid from a broad range of perspectives. Diffusionists have searched (in vain) for a continuous line of descent of the grid from a singular "origin"; formalists have devised typologies to distinguish the grid from other morphological patterns; humanists have sought to decipher the essential meaning of the grid by decoding the intentionality of urban design; political economists have critiqued the use of the grid as a template for the commodification of urban space in the capitalist city; social and political theorists have examined the uses of the grid as a mechanism of social control and a strategy of asserting sovereign authority over populations and territories; and historians of empire have documented the many instances in which the grid has served as a political technology of imperialism.

These approaches, of course, are not necessarily all mutually exclusive, since most diffusionists have also subscribed to a formalistic conception of the grid, and most formalists have embraced a humanistic approach to understanding the meaning of urban forms. This diffusionist-formalist-humanistic approach to the grid was the predominant paradigm for studying urban spatial formations more generally throughout the first three-quarters of the twentieth century. Since the 1980s, however, the urban grid has not only been an object of study for specialists in the field of urban morphology; it has also become a topic of broader interdisciplinary interest, gaining attention from sociologists and anthropologists, political scientists and geographers, philosophers and literary theorists, historians and urban planners. This wider interest in the grid as a technique of urban spatial ordering coincided with the "spatial turn" in the social sciences and humanities, which emphasized the importance of space and place in all facets of social life. Given the significant role that the grid has played as both a mechanism in the capitalist production of urban space as well as a political technology of urban governmentality, Marxian and poststructuralist theorists alike have highlighted the significance of the grid as a spatial strategy of modern urbanism. Yet these contrasting perspectives on the grid have rarely come into direct dialogue with one another.

For much of the past century, different interpretations of the grid have largely been confined to their respective disciplinary silos, each with its own philosophical traditions and interpretive norms. It is our hope that by bringing together a diverse array of writings on the urban grid in a single book, the present anthology can serve as a bridge across such disciplinary divides and will hopefully inspire present and future scholars to cultivate a more transdisciplinary understanding of gridded space. The purpose of this collection is therefore not to solidify a "canon" of great works on the grid. On the contrary, the juxtaposition of contrasting perspectives on the grid in a single volume is meant to stimulate *critical* encounters across different traditions of scholarship and encourage readers to critically engage with—and move beyond—existing conceptions of the grid.

For this collection, we have included many of the writings discussed in the previous section with the aim of highlighting the diversity of approaches to theorizing the grid while also tracing common threads across different paradigms. Given the global history of the grid, we have made our best attempt at temporal and geographical inclusion—with studies examining the grid from antiquity to the present drawing upon a diverse array of case studies from Europe, Asia, Africa, and the Americas. They explore the grid as both an indigenous urban form and a colonial imposition, a symbol of Confucian ideals and a spatial manifestation of the Protestant ethic, a replicable model for real estate speculation within capitalist societies and a spatial framework for the design of socialist cities. By bringing together scholarship from history, geography, anthropology, sociology, architecture, urban planning, and literary studies, this anthology illustrates how a critical genealogy of the grid is not reducible to a singular narrative of global modernity but must take into account the multiple trajectories and entangled histories of urban differentiation that underlie the apparent sameness and repetition of the grid as an urban spatial form.

One of the commonalities shared across all of the contributions in this collection is a focus on the grid as an urban spatial formation. This can easily lend itself to a fetishization of "form" over "process," which has led some contemporary urban theorists to call for the wholesale abandonment of studying different essential types of "settlement space," which is to be "superseded by the analysis of sociospatial processes (constitutive essences)" (Brenner 2013, 98, italics omitted). We agree that the search for the "essence" of spatial forms should be abandoned; however, we are less convinced that socio-spatial processes are themselves reducible to "essences," whether constitutive or otherwise. Instead, we seek to cultivate non-essentialist conceptions of both spatial forms and socio-spatial processes in order to develop more nuanced understandings of historical and contemporary urbanism. By way of conclusion, then, we would like to propose a number of interpretive reorientations that may inform future scholarship on the urban grid.

First, *one way to avoid fetishizing the grid as an urban form is to shift the focus from the grid as a spatial structure to the act of gridding as a practice of spatial reproduction.* This conceptual move underscores how spatial forms are temporal phenomena resulting from a myriad of socio-spatial processes. The practice of gridding entails the foundational acts of surveying, mapping, and partitioning gridded spaces, but it also involves the maintenance of such spaces through the repetitious enactment of everyday practices that normalize the "order" of the grid. The production of gridded space is thus not solely the result of a singular imposition of a spatial plan but is rather an ongoing process of spatial reproduction. The day-to-day reproduction of gridded spaces includes everything from the legal codification of land titles and the maintenance of infrastructural systems to the spatial narratives of popular culture and the habitual practices of urban inhabitants. Although the formal geometric qualities of the grid may appear equivalent from one context to another, the socio-spatial practices of gridding often differ significantly, which is why the grid has been interpreted as a symbol of contrasting political ideologies, economic systems, and cosmological worldviews.

Second, *the quest for decoding the essential meaning of the grid is a dead-end street and should be replaced with a critical analysis of the politico-economic and socio-cultural effects of urban gridding.* The ultimate dream of morphological essentialism is to uncover a foundational text in which the initial designers of a city plan clearly explain the precise reasons why they selected a given spatial form, thereby providing a definitive explanation of a plan's meaning and significance. This desire for interpretive transparency is comparable to the conservative legal doctrine known as "originalism," which is based upon the belief that meaning is stable over time and that an author's original intentions define the meaning of a text. This originalist approach to hermeneutics might still have adherents in courts of law, but it is widely recognized as hopelessly naïve among most literary theorists, cultural geographers, and other scholars. However, when it comes to interpreting the meaning of the grid, urban commentators have nevertheless regularly privileged the "official" statements of city planners in an attempt to uncover the definitive interpretation of the grid plan. Of course, many scholars acknowledge that the meaning of spatial forms is multiple, not singular. Yet the obsession with the meaning of spatial forms unnecessarily narrows the scope of attention to the realm of representation and signification when what is needed is a more detailed analysis of the *effects* that gridding has had on the political, economic, social, and cultural practices of urban life.

Third, *the grid is not only a tool of social control and political repression, since the act of gridding is also a performative practice of world-making that brings new "worlds" into being.* Many of the contributions in this anthology portray the urban grid as a political technology of social control and repression. Following Foucault (1990 [1976]), we might call this the "repressive hypothesis" of the grid. And, indeed, there seems to be considerable evidence supporting such a claim given the role that the grid has played as a spatial strategy of colonial governmentality, imperial domination, capitalist property regimes, and socialist planning schemes. Yet if we only consider what Grant (2001) calls the "dark side of the grid," we miss a crucial part of the story, which is that gridding is a form of world-making, or "worlding" (Roy and Ong 2011). The making of gridded spaces is performative in the sense that it brings new worlds into being. These "gridded worlds" are not simply imposed upon pre-existing urban spaces and populations; rather, they have the effect of reconfiguring the very experience of urban spatiality itself. Moreover, individuals and populations come to "inhabit" gridded worlds and thus live what Brown (2001) calls "gridded lives." This may sound sinister—and it certainly can be in some contexts—but it also produces new subjectivities for which the grid acquires the appearance of the "natural" order of the world. This taken-for-granted spatial order constrains some while enabling others, which is why it is crucial to examine the differential effects that accompany the production of gridded worlds.

Lastly, *if we are to move beyond Eurocentric-colonialist narratives of the grid, we need to develop more sophisticated theories and methods for analyzing the entangled histories of indigenous, colonial, and postcolonial gridded spaces in both the Global North and Global South.* It is now well-established that orthogonal layouts pre-dated the arrival of Europeans in the Americas (Smith 2007) and Sub-Saharan Africa (Ross 2006), so the Eurocentric claim that the grid was solely a product of European colonial planning in South and Central America or Africa must be rejected (Low 1995; Goerg and de Lemps 2003). Even in cases where the grid plan was largely a European colonial imposition, prior indigenous modifications of the landscape have often been incorporated into the gridded spaces of colonial urban settlement. From the Lebou's *péncs* in Dakar to Wickquasgeck (Broadway) in New York, the entanglements between indigenous and colonial morphologies of landscapes are manifold. Given the extent to which indigenous spatial forms are interwoven into colonial and postcolonial gridded spaces, the indigenous influences on contemporary urban landscapes should be viewed not as relics of a distant past but rather as integral to the geographies of the present.

These conceptual reorientations have been underway, in some quarters at least, for the past few decades, but their acceptance is by no means universal. In fact, the majority of the contributions to this collection do *not* align with one or more of the reconceptualizations outlined above. Indeed, one of our aims as the editors of this anthology is to *disrupt* the ritualistic narrations that have come to pervade the interdisciplinary literature on the grid. By unsettling conventional understandings of the urban grid, this collection seeks to inspire a new generation of urban scholars to pose the question of the grid anew, navigating around the dead-ends of prior scholarship in order to develop a more critical engagement not only with the urban grids of the past but also with the gridded worlds of the future that have yet to be imagined.

References

AlSayyad, N. (1991). *Cities and caliphs: On the genesis of Arab Muslim urbanism*. New York: Greenwood Press.

Aristotle. (1998). *Politics* (trans: C.D.C. Reeve). Indianapolis: Hackett Publishing Co.

Ballon, H. (Ed.). (2012). *The greatest grid: The master plan of Manhattan, 1811–2011*. New York: Columbia University Press.

Beresford, M. (1967). *New towns of the middle ages: Town plantation in England, Wales and Gascony*. London: Lutterworth Press.

Bigon, L., & Hart, T. (2018). Beneath the city's grid: Vernacular and (post)colonial planning interactions in Dakar, Senegal. *Journal of Historical Geography, 59*, 52–67.

Brenner, N. (2013). Theses on urbanization. *Public Culture, 25*(1), 85–114.

Brown, K. (2001). Gridded lives: Why Kazakhstan and Montana are nearly the same place. *American Historical Review, 106*(1), 17–48.

Butzer, K. (1992). From Columbus to Acosta: Science, geography, and the New World. *Annals of the Association of American Geographers, 82*(3), 543–565.

Cameron, D. (2003). *Living inside the grid*. New York: New Museum for Contemporary Art.

Carter, P. (1988). *The road to Botany Bay: An exploration of landscape and history*. New York: Knopf.

Castagnoli, F. (1971 [1956]). *Orthogonal town planning in antiquity*. Cambridge, MA: MIT Press.

Çelik, Z. (1997). *Urban forms and colonial confrontations: Algiers under French rule*. Berkeley: University of California Press.

Cohen, P., & Augustyn, R. (1997). *Manhattan in maps, 1527–1995*. New York: Rizzoli International Publications, Inc.

Cozens, P., & Hillier, D. (2008). The shape of things to come: New urbanism, the grid and the cul-de-sac. *International Planning Studies, 13*(1), 51–73.

Culot, M., & Thiveaud, J. M. (Eds.). (1992). *Architecture française outre mer*. Liège: Pierre. Mardaga.

Deleuze, G. (1997). Postscript on the societies of control. In N. Leach (Ed.), *Rethinking architecture: A reader in cultural theory* (pp. 309–313). London / New York: Routledge.

Denoix, S. (1992). *Décrire le Caire Fustāṭ-Miṣrd'après Ibn Duqmāq et Maqrīzī: l'histoire d'une. partie de la ville du Caire d'après deux historiens égyptiens des XIVe-XVe siècles*. Cairo: Institut français d'archéologie orientale du Caire.

Foucault, M. (1990 [1976]). *The history of sexuality: An introduction, volume 1*. New York: Vintage Books.

Foucault, M. (1995 [1975]). *Discipline and punish: The birth of the prison*. (trans: A. Sheridan). New York: Vintage Books.

Gasparini, G. (1993). The pre-Hispanic grid system: The urban shape of conquest and territorial organization. In R. Bennett (Ed.), *Settlements in the Americas: Cross-cultural perspectives* (pp. 78–109). Newark: University of Delaware Press.

Gasparini, G., & Margolies, L. (1980). *Inca architecture* (trans: P. Lyon). Bloomington: Indiana University Press.

Geyh, P. (2009). Urban grids and urban imaginary: City to cyberspace, cyberspace to city. In P. Geyh (Ed.), *Cities, citizens, and technologies: Urban life and postmodernity* (pp. 63–91). New York: Routledge.

Goerg, O., & de Lemps, X. H. (2003). La ville européenne outre-mer. In J. L. Pinol (Ed.), *Histoire de l'Europe urbaine* (Vol. II (II vols.), pp. 277–551). Paris: Seuil.

Grant, J. (2001). The dark side of the grid: Power and urban design. *Planning Perspectives, 16*(3), 219–241.

Guèye, C. (2002). *Touba. La capitale des mourides*. Paris: Karthala.

Hakim, B. S. (1986). *Arabic-Islamic cities: Building and planning principles*. London: Routledge Kegan Paul.

Haverfield, F. (1913). *Ancient town-planning*. Oxford: Clarendon Press.

Higgins, H. (2009). *The grid book*. Cambridge, MA: MIT Press.

Johnson, H. B. (1976). *Order upon the land: The U.S. rectangular land survey and the upper Mississippi country*. New York: Oxford University Press.

Kostof, S. (1991). *The city shaped: Urban patterns and meanings through history*. London: Little, Brown, and Co.

Krauss, R. (1979). Grids. *October, 9*, 50–64.

Lefebvre, H. (2004). *Rhythmanalysis: Space, time and everyday life* (trans: S. Elden and G. Moore). London: Continuum.

Low, S. (1995). Indigenous architecture and the Spanish American plaza in Mesoamerica and the Caribbean. *American Anthropologist, 97*(4), 748–762.

Low, S. (2000). *On the plaza: The politics of public space and culture*. Austin: University of Texas Press.

Malverti, X., & Picard, A. (1991). Algeria: Military genius and civic design (1830–70). *Planning Perspectives, 6*(1), 207–236.

Marcuse, P. (1987). The grid as city plan: New York City and laissez-faire planning in the nineteenth century. *Planning Perspectives, 2*(3), 287–310.

Mazza, L. (2009). Plan and constitution: Aristotle's Hippodamus – Towards an 'ostensive' definition of spatial planning. *Town Planning Review, 80*(2), 113–141.

Morris, A. E. J. (1972). *History of urban form: Before the industrial revolutions*. New York: Wiley.

Pattison, W.D. (1957). *Beginnings of the American rectangular land survey system, 1784–1800*. University of Chicago, Department of Geography, Research Paper No. 5. Chicago.

Pinol, J. L. (Ed.). (2003). *Histoire de l'Europe urbaine* (2 vols). Paris: Seuil.

Pinon, P. (1996). Raisons et formes de villes: approche comparée des fondations coloniales française au début du xviii siècle. In C. Coquery-Vidrovitch & O. Goerg (Eds.), *La ville européenne outre-mers* (pp. 27–56). Paris: l'Harmattan.

Pope, A. (1996). *Ladders*. New York: Princeton Architectural Press.

Robinson, J. (1990). A perfect system of control? State power and 'native locations' in South Africa. *Environment and Planning, 8*(2), 135–162.

Rose-Redwood, R. (2008). Genealogies of the grid: Revisiting Stanislawski's search for the origin of the grid-pattern town. *Geographical Review, 98*(1), 42–58.

Rose-Redwood, R. (2011). Mythologies of the grid in the Empire City, 1811–2011. *Geographical Review, 101*(3), 396–413.

Rose-Redwood, R. and Li, L. (2011). From island of hills to Cartesian flatland? Using GIS to assess topographical change in New York City, 1819–1999. *The Professional Geographer, 63*(3), 392–405.

Ross, E. (2006). *Sufi city: Urban design and archetypes in Touba*. Rochester: Rochester University Press.

Ross, E., & Bigon, L. (forthcoming). The urban grid and entangled planning cultures in Senegal. *Planning Perspectives*.

Roy, A., & Ong, A. (Eds.). (2011). *Worlding cities: Asian experiments and the art of being global*. Chichester, West Sussex: Wiley-Blackwell.

Scobey, D. (2002). *Empire City: The making and meaning of the New York City landscape.* Philadelphia: Temple University Press.

Scott, J. (1998). *Seeing like a state: How certain schemes to improve the human condition have failed.* New Haven, CT: Yale University Press.

Sennett, R. (1990). American cities: The grid plan and the Protestant ethic. *International Social Science Journal, 42*(3), 269–285.

Siegert, B. (2015). *Cultural techniques: Grids, filters, doors, and other articulations of the real* (trans: Geoffrey Winthrop-Young). New York: Fordham University Press.

Sinou, A. (1993). *Comptoirs et villes coloniales du Sénégal: Saint-Louis, Gorée, Dakar.* Paris: Éditions Karthala, ORSTOM.

Smith, M. (2007). Form and meaning in the earliest cities: A new approach to ancient urban planning. *Journal of Planning History, 6*(1), 3–47.

Soulillou, J. (Ed.). (1993). *Rives colonials: Architecture de Saint-Louis à Douala.* Paris: ORSTOM.

Stanislawski, D. (1946). The origin and spread of the grid-pattern town. *Geographical Review, 36*(1), 105–120.

Stanislawski, D. (1947). Early Spanish town planning in the New World. *Geographical Review, 37*(1), 94–105.

Stelter, G. (1993). Military considerations and colonial town planning: France and New France in the seventeenth century. In R. Bennett (Ed.), *Settlements in the Americas: Cross-cultural perspectives* (pp. 210–237). Newark: University of Delaware Press.

Trachtenberg, A. (1964). The rainbow and the grid. *American Quarterly, 16*(1), 3–19.

Vance, J. (1977). *This scene of man: The role and structure of the city in the geography of Western civilization.* New York: Harper's College Press.

Vance, J. (1990). *The continuing city: Urban morphology in Western civilization.* Baltimore: Johns Hopkins University Press.

Wheatley, P. (1971). *The pivot of the four quarters: A preliminary enquiry into the origins and character of the ancient Chinese city.* Edinburgh: Edinburgh University Press.

Young, M. (2015). *Broadway.* Charleston: Arcadia Publishing.

Zhu, J. (2004). City plan as ideology. In J. Zhu (Ed.), *Chinese spatial strategies: Imperial Beijing, 1420–1911* (pp. 28–44). London: RoutledgeCurzon.

Chapter 2
The Origin and Spread of the Grid-Pattern Town

Dan Stanislawski

Abstract Originally published in 1946, this chapter is a classic diffusionist account of the origin and spread of the grid as an urban spatial form. The author examines a variety of arguments in favor and opposed to the use of the grid as an urban plan. The chapter then proceeds to trace a genealogy of the grid's origin in the ancient Indus Valley settlement of Mohenjo-Daro as part of the author's effort to support the claim that the grid plan was a one-time invention which subsequently spread from its source region to become a global urban phenomenon.

Keywords Grid · Urban history · Mohenjo-Daro · Indus Valley civilization · New World · Antiquity · Middle Ages · Renaissance

Introduction

Many geographers have concerned themselves with the study of towns, their distribution, position, site, function, and anatomy, and yet, of the innumerable articles and books written on this subject, none, to my knowledge, has been devoted to the origin and spread of the design that is now standard throughout much of the world—the grid pattern with straight streets (parallel or normal to one another) and rectangular blocks. It is true that some writers have casually considered this pattern, concluding that it spontaneously recommended itself to the town builder whoever or

This chapter was originally published as Stanislawski, D. (1946). "The Origin and Spread of the Grid-Pattern Town." *Geographical Review*, 36(1): 105–120. Copyright © 1946 by the American Geographical Society of New York. Reproduced with permission of John Wiley & Sons, Inc.

D. Stanislawski (✉) (deceased)
e-mail: permissions@wiley.com

© Springer International Publishing AG, part of Springer Nature 2018   21
R. Rose-Redwood, L. Bigon (eds.), *Gridded Worlds: An Urban Anthology*,
https://doi.org/10.1007/978-3-319-76490-0_2

wherever he might be. I likewise made this assumption at first. But the obviousness of the grid is more apparent than real. In the record of its use it seems to have been no more obvious than, for example, the wheel.

My interest started in the Spanish towns of the New World, where I soon found that not only did native towns fail to exhibit such a pattern but during the earliest period of Spanish settlement it was lacking also,[1] and subsequent Spanish cities, except when constructed under direct orders, were likely to vary greatly from the simple rectangular design.[2] It was this that indicated the need for further inquiry into the background of grid towns. My investigation led me into the Middle East and into the third millennium before Christ. That the grid may have an even longer history awaits further archeologic investigation. It may have been a one-time invention which has spread from its source region until at present it encompasses the globe.

Arguments For and Against the Grid

The casual assumption that the grid almost automatically becomes the pattern of a new settlement cannot hold up in the light of the history of its distribution. Only those regions directly associated with, or accessible to, areas of earlier use have shown evidence of its existence. I know of no region in the world that will clearly contradict this thesis. But when once known and recognized and fitted into the culture pattern, the grid has both obvious advantages and some disadvantages. Let us consider the disadvantages first. From the point of view of the individual there are many reasons for a man to place his building, whether it be dwelling or workshop or temple, at an angle with buildings nearby and at some distance from them rather than directly in line and adjoining. Such placement offers advantages in terms of circulation of air and exposure to sunlight, as well as accessibility of the various parts, whereas in the grid efficiency is largely lost without the alignment and juxtaposition of buildings. Secondly, again as regards the individual, there are other plans that would have greater utility. For example, the radial plan with streets leading out from a center like spokes from the hub of a wheel offers certain advantages over the grid in communication from the periphery to the center. Thirdly, the topography very frequently indicates easier street planning than the insistence upon straight lines mounting hills and falling steeply into valleys.

To consider the advantages of the grid plan is to consider a longer, and from many points of view, a superior list. Perhaps its greatest single virtue is the fact that as a generic plan for disparate sites it is eminently serviceable, and if an equitable

---

[1] There is no record of the use of the grid pattern for a generation and a half after the Spaniards arrived in the New World. They founded many new towns during this period, but the grid did not appear until the third decade of the sixteenth century.

[2] After the restrictions were weakened—for example, in the eighteenth century—many towns came into being, but, with examples of the grid all around them, they grew with hardly a suggestion of that pattern.

distribution of property is desirable, there is hardly any other plan conceivable. It can be extended indefinitely without altering the fundamental pattern or the organic unity of the city. Property can be apportioned in rectangular plots fitting neatly into a predetermined scheme of streets and plazas. It can be sketched on the drawing board and, within certain obvious limitations, made serviceable. It is also far the easiest plan to lay out with crude instruments of measurement. For a *compact* settlement of rectangular buildings this scheme is the only one that lends itself to the efficient use of space. Moreover, a distinct advantage for the grid-plan town under certain political conditions is that of military control. This would apply in the case of subject towns to be held under control; for it has been clearly recognized, not only by the Spaniards in the New World[3] but by Romans and early Greeks before them (Morgan, 1914; Martienssen, 1941), that a tortuous street facilitates defense by individuals and a straight street lends itself to control from without.[4]

Theories of Origin

One theory as to the origin of the grid is based on its obvious efficiency in the use of space where rectangular buildings are involved. The reasoning is seductive but not borne out by facts. Examples of strict rectangularity of buildings with a highly irregular street pattern are far too common. They long predate the first use of the grid and continue to the present in large areas of the world.[5] Another point of interest with regard to theories of the origin of the grid-pattern town concerns the straight processional street. Another far too casual assumption was likewise made here that such a street would suggest the advisability of others parallel or at right angles to it. This also fails to be borne out, both in Egypt and through the long history of early Mesopotamia (Hughes and Lamborn 1923; Von Gerkan 1942).

The theory that the grid stemmed from an orientation toward the points of the compass, probably based on religion, has proved equally inadequate. In Mesopotamia, Egypt, and early Greece the orientation of a building and even a street was common, but it did not lead to the laying out of other streets in accor-

---

[3] In these orders of Philip II it is suggested that where horses are available the wide street is better for defense. Obviously "defense" meant defense of Spaniards, not of natives, for the former were possessors of horses (*caballeros*). A narrow, tortuous street would have meant the doom of Spanish horsemen in a native revolt ("Fundación de pueblos en el siglo XVI" 1935).

[4] It is sometimes assumed that the grid was the product of military thought. That it recommended itself to military thinking is not, however, proof that it was originated by soldiers. Polybius says: "The whole camp [Roman] is a square, with streets and other constructions regularly planned like a town" (Hultsch 1889, 484). Note the last words. The prior existence of the nonmilitary organization is implied.

[5] Throughout the long early history of Mesopotamia the rectangular building was common (see Langdon 1923). Nevertheless, irregularity of streets is also typical (see Speiser 1935). Egypt, for an even longer time than Mesopotamia, showed, with one exception, this combination of rectangular buildings and irregular streets (see Maspero 1892; Martienssen 1941; von Gerkan 1942).

dance (Maspero 1892; Langdon, 1923; Speiser 1935; von Gerkan 1942). On the other hand, in Mohenjo-Daro, in northwestern India, there was obvious orientation of all the streets and rectangularity of blocks, yet excavation has shown no temple, and there may have been none (Marshall 1931). It seems, then, that religious significance as basic to the grid can likewise be written off as inapplicable.

In weighing these advantages and disadvantages of the grid pattern certain things seem clear:

1. It is possible only in either a totally new urban unit or a newly added subdivision. This pattern is not conceivable except as an organic whole. If the planner thinks in terms of single buildings, separate functions, or casual growth, the grid will not come into being; for with each structure considered separately the advantage lies with irregularity. History is replete with examples of the patternless, ill-formed town that has been the product of growth in response to the desires of individual builders. Nor is it simple to rectify an older city. The difficulty, and probably the impossibility, of this has been demonstrated by Von Gerkan (1942).[6]

2. Some form of centralized control, political, religious, or military, is certainly indicated for all known grid-plan towns. When centralized power disintegrates, even if the grid pattern has been established it disappears. This is indicated clearly by medieval Europe as compared with Europe under Roman rule.

3. It may indicate colonial status, not necessarily a situation in which the younger settlement is bled by the older, but more frequently an amiable association for mutual benefit between mother and daughter settlements.

4. Desire for measured apportionment of land. But none of the foregoing can be said to indicate that a strongly organized political group desirous of founding a colony will, because of its obvious virtues, set up a grid town. The virtues are obvious only when demonstrated. This is confirmed by history. According to the evidence, only those exposed to the idea will utilize this pattern. Hence another requirement must be added:

5. Knowledge of the grid.

The City of Mohenjo-Daro

The earliest record we have of this street pattern is that of Mohenjo-Daro, a city which flourished in the first half of the third millennium before Christ (Mackay 1938).[7] This city was not casually built. The precision of its plan could not have been accidental. It was a well-rounded concept designed to fit the needs of a highly

---

[6] This fact was recognized by the Spanish king in his instructions to Cortes (see "Colección de documentos in éditos relativos aldescubrimiento, conquista y organización de las antiguas posesiones españolas de ultramar" 1885–1925).

[7] The dates here given—2800-2500 BC—correct an earlier assumption. But these dates do not indicate the earliest establishment or the end of the city. It may be far older than these dates suggest and may have continued its existence for many centuries after 2500 BC.

organized, highly urbanized people. The streets were straight and either parallel or at right angles to one another, as far as the inaccurate instruments of the time permitted. This was not a placing of buildings merely with the idea of the individual in mind. The concept was that of an organic city in which all parts were designed to function within the whole.

Trade was of enormous importance to the people of the city (Mackay 1933, 1935). The very high quality of the manufactures makes evident that it was indubitably the home of men of skill with a long background of training and organization. That Mohenjo-Daro does not represent the earliest settlement of this people may be indicated by the fact suggested above, that the grid city is completely planned and established as a new unit. We can, therefore, postulate that the ancestors of the people inhabiting Mohenjo-Daro had a long history of social organization in this region or elsewhere (see also Marshall 1931).

For the next known example we must seek much later times,[8] although there may be Oriental material that will, when known, alter opinion with regard to this intervening period. There is at present no reason to suppose that any Oriental settlement with anything suggesting a grid pattern could rival Mohenjo-Daro in antiquity. However, Creel (1936) has some interesting though inconclusive statements on early Chinese planned buildings and streets.[9] The next record of the grid is found at the eastern Mediterranean in the eighth century before Christ. Sargon of Assyria, tiring of his old capital, decided to perpetuate his glory by the establishment of a new one, Dur-Sarginu. For its site he chose the unimportant and formless little village of Magganuba, where he laid out his new capital precisely in terms of the grid. This was not destined to last, but the gap in time was not to be long until Hippodamus, and undoubtedly his predecessors, would take up the idea in Greece and Greek lands and establish it in such fashion that it was not again to be lost to the record.[10]

---

[8] Had this paper been written somewhat earlier, there would have been included settlements of Italy that were originally described by L. Pigorini (see various publications in the *Bulletino di Paletnologia Italiana*, Parma) and accepted and further developed by many serious writers. The description of how a Bronze Age people crossed the Alps to the Italian plain took with them, even to Taranto, their pile construction, using it in precisely planned towns, makes a fascinating story, but unfortunately it holds little truth. This has been demonstrated by the exhaustive work of Gösta Säflund (1939), reviewed by Hawkes and Stiassny (1940). There is no proof of systematic planning of the town pattern or of most of the other features attributed by Pigorini to the settlers of the second millennium before Christ. No migration from the lake country is proved, or any connection of Hungarian and South Italian settlements with those of North Italy. David Randall-MacIver (1939) refers to the uneasy feeling he had had concerning the terremare theories and writes in praise of Säflund's conclusions.

[9] Creel (1936) says that buildings in a settlement of the fourteenth century before Christ were carefully oriented but that their arrangement otherwise has not yet been determined. He quotes a poet of a later period who, in describing the city, said that land was distributed in predetermined plots and that, under central supervision, houses were planned along streets that presumably were straight.

[10] Babylon and its form are a matter of question. Herodotus credited it with a grid form—or at least so he seems to imply. Robert Koldewey (1914, 242) says: "The streets, though not entirely regular, show an obvious attempt to run them as much in straight lines as possible, so that Herodotus was able to describe them as straight. They show a tendency to cross at right angles."

A Continuing Tradition in India?

The question may be raised why one should attribute to a single invention a plan that has appeared in places far distant from one another with a gap of long centuries between. The question is not an unreasonable one. A further inquiry into Indian sources might yield the answer. The data that we have at hand, although inaccurate as to dating, seem to indicate a strong possibility that the tradition of Mohenjo-Daro has been continued in India, perhaps unbrokenly. If one were to accept the claims of recent Indian writers with regard to town planning in their country, one would need to seek no further; for it is their contention that town planning existed in India long centuries before the Christian Era.[11] The brilliance and completeness of Indian town planning indicated in the Silpa Sastra is not an overnight creation.[12] It is the outcome of the thought of many men and must have evolved through many centuries. The casual assumption that Indian town planning derives from Alexander's generals, the Greek Bactrian kings, or Vitruvius and the Romans may not be a fair one, in view of the great elaboration of Indian thought, and in view of the indicated contribution of architectural types from the Iranian plateau as well as of the possible development of town planning, even among the Dravidians (Venkatarama-Ayyar 1916). India may have carried the tradition of this town pattern for all later ages to accept at their leisure.

One regrets that Sargon, in the eighth century before Christ, did not record why he chose the grid or where he found his sources for such a plan, but again, eyes may have been turned to the East. The trade from Mesopotamia through Persia and even into India cannot be questioned.[13] That the East was contributing ideas, specifically in architecture, which might suggest a contribution to broader planning is shown by Herzfeld's (1935) demonstration that even the Ionic pillar was a product of lands to the east of Greece.

To those who question the assumption of Indian derivation it can be asked: "Where has the pattern of the grid town appeared without possible connections with India?" No part of Europe or Asia except those regions that had contact with this

---

[11] There is no doubt of the fact that the Greek Megasthenes wrote glowingly in the third century of the city of Pataliputra. It was described by him as an elongated rectangle (see McCrindle 1877; Bogle 1929). This was after the invasion of Alexander, but hardly a long enough time had intervened for the construction of the city by order of the Greeks. Indian writers, however, would push their dates even further back on the basis of their evidence. It is unfortunate that there is a certain "timeless" quality to Indian scholarship that casts some doubt upon its usefulness. The dating of the records is far from conclusive. See the following: Raz (1834); Venkatarama-Ayyar (1916); Tarn (1938, esp. 419); Rhys-Davids (1894).

[12] Concerning this and collateral subjects, see Acharya (1933). Śilpa Śastra is a collective term for numerous old treatises on the manual arts of the Hindus.

[13] Trade between these countries was well established at the time of Mohenjo-Daro and probably even before that. See Langdon (1923); Mackay (1925); Grousset (1929); Hall and Woolley (1927); Stein (1934); and Sykes (1934).

area of oldest appearance has given evidence of the grid pattern.[14] Nor did any part of Africa exhibit this pattern until Alexander introduced it as derived from eastern Mediterranean lands.[15]

No Proven New World Examples

Nowhere did this plan appear in the New World, statements to the contrary notwithstanding. The Chimu city of Chan Chan on the Peruvian coast certainly was, it is true, one of straight lines and right angles (Holstein 1927; Rich 1942). Some of these lines were maintained for a notable length, but they did not carry on through; the organic quality of the grid plan was broken by irregularities. It was rather a series of blocks, many rectangular, but not communicating with other blocks in the functional way necessary to the grid.

Many contentions have been made concerning the use of the grid in Mexican towns, but here again the evidence does not support it. The famous "Plano en Papel de Maguey," despite some theories to the contrary (Kubler 1942), is obviously a post-Conquest design drawn to the order of Europeans (Toussaint et al. 1938). The theory that Tenochtitlan had rectangular blocks because of the rectangularity of its temples and temple squares does not stand up, in view of the fact that so many places in the Old World had square temples and corresponding courtyards, with the remainder of the settlement clearly at variance. Certainly Cortes and Bemal Diaz remarked about the straightness of the passageways leading into Mexico, but nowhere did they suggest more than the straightness of single streets.[16] It might also be indicated that in their apparent surprise at first sight of this straight passageway these Spaniards, who were used to the tortuous streets of sixteenth-century Spain, surely should have been even more struck with the rectangularity of blocks. Failure to mention such a condition may well be taken to indicate that it did not exist.[17]

---

[14] It has been mentioned above that new material on the Orient may yet alter conclusions. But note the irregularity of Khotan, a settlement of Central Asia earlier than the Christian Era (Stein 1907). Neither the cities of Phoenicia nor her colonies exhibited the pattern (see Whitaker 1921; Von Gerkan 1942). The grid was not known in Minoan Crete (Martienssen 1941) or in Greece during its early centuries. Pre-Roman Spain lacked it, as did pre-Roman France (Gantner 1928).

[15] There is one exception to be noted here, the little settlement of Kahun in Egypt, which was planned and set up as a unit by Pharaoh Usertesen II as a settlement for the workmen on the pyramid being constructed at that time (see Flinders-Petrie 1890). However, this settlement was established some centuries after the establishment of Mohenjo-Daro, when the connections of Egypt with Sumeria and those of Sumeria and Mohenjo-Daro were clear. Moreover, Kahun was not an organic unit but rather like a barracks.

[16] Hernán Cortés (1932, 98): "Son las calles della [referring to Temixtitan—site of present Mexico City], digo las principales, muy anchas y muy derechas." By his limiting phrase he specifically excludes all but the main streets as being wide or straight (also, see Díaz del Castillo 1939).

[17] Note also in Saville (1917), the failure to indicate anything resembling a grid and also the comparison of various cities of Mexico with cities of Spain. This may not be proof that the pattern of streets in Mexican cities was as amorphous as those of sixteenth-century Spain, but it certainly does not suggest the striking difference that would immediately be apparent to a Spaniard if they were straight.

According to present evidence, the rectangular grid was nowhere a casual, spontaneous thing. In spite of its apparent obviousness, it would seem that it was not put into practice by any except those who had known it previously or who had access to regions of its occurrence.

The Greek Record

The continuous record starts in the sixth century before Christ, in Greek lands (Robinson and Graham 1938). Before this time the regular pattern was clearly not a typical feature of Greek settlement (Lanchester 1925; Gantner 1928; Goldman 1931; Martienssen 1941). There are many examples of earlier Greek cities showing anything but the regularity of the grid plan, and a definite record of cities settled at least as late as the middle of the seventh century before Christ shows that irregularity was typical. In fact, according to Von Gerkan, as late as the early part of the fifth century some cities were settled without a standard pattern. Hippodamus, a Milesian, is credited by Aristotle with being the planner of the grid-pattern harbor of Athens, the Piraeus (Gardner 1911; Ellis 1912), but even earlier than the Piraeus—probably also of the fifth century—was the grid design of Hippodamus' own birthplace, Miletus. There can be no doubt that the plans of Hippodamus were not born in his brain but derived from earlier times—there is at least one clear example, Olbia— and perhaps distant places. It is interesting to note that the earliest plans are associated with Ionic Asia Minor and settlements by Ionians on the Black Sea, and not nuclear Greece. So the first appearance among Greeks was in the western extension of Asia, where it could have been based on earlier knowledge and use.

Long before the time of Hippodamus, Greeks had been expanding their knowledge of the world through their growing trade connections. For several centuries these connections were those of "tramp" traders, who either settled among "barbarian" peoples, taking more and more control of the region by reason of their superior training, or merely came temporarily to these regions to exchange merchandise. This did not involve planning. It was simple contact for the purposes of exchange and profit.

The Greeks pursued their course westward through the Mediterranean, making contacts with the present Italian mainland and islands. Many different groups were involved in this trade until the latter part of the eighth century, when Corinth was infected with the virus of what might be termed precocious imperialism. Whereas before the founding of Syracuse all Greeks, so far as can be determined, traded with the west, after 734 BC Corinthian goods became dominant in the market and eventually were far more important than the materials from all other Greek traders combined (Blakeway 1935).

Corinth was operating according to a plan. Whereas theretofore settlements had, presumably, been made rather casually, Syracuse was founded under authority from the mother city and by settlers who were dispatched to the place with orders based on careful planning. These orders included instructions for the division of land for use by the settlers. Here was a clear indication of the growth of centralized control. It was likewise an indication of increasing importance of trade as well as of a possible pressure of population at home.

To the east the Greeks were making other contacts. Miletus sent out secondary colonies, particularly after the middle of the eighth century, to take over the trade of the Black Sea. The "great Asiatic mother of colonies," like Corinth, was not averse to the use of force to maintain trade supremacy. She was, however, the greatest center of Oriental influence, and the attainments of these Asiatic Greeks are thought by some to have been far superior to those of the European homeland. Their contacts with the interior of Asia Minor and the countries of high civilization to the east of the Mediterranean were a liberal education (Hogarth 1924).

The drive of colonization both in the Mediterranean and in the Black Sea was temporarily reduced during the period of the Tyrants (Hogarth 1925). During their regime, however, there was an even greater centralization of control, and part of this remained to contribute to the colonization that increased again after their decline. After the epoch of the Tyrants, the trade of the Asiatic Greeks spread greatly through the lands of the friendly Lydian king Alyattes. This monarch controlled a considerable part of the interior of Asia Minor and had alliances with Mesopotamia, Egypt, and others. His son, Croesus, likewise a Hellenophile, offered continuing opportunities for Greek traders, which were only partly broken by his defeat at the hands of the Persians just after the first half of the sixth century.

The planning that is called Hippodamic was a product of the period following that of the concentration of power in the hands of the Tyrants, and also following the period of greatly expanded trade through Lydian country into Mesopotamia and other eastern lands where examples of the grid were to be seen. Olbia was laid out in grid form at the end of the sixth century, Miletus not long afterward, in the fifth century, after the destruction of the old city by Cyrus of Persia.

By this time all of the factors favoring the grid had come into being: (1) there was centralized control, and a background of town planning; (2) totally new units were being founded, with dependent—"colonial"—status; (3) knowledge of the grid was available from the East; and (4) desirability of the grid as a general plan would have been apparent, especially with regard to the distribution of land, which was important to the land-hungry Greeks.

It is likewise interesting to note, and perhaps it is the explanation of the Greek acceptance of this plan, that its methodical regularity and orderly quality well suited the Greek philosophic view of worldly order created out of variety. The idea of a corporate whole is typical of Greek thought of the period (Kroeber 1944). During this period the settlement of towns was widespread, and the grid was used by Greeks not only in their homeland but in western places as well. For example, there is Thurii in southern Italy, commonly attributed to Hippodamus; there is Selinus in Sicily, and Naples on the peninsula. These undoubtedly made their contribution to, and saw their continuance in, Roman planning of a somewhat later date.

Effects of Alexander's Conquests

After the period of Hippodamus the next striking development of the use of the grid plan is in the Alexandrian age, when it was spread so widely by the conqueror and his heirs. Again it is of interest to speculate whether the strengthening of interest in the plan at this time was not a product both of the background in Greek lands and of further knowledge acquired in eastern lands. Alexander brought in his entourage not only fighting men but men of intellectual attainment who might easily have been struck by urban developments in the lands they visited.

The cities that remain from the time of Alexander or his successors present us with excellent examples of the planning of the period. Many were founded in Anatolia. Priene, the best known, through the work of Wiegand and his associates (Wiegand and Schrader 1904), is a perfect example of the grid pattern, its buildings precisely oriented and carefully aligned with the streets. In the more distant lands are the cities of the Greek Bactrian kings and those of India proper, which, although commonly accepted to be of Alexandrian age or later, may indeed show an earlier history.

The transfer of knowledge along the Mediterranean by Greeks, however, was a matter of early centuries—long proceeding the Alexandrian age—and the technique of town planning was carried into lands that were to become Roman. Here it became basic to later Italian settlement form. Greek traders were in Italy centuries before the rise of Rome. During this early period, probably in the eighth century, the Etruscans arrived from the east and settled in the peninsula (Dohan 1942).

The early Etruscan settlements were certainly not neatly plotted grids, though, within the exigencies of the hill locations which they chose for their settlements, they may have striven for greater regularity than appears at first glance.

Greek influence was felt throughout Etruria from the outset. After the middle of the seventh century, however, the influence became more strongly Ionic (Mühlestein 1929). This was the period of the first definite Etruscan grid town, Marzabotto, built at the end of the sixth century, and perhaps the first real grid town in Italy. Here the *cardo* and *decumanus* of later Roman cities clearly appear (Ducati 1927).

It is to be recalled that Ionic influence in Italy coincides not only with Marzabotto but with Olbia, and roughly with Miletus, all of which used the grid plan that had had earlier exemplification in parts of western Asia. It is to be recalled likewise that Ionian Greeks had wide experience and knowledge of these regions of western Asia.

In the early period of Roman development there is little, if any, evidence of awareness of the grid—or of town planning at all. It was the late Republic and the early Empire that saw the rapid development of the form. Then it spread through Roman colonies to near and distant points in the Empire.

The Roman Grid

The grid plan as used by the Romans was not precisely that of the Greeks. It was an adjustment of the plan used by Greek traders to the demands of a Roman order, perhaps with influences derived from Etruscan practices, with an interesting association of the Roman block and the *jugerium*, the rural unit of surveying (Bosanquet 1915). The town block was clearly rooted in history, and linked with the distribution of agricultural plots.

This rigorous, clear pattern lent itself smoothly to the necessities and point of view of the Roman state. Here was an intense centralization of power in the hands of men faced with the pressure of population and the necessity of protecting exposed frontiers of the Empire. For both these problems daughter colonies were an obvious solution. Particularly after the civil wars of Sulla, Caesar, and Octavian, who had amassed great armies to support their causes, there was a pressing necessity for the absorption of these soldiers into a peacetime economy. This was largely achieved through the establishment of newly planned urban units in various parts of the Empire. Given the necessities of the Roman state, the psychology of its rulers, the background of its history, what was more logical than to establish the grid wherever new urban units were planned?

Following the downfall of the Western Empire, the era of city planning came to a close, and, more important, even those cities that were completely planned and built before the dissolution of the Empire fell into other ways and forms, so that the end of the medieval period saw hardly an example of Roman planning in the cities that she had established (Jürgens 1926; Pidal 1935).

The Medieval Collapse

Following upon the organized control and planning of the Romans, the early medieval period saw a degree of collapse in which the factors militating against the serviceability of the grid pattern town became dominant. Centralized power, basic to its establishment, no longer existed. Division of power and localization of authority came into being. No longer was the broad power present which tends to maintain a single pattern. Secondly, as has been indicated, defense of the local unit was facilitated by tortuous lanes; straight thoroughfares lent themselves to control by centralized power. Thirdly, with local control each unit used its topography as individuals saw fit. There was no necessity for following the rigorous grid plan. Indeed, for many topographic situations it would have been costly and excessively difficult, and it served no real purpose in this feudal period. Fourthly, this was a period in which trade was greatly restricted, and the grid plan, which had functioned well for a trading center, was no longer needed for that purpose. Perhaps more important than all others is the fact that there was no longer the idea of equitably distributed plots of ground. This was not a period of small holders asserting their rights over definite recognized portions of territory. The feudal order operated on an entirely different basis.

However, in spite of all these tendencies toward breakdown, the pattern was never completely lost in the former Roman lands. Several examples remain in northern Italy—Turin, for example. Traces remain in such places as Braga in Portugal, Chester in England, Tarragona and Mérida in Spain, and Cologne and Trier in Germany. Some would place Oxford in this category, though this now seems dubious (Hughes and Lamborn 1923). It has been fortunate for the planners of later centuries that these examples remain.

The Renaissance

If the early part of the Middle Ages saw the decline and almost the obliteration of this pattern, the later Middle Ages saw its adumbration again, and the Renaissance its establishment. Again political conditions had changed so that central power, planning, and trade re-emerged and local units existing in the feudal structure began to lose their dominance—in short, the trend again contributed to the utility of the grid (Brinckmann 1911).

Particularly was there a striking advance in the use of the pattern in the thirteenth century. In this century at least one urban unit using the grid was made by Italians in Sicily. The Germans, in establishing cities on the Slavic frontiers and beyond, such as some of those in Prussia, Breslau, and Cracow, used this plan as their basis.

The Grid in France and England

But most important during this period was the establishment in France of the bastides, the *villes-neuves*. The record is clear. The site was plotted into rectangular blocks, divided by streets parallel to one another or at right angles, in which the main roads running from the gates led to a large square or market place at the center. Around this square were the homes of the more important residents, with arcades giving shade to the walk (de Verneilh 1847).

The most important founders of the French bastides were St. Louis and his brother, Alfonse of Poitiers. Kings of England who possessed French territory at this time also built towns of a similar order in France.

Again the function and desirability of the pattern are apparent with the change in the political and social order. Again power was centralized, and it was those individuals that exerted power over a large area of land who were responsible for the establishment of the towns. Again it is to be noted that it was not the replotting of existing towns. This is virtually impossible. These were completely new units founded under the direction of centralized power, and all at one time. They were under military control and functioned as military centers. Also, the plots in town were distributed on the basis of standardized units, and again it is to be noted that the agricultural plots beyond the city were likewise distributed in terms of standard units.

The situation in England is probably not as clear as that in France, but perhaps it is even more interesting. Although English settlement of this period was clearly influenced more strongly by France than by any other source, there are still the yet undetermined possibilities of an earlier development within England itself. As was mentioned above, Oxford is thought by some to be a Roman foundation. This seems a dubious postulate. It appears now that Oxford was clearly later than Roman times, but almost as clearly it seems indicated that it may have been earlier than the period of the French bastides, and may perhaps have reached back into Saxon times. Ludlow is another example of a town that was clearly earlier than the period of the bastide. It is a foundation of early Norman time, settled during the twelfth century, and probably using the grid plan. This, of course, suggests knowledge brought in from the continent. It may well have served as a partial inspiration for later models.

The real development of towns in England, mostly in the pattern of the grid, began with Edward I. It should be noted that Edward possessed territories in France, his training was French, his language was French. He knew well the town planning of thirteenth-century France, and it is clear that this was the model he had in mind in setting up the so-called Welsh bastides and other towns in England. Again the factors contributed to the utility of this plan; for now England with a centralized authority felt itself in need of totally new units and had the experience of France before it.

With one exception nothing more need be said regarding the grid in Western Europe. Its serviceability in the period of expanding settlement both within Europe and in European colonies was obvious. Never has it been lost since the time of its redevelopment toward the end of the medieval period.

Spain and the New World

The exception to be noted is Spain. Isolated from the rest of Europe during the long period when she was involved in internecine warfare, she failed for the most part to take part in developments of neighboring countries. It is unfortunate that she lacked their experience with Renaissance planning; for it was she that conquered the New World and established thousands of completely new settlements there. As she was uninitiated in the methods of town planning, her settlements were amorphous for about three decades after the beginning of her control. Finally she realized the necessity for a plan, and for this she turned to her neighbors and beyond them to the Roman and Greek sources from which they had profited. But this is a subject in itself and must be treated in a separate paper.

References

Acharya, P. (Trans. from Sanskrit, 1933). *Architecture of Manasara*. 7 vols. London: Oxford University Press.

Blakeway, A. (1935). Prolegomena to the study of Greek commerce with Italy, Sicily and France in the Eighth and Seventh Centuries, B.C. *British School at Athens Annual No. 33*, Session 1932–1933, 170–208.

Bogle, L. (1929). *Town planning in India today*. 10 vols. London: Oxford University Press.

Bosanquet, R. (1915). Greek and Roman towns. *Town Planning Review, 5*(4), 286–293.

Brinckmann, A. (1911). The evolution of the ideal in town planning since the renaissance. In *Transactions of the Town Planning Conference, London, October 10–15, 1910*. London: Royal. Institute of British Architects.

Colección de documentos in éditos relativos aldescubrimiento, conquista y organización de las antiguas posesiones españolas de ultramar. Ser. 2, 17 vols. (1885–1925). Madrid.

Cortés, H. (1932). *Cartas de relación*. Madrid: Espasa-Calpe.

Creel, H. (1936). *The birth of China*. London: Jonathan Cape.

Díaz del Castillo, B. (1939). *Historia verdadera de la conquista de la Nueva España* (3 vols). Madrid: Edición Critica.

Dohan, E. (1942). *Italian tomb groups in the university museum*. Philadelphia: University of Pennsylvania Press.

Ducati, P. (1927). *Storia dell' arte Etrusca* (2 vols). Florence: Rinascimento del Libro.

Ellis, W. (trans. from Greek, 1912). *A treatise on government*. New York: E.P. Duton & Co.

Flinders-Petrie, W. (1890). *Kahun, Gurob, and Hawara*. London: Keegan Paul.

Fundación de pueblos en el siglo XVI. (1935). *Boletín del Archivo Generál de la Nación* 6: Section 116.

Gantner, J. (1928). *Grundformen der euro-päischen stadt*. Vienna: A. Schroll.

Gardner, P. (1911). The planning of Hellenistic cities. *Transactions of the Town Planning*. Conference, London, October 10–15, 1910, London: Royal Institute of British Architects.

von Gerkan, A. (1942). *Griechische städteanlagen*. Berlin and Leipzig: Städteanlagen.

Goldman, H. (1931). *Excavations at Eutresis in Boeotia*. Cambridge, MA: W. Green.

Grousset, R. (1929). *Les civilisations de l'Orient*. 4 vols. (vol. I: L'Orient). Paris: G. Crès.

Hall, H., & Woolley, C. (1927). *Ur Excavations. 2 vols. (vol. I: Al Ubaid)*. Oxford University Press: London.

Herzfeld, E. (1935). *Archaeological history of Iran*. London: Oxford University Press.

Hogarth, D. (1924). Hellenic settlement in Asia Minor. In J. Bury, S. Cook and F. Adcock (Eds), *The Cambridge ancient history* (vol. 2, pp. 542–562), 12 vols. New York: Cambridge University Press.

Hogarth, D. (1925). Lydia and Ionia. In J. Bury, S. Cook and F. Adcock (Eds. vols. 1–6), *The Cambridge ancient history* (vol. 3, pp. 501–526), 12 vols. New York: Cambridge University Press.

Holstein, O. (1927). Chan-Chan: Capital of the great Chimu. *Geographical Review, 17*(1), 36–61.

Hawkes, C., & Stiassny, E. (1940). Review of Säflund's Le terremare delle provincie do modena, Reggio, Emilio, Parma, Piacenza. *Journal of Roman Studies, 30*(1), 89–97.

Hughes, T., & Lamborn, E. (1923). *Towns and town-planning, ancient & modern*. Oxford: Clarendon Press.

Hultsch, F. (1889). *The histories of Polybius* (Vol. 2. Edited and translated by E. Shuckburgh). London: Cambridge University Press.

Jürgens, O. (1926). Spanische städte: Ihre bauliche Entwicklung und Ausgestaltung Hamburgische Universität Abhandl. aus dem Gebiet der Auslandskunde, 23 (B). Hamburg: Friederichsen & Co.

Koldewey, R. (1914). *The excavations at Babylon*. Translated by A. Johns. London: Macmillan.

Kroeber, A. (1944). *Configurations of culture growth*. Berkeley: University of California Press.

Kubler, G. (1942). Mexican urbanism in the sixteenth century. *Art Bulletin, 24*, 160–171.

Lanchester, H. (1925). *The art of town planning*. London: Chapman and Hall.

Langdon, S. (1923). Early Babylonia and its cities. In J. Bury, S. Cook, & F. Adcock (Eds.), *The Cambridge ancient history* (Vol. 1, pp. 356-401), 12 vols. New York: Cambridge University Press.

Mackay, D. (1933). Mohenjo-Daro and the ancient civilization of the Indus Valley. *Annual Report of the Smithsonian Institute 1932* (Washington), pp. 429–444.

Mackay, E. (1925). Sumerian connections with ancient India. *Journal of the Royal Asiatic Society of Great Britain and Ireland* (London), October: n.p.

Mackay, E. (1935). *The Indus civilization*. London: Clay and Sons.

Mackay, E. (1938). *Further excavations at Mohenjo-Daro*. New Delhi: The Government of India.

Marshall, J. (Ed.). (1931). *Mohenjo-Daro and the Indus civilization* (Vol. 3). London: Arthur Probsthain.

Martienssen, R. (1941). Greek cities. *South African Architectural Record* (Johannesburg), January: 1–58.

Maspero, G. (1892). *Life in ancient Egypt and Assyria*. New York: D. Appleton and Company.

McCrindle, J. (1877). *Ancient India as described by Megasthenes and Arrian*. Calcutta: Thacker, Spink.

Morgan, M. (Ed. and Trans.). (1914). *Vitruvius: The ten books on architecture*. Cambridge/Oxford: Humphery Milford and Oxford University Press.

Mühlestein, H. (1929). *Die kunst der Etrusker*. Berlin: Frankfurter Verlags-Anstalt.

Pidal, R. (1935). *Historia de España*. 31 vols. (vol. 2, España Romana). Madrid: Espasa-Calpe.

Randall-MacIver, D. (1939). Modern views on the Italian Terremare. *Antiquity, 13*, 320–323.

Raz, R. (1834). *Essay on the architecture of the Hindus*. London: Reid.

Rhys-Davids, T. (Trans. from the Pali, 1894). The questions of king Milinda. In M. Müller (Ed.), *The sacred books of the East* (Vol. 36, part II, p. 208). Oxford: Oxford University Press.

Rich, J. (1942). The face of South America: An aerial traverse. In *American Geographical Society's Special Publication No. 26*.

Robinson, D., & Graham, J. (1938). *Excavations at Olynthus*. Baltimore: Johns Hopkins Press.

Säflund, G. (1939). Le terremare delle provincie do modena, Reggio, Emilio, Parma, Piacenza. *Acta* of the Swedish Institute in Rome, 7: n.p.

Saville, M. (Trans.) (1917). *Narrative of some things of New Spain by The Anonymous Conqueror: Documents and narratives concerning the discovery and conquest of Latin America*. New York: Cortes Society.

Speiser, E. (1935). *Excavations at Tepe Gawra* (Vol. 2). Philadelphia: University of Pennsylvania Press.

Stein, A. (1934). The indo-Iranian borderlands: Their prehistory in the light of geography and of Recent Explorations. *Journal of the Royal Anthropological Institute, 64*, 179–202.

Stein, M. (1907). *Ancient Khotan* (Vol. 2). Oxford/London: Clarendon Press.

Sykes, P. (1934). *A history of exploration from the earliest times to the present day*. New York: Macmillan.

Tarn, W. (1938). *The Greeks in Bactria and India*. Cambridge: Cambridge University Press.

Toussaint, M., Gomez de Orozco, F., & Fernandez, J. (1938). *Planos de la ciudad de Mexico*. Mexico: UNAM.

Venkatarama-Ayyar, C. (1916). *Town planning in ancient Dekkan*. Madras: Law Printing House.

de Verneilh, F. (1847). Architecture civile au Moyen Age. *Annales Archeologiques (Paris), 6*, 94–88.

Whitaker, J. (1921). *Motya: A Phoenician colony in Sicily*. London: G. Bell and Sons.

Wiegand, T., & Schrader, H. (1904). *Priene*. Berlin: Staatliche Museen.

Chapter 3
Genealogies of the Grid: Revisiting Stanislawski's Search for the Origin of the Grid-Pattern Town

Reuben Rose-Redwood

Abstract This chapter provides a genealogy of the grid and a critical reassessment of the limitations of Stanislawski's theory of the grid's origin as a means of challenging the doctrine of geographical diffusionism more generally. It then offers a selective overview of recent approaches to understanding the grid and calls for a comparative genealogy of gridded spaces.

Keywords Diffusionism · Genealogy · Grid · Orthogonal planning · Dan Stanislawski · Urban form

Introduction

More than half a century has passed since Dan Stanislawski (1903–1997) published his landmark study in the *Geographical Review* on the geography of the grid settlement plan, "The Origin and Spread of the Grid-Pattern Town" (1946). In it, he attempted to trace the origin and diffusion of the grid plan from antiquity to the Spanish conquest of the "New World." The main assumption underlying Stanislawski's analysis was that the grid "may have been a one-time invention which has spread from its source region until it encompasses the globe" (1946, 105). The search for the true "origin" of the grid led Stanislawski to the ancient city of Mohenjo-Daro—in British India at the time of his writing, now in Pakistan—and he argued that all subsequent grid plans derived from the tradition of Indus Valley town planning in the third millennium BCE. The grid emerged from his analysis as

This chapter was originally published as Rose-Redwood, R. (2008). "Genealogies of the Grid: Revisiting Stanislawski's Search for the Origin of the Grid-Pattern Town." *Geographical Review*, 98(1): 42–58. Copyright © 2008 by the American Geographical Society of New York. Reproduced with permission of John Wiley & Sons, Inc.

R. Rose-Redwood (✉)
University of Victoria, Victoria, BC, Canada
e-mail: redwood@uvic.ca

© Springer International Publishing AG, part of Springer Nature 2018
R. Rose-Redwood, L. Bigon (eds.), *Gridded Worlds: An Urban Anthology*,
https://doi.org/10.1007/978-3-319-76490-0_3

a quasi-Platonic Ideal Form that became manifest through the continuity of tradition, and the scholar's task was to trace this continuity back to its original fountain of purity in order to decipher the inherent meaning of the grid.

It is important to bear in mind that Stanislawski was writing at a time when many geographers and other scholars were embracing the doctrine of diffusionism. This doctrine is based on the belief that cultural innovations generally spread or diffuse outward from a single source region rather than being independently invented in multiple locations. The debate over cultural diffusion and "single" versus "multiple" invention has a long history (Childe 1962 [1937]; Jett and Carter 1966; Rowe 1966; Blaut 1977, 1987, 1993; Hugill and Dickson 1988), and Stanislawski's search for the origin of the grid is but one example of the diffusionist attempt to trace an innovation back to a single source. From this perspective, the origin holds the key to understanding the meaning of a cultural phenomenon or spatial form and is therefore of primary importance.

I argue in the current chapter that this privileging of the "origin" should be rejected as symptomatic of a metaphysics of essentialism based on the belief that "what stands at the beginning of all things is also what is most valuable and essential" (Nietzsche 1996 [1880], 302). The main point, as Blaut (1987) rightly contended, is not to deny that spatial diffusion occurs in many contexts. Rather, it is to call into question the essentialist assumptions that underpin diffusionism as a mythology of the "authentic origin." That is, even if we can determine that a particular innovation has a single source, we should not conclude that the origin itself is essential and that all subsequent adaptations are merely imperfect copies of an original Ideal Form. Instead, we should focus on understanding the particularities of how and why a given innovation was adopted within a specific historico-geographical context.

Such a critique also opposes the doctrinaire application of diffusionism, especially in cases where the evidence does not warrant such an explanation, a phenomenon Blaut (1987, 37) referred to as "phantom diffusion." Stanislawski's writings on the grid plan serve as a useful exemplar of the pitfalls associated with doctrinaire diffusionism. Yet Stanislawski was certainly not the only scholar to "succumb to diffusionism" (Blaut 1987, 30); nor should we dismiss his contribution to geography on this basis alone. He was not unaware of the dangers of embracing speculative theories, although this might not be evident from the rhetorical tone of his writing on the grid. But, as Stanislawski himself noted in a different context, "it seems that a romantic theory can receive widespread acceptance, even though it is based on a total disregard of realities" (1976, 36). Few contemporary geographers or anthropologists would readily accept Stanislawski's conclusion that the grid was a "one-time invention." It is important, therefore, not to overstate his influence on current scholarship. Yet the purpose of critically engaging Stanislawski's theory of the grid's origin over seventy years after its initial publication is to explicitly challenge the essentialism of the doctrinaire diffusionist's "model of the world" (Blaut 1993), which continues to shape geographical imaginations today.

Although research has broadened the scope of comparative historico-geographical analysis concerning orthogonally-planned cities, few scholars have directly challenged Stanislawski's interpretation of the grid. Now, two decades after his death, a critical reassessment of Stanislawski's contribution to the historical geography of the grid plan is long overdue. I open this chapter with a summary of Stanislawski's general framework for explaining the grid pattern and examine the manner in which scholars have drawn upon and critiqued this approach. I then consider a number of theoretical perspectives that more recent scholars have developed to better understand the grid as a spatial form. Finally, I conclude by suggesting that geographical accounts of the grid should be situated within broader interdisciplinary discussions and genealogies of the grid.

Stanislawski and the Origin of the Grid

After completing his doctoral studies under the direction of Carl Sauer at the University of California-Berkeley, in 1944, Stanislawski (1946) published his first article on the "origin" of the grid pattern as a form of urban settlement. The article quickly drew the attention not only of geographers but also of architectural historians and other scholars (e.g., Kubler 1972 [1948]), and it has become a standard reference for works that examine the grid pattern.

During the early-1960s, Stanislawski's study of the grid was reprinted in two important anthologies: George Theodorson's *Studies in Human Ecology* (1961) and Philip Wagner and Marvin Mikesell's *Readings in Cultural Geography* (1962). The former uncritically praised Stanislawski's contribution to understanding "a basic factor in the ecological structure of most American cities" (1961, 133), whereas the editors of the latter were more cautious about fully endorsing Stanislawski's conclusions: "As new archeological evidence is exposed, some features of [Stanislawski's] ... reconstruction may have to be changed, but revision or refinement will also have to be based on analysis of form and function through time" (1962, 207). As a reference that contradicted Stanislawski's diffusionist model, they called on George Foster's suggestion that the use of the grid plan in the Spanish colonial towns of the Americas should be seen "not [as] the diffusion of a material trait, but the utilization of an idea in a new context, with specific goals in mind" (Foster 1960, 49; also, see Wagner and Mikesell 1962, 207). Others have also questioned the need to search for the "origin" of the grid plan (Pattison 1957; Johnson 1976; Low 1993, 1995, 2000). Yet, as late as 1998, Stanislawski's study of the grid was described by one geographer as "a masterful treatment of questions of origin and diffusion of innovation, of independent invention versus borrowing" (Pederson 1998, 700). What exactly did this "masterful treatment" entail?

Stanislawski began by explaining how his interest in the origin of the grid plan initially developed from his regional studies of Spanish colonial settlement patterns in the Americas. His investigations of Spanish colonial towns compelled him to consider when, where, and why the grid plan originated and how it eventually "spread from its source region." As I noted above, Stanislawski suggested that the grid plan was likely a "one-time invention" that later diffused across the world

(1946, 105). He then proceeded to elaborate on and justify such a diffusionist approach to studying the grid-pattern town.

Before examining the precise geographical location of the grid's "source region," Stanislawski weighed the advantages and disadvantages of the grid plan. He skipped rather quickly through the disadvantages, clearly viewing the benefits as a "superior list" (1946, 106). Those criticisms of the grid included its lack of accommodation to local topography, the conformity of building alignment imposed on individual property owners, and the greater efficiencies of the radial plan with respect to "communication from the periphery to the center" (1946, 106). In terms of the grid's advantages, he emphasized that the plan was ideal for the "equitable distribution of property" by virtue of its "efficient use of space," yet it was also a strategic mode of spatial organization that enabled military control of populations at a distance (1946, 106). As Stanislawski maintained, "It has been clearly recognized ... that a tortuous street facilitates defense by individuals and a straight street lends itself to control from without" (1946, l06–7). Additionally, the fact that the grid simplifies the calculations of the surveyor, can easily be "sketched on the drawing board," and is capable of being "extended indefinitely" are all listed as key advantages of rectilinear plans (1946, 106).

With the advantages of the grid explained, Stanislawski proceeded to consider several theories regarding its origin. Theories that derive the grid plan from the prior use of rectangular buildings or a processional axis, he insisted, could not be maintained in light of the historical evidence of ancient town planning. He then tackled the question of military and religious explanations. Although the military advantages of the grid were not in doubt, Stanislawski contended that Roman military camps were modeled on pre-existing grid-patterned towns, not the other way around. The religious use of compass directions as a means of spatial orientation was also deemed "equally inadequate," because not all ancient grid settlements included a religious temple as part of their design. In particular, Stanislawski interpreted the lack of a temple at Mohenjo-Daro, one of the earliest grid settlements in history, as sufficient evidence to conclude that "religious significance as basic to the grid can likewise be written off as inapplicable" (1946, 107). The notion that religion is, or is not, a "basic" quality of the grid betrays an ontological essentialism, implying that only those meanings found at the origin of a cultural phenomenon are authentic and essential. Yet, to his credit, Stanislawski cautiously avoided the lure of reductionism when it came to ultimate causation.

Rather than reducing the logic of the grid to one unifying explanatory cause, Stanislawski outlined a fivefold set of circumstances that generally accompanied, in one permutation or another, the adoption of the grid plan. The first factor involved envisioning the city as a pre-conceived "organic whole" rather than as a conglomeration of individual buildings. This was only possible, he suggested, when developing "a totally new urban unit or a newly added subdivision" (Stanislawski 1946, 108). If the job of planning was left to individual property owners alone, Stanislawski contended that "the grid will not come into being," at least not at the citywide scale (1946, 108). His second key factor, then, was the existence of some type of centralized authority that could ensure the implementation of a systematic layout. The classic example alluded to here is the Roman imperial tradition of town planning and the morphological disintegration of many Roman grid plans after the empire fell.

Given its historical use as a technique of social control from a distance, Stanislawski's third point was that the grid commonly signified the "colonial status" of a given settlement. Without elaborating in any detail or providing historical evidence, he argued that the grid plan was often aligned with a benevolent colonialism of "amiable association for mutual benefit between mother and daughter settlements" rather than "a situation in which the younger settlement is bled by the older" (Stanislawski 1946, 108). One can only assume that Stanislawski was referring to the examples of Greek, Roman, and Spanish colonial towns. Yet, certainly the Libertadores who fought against the Spanish for their independence—not to mention the indigenous populations that were dispossessed and enslaved—might find such notions of colonial amiability rather perplexing.

The final two factors that Stanislawski highlighted were a "desire" for the systematic measurement of land and prior knowledge of the grid plan. The latter point was crucial to Stanislawski's diffusionist hypothesis, for if grid plans were devised independently in multiple locations—without knowledge of prior grid layouts— then the diffusionist theory of the grid's origin as a "one-time invention" would fall apart. Stanislawski sought to prevent such an intellectual travesty from besetting the geographical imagination, so he searched for the earliest city known to have been laid out as a grid in the hope that he could trace a "continuing tradition" throughout the ages (1946, 110). This led him to the city of Mohenjo-Daro, which, recent archaeological excavations at the time had suggested, was one of the earliest known settlements with an orthogonal morphology.

The possibility was left open that future historical or archaeological evidence might reveal grid-plan cities in East Asia, but he confidently maintained that "there is at present no reason to suppose that any Oriental settlement with anything suggesting a grid pattern could rival Mohenjo Daro in antiquity" (1946, 109). After establishing the "first" grid-pattern town in history, Stanislawski pursued a diffusionist argument by noting the chain of subsequent grid-plan settlements of the Assyrians, Greeks, and Romans, which were followed during the European Renaissance by the grid plans of the Italians and Germans as well as the French bastides and the development of new towns in England under Edward I. "The question may be raised," Stanislawski acknowledged, "why one should attribute to a single invention a plan that has appeared in places far distant from one another with a gap of long centuries between" (1946, 110). His answer relied on the following logic: a continuous tradition of town planning in India can be traced back at least as far as Mohenjo-Daro in the third millennium BCE, and subsequent civilizations that utilized the grid plan had either direct or indirect contact with India. Therefore, he concluded, "India may have carried the tradition of this town pattern for all later ages to accept at their leisure" (Stanislawski 1946, 111).

Stanislawski provided surprisingly little concrete evidence of the link between Indian town planning and later developments. His interpretation of the diffusion of the grid from India to Assyria—which he viewed as one of the earliest appropriations of the grid after Mohenjo-Daro— borders on the speculative as he contemplated the original intentions of Sargon, the Assyrian leader. "One regrets that Sargon, in the eighth century before Christ, did not record why he chose the grid or where he found his sources for such a plan," Stanislawski mused, "but again, eyes may have been turned to the East" (1946, 111). He interpreted the fact that trade connections among Mesopotamia, Persia, and India were indisputable as sufficient evidence of the Indian derivation of Assyrian town planning. However, according to more recent studies, the presence of temples and monumental structures in Mesopotamia, and their absence in Indus Valley settlements, indicates that "the fundamental organizing and operational principles [in the Indus Valley] ... were different from those of Egypt and Mesopotamia" (Possehl 2002, 148).

The theory of the grid's diffusion from India, then, is based not on solid historical and archaeological evidence but on speculation on possible connections among disparate gridded sites. For that reason Stanislawski qualified all of his substantive claims by noting that they "may have" occurred, without offering a more definitive assessment. Nevertheless, he defended his position against skeptics by remarking that:

> to those who question the assumption of Indian derivation it can be asked: "Where has the pattern of the grid town appeared without possible connections with India?" No part of Europe or Asia except those regions that had contact with this area of oldest appearance has given evidence of the grid pattern. Nor did any part of Africa exhibit this pattern until Alexander introduced it as derived from eastern Mediterranean lands. (Stanislawski 1946, 111)

Stanislawski went even further by claiming that no settlements in the Americas were laid out as a grid prior to European contact in the fifteenth century, "despite some theories to the contrary" (1946, 112). He dismissed evidence put forward by other scholars, such as George Kubler (1942), which supported the thesis that a number of pre-Columbian sites were based on some form of orthogonal pattern. Remarkably, Stanislawski suggested that, because the early Spaniards did not explicitly mention the presence of grid-pattern towns in their written accounts, we can therefore assume that no pre-contact grids existed. As he put it, "failure to mention such a condition [of rectilinear street patterns in pre-contact settlements] may well be taken to indicate that it did not exist" (Stanislawski 1946, 112). This rather dubious claim of the non-existence of grid-pattern towns in pre-Columbian America is perhaps the weakest link in Stanislawski's argument and raises serious questions about his diffusionist approach.

Stanislawski was on more solid ground when he discussed the influence of Roman town-planning principles on the Spanish colonial settlement tradition. In a companion piece, "Early Spanish Town Planning in the New World" (1947), published in the *Geographical Review* a year after his initial study of the grid, he documented the Roman inspiration of Spanish colonial settlement patterns in the Americas. First, Stanislawski reiterated his fivefold set of "basic conditions" that accompanied the use of the grid plan. He then convincingly demonstrated the parallels between the instructions for Spanish colonial settlement outlined by Philip II in

1573, generally known as the "Laws of the Indies," and the recommendations offered by the ancient Roman writer Vitruvius in *The Ten Books on Architecture* (1999 [ca. 30–20 BCE]), which was itself inspired by the Greek experience of town planning. He used this Spanish-Roman-Greek connection, which is well documented, to support his broader diffusionist hypothesis. Some scholars, however, have questioned the importance of this evidence, referring to it as a "divertingly pointless comparison" (Morris 1994, 306). Nevertheless, it was one of Stanislawski's chief sources of evidence, and he also re-emphasized the claim that "there is no convincing evidence of any grid-pattern town in the New World before Cortes rebuilt Mexico City" (Stanislawski 1947, 97). Again, this claim was essential if the diffusionist theory was to be sustained.

Challenges to Stanislawski's Diffusionist Theory of the Grid

One of the first responses to Stanislawski's theory of the grid's origin came, not surprisingly, from George Kubler (1972 [1948]). In both of his studies of the grid plan, Stanislawski criticized Kubler's earlier dismissal of the diffusionist hypothesis with respect to the origin of the grid. In an article on sixteenth-century Mexican urbanism, Kubler remarked that it had been established "long ago that [the grid] ... is a generic urban solution, independently achieved by many peoples" (1942, 166). Kubler insisted not only that the grid had multiple origins but also that it emerged independently in pre-Columbian America. "In Mexico, the [Spanish] colonial checkerboard thus represents no invention or major departure," Kubler confidently declared, "but a repetition of the system used *before the Conquest on both continents*" (1942, 167, italics added). Given Stanislawski's commitment to a diffusionist framework, it is little wonder that Kubler's anti-diffusionism rubbed him the wrong way. In fact, it is quite likely that the desire to challenge Kubler's work was one of the chief impetuses that drove Stanislawski to develop his own theory of the grid's diffusion.

Shortly after the appearance of Stanislawski's two articles on the grid plan, Kubler published his *Mexican Architecture of the Sixteenth Century* (1972 [1948]), which included revised material from his previous article that Stanislawski had singled out for criticism. Kubler took Stanislawski's work quite seriously, for he scaled back and qualified his initial claim by remarking that the Mexican "colonial checkerboard *may* represent less an invention or major departure, than a repetition of the system used before the Conquest on both continents" (1972 [1948], 94, italics added). Though not fully conceding to his rival's approach, Kubler did acknowledge Stanislawski as the leading advocate of the "diffusionist point of view" with respect to the grid plan. Nevertheless, he continued to insist that "Pre-Conquest American examples [of the grid] are not unlikely" and provided additional citations to support his anti-diffusionist and pre-contact claims against Stanislawski's critique (1972 [1948], 94).

Moreover, Kubler even suggested that pre-Columbian Indian settlement designs likely influenced the urban form of some Spanish colonial towns. "After the Conquest," he argued,

> the form of the Indian towns may have affected and conditioned the Spanish layouts. Mexico City still reveals the form of the Aztec capital. Many central streets follow the pattern of otherwise obliterated Indian canals .... The plaza of modern Texcoco occupies the site of the patio of this residence, where the ball court of the Indian town was located. Thus colonial Texcoco drifted in among the ruins of the old city, and the modern reticulated appearance of the town may derive from a pre-Conquest plan. (Kubler 1972 [1948], 102)

This argument of pre-Columbian influences on Spanish colonial town planning has drawn increased attention in recent years, but in Kubler's (1978) later work, he appeared to have shifted his emphasis toward analyzing the European roots of the Spanish colonial grid-plan town (yet, see Kubler 1993).

In the mid-1960s, John McAndrew (1965) discussed the indigenous influence on Spanish colonial grid-plan towns, but he acknowledged the speculative nature of his conclusions. "All that is certain," McAndrew noted, "is that there was a successful fusion … [between] pre-conquest planning and European theory" (1965, 110). However, the very existence of pre-Columbian grid designs, such as that of Tenochtitlin, was not in doubt, despite Stanislawski's (1946, 1947) earlier suggestions to the contrary. This view was later supported by Dora Crouch, Daniel Garr, and Axel Mundigo in their now-classic *Spanish City Planning in North America* (1982). They drew inspiration from Stanislawski's interpretation of the Vitruvian influence on the Spanish Laws of the Indies yet pointed out that Vitruvius himself never explicitly recommended a grid layout, preferring a radial plan instead. They also recognized that symmetrical designs existed prior to the Spanish conquest, which undermined Stanislawski's "one-time invention" hypothesis even further. Although the "cultural preadaptation" (Newton 1974) of the Spanish to utilizing a grid plan in their colonies can be traced back to Roman and Greek precedents, this process of spatial diffusion does not account for the pre-contact orthogonal settlements in the Americas.

In the 1980s and early-1990s, a number of scholars began to re-evaluate the possibility of pre-Columbian antecedents of the Spanish colonial grid. One of the most intriguing cases was made by Graziano Gasparini (1993). He noted that most scholars had focused primarily on the European inspirations for the Spanish colonial grid plan, whereas "the pre-Columbian contribution has received little attention and has been considered scarcely relevant as an influence" (Gasparini 1993, 78). In contrast, Gasparini (1993) pointed to the Incan grid designs of Ollantaytambo, Chucuito, Hatunqolla, and Paucarqolla, all of which pre-date European contact (also, see Gasparini and Margolies 1980). More controversially, he developed a theory that the pre-Columbian grid design of Cholula directly influenced the layout of the nearby Spanish town of Puebla during the sixteenth century (yet, see Smith and Schreiber 2006).

To date, Setha Low has provided the most compelling critique of the Eurocentric bias with respect to interpreting the "cultural meaning" of the Spanish American grid-pattern design (1993, 1995, 2000). Low has maintained that previous accounts of the Spanish colonial grid are self-contradictory:

> The interpretation of the evidence is contradictory, with some researchers arguing for a solely European derivation of the gridplan-plaza complex while at the same time presenting evidence that a large number of towns, including Mexico City, Cholula, and Cuzco, were built isomorphic to the indigenous ruins .... The correspondence between the indigenous forms and the Spanish reconstruction is so clear that the denial of its significance is startling. (1993, 76–7)

This is not to say that no "European derivation" of the grid existed; it is rather to suggest, as McAndrew (1965) argued, that a complex "fusion" of cultural influences should be taken into account in some, but certainly not all, cases in the Americas. Or, as Low put it, "there are multiple cultural sources and architectural and planning models for the gridplan plaza urban design of the Spanish New World" (1993, 79). What effect might such a realization of the "multiple sources" of the grid plan— especially its usage in pre-Columbian America—have on the standing of Stanislawski's diffusionist hypothesis of the grid's singular origin?

One strategy that diffusionists might adopt to sustain a "single-origin" hypothesis is the argument that pre-Columbian grid layouts themselves may be traceable to the Indus Valley via East Asian diffusion. However, from Low's standpoint, as well as my own, the search for a unitary "origin" of the grid is not only historically questionable but also rendered theoretically irrelevant. In its place, I would argue, what is needed is a comparative genealogy of the grid, in the Nietzschean-Foucauldian sense, rather than a diffusionist approach that seeks to trace the idea of the grid back to a single "origin" and thereby capture the pure essence of the grid at the precise moment of its first conception. "From this perspective," Low argued, "the question of the origin of the gridplan disappears, and its continuous existence from many cultural sources emerges. The more relevant questions are what is the meaning of the grid-plan, and why is it so pervasive?" (1993, 79). This critique of the search for the grid's "origin" was raised as early as the 1950s and has gained a growing number of adherents in recent years (Pattison 1957; Johnson 1976; Kostof 1991; Butzer 1992; Low 2000).

In his account of the U.S. Rectangular Survey System, William Pattison instructed his readers that "until further research produces final answers, the present author would suggest that the issue of origins is likely to be more entertaining than instructive" (1957, 64). Similarly, Karl Butzer called on geographers to stop the "endless and inconclusive search for specific antecedents" and instead to concentrate on producing "particular urban histories" that take into account the functions of town planning under the conditions of colonial expansion (1992, 555). What is needed, according to Low (1995, 2000), is a critical analysis of the multiple meanings that urban forms acquire through the struggle over their production, interpretation, and use (also, see Lefebvre 1991 [1974]; de Certeau 1984). A growing number of geographers, historians, and other scholars have provided useful starting points for a critical spatial history of the grid, and it is to these formulations that I now turn.

Approaching Gridded Spaces and Places Beyond the Search for Origins

Much of the literature on the grid is either descriptive, polemical, or an attempt to construct typologies of the grid as a morphological pattern. To summarize all that has ever been written about the grid would be pointless—not to say impossible. However, a number of theoretical approaches to the study of gridded spaces and places are worth considering. What follows, therefore, is a selective overview of different interpretations of the grid as a spatial form.

Recent critical analyses address a number of important issues, including: the multiplicity of cultural meanings and politico-economic uses associated with the grid in different historico-geographical contexts (e.g., Marcuse 1987; Kostof 1991; Low 2000); the role of the grid as part of the initiation and naturalization of property regimes (Blomley 2003); the discontinuities and radical ruptures that mark the spatial history of gridded spaces (Pope 1996); the linkages between the grid and related practices of socio-spatial rationalization (Scott 1998; Hannah 2000; Pickles 2004; Rose-Redwood 2006a);   and the production of "place" within the confines of abstract gridded space (Cresswell 2004). These themes are by no means exhaustive but, rather, suggest numerous productive lines of inquiry that attempt to move beyond the diffusionist search for "origins."

Even though many scholars have abandoned the quest to determine the grid's origin, Stanislawski's argument that the grid plan facilitates the social control of populations by a centralized state authority has gained much wider acceptance (Kostof 1991; Scott 1998; Brown 2001; Grant 2001). Such accounts challenge the popular mythology which holds that the grid symbolizes a universal democratic ethos of egalitarianism. For instance, Richard Sennett (1990) drew on the Weberian "Protestant ethic" thesis to explain the grid in modern America, whereas other writers have highlighted the importance of the grid as an instrument of real estate speculation and the commodification of space (Mumford 1961; Reps 1965; Lefebvre 1991 [1974]; Harvey 1990; Marcuse 1987; Scobey 2002). As Blomley (2003, 131) has argued, "the codes of access and exclusion that structure the uses of the grid are saturated by conceptions of property .... The grid clearly has an instrumental importance to the second nature of property, making possible a capitalist market in parcels of land and facilitating the creation of the boundaries that are so vital to a liberal legal regime." The violence of sovereign power, according to Blomley, is fundamental to the grid as a spatial strategy of disciplinary rule.

However, as Kostof (1991) rightly argued, general statements that universally align the grid plan with a specific political ideology or economic practice are bound to be reductionistic and misleading. The grid can serve the interests of authoritarian dictatorships or liberal democracies just as easily as capitalist or socialist regimes (Brown 2001). As Marcuse (1987, 289) maintained, "the same form can be produced by quite different interests whose conflicts result in quite different compromises." Conversely, the historical record also demonstrates, as Newton (1974, 148) aptly remarked, that "different forms can discharge the same functions." He further asked us to question the functionalist fallacy of privileging the original function of a spatial form. As Newton put it, "the reasons for origin and the reasons for persistence may be quite different" (1974, 148). To view the morphology of the grid as having an intrinsic ideological essence or transcendental meaning, therefore, is to universalize the intentionality of spatial pattern and geometric form. It is with this realization in mind that Kostof insisted that "the political innocence of the grid in the West is a fiction" (1991, 99). The grid has historically been associated with contrasting politico-economic regimes and has acquired a diverse array of cultural meanings. It is thus crucial to consider the particularities of how the grid has been utilized within different historico-geographical conjunctures without losing sight of shared spatial histories and the intersecting geographical trajectories of planning practices.

When discussing the "grid plan" it is easy to assume that all grids are basically the same—indeed, Stanislawski's model is predicated on the self-identical nature of the grid as an ideal urban form. But this assumption is far from self-evident. Marcuse distinguished between the closed grid of the pre-capitalist city and the open grids of both laissez-faire and mature capitalist urbanism, where closed grids are:

> laid out for a clearly limited area defined by city walls, fortifications, major outer termini for central streets, greenbelts etc., whereas the open grid is laid out with a view towards expansion and reduplication, in one or more directions, theoretically without limit. A closed gridiron plan is a complete and encompassing plan for a physically defined and bounded area; the open gridiron is an initial step towards plotting an unknown and perhaps unlimited area capable of indefinite expansion. (1987, 290–1)

Marcuse's contrast between open and closed grids is not unlike Rosalind Krauss's (1985) distinction between the centrifugal (outward-oriented) and centripetal (inward-oriented) grids of modern art. In his provocative study, *Ladders* (1996), Albert Pope drew on both Marcuse's and Krauss's work to argue that the nineteenth-century centrifugal grid of American cities gave way during the mid-twentieth century to a centripetal form of urban design that privileged an enclosed and privatized grid-based morphology, which Pope referred to as a "ladder."

Another key distinction to consider is that between a simple rectilinear geometric pattern on the one hand and a systematized coordinate grid on the other. The latter combines rectilinear geometry with a coordinated system of numbered streets, lots, and houses. Most commonly associated with the gridiron cities of the United States (Rose-Redwood and Kadonaga 2016), the spatial practice of numbering streets can actually be traced back more than 1000 years, with the ancient Japanese city of Heian-kyo—present-day Kyoto—founded in 794, serving as a classic example (Steinhardt 1990; Knapp 2000). The similarities between ancient Japanese land-division patterns and that of the United States are striking, yet it is not entirely clear what influence, if any, the Japanese tradition had on the practice of orthogonal planning in the United States (Kornhauser 1984). What is of interest is not so much the potential continuity between these two sets of practices as the discontinuity that marks the spatio-temporal distance between them.

Geographers often maintain that the numerical coordinates of locational grids are integral to the production of abstract space, whereas "replacing a set of numbers with a name means that we begin to approach 'place'" (Cresswell 2004, 2). This is consistent with the standard view of "place" as space imbued with meaning. Yet the romanticization of name over number obscures the symbolic capital that numbers can acquire as well as the cultural attachments to specific numerical designations that may be viewed as fundamental to a sense of place (e.g., Esterow 1955). Simplistic theories that categorically align the coordinate grid with abstract space in contrast to the meaningfulness of place should be re-examined from a critical perspective.

The search for the grid's origins may have been a dead-end in theoretical terms, but critical analyses of the "inhabited grid" are as relevant as ever, for the grid continues to enable and constrain everyday life for millions of urban inhabitants (Cameron 2003, 12). In the current global historical conjuncture, however, the expanding megacities of the present are coping less with the constraints of an all-encompassing "grid" than with the limitations imposed by the brutalities of global inequality that have all but ruptured the morphological structures of metropolitan areas (Davis 2006). Genealogies of the grid must certainly be attentive to the contradictions that lie just below the surface of any apparently "rational" spatial order as well as to the processes of socio-spatial ordering that underpin the appearance of seemingly random, chaotic assemblages.

Comparative Genealogies of the Grid: Crossing the Disciplinary Divide

Scholars from many academic disciplines—ranging from modern art, graphic design, and architecture to archaeology, urban planning, and geography—have explored the role of the grid within their respective fields of inquiry (Reps 1965; Castagnoli 1971; Johnson 1976; Hurlburt 1978; Krauss 1985; Williamson 1986; Carter 1988; Swann 1989; Rama 1996; Conzen 2001; Lucas 2001; Chadha 2002; Cameron 2003; Baird 2005). Yet few have attempted to link these different discussions together in an interdisciplinary genealogy of the grid (yet, see McNamara 1992; Berman 1993; Pope 1996). What is the relationship, for instance, between discussions of the grid in urban planning or historical geography and the use of the grid as the epistemological basis of modern archaeological excavations, cartography, and modern science more generally? How does a genealogy of the grid within the fields of architecture or modern art intersect with its function as a conceptual device in graphic design? More generally, how and why has the grid become a metaphor for modernity at large, and to what extent has the grid been deployed as a technology for the reproduction of Cartesian subjectivities? By considering such questions we can move beyond a search for the grid's definitive "origin" and toward a critical account of the multiple genealogies of the grid.

A genealogical approach, as developed by Foucault and inspired by Nietzsche, is particularly useful in critiquing the search for origins. In his essay entitled,

"Nietzsche, Genealogy, History," Foucault (1984 [1971]) explained the fundamental epistemological and ontological issues that are at stake in the methodological task at hand, and his critique has significant implications for Stanislawski's obsession with Mohenjo-Daro as the birthplace of the grid. The "pursuit of the origin," argued Foucault,

> is an attempt to capture the exact essence of things, their purest possibilities, and their carefully protected identities; because this search assumes the existence of immobile forms that precede the external world of accident and succession. This search is directed to "that which was already there," the image of a primordial truth fully adequate to its nature, and it necessitates the removal of every mask to ultimately disclose an original identity. (1984 [1971], 78)

Against this version of historical essentialism, Foucault posited a genealogical analysis based on the recognition that "there is 'something altogether different' behind things: not a timeless and essential secret, but the secret that they have no essence or that their essence was fabricated in a piecemeal fashion from alien forms" (1984 [1971], 78). This is why a Foucauldian-inspired genealogy "opposes itself to the search for 'origins'" (1984 [1971], 77).

Opposing the pursuit of the origin by no means precludes a critical analysis of the spatial histories of ancient cities, such as Mohenjo-Daro and other early urban settlements (Smith 2007). Yet the purpose of considering ancient urban morphologies is no longer to rediscover the ultimate meaning of geometric forms. It is, rather, to examine the political, economic, and cultural contingencies associated with particular spatial practices. Of course, continuities between different uses of the grid throughout history are undeniable, and these connections should be explored. However, a genealogical analysis is equally concerned with the discontinuities, contingencies, reversals, contradictions, failures, and reformulations that have accompanied the use of the grid as a spatial pattern.

A comparative genealogy of the grid is particularly relevant today, because the grid has allegedly made a "comeback," at least in North America, with the growing prominence of New Urbanist principles of neotraditional urban design (Grant 2001). If the grid has come to signify the "traditional" in some urban-design circles, it is more commonly viewed as the quintessential symbol of modernity: a metaphor for all things "modern." For instance, in "Grids," a celebrated essay on modern art, Krauss maintained that "the grid is an emblem of modernity" and insisted that it is "so stridently modern to look at" (1985, 10–2). Such a claim rests on the circular logic of defining modernity as characterized by the grid and then proceeding to argue that the grid, therefore, is emblematic of the modern. Recognizing the self-referential circularity of Krauss's argument, however, should not be taken as a refutation of such a view. To the contrary, such circularity can be self-reinforcing and has the potential to materialize itself as "reality" (Berman 1993; Scott 1998; Sluyter 1999).

Nevertheless, we should not insist too strongly on the strictly "modern" connotations of the grid. The grid pattern has been used as a mechanism of spatial ordering for centuries in many different cultural contexts, which complicates those narratives that see the grid as the essence of modernity alone. Although the grid is not unique to European modernity, the proliferation of gridded spaces and the unprecedented scale of such spatial projects, especially since the latter half of the eighteenth century, may go a long way toward explaining why the grid has been perceived as a fundamental characteristic of modern spatial organization.

Yet, as time has passed, what once epitomized the "modern" now takes on the emblem of the "traditional." Is this not sufficient evidence to justify the point that the grid is associated with contrasting meanings at different historical moments? If this is the case, then the grid of New Urbanism is fundamentally not the same grid as that of Le Corbusier. Nor is it identical to the grid of Spanish, Roman, and Greek colonial settlements, or the imperial cities of ancient China, Korea, and Japan. Rather, the New Urbanist's grid is inseparable from late-twentieth-century reactions to suburban life and the nostalgia for a lost sense of community that haunts many privileged souls in the post-industrial world. We should also question whether it is actually the "grid" and not what Pope (1996) has called a "ladder" formation, with its centripetal zones of privatized security, that the New Urbanism is truly espousing.

The grid, then, is not an eternal Platonic Ideal Form that manifests itself throughout history. The general resemblances of geometric forms need not imply a correspondence of strategic function, meaning, or the continuity of an unbroken tradition. In fact, the obsession with geometric form—be it rectilinear, radial, curvilinear, or the less rigidly defined morphology of a so-called organic layout—can easily obscure the importance of other socio-spatial ordering practices as well as the contradictions that underlie the legibility of surface appearances (Rose-Redwood 2006b). In contrast to more formalistic approaches to examining space, Lefebvre insisted that there should be a "recognition of conflicts internal to what on the surface appears homogenous and coherent— and presents itself and behaves as though it were" (1991 [1974], 352). From such a dialectical perspective, it is essential to critically examine the production of spaces rather than merely interpreting such spaces as legible, finished products.

As I have shown in this chapter, the partitioning of spaces into grids has a long but discontinuous history. Early attempts to pinpoint the precise origin and linear diffusion of the grid have largely been abandoned given the accumulation of evidence suggesting the inadequacies of the diffusionist line of argumentation as well as the theoretical shift away from a metaphysics of essentialism. I have argued that Foucault's genealogical critique of the pursuit of "origins" provides a useful set of conceptual tools for grappling with the spatial history of the grid. Foucault's own analyses of spatial partitioning highlight the utilization of the grid as an instrument of disciplinary power beginning in the late-sixteenth century (1995 [1975]; 2003; 2007). This emphasis on the disciplinary dimension of the grid has not gone unnoticed among geographers and urban planning historians (Hannah 2000; Grant 2001; Blomley 2003; Crampton 2007). But too strict of a disciplinary reading of the grid—of which Foucault himself is at times guilty—risks falling back into an unproductive reductionism. Again, it is crucial to recognize that "the historical record shows that [the grid] ... can represent a wide array of meanings in societies with divergent objectives and organizing strategies" (Grant 2001, 221). If we have learned nothing else since Stanislawski's initial mid-twentieth-century foray into the terrain of the inhabited grid, it is certainly that the "essential secret" of the grid is that it has no essence—we are left with only a series of spatial formations whose definitive identity continues to elude us.

References

Baird, E. (2005). The reordering of space in sixteenth-century Mexico: Some implications of the grid. In E. H. Boone (Ed.), *Painted books and indigenous knowledge in Mesoamerica: Manuscript studies in honor of Mary Elizabeth Smith* (pp. 289–300). New Orleans: Middle American Research Institute.

Berman, I. (1993). [Im]material events and the emergence of smooth space at the limits of contemporary architecture. Ph.D. diss., Harvard University.

Blaut, J. (1977). Two views of diffusion. *Annals of the Association of American Geographers, 67*(3), 343–349.

Blaut, J. (1987). Diffusionism: A uniformitarian critique. *Annals of the Association of American Geographers, 77*(1), 30–47.

Blaut, J. (1993). *The colonizer's model of the world: Geographical diffusionism and Eurocentric history*. New York: Guilford Press.

Blomley, N. (2003). Law, property, and the geography of violence: The frontier, the survey, and the grid. *Annals of the Association of American Geographers, 93*(1), 121–141.

Brown, K. (2001). Gridded lives: Why Kazakhstan and Montana are nearly the same place. *American Historical Review, 106*(1), 17–48.

Butzer, K. (1992). From Columbus to Acosta: Science, geography, and the New World. *Annals of the Association of American Geographers, 82*(3), 543–565.

Cameron, D. (2003). *Living inside the grid*. New York: New Museum for Contemporary Art.

Carter, P. (1988). *The road to Botany Bay: An exploration of landscape and history*. New York: Knopf.

Castagnoli, F. (1971). *Orthogonal town planning in antiquity*. Cambridge, MA: MIT Press.

Chadha, A. (2002). Visions of discipline: Sir Mortimer Wheeler and the archaeological method in India (1944-1948). *Journal of Social Anthropology, 2*(3), 378–401.

Childe, V.G. (1962 [1937]). A prehistorian's interpretation of diffusion. In P. Wagner and M. Mikesell (Eds.), *Readings in cultural geography* (pp. 209–217). Chicago: University of Chicago Press.

Conzen, M. P. (2001). The study of urban form in the United States. *Urban Morphology, 5*(1), 3–14.

Crampton, J. (2007). Maps, race, and Foucault: Eugenics and territorialization following World War I. In J. Crampton & S. Elden (Eds.), *Space, knowledge and power: Foucault and geography* (pp. 223–244). Burlington: Ashgate.

Cresswell, T. (2004). *Place: A short introduction*. Oxford: Blackwell Publishing.

Crouch, D., Garr, D., & Mundigo, A. (1982). *Spanish city planning in North America*. Cambridge, MA: MIT Press.

Davis, M. (2006). *Planet of slums*. London: Verso.

de Certeau, M. (1984). *The practice of everyday life*. Berkeley: University of California Press.

Esterow, M. (1955). After ten years, it's still 6th Ave. *New York Times*. October 3, p. 12.

Foster, G. (1960). *Culture and conquest: America's Spanish heritage*. New York: Wenner-Gren Foundation for Anthropological Research.

Foucault, M. (1984[1971]). Nietzsche, genealogy, history. In P. Rabinow (Ed.), *The Foucault Reader* (pp. 76–100). New York: Pantheon Books.

Foucault, M. (1995 [1975]). *Discipline and punish: The birth of the prison* (trans: A. Sheridan). New York: Vintage Books.

Foucault, M. (2003). *Society must be defended: Lectures at the Collège de France, 1975–1976* (trans: D. Macey). New York: Picador.

Foucault, M. (2007). *Security, territory, population: Lectures at the Collège de France, 1977–1978* (trans: G. Burchell). New York: Palgrave Macmillan.

Gasparini, G. (1993). The pre-Hispanic grid system: The urban shape of conquest and territorial organization. In R. Bennett (Ed.), *Settlements in the Americas: Cross-cultural perspectives* (pp. 78–109). Newark: University of Delaware Press.

Gasparini, G., & Margolies, L. (1980). *Inca architecture* (trans: P. Lyon). Bloomington: Indiana University Press.

Grant, J. (2001). The dark side of the grid: Power and urban design. *Planning Perspectives, 16*(3), 219–241.

Hannah, M. (2000). *Governmentality and the mastery of territory in nineteenth-century America.* New York: Cambridge University Press.

Harvey, D. (1990). *The condition of postmodernity: An enquiry into the origins of cultural change.* Cambridge, England: Blackwell Publishing.

Hugill, P., & Dickson, D. (Eds.). (1988). *The transfer and transformation of ideas and material culture.* College Station: Texas A&M University Press.

Hurlburt, A. (1978). *The grid: A modular system for the design and production of newspapers, magazines, and books.* New York: Van Nostrand Reinhold.

Jett, S., & Carter, G. (1966). A comment on Rowe's diffusionism and archaeology. *American Antiquity, 31*(6), 867–870.

Johnson, H. B. (1976). *Order upon the land: The U.S. rectangular land survey and the upper Mississippi country.* New York: Oxford University Press.

Knapp, R. (2000). *China's walled cities.* Oxford: Oxford University Press.

Kornhauser, D. (1984). Common imprints on the landscapes of Japan and America: Invention or diffusion? *Asian Profile, 12*(5), 465–472.

Kostof, S. (1991). *The city shaped: Urban patterns and meanings through history.* London: Little, Brown, and Co.

Krauss, R. (1985). Grids. In R. Krauss (Ed.), *The originality and the avante-garde and other modernist myths* (pp. 9–22). Cambridge, MA: MIT Press.

Kubler, G. (1942). Mexican urbanism in the sixteenth century. *Art Bulletin, 24*(2), 160–171.

Kubler, G. (1972 [1948]). *Mexican architecture of the sixteenth century.* Westport: Greenwood Press.

Kubler, G. (1978). Open-grid town plans in Europe and America. In R. Schaedel, J. Hardoy, & N. Kinzer (Eds.), *Urbanization in the Americas from its beginning to the present* (pp. 327–341). The Hague: Mouton Publishers.

Kubler, G. (1993). Cities of Latin America since discovery. In R. Bennett (Ed.), *Settlements in the Americas: Cross-cultural perspectives* (pp. 17–27). Newark: University of Delaware Press.

Lefebvre, H. (1991 [1974]). *The production of space.* Cambridge: Blackwell Publishing.

Low, S. (1993). Cultural meaning of the plaza: The history of the Spanish-American gridplan-plaza urban design. In R. Rotenberg & G. McDonogh (Eds.), *The cultural meaning of urban space* (pp. 75–93). Westport, CT: Bergin & Garvey.

Low, S. (1995). Indigenous architecture and the Spanish American plaza in Mesoamerica and the Caribbean. *American Anthropologist, 97*(4), 748–762.

Low, S. (2000). *On the plaza: The politics of public space and culture.* Austin: University of Texas Press.

Lucas, G. (2001). *Critical approaches to fieldwork: Contemporary and historical archaeological practice.* New York: Routledge.

Marcuse, P. (1987). The grid as city plan: New York City and laissez-faire planning in the nineteenth century. *Planning Perspectives, 2*(3), 287–310.

McAndrew, J. (1965). *The open-air churches of sixteenth-century Mexico: Atrios, posas, open chapels, and other studies*. Cambridge, MA: Harvard University Press.

McNamara, A. (1992). Between flux and certitude: The grid in avant-garde utopian thought. *Art History, 15*(1), 60–79.

Morris, A. E. J. (1994). *History of urban form: Before the industrial revolutions* (3rd ed.). New York: John Wiley & Sons.

Mumford, L. (1961). *The city in history: Its origins, its transformations, and its prospects*. New York: Harcourt, Brace & World.

Newton, M. (1974). Cultural preadaptation and the upland South. In H. J. Walker & W. G. Haag (Eds.), *Man and cultural heritage: Papers in honor of Fred B. Kniffen* (pp. 143–154). Baton Rouge: Louisiana State University, School of Geoscience.

Nietzsche, F. (1996 [1880]). The wanderer and his shadow. In *Human, all too human: A book for free spirits* (pp. 301–395) (tans R. J. Hollingdale). London: Cambridge University Press.

Pattison, W.D. (1957). *Beginnings of the American rectangular land survey system, 1784-1800*. University of Chicago, Department of Geography, Research Paper No. 5o. Chicago.

Pederson, L. (1998). Memoriam: Dan Stanislawski, 1903–1997. *Annals of the Association of American Geographers, 88*(4), 699–705.

Pickles, J. (2004). *A history of spaces: Cartographic reason, mapping, and the geo-coded world*. New York: Routledge.

Pope, A. (1996). *Ladders*. New York: Princeton Architectural Press.

Possehl, G. (2002). *The Indus civilization: A contemporary perspective*. Walnut Creek: AttaMira Press.

Rama, A. (1996). *The lettered city* (trans: J. Chasteen). Durham: Duke University Press.

Reps, J. (1965). *The making of urban America: A history of city planning in the United States*. Princeton: Princeton University Press.

Rose-Redwood, R. (2006a). Governmentality, geography and the geo-coded world. *Progress in Human Geography, 30*(4), 469–486.

Rose-Redwood, R. (2006b). Governmentality, the grid, and the beginnings of a critical spatial history of the geo-coded world. Ph.D. diss., Pennsylvania State University.

Rose-Redwood, R., & Kadonaga, L. (2016). "The corner of Avenue A and Twenty-Third Street": Geographies of street numbering in the United States. *The Professional Geographer, 68*(1), 39–52.

Rowe, J. (1966). Diffusionism and archaeology. *American Antiquity, 31*(3), 334–337.

Scobey, D. (2002). *Empire City: The making and meaning of the New York City landscape*. Philadelphia: Temple University Press.

Scott, J. (1998). *Seeing like a state: How certain schemes to improve the human condition have failed*. New Haven, CT: Yale University Press.

Sennett, R. (1990). American cities: The grid plan and the Protestant ethic. *International Social Science Journal, 42*(3), 269–285.

Sluyter, A. (1999). The making of the myth in postcolonial development: Material-conceptual landscape transformation in sixteenth-century Veracruz. *Annals of the Association of American Geographers, 89*(3), 377–401.

Smith, M. (2007). Form and meaning in the earliest cities: A new approach to ancient urban planning. *Journal of Planning History, 6*(1), 3–47.

Smith, M., & Schreiber, K. (2006). New World states and empires: Politics, religion, and urbanism. *Journal of Archaeological Research, 14*(1), 1–52.

Stanislawski, D. (1946). The origin and spread of the grid-pattern town. *Geographical Review, 36*(1), 105–120.

Stanislawski, D. (1947). Early Spanish town planning in the New World. *Geographical Review, 37*(1), 94–105.

Stanislawski, D. (1976). Commonsense geography: The case of the Greek war chariot. *Landscape, 20*(2), 33–36.

Steinhardt, N. (1990). *Chinese imperial city planning*. Honolulu: University of Hawaii Press.

Swann, A. (1989). *How to understand and use grids*. Cincinnati: North Light Books.

Theodorson, G.A. (Ed.). (1961). *Studies in human ecology*. Evanston: Row, Peterson.

Vitruvius. (1999 [ca. 30–20 BCE]). *Vitruvius: Ten books on architecture*. I. D. Rowland and T.N. Howe (Eds.) (trans: I.D. Rowland). New York: Cambridge University Press.

Wagner, P., & Mikesell, M. (Eds.). (1962). *Readings in cultural geography*. Chicago: University of Chicago Press.

Williamson, J. (1986). The grid: History, use, and meaning. *Design Issues, 3*(2), 15–30.

Chapter 4
The City Shaped: The Grid

Spiro Kostof

Abstract This chapter is an abridged version of Spiro Kostof's chapter on "The Grid," which was originally published in the author's landmark book, *The City Shaped: Urban Patterns and Meanings Through History* (1991). Kostof's account of the grid layout has had a significant influence on subsequent scholarship related to the historical geography of the grid. The excerpts reprinted in this chapter highlight Kostof's key contributions with a focus on the relation between the grid and political ideology.

Keywords Grid · Politics · History of surveying · Town planning · Aesthetics · Urban patterns

The grid—or gridiron or checkerboard—is by far the commonest pattern for planned cities in history. It is universal both geographically and chronologically (though its use was not continuous through history). No better urban solution recommends itself as a standard scheme for disparate sites, or as a means for the equal distribution of land or the easy parcelling and selling of real estate. The advantage of straight through-streets for defense has been recognized since Aristotle, and a rectilinear street pattern has also been resorted to in order to keep under watch a restless population. Refugee and prisoner camps are obvious settings. The grid of the *barrio* of Barceloneta may appear less strict now that the citadel of Philip V, who conquered Barcelona in 1714, is gone; but the siting of this planned *barrio* on a spit of harbor land outside the citadel's bastions, and the direction of the fifteen straight streets of long, narrow blocks, was an intentional strategy that permitted surveillance of these

This chapter is an abridged version of Kostof, S. (1991). "The Grid." In S. Kostof, *The City Shaped: Urban Patterns and Meanings through History* (pp. 95–157). London: Little, Brown, and Co. Copyright © 1991 by Spiro Kostof. Reproduced with permission of Thames and Hudson Ltd.

S. Kostof (✉) (deceased)
e-mail: permissions@thameshudson.co.uk

© Springer International Publishing AG, part of Springer Nature 2018   55
R. Rose-Redwood, L. Bigon (eds.), *Gridded Worlds: An Urban Anthology*,
https://doi.org/10.1007/978-3-319-76490-0_4

"people of the sea" whose old houses had been demolished to make room for the citadel.

Yet, ubiquitous as the grid has always been, it is also much misunderstood, and often treated as if it were one unmodulated idea that requires little discrimination. Quite the contrary, the grid is an exceedingly flexible and diverse system of planning: hence its enormous success. About the only thing that all grids have in common is that their street pattern is orthogonal—that the right angle rules, and street lines in both directions lie parallel to each other. Even this much is not immutable; the system can curve around irregularities on the ground without betraying its basic logic.

Two singular, and well-preserved, grid schemes from unrelated cultural contexts—Sung China and Colonial America—should demonstrate the wisdom of studying this urban commonplace with particular care.

Suzhou, an ancient Chinese city in southern Jiangsu province, was thoroughly overhauled under the Sung Dynasty, and its extraordinary new design survives on record in a beautiful stone engraving prepared in 1229. The planning is indeed orthogonal, but the overall pattern is of a supple rhythmic complexity free of dogmatic symmetry, continuous straight lines, or uniform divisions into blocks. Yet both in terms of a dimensional order and in the consistent articulation of a spatial structure, the plan was clearly premeditated, and executed according to precise calculations of measurements and levels. The street lines throughout the city were paralleled by a system of canals: 6 canals ran north-south and 14 east-west. Some 300 bridges crossed these canals, artfully grouped at junctions. The double network of transportation was enlivened by frequent cranked intersections and zig-zags. In shape, the city was a walled rectangle. But the frame had projecting sections mindful of the topography, and three corners of the wall were splayed to go with the direction of the water flow in the canals. Five gates were situated asymmetrically around the periphery. The focus of the city was the large walled and moated enclosure of the government complex; it lay southeast of dead center. All public buildings formed sealed compounds of this sort, their high walls reinforced, in the case of the most important institutions, with a band of water. North of the government complex, residential strip blocks provide the only passage of relative uniformity in the plan. They are divided into long narrow plots, with the house fronts lined along a street and the garden walls at the back lined along a canal (Johnston 1983).

Savannah, in the new colony of Georgia, was laid out in 1733, the unwalled core of a sophisticated regional plan. The city grid was organized into wards, each with its own square. On the east and west sides of each square, lots were set out for public buildings like churches and stores. The other two sides were divided into forty house lots. Darby Ward, with its Jackson Square, was the first to be built, and became the center of town. "Ward," of course, is a political term. The plan was the blueprint of a political system. Ten freeholders formed a tything: four tythings made up a ward whose political officer was the constable. The tythings were grouped in two rows of five house lots, back to back, sharing a lane or alley. Since the houses all faced along east-west streets, the wards were united visually, as they were interdependent socially in the shared use of public buildings and the like. So the inner-oriented ward system around squares also had a street-oriented linear reading. The streets linking the squares and the squares themselves were tree-lined fairly early, while the north-south thoroughfares and the small streets within the wards remained treeless. The ward unit was repeatable, and Savannah extended its primary pattern unvaryingly well into the 19th century.

This arbitary choice of two intricate rectilinear plans points up the scope of the historical analysis that follows. Some of the issues that have to be taken into account are the following:

1. the size and shape of the blocks, and their internal organization
2. the open spaces and their distribution
3. the accommodation of public buildings
4. the nature of the street grid, that is, whether any emphasis is created (by stressing a cross-axial focus, for example), or whether a systematic distinction is made between primary and secondary streets
5. the termination of the grid: open-ended? Fitted into a walled precinct? Locked into a system of city gates?
6. the relation of the grid to the surrounding country and the features of the topography
7. most critically, the effect of the grid in three dimensions, for example, Manhattan versus a small railroad town

All of these points are not only essential to conduct a discussion of form: they also go to the heart of the motivation of grids, the kind of life the grids are designed to play host to.

In addition, the subject is crowded by impure, composite, or other sorts of hybrid uses of the grid. I might single out:

1. loose approximations, where the lines are not strictly parallel or the angles strictly right (a good many of the medieval *bastides* fall into this category)
2. gridded extensions of "organic" city forms (e.g., Berlin, Cracow, etc.)
3. gridded additions to an original grid plan (e.g., San Francisco, New Orleans, Turin)
4. grids combined with other geometric planning principles, most commonly diagonal avenues, as in the famous instance of L'Enfant's Washington, or in the 18th-century scheme for St. Petersburg
5. the curvilinear grid of the modern residential development

The Grid and Politics

Generally speaking, gridded towns serve most of the purposes of towns *per se*: defense, agricultural development, trade. There is little premeditation in the choice of this street layout beyond the fact that it is, for certain periods in history, the most practical way to plan new cities. This was the case, for example, in the later Middle

Ages. So when the philosophers and Church fathers insisted that the founding of cities was the duty of pious sovereigns, the model that stood before them had to be some type of orthogonal planning. Francesco Eiximenes, the Catalan philosopher of the 14th century, in the description of city-form he gives in his *Crestià*, recreates a generic version of the Classical grid (Puig i Cadafalch 1936).

Simple equations common to surveys of Western urban history—the grid with democratic societies, and the Baroque aesthetic with regimes of a centralist structure—are easily overdrawn, not to say fundamentally misleading. They do not account, for one thing, for the extensive use of the grid by absolutist powers like Spain and France in their colonial enterprises.

The grid has served the symbolic needs of the most absolute governments, China and Japan chief among them. The Chang'an of the Tang Dynasty ranks among the strictest of grids, and its example was exported to Japan to guide the planning of Heijo-kyo (modern Nara) in the early 8th century. In the first centuries of Chinese imperial history, the administrative capital was an act of total creation; it was a place of enforced residence under political control. The city symbolized power, and was in the service of the needs of power. The orthogonal plan froze the spatial structure to reflect an unalterable hierarchy: it put in isolated urban envelopes the palace precinct, administration, religion, and housing according to class. Trade was of secondary concern and was strictly regimented within the political grid. That is what makes Suzhou fascinating. Its sprightly grid is a vivid record of that slow loosening up of the Chinese administrative city after the 10th century, and the acceptance of commerce and pleasure as constituents of city-form.

These are famous episodes which, because of the remoteness and insularity of their cultures, are treated as exceptions to mainstream urban history. But the political innocence of the grid in the West is a fiction. In the early Greek colonies, for example, the grid, far from being a democratic device employed to assure an equitable allotment of property to all citizens, was the means of perpetuating the privileges of the property-owning class descendent from the original settlers, and bolstering a territorial aristocracy. The first settlers who made the voyage to the site were entitled to equal allocations of land both inside and outside the city walls. These hereditary estates were inalienable; the ruling class strictly discouraged a land market. The estates were huge, as much as 2 ½ acres for some families. They were then subdivided by the owner. Within the city, private land could only be used for housing. Any alienation of land, or any agitation for land reform, was severely dealt with, and could be punishable as for murder (Métraux 1978).

Centuries after Chang'an and Heijo-kyo, the special arrangement of public buildings and other planning devices could still be used to cast a grid unmistakably in a mode that celebrates centralized political structure. Take Brest in Brittany, one of four new port cities sponsored by the administration of Louis XIV as part of a calculated extension of French sea power. The 1680s scheme of Colbert's engineer Sainte-Colombe was "a regimented, unbroken, unembellished grid pattern of blocks," as the student of these cities, Josef W. Konvitz, describes it. The next year Vauban introduced some improvements—specifically, the insertion of a unified composition of church, market and formal residential square, which distinguished this grid as a governmental creation. By placing this monumental episode between the city and the arsenal, Vauban effectively expressed that the new Brest was a royal initiative—without having to resort to great Baroque diagonals and the other obvious apparatus of absolutist planning. The *place d'armes* of French colonial plantations in America, situated on the waterfront and meant to carry an assortment of institutional buildings (palaces for governor, bishop and intendant, barracks, hospitals, etc.), similarly marked the simple linear grid of New Orleans or St. Louis as a royal undertaking.

By the same token, to say that Holland's use of the grid in the 17th century represents "Calvinist dogmatism and democratic equalitarianism," as E.A. Gutkind (1971, 35) does, is to attribute simple political messages to an urban diagram that was largely motivated by matter-of-fact economic considerations. The Dutch furthered a pragmatic bourgeois mercantilist culture, to which Baroque diagonals and formal places marked by equestrian monuments were irrelevant.

The fact is that egalitarianism is no more natural to gridded patterns than to any other urban form. However noble the original premise, inequities will creep in sooner or later. In accordance with the free society they promoted, medieval new towns had honorable intentions about the equality of their parcels. The smaller lots on the market square in a town like Villeneuve-sur-Lot were intended to make amends for the advantages of this privileged situation. Towns on hilly terrain were so laid out that every settler would encounter the same conditions in relation to the slope. But half-lots materialized soon enough, and select inhabitants were given the chance to build on double or triple lots.

The most persistent belief that urban grids represent an egalitarian system of land distribution is expressed in the context of modern democracies, principally the United States. The point is made regularly that grids, besides offering "simplicity in land surveying, recording, and subsequent ownership transfer," also "favored a fundamental democracy in property market participation. This did not mean that individual wealth could not appropriate considerable property, but rather that the basic initial geometry of land parcels bespoke a simple egalitarianism that invited easy entry into the urban land market" (Conzen 1990, 146). The reality is much less admirable. The ordinary citizen gains easy access to urban land only at a preliminary phase, when cheap rural land is being urbanized through rapid laying out. To the extent that the grid speeds this process and streamlines absentee purchases, it may be considered an equalizing social device. Once the land has been identified with the city, however, this advantage of "the initial geometry of land parcels" evaporates, and even unbuilt lots slip out of common reach. What matters in the long run is not the mystique of grid geometry, but the luck of first ownership.

It may be that the most genuinely egalitarian use of the grid came most naturally to religious confraternities. Two celebrated cases will make this point.

The first is a late outcome of the great schism in the Catholic Church. After the repeal of the Edict of Nantes in 1685, over 200,000 Huguenots fled from France. They settled and founded towns and suburbs in Protestant Germany, and in England, Holland, and Switzerland. All the towns had the same form: a regular street grid on a square site, uniform houses of identical shape, size, and color, a small church, and identical manufactories. Among the best known Huguenot settlements are Karlshafen near Kassel, and Erlangen in the territory of the Margrave of Ansbach (Braunfels 1988). Here unequivocally the sameness was meant to express the social equality of all inhabitants.

So it was with the Mormons two centuries later. God informed these followers of the Church of Jesus Christ of the Latter Day Saints, through Joseph Smith, that the Second Coming would take place in America at a "perfect time and place," and that their mandate was to prepare a fitting city for this millennial event. In 1833, Smith drew up a scheme for the ideal Mormon city, known as the "Plat of the City of Zion." The Plat was one square mile in surface, divided by a grid of streets. The houses, to be built of brick and stone, were to be set back from the street line. The plan would grow infinitely as the faithful increased. All property would be deeded to the Church, and one would then be assigned an inheritance or stewardship—a farm, a store or shop, a ministerial mission.

The Mormons laid down the Plat of Zion twice (at Caldwell County, Missouri, and Nauvoo, Illinois) before their final stop, in the valley of the Great Salt Lake. Salt Lake City grew fast, around the Temple erected in one of the central squares. Beyond the monumental checkerboard sheltered by the Wahsatch Mountains stretched the garden and farm lots, also within the lines of an undeviating grid. The houses were built at the corners of their spacious plots, grouped in fours at street intersections. The successor of the square city of the Levites described in Numbers and Leviticus, and of Ezekiel's square city of Jerusalem, spread out in the Territory of Deseret, in the primordial rockscape of Utah. The Latter Day Saints were ready for the Second Coming (Reps 1969).

"Better Order" or Routine

Historically, the grid has served two main purposes. The first is to facilitate orderly settlement, colonization in its broad sense. This involves both the acquisition of distant territory—by the Greeks in Sicily, Spain in the New World—and the settlement of reclaimed or newly opened-up land, as happened in the Spanish peninsula with the *reconquista* or in the American Midwest after about 1800.

The other application of the grid has been as an instrument of modernization, and of contrast to what existed that was not as orderly. Romans tidied up native Iberian or Germanic settlements this way. In the Renaissance, princes extended the fabric of their medieval cities with exemplary gridded quarters; Ercole d'Este's addition to Ferrara designed by Biagio Rossetti at the end of the 15th century is an early example. A royal decree of 1628 provided that all existing towns in Finland were to be reshaped as grids, so that they could be brought into "better order," and all new towns were to be cast in this same mold (Lilius 1985). Modern Europe used the grid for new quarters next to the native cities of its colonial empires—in Cyprus, Morocco, or Vietnam. Newly established modern nations updated their territory with the help of the grid—witness 19th-century Greece after Independence and the contemporary versions of ancient cities like Corinth or Sparta. The Modern Movement developed its own basic grid to serve as matrix for a revolutionary new way of planning or replanning cities in different countries and climates. Lucio Costa's plan for Brasilia, the new capital of Brazil, was said by him to be a perfect example of Modernist principles. Chandigarh too, except for the famous group of civic buildings by Le Corbusier, is an anonymous Modernist grid in sharp contrast to the congested tangle of the old cities of India.

The actual motivation for the grid has also varied. It served military arrangements (Roman *castra*, British cantonments), religious covenants, mercantile capitalism (railroad towns), and industrial planning. This versatility of program within what it is possible to see as a simple-minded, uninspired, unvarying formula has brought the grid many detracters. Advocates of the Grand Manner, from Baroque urbanists to the theorists of the City Beautiful movement in the United States, have faulted it for its timidity and its failure to provide distinctive sites for public buildings. Those who defended the visual interest and social richness of the old European towns could think of orthogonal planning only as a symptom of a primitive state of culture, or proof of the impoverishment of the urban experience in modern times. Charles Dickens, during his visit to the United States in 1842, complained that Philadelphia was "distractingly regular. After walking about it for an hour or two, I felt that I would have given the world for a crooked street" (1850, 67). Compared to the old core of Belgian cities, the reformist mayor of Brussels Charles Buls wrote in 1893, the modern additions with their streets running parallel or perpendicular to each other have "the character of an artificial crystallization, dry, mathematical" (Buls 1893, 8–9). And Camillo Sitte's slightly earlier appraisal of the Jeffersonian gridding of America was none too kind:

> This [division] is obviously due to the fact that the terrain was not well-known at the time and its future development could not be predicted, since America lacked a past, had no history, and did not yet signify anything else in the civilization of mankind but so many square miles of land. For America, Australia, and other unopened lands the gridiron plan may for the time being still suffice. Wherever people are concerned merely with colonizing land, live only for earning money and earn money only in order to live, it may be appropriate to pack people into blocks of buildings like herring in a barrel. (Sitte in Collins and Collins 1986 [1965], 126)

This prejudice against the grid was nurtured by American planners and scholars in more recent days. The grid was an easy target for Garden City apologists like Lewis Mumford, for formalist urban historians who could appreciate the beauty of Savannah's pattern but saw no merit in the mean layouts of speculative towns, and for social historians eager to make the grid synonymous with greed and the unfeeling, mechanized production of mock-communities.

But of course to blame the grid for the shallowness and callousness of urban experience is surely to miss the point. Any grid holds the potential to become a beautiful city over time depending on how it is fleshed out. The architect, the social planner, the politician, the residents themselves have their chance once the two-dimensional diagram is in place. If grids serve up a routinized, alienating urban setting, it is largely because of what was allowed to happen or was not encouraged to happen after the initial lines were drawn (Groth 1981). Without collective control even model grids like Savannah's will quickly squander their initial advantages. With care and imagination, the initial sameness of the most prosaic of grids may become the matrix within which interest, diversity, and human richness can be provided for. And of course the original intention for the grid can itself ensure against tedium and trivialization. Against the profit-mongering of speculative towns we can pit communitarian experiments. The grids which Mormons planted along the trail of their persecution, though on paper no more enticing than the speculative diagrams of land development and railroad companies, were resonant with the force of faith. Perhaps it is indeed time to stop condemning the grid plan out of hand as "dull-witted, unesthetic, and somehow speaking of a lower use of man's intellect," and to see it rather as "one of the great inventions of the human mind" (Vance 1977, 44–45).

Laying Out the Grid

The word "grid" as it has been used so far in this chapter is a convenient, and imprecise, substitute for "orthogonal planning." "Gridiron," in the United States at least, implies a pattern of long narrow blocks, and "checkerboard" a pattern of square blocks. These are the two commonest divisions of a grid plan. The basis of a true checkerboard is bound to be modular, since the quadratic units produced by the coordinates are equal. A gridiron may prove to be modular or not, depending on the regularity of the long narrow blocks and the relation of their size to the public buildings and open spaces.

True checkerboards are rare. One thinks, in chronological order, of the unfinished Urartian town of Zernaki Tepe in eastern Turkey (8th century BC); early Roman colonies in northern Italy such as Verona; Kyoto; a smattering of medieval planted towns like Lalinde (Périgord, France); the towns of New Spain; the initial schemes of American towns like Omaha, Nebraska; and Cerdà's Barcelona. Rectangular blocks are much commoner. But as a rule, a grid plan will contain a mixture of different-sized blocks, if not initially, then through units added after the fact.

But the street grid and block pattern, the object of primary concern for historians of urban planning, do not in themselves explain the character of the city-form. At the time that this overall grid is laid out, a second, more detailed grid is put in place—that of plot parcels within the block. Decisions affecting allocation of land to owners or renters need to be made before, or at the same time as, the drawing of the street lines. If in the city's history the street grid is likely to endure longer than this closer-grained, and less visible, division, it is because streets, as public space, are under official scrutiny while private parcels can stage their own internal transformations. Nonetheless, street grid and plot grid will always interlock and be interdependent.

Two other important considerations affect the quality of gridded urban form. The shape of the land is one of them; the technology of surveying and its relative sophistication at a given time and place is the other.

On the Site

As always, one begins with the land. Where the land is flat, the grid is on its own. This is the closest the city planner will come to a blank sheet of paper. On level ground a standardized format can be painlessly repeated. The planning agency may indeed decide to create a level site, filling in depressions and shaving off swells. Roman towns in Gaul, it has been observed, "demonstrate a quite remarkable disdain for existing features, either natural or manmade. The demand was for a virtual *tabula rasa* … [so that] the new city could be shown in a condition of 'perfect horizontality'" (Drinkwater in Grew and Hoblet 1985, 53).

Even on flat land, gridded settlement patterns may reflect the broad physical facts of the site. River towns, for example, will tend to run their main streets parallel to the waterfront, with a small number of connecting cross-streets. The *bastide* of Castelsarrasin on the Garonne in southwestern France is a case in point. Later, the river ports of colonial France in North America, grids of long and narrow shape, exemplified more formal castings of this sympathetic street alignment.

The incidence of a pure, uncompromising grid over rolling topography is rare. The most celebrated instance from antiquity is Priene's well thought-out grid, from the 4th century BC. The original town had been at the mouth of the Meander which had silting problems. The new city, meant for a population of about 4000 people, was built on high ground at the southern end of a spur sloping south, east and west. The city blocks were terraced like the seats of a theater along the main east-west streets, and the north-south streets for pedestrians were cut into steps in places. At medieval Lübeck, the disregard for natural topography can be rationally explained. The city was surrounded by the River Trave, the city core was along a ridge at the high point of the site, and straight streets down the slope were the shortest distance between the center and the river piers. Modern instances like San Francisco are speculators' shortcuts; the challenge of coping with lots on slopes is passed on to the buyers.

The common rule about street grids is to seek a compromise between natural irregularities and the abstract rigor of the right angle. We need look no further than medieval new towns to find a wealth of intuitive and expedient adjustments of reticulate city-form to the facts of local terrain. Among hundreds of *bastides*, uncompromised grids like Monpazier and Aigues-Mortes in France and Flint in Wales are extremely rare. They occupy level ground, and are usually framed by the rectangle of city walls. The majority of new towns never were fortified, and not being so delimited at the start, their overall appearance was frayed at the edges. They sat on uneven terrain, sometimes next to an extant castle settlement which had chosen its rough perch advisedly. For the most part, therefore, the layout was the product of "a primarily local, empirical approach in which a general familiarity with the bastide form was adapted to the exigencies of local conditions" (Carter 1990, 193). Ridges yielded simple linear grids of one main street and a parallel set along the slopes (e.g., Villefranche-du-Queyran, St.-Pastour). On rounded hilltops, the annular plan which would have resulted from "organic" growth was simply squared (e.g., Donzac). The planners of New Winchelsea gridded as much of the hilltop as they could, and left the irregular edges for odd-shaped house lots and grazing ground. Beaumont acknowledged the shape of its hill-back by bending the grid blocks north of the marketplace so that they are a few degrees out of line with those to the south. Prior settlements and major roads affected the new town to the extent that it was expeditious and economical to conserve street surfaces. The two *bastides* of Villeneuve-sur-Lot, built on opposite banks of the river ten years apart, demonstrate this dependence: the older town on the right bank, built on virgin ground, is quite regular; its companion on the left bank, where a village and two strongholds of the lord of Pujols already existed, has a much looser form with large angular blocks.

As regards the general orthogonality of these hundreds of plans, it is well to remember that this was the only option for rational urban design open to the Middle Ages. It was the only system that facilitated the calculation of area and the coordination of parts. Until the Renaissance, planners did not have the instruments to construct mathematically accurate maps of geographic or urban forms. "In the Middle Ages," David Friedman writes, "it is only on an orthogonally articulated plane that the precise location of a point could be known" (1988, 51). Siena's planned organicism was achieved within an extant scheme. Out in the open, this was a different story. It was only during the Renaissance that the possibility opened up to survey and record geographic features and irregular city shapes.

Surveyors and Theorists

The simplicity of marking out an orthogonal street pattern made the grid a feasible city-form even for technologically unsophisticated cultures. The training of those who did the actual division on the site could be fairly basic. The tools remained in use for long spans of time, with periodic improvements that made their performance more accurate. Ropes and pegs marked straight lines at all stages of history. Alberti's *hodometer* or "road-measurer" was described in Vitruvius fifteen hundred years earlier: an ordinary cart wheel of known circumference, the revolutions of which are recorded automatically.

Egyptians could determine the horizontal and the difference in height between two points. They had a simple sighting instrument, and used a primitive form of the transit, called *groma*, which was passed on to the Greeks and Romans and remained the standard land-surveyor's instrument until improved versions were developed in the Renaissance. In this transit, one of the lineals was used for sighting a main direction, and the other to determine the direction in the field at right angles to it.

In Greek colonial enterprises, the *horistes* was a key member of the original expedition; the word literally means the establisher of boundaries (*horoi*). He was a man of practical skills. The division was done in long narrow strips.[1] Diodorus in the late 1st century BC describes the founding of a colony: first, the ritual consultation of an oracle (the religious component); then, the location of a spring (water supply); the building of a city wall (defense); the laying out of a grid of broad avenues or *plateiai* (for Thurii which he is describing, there were four in one direction and three others at right angles to them); and after this primary order, the subdivision into narrow blocks for houses, served by lesser streets called *stenopoi*, basically footpaths between lots. The houses fronted on *stenopoi*, public buildings on *plateiai*. A portion of the city was strictly reserved for civic and commercial buildings; some economic activity was also incorporated in the residential zones. As for public buildings, the temples sometimes fitted the grid and sometimes were oriented independently (e.g., Agrigento, Paestum), presumably for religious reasons. The theater often took advantage of a natural slope for the arrangement of seats.

The case of Hippodamus of Miletus is puzzling. We have no working details for the system attributed to him, but what distinguished it, it seems fairly certain, was the fact that it relied on a theoretical formula of geometry, more so than the purely technical (and empirical) practice of land surveyors, and that it was carefully adjusted to the specific demands of the site. If we can judge from Piraeus, the system involved the division of the territory into sectors, each with its own rectilinear street pattern; the setting aside of public areas, delimited by boundary markers, for specific public functions; and provision for the placement of public buildings. From the example of Rhodes, to the extent that its ancient street pattern can be reconstructed, we might deduce that the Hippodamian geometric system had a triple order of division. The largest element was a square of which the sides measured one *stadion* each (a variable unit of about 600 feet). Each of these squares was quartered to produce squares one-half *stadion* to a side; and each of these was in turn divided into six parts to form rectangles measuring 100 by 150 feet. Whether the system became established as a school of urban design after the death of Hippodamus, or simply refined the *modus operandi* of the common surveyor, is impossible to say.

We know a lot about the training of Roman surveyors. It involved knowledge of arithmetic, geometry, and law. On the whole, they worked with squares and rectangles, and applied triangles, which they used not for surveying by triangulation but for things like finding the width of a river without crossing it and possibly for calculating height. Other instruments of the trade were the set-square, of most use to building surveyors, the water-table to establish precise horizontality, the portable sundial which helped with orientation, and of course measuring-rods and chains.

---

[1] The term used for this division, *per strigas*, was actually coined by a modern scholar (Castagnoli 1971). *Striga* in Latin means "a long line of grass or corn cut down, a swath," by extension a "plough furrow." In Roman parlance the system of *strigae* and *scamnae* referred to an old method of land division adopted especially in public arable land in the provinces, where strips were arranged lengthwise (*strigae*) and breadthwise (*scamnae*) in relation to the surveyor's orientation (Dilke 1961, 424n).

There was no strict separation between planned cities and the rectangular land survey of the agricultural land around them, nor between surveyors of rural land and military, or urban, surveyors (Dilke 1961). It was customary to set up a *groma* in the center of a military camp.

Until the Renaissance, rectilinear layouts were generated by simple rotes of surface geometry. The surveyors knew how to create a perpendicular to a given line on the ground, and so establish the two coordinates to which parallel survey lines could be drawn. In many *bastides*, the Pythagorean triangle with sides of 3-4-5, which permitted the tracing of right angles with the help of a cord of 12 knots, was widely used. More complicated patterns based on constructive geometry, quite familiar in the design of Gothic cathedrals, could be transferred to the field but were not. In other words, the laying out of cities was not looked upon as an elevated problem of architectural design.

Coordinated Systems of Town and Country

Rural Grids

The control of their countryside has always been a main worry of cities. A program of colonization or land reclamation is particularly dependent on the equitable distribution of agricultural land if it is to attract settlers. This often entails a large-scale grid of some sort. The two rectilinear systems of town and country are likely to follow similar rules applied at different scales, and the same units of measurement.

In early imperial China, this unit was the *li*, which roughly corresponds to the Greek *stadion* (ca. 600 feet). The rural grid divided the cultivated fields, with eight families in each square. The square was actually divided into 9 parts; the lord collected a tax from the cultivation of the ninth part. The relation of this agricultural division to a military system of conscription is unclear, but the fields were grouped into multiples of 5 for that purpose. In Japan, the *jori* system, introduced in the 7th century in connection with a new political order, was intended to ensure the equitable distribution of rice lands. The main squares measured roughly half a mile to a side. These were subdivided into 36 equal squares called *tsubo*, and each of these was further cut up into 10 strips, modest portions of land that were allotted by the State to the cultivators on a periodic basis. The outlines of the *jori* system are still in evidence today in parts of southern Japan (Hall 1970).

Roman land survey followed several methods, of which the commonest was centuriation. Two axial roads at right angles to each other started the survey; then field tracks (*limites*) were driven parallel to their course until a grid of squares or rectangles had taken shape. The squares were meant to contain one hundred small holdings (*centuriae*).

In the French *bastides*, a triple system of land division prevailed. Settlers received building lots called *ayrals* (between ca. 1000 and 3300 square feet each), vegetable gardens called *cazals* (6500 to 7500 square feet), and arable land for fields and vineyards called *arpents* or *journaux* after the units of measurement (about two-thirds of an acre per settler). These allotments formed three concentric zones. The urban parcels stretched to the limits of the town, or the walls if they existed. The gardens were within or immediately outside the walls. Arable land and pastures might not always lie adjacent to the town.

When the Spaniards arrived in the New World, land management was practiced on a regional basis. The jurisdiction of the original colonial cities was extraordinarily large. The territory of Asunción stretched for some 300 miles in every direction: the whole of present-day Paraguay thus belonged to this one city. Land tracts were generally square, 10,000 *varas* or 5 ¼ miles on each side; these tracts were called *sitios*. The town proper was in or near the middle of the tract. Around the town, on one or more sides, were the *ejidos*—common lands reserved for the enlargement of the town. Then came farming plots, most of them allotted to the original settlers, some reserved for latecomers, and some rented out to produce income for community purposes. There were also common pasture lands and common woodlands. Each settler got a farming plot and a house lot in the town. The land could not be sold. The similarity here to the ancient Greek practice in Sicily is obvious. I should also note that the land division pattern of the farmland—a large grid—made it possible to integrate the later urban development and the original town core, since the town grid could be systematically extended, and fitted into, the larger grid of the countryside. In South America, streets of 19th-century extensions are dead-straight continuations of the original grid lines, sometimes (as in Buenos Aires) stretching out for as long as 10 miles. Only since the First World War have suburban streets in more irregular patterns appeared.

The colonial experience of the English in North America had its own rural/urban order. Savannah, to take a celebrated case, was conceived as part of a regional plan. Beyond the town limits were garden lots (half-squares in the form of triangles), and further out still, larger plots for farms of major contributors. In New England, the pattern of farm fields, like that of the towns themselves, did not aspire to a disciplined grid.[2] Towns were organized as nucleated villages, a cluster of house lots around the common, or along the spine of a single street. Less commonly we get a compact "squared" town, like Cambridge in Massachusetts, or Fairfield and Hartford in Connecticut. In the South, holdings were isolated, and the settlement pattern diffuse. Then after 1785 came the National Survey. The townships measured 6 by 6 miles. Every other township was subdivided into plots one square mile, or 640 acres, in area, called sections, and the 36 sections were eventually broken down further into more manageable halves and quarters. The distant precedents were Roman centuriation, the *sitios* of New Spain, the Japanese *jori* system, and the land division applied by Dutch engineers to land reclaimed from the sea (*polders*). In all

---

[2] The township was divided and distributed according to merit, the size of each allotment reflecting either the relative amount each settler contributed to the initial expense of the enterprise, or the extent of his personal property. There was a class hierarchy of proprietors, first settlers, and latecomers.

these cases, the survey adjusted to topography. Only the National Survey of the United States was strictly oriented to the points of the compass.

The Jeffersonian gridding of America was based on the notion of "freehold," by which was meant property of a certain size or value, or that produced a specified taxable income. This is to be distinguished from leasehold, which signifies a condition of tenancy. Freeholders had political rights. They were enfranchised: they could hold office or they could vote. Property is the key to citizenship and suffrage. In the Colonial period, freehold qualification was about 50 acres. Jefferson wanted Americans to have more. At the time of the Survey, most of the Thirteen Colonies had abandoned the literal sense of freehold for a tax equivalent. So Jefferson was being conservative. But his dream was to make of all Americans (white males at any rate) citizens with voting rights on the strength of being landowners. The National Survey grid has been considered, in that sense, the equivalent of the Constitition (Hurtt 1983). Under the circumstances, it was providential that the Constitution was indeed enacted, for the Jeffersonian land democracy, like almost all such experiments of history, proved exceedingly short-lived.

Gridded Extensions

The existence of a coordinated array of town and country did not ensure an orderly extension of town grids into the surrounding territory. As a rule, only when city authorities had the power to oversee the development of the suburban region could gridded extensions obey a coherent design and establish rational links to the urban core.

The suburban grid could be appended to an "organic" town, or to an original grid. Some *bastides* were gridded extensions grafted onto earlier castle towns. Culemborg in Holland is a good instance. The old nucleus dates from the early 12th century, the castle from 1271, the "Nieuwstad" to the southwest from 1385–92. A street stretches from the marketplace in the old town, through the south gate, across the drainage canal and into the new town, strapping the two urban units together (Burke 1956).

This is the standard device of junction, both between an "organic" core and a subsequent grid and between two grids of separate date. Examples at random would include Le Havre, where the main axis of the old town is extended into the gridded *ville neuve*, and Renaissance Ferrara where linear connections are made between the old market and the piazza of the Herculean Addition. If the gridded extension came after the old town had received bastioned walls, the problem of grafting was more difficult. Berlin, and its 17th–18th century additions of Dorotheenstadt and Friedrichstadt, are a case in point; despite the strong cord of Unter den Linden, the gridded suburbs could not mesh with the medieval core until its walls came down.

Turin is the most lucid demonstration of an original gridded town of Roman descent able smoothly to graft on later grids. Having been chosen to be the capital of Piedmont under the Savoy dynasty, Turin added no fewer than three gridded quarters to the old Roman core—a group of 12 new blocks outside the walls to the south in the early 17th century, an eastward extension to meet the banks of the Po beginning in 1673, and finally an addition to the west in 1712.

Amsterdam is a special case. This great northern port, which always exercised a remarkable element of public control over city-form, borrowed the best of the "organic" system and the grid, to ensure a rational, long-range development. A major master plan launched in 1607 increased its area fourfold. The city had started in the 13th century with a sea-dyke along the south side of the Ij estuary and a dam across a little stream called the Amstel. Ditches were built parallel to this line of estuary and the Amstel, to the east and the west of the settlement—two sets of them between the end of the 14th and the middle of the 15th century. These converged south of town, and houses were aligned along them and along the river itself. The 1607 plan simply took the canals that then formed the city's edge, and retraced them in three encircling canals across empty land. The first of these—the Heerengracht— was built over the bastioned walls of 1593, and the two others ran parallel to them. Each of these canals was to serve as the new city edge during successive enlarge- ments of the urban core. So you had both an overall extension plan, with land uses determined from the start, and the possibility of construction in stages. The narrow strips between the canals were gridded, but because of their concentric disposition a good proportion of the blocks were trapezoidal. The city itself decided the position of the three canals, but the development between them and the new walls beyond was left to private enterprise. On the western section of this area, a workers' district was laid out (the Jordaan), with housing, tanneries, woolen and velvet mills, and dye works. Its street grid, laid over existing paths and ditches, was aligned obliquely in relation to the new canals.

Without the centralized authority of cities like Turin and Amsterdam, or of German municipalities in the modern period, gridded extension degenerates into a patchwork of small developments that meet at ownership boundaries of rural hold- ings. This is the common reality of American city growth, rather than the uniform 1811 grid of Manhattan. The impression of an "infinitely extendable grid" is in most cases indebted to the streamlining of this *ad hoc* patchwork by the traffic engineer's "supergrid" of through-streets assembled for the automotive age.

The Grid in the 20th Century

The coming of the Modernist era marked the end of experimentation to salvage the traditional gridiron city through new building typologies. For urban designers of the Modernist stripe, the grid could not serve as the frame for socially equitable devel- opment. Advocates of housing reform—Werner Hegemann in his scathing indict- ment of Berlin's tenements, *Das steinerne Berlin* (Stony Berlin) of 1930, and Catherine Bauer in her influential *Modern Housing* of 1934—represented the grid- iron block as an intractable source of urban misery. Modernist ideologues con- demned high density block development on the grounds that it denied tenants their inalienable rights to *Licht, Luft und Sonnenschein* (light, air, and sunshine). But the seemingly boundless increase in modern city traffic was perhaps the most persuasive indictment of the grid. It was now argued that the grid was essentially made for carriage traffic. The automobile had changed its character for the worse, turning city blocks into besieged islands. An estimate of 1933 claimed that the automobile had tripled the radius of the metropolitan area, and increased the daily traffic area ninefold (McKenzie 1933). The volume and speed of this traffic made streets extremely dangerous, especially for children.

All this provided the rationale for abandoning the grid as such, and embracing the idea of an inturned superblock bounded by major traffic arteries. Now the use of the grid as a frame for separate communities, rather than as a means of organizing individual building lots, has non-Western precedent. In a number of cultural situations, the rigorous block structure forms the overall urban matrix within which a tracery of finer scale and more lively intercourse takes shelter. In Chinese imperial cities up to the 10th century or so the periphery of the large blocks was merely a screen—in the early Empire sometimes literally a wall—beyond which a complex local organization prevailed. Similarly, the great square subdivisions of old Jaipur, of about one-half mile on a side, might best be called "sectors" rather than blocks. Within each one is a closer-grained and looser "minigrid" defining neighborhoods (*mohallas*). These neighborhood blocks accommodate 40 to 50 residential plots, and hold a homogeneous population based on caste, trade, or ethnic/religious affiliation.

The Modernist superblock has a different edge. In Europe, one common arrangement is to set freestanding terraces (*Zeilenbau*) in parallel rows, the long pared-down façades looking onto strips of greensward, the short end-faces, often blank, turned to the circuit of major streets that create a moat around the development. American advocates of the residential superblock had a specific social agenda: to build community spirit. The conventional street grid stranded residents on "rectangular islands surrounded by noise, dirt, fumes, and danger" (Dahir 1947, 22). Denied easy access to a rewarding social life, city dwellers were depicted as isolated and anomic, afloat in a "great sea of despondency" (Dahir 1947, 38). The solution was to promote social intercourse in superblocks designed as self-contained neighborhoods, each with its own shops, schools and community facilities.

An early formulation of these ideas was in Chicago around 1915. A competition sponsored by the City Club sought out innovative designs for the development of outlying portions of large cities—designs that would abandon the conventional grid and its small blocks for a unified treatment of parcels as large as a quarter-section. "The temperamental nervousness that charaterizes us as a people must find an outlet in variety and not in monotony," a jury member wrote, "[and] this should be expressed by the foiling of ... playfulness and charm against severity" (Yeomans 1916, 105). All the winning projects kept the rectilinear section roads as a stable frame, while introducing broad curves and a looser block structure. All emphasized landscaping, and focused their inward-looking parcel with public buildings like schools and churches.

But the first major policy statement of the "neighborhood unit for the family-life community" came in a 1929 paper by the sociologist Clarence A. Perry for the

Russell Sage Foundation. Focused on a "community center" and endowed with a freewheeling system of interior streets, the Perry scheme generalized the select experience of American picturesque suburbs and English Garden Cities. Architects like Henry Wright (1935), the American advocate of Garden City principles, went so far as to argue for a legal modification of the American grid as the matrix of land development.

From the 1930s onward, American concepts of superblock planning became increasingly allied with theories emanating from the International Congresses of Modern Architecture, or CIAM. According to Modernist canons set down in CIAM's 1933 position paper known as the Athens Charter, traffic flow and its design was the primary determinant of city form. CIAM dogma focused on the incompatibility of the sleek new transportation technologies with the slowly evolved husks of existing cities. In practice, the Modernist alternative was a composition of free-standing buildings, set in a diffuse landscape of foliage and organized by a loose grid of high-speed arteries. In Detroit and Minneapolis, planners had envisaged a maxigrid of this kind, as an adjunct to the gridiron of streets rather than its replacement, as early as the 1920s.

A more comprehensive proposal to reshape the American gridiron came from a Chicago-based luminary of the Bauhaus diaspora, Ludwig Hilbersheimer. His "settlement unit," inspired by both American neighborhood unit planning and the more radical urban proposals of European Modernism, was predicated on the gradual transformation of the conventional gridded city through an orderly program of street closings and selective demolition. In the new pattern, neighborhoods would be separated by park belts and made safe from traffic through the provision of residential cul-de-sacs as a part of an overall street hierarchy (Hilbersheimer 1955).

In contrast to Hilbersheimer's accommodation of the historic settlement pattern, orthodox Modernist projects for high-speed maxigrid cities were plotted against vacant backgrounds. New towns held the best chance for unencumbered city-making of this sort; bombed postwar cities provided a less tidy but workable slate.

At Chandigarh (founded in 1951), the first Modernist city to be realized *ab ovo*, the sophisticated residential pattern is characterized by the interpenetration of green landscape and a loose grid pattern of primary roads defining superblocks. The superblocks, or "sectors" as they are called, measure half by three-quarters of a mile each, proportions based on the Golden Section. The blocks are controlled communities oriented inward, so that the primary traffic roads have little if any street life. Each block is bisected lengthwise by one major local through-street, the market street; together, these form a linear shopping system, Modernism's homage to the bazaar.

The most thoroughly worked out Modernist grid of recent years is in Milton Keynes (founded in 1967), the last of the English New Towns. This grid system is made up of motorways defining 0.6 mile squares, and it is far from being rigid. The lines gently undulate, at the same time that they rise and fall, in sympathy with the gently contoured land. Moreover, the roads are bordered by thick tree-walls intended to absorb traffic noise. The imagery is hybrid: the picturesque green effects of the Garden City are made to civilize a rational grid, with the road engineers "trying in vain to give a useful structure a look of self-grown beauty" (Rasmussen in Walker 1982, 7). There is no specific road center, and therefore the congestion of traffic that is inevitable in a centralized plan like Ebenezer Howard's original diagram of the Garden City, subsequently respected in all the New Towns, is here avoided. The town center is in the nature of a shopping mall, and one of the motorways runs through it at upper-story level.

Within the grid squares, private development has a free hand. Both apartment blocks and detached houses are acceptable, and some of the squares are of course relegated to industrial and commercial buildings, to leisure and recreation. Despite the planners' espousal of mixed use, the Modernist dogma of breaking the city into "functions" prevails. A network of local traffic accommodates pedestrians and bicyclists. But the grid squares are not conceived as inturned "planned residential neighborhoods" in the Garden City mode. If anything, the desire here is to revert to the open grid, and use the motorways and local streets to move freely over the entire city. At Milton Keynes, it might be fair to suggest, the experiences of Modernism and the Garden City are redirected to traditional ends.

Indeed, the crusade of the last two decades to bring back the historic city, conserve what is left of it and rehearse its lessons, also entails the recovery of the traditional block. The grid, in fact, never quite disappeared. The Modernist cityscape had displaced two other urban traditions that were now being reclaimed: the "organic" townscape with its picturesque effects and irregularities all within a system of spatial closure, of tight spatial sequences; and the Baroque townscape with its complete compositions, its visual drama, its showcasing of monuments in formal squares and at the ends of vistas, its scenographic hierarchies.

It is the great virtue of the grid, of its ceaseless usefulness, to resist both of these contrived urban experiences. Their champions hold as an article of faith that the complexity of social life requires complex street systems to seek its fulfillment. The premise of the grid is that city-form, as a tissue of lines on the ground, is the inscribed set on which our lives are played. How well we play on this set, what progress we register towards creating a decent and proud community, is in our hands. The proof of our intentions will be in the streets and public places as we shape them in our progress. The virtue of the grid is precisely in being a conceptual formal order, non-hierarchical, neutral, until it is infused with specific content. The grid is free both of *malerisch* incident and of ideological posturing. It is repetitive, homogeneous, even redundant. And because it is so, it calls us both to respect it and to complete it. Our task as designers becomes one of celebrating its commonality while teasing it into calibrations it does not promise as a two-dimensional plan on the ground. The grid carries no inherent burden of its own. The grid is what you make it.

References

Braunfels, W. (1988). *Urban design in Western Europe: Regime and architecture, 900–1900* (trans: K. Northcott). Chicago: University of Chicago Press.

Buls, C. (1893). *Esthétique des villes*. Bruxelles: Imprimerie Bruylant-Christophe.

Burke, G. (1956). *The making of Dutch towns: A study in urban development from the tenth to the seventeenth centuries*. London: Cleaver/Hume Press.

Carter, H. (1990). Parallelism and disjunction: A study in the internal structure of Welsh towns. In T. Slater (Ed.), *The built form of Western cities: Essays for M.R.G. Conzen* (pp. 189–209). Leicester: Leicester University Press.

Collins, G., & Collins, C. (1986 [1965]). *Camillo Sitte: The birth of modern city planning*. Mineola: Dover Publications.

Conzen, M. (1990). Town-plan analysis in an American setting: Cadastral processes in Boston and Omaha, 1630–1930. In T. Slater (Ed.), *The built form of Western cities: Essays for M.R.G. Conzen* (pp. 142–170). Leicester: Leicester University Press.

Dahir, J. (1947). *The neighborhood unit plan*. New York: Russell Sage Foundation.

Dickens, C. (1850). *American notes*. London: Chapman and Hall.

Dilke, O. (1961). Maps in the treatises of Roman land surveyors. *Geographical Journal, 127*(4), 417–426.

Friedman, D. (1988). *Florentine new towns: Urban design in the late middle ages*. New York: MIT Press.

Grew, F. and Hoblet, B. (Eds.). (1985). Roman urban topography. CBA Research Report 59.

Groth, P. (1981). Streetgrids as frameworks for urban variety. *Harvard Architectural Review, 2*, 68–75.

Gutkind, E. (1971). *Urban development in Western Europe, Great Britain, and the Netherlands*. New York: Collier-Macmillan.

Hall, J. (1970). *Japan from prehistory to modern times*. New York: University of Michigan Center for Japanese Studies.

Hilbersheimer. (1955). *The nature of cities*. Chicago: Paul Theobald & Co.

Hurtt, S. (1983). The American continental grid: Form and meaning. *Threshold, 2*, 32–40.

Johnston, R. (1983). The ancient city of Suzhou. *Town Planning Review, 54*(2), 194–222.

Lilius, H. (1985). *The Finnish wooden town* (trans: R. Riska and E. Hawkins). Rungsted Kyst: Anders Nyborg.

McKenzie, R. (1933). *Metropolitan community*. New York: McGraw-Hill.

Métraux, G. (1978). *Greek land use and city-planning in the archaic period*. New York: Garland.

Puig i Cadafalch, J. (1936). Idees teòriques sobre urbanisme en el segle XIV: un fragment d'Eiximenis. In Homenatge a Antoni Rubio i Lluch. Barcelona.

Reps, J. (1969). *Town planning in frontier America*. Princeton: Princeton University Press.

Vance, J., Jr. (1977). *This scene of man*. New York: Harper & Row.

Walker, D. (1982). *The architecture and planning of Milton Keynes*. London: Architectural Press.

Wright, H. (1935). *Rehousing urban America*. New York: Columbia University Press.

Yeohmans, A. (Ed.). (1916). *City residential land development*. Chicago: University of Chicago Press.

Chapter 5
The Dark Side of the Grid Revisited: Power and Urban Design

Jill L. Grant

Abstract In contemporary discussions of preferred urban form, many planners and designers advocate a return to the grid. Proponents of the grid see it as legible, accessible, efficient, traditional, and, perhaps, even egalitarian. This chapter examines the grid in the context of traditions which have used it as a dominant form in city building. A brief historical review shows that the grid has emerged in some societies seeking to diffuse authority among citizens, but appears most commonly in the context of centralizing or globalizing power. The author illustrates that the extraordinary symbolism of the grid as a "rational" built form imposed on landscapes can convey a range of meanings, both positive and negative.

Keywords Grid design · Political authority · Power · Global history · New Urbanism

Introduction

When I began writing an earlier version of this chapter in 1999 (Grant 2001), the advocates of new urbanism—a planning and design movement that promoted a return to "traditional" town-building principles, including the grid street pattern— was rapidly gaining ground in North American planning (Grant 2006). Although many of the benefits the New Urbanists attributed to the grid—including efficient servicing, ease of access, and legibility—made sense, one of their claims struck me as highly problematic and even ethnocentric. In public presentations, and in some of the written materials associated with the movement (Krieger 1991; Duany and Plater-Zyberk 1992), spokespersons suggested or implied that the grid was by its

This chapter is a revised version of Grant, J. (2001). "The Dark Side of the Grid: Power and Urban Design." *Planning Perspectives*, 16(3): 219–241. Copyright © 2001 by Taylor & Francis Ltd. Reproduced with permission of Taylor & Francis Ltd.

J. L. Grant (✉)
Dalhousie University, Halifax, NS, Canada
e-mail: Jill.Grant@Dal.Ca

nature egalitarian. Having taught planning history for several years, I linked the grid with colonizing regimes such as the Romans and the Spanish. Engaging discussions with students in my classes motivated me to begin a systematic evaluation of the literature to understand the relationship between urban form and power. I was fortunate during the paper's review (at *Planning Perspectives*) to be pushed by reviewers and the editor, Anthony Sutcliffe, to delve deeply for patterns and to theorize from the results. That led me to a three-fold categorization of the way the grid was used under three kinds of political regimes: diffusing authority, centralizing authority, and globalizing authority.

Through ten millennia of urban development, the grid appears with considerable frequency, but it is arguably less common and more recent than are organic layouts, which feature winding lanes and dead-end streets. Moreover, the grid and other patterns of urban form that derive from geometric principles and surveying technology are more frequently associated with the concentration of military power and wealth than with egalitarian traditions. Settlement history reveals vibrant and successful cities of all shapes and sizes. The grid has appeared in societies with divergent systems of authority. It can be linked to tyranny and monarchy as well as to democracy. It appears in association with many economic adaptations. While we do find the grid associated with some societies that attempt to diffuse authority (by empowering citizens politically, economically, or socially), we find it more often in conjunction with societies that concentrate power and wealth by centralizing authority or even globalizing authority. People choose to use the grid layout for various reasons to serve multiple functions. The record offers no simple correlation between specific physical forms and social patterns or aspirations.

Scholars too rarely get the opportunity to return to key works written long ago. I have found it invigorating to have the chance to re-evaluate the evidence, reconsider my stance, and refine my thinking on this complex topic. A few years after my original paper on the grid and power came out I had some energizing discussions with Michael E. Smith and his colleagues at Arizona State that led me to alternative sources and further reading to clarify my thinking on some urban traditions I discussed. While my interest in this theme came from concerns about contemporary claims in urban planning, Smith (2007) addresses similar issues from the perspective of the archaeologist. His views offer important nuance and arguments that have influenced my thinking. The many revisions of my analysis expressed in this version of the paper owe a debt of gratitude to some of the challenges that recent research in archaeology present to overly simplified theoretical paradigms.

In 2001, I optimistically argued that the pre-historical record offered examples of societies using the grid in ways that diffused power. I am no longer as confident that the grid has been used widely in that way. Further reading led me to sources that changed my thinking about some traditions I thought had been diffusing authority. Of course, the meaning of the grid and its associations with specific power regimes do not last forever. A grid could be used to plan settlements in a society committed to power sharing, but then the form could continue in practice as a republic becomes a tyranny. Or vice versa. There is nothing implicit in the form that commits its use to any power arrangement. As history shows, however, regimes that concentrate

Table 5.1 Approaches to power

Diffusing authority	Centralizing authority	Globalizing authority
Promoting a communitarian or egalitarian philosophy	Promoting the interests of a relatively small elite for aggrandizement	Promoting control over territory for efficient concentration of capital and expansion of wealth
Creating a system of towns or cities to accommodate population	Creating a central nodal capital	Creating key regional capitals, with possible nodal centre
Community members consent to order	Military authority imposes or enforces order (control may be ideological)	Military and economic power impose order (control may be hidden, subtle)
Land linked to liberty, security, identity	Land controlled and used to support the needs of central authorities	Land as commodity and resource

power and wealth seem commonplace, and it is those that have systematically found the grid most useful for town planting.

Developing a Typology of Approaches to Power

Any attempt to create a framework for analyzing the ways in which societies approach power must recognize the diversity of experience that renders classification precarious. The record offers a continuum of approaches within which societies may transform themselves from one to another and back again, even over relatively brief periods of time. Accordingly, any schema which seeks to generate an "evolutionary" framework that postulates progression over time runs headlong into defiant history: while change is inevitable, "progress" is not. For purposes of this analysis, I argue that it is reasonable to present a typology of three basic approaches that characterize urban traditions deploying the grid in history. These categories represent significant differences in social and political structure and provide a useful differentiation for purposes of analysis, but the reader should be cautious to avoid concluding any evolutionary progression between them. Any of these strategies may appear at various times and places through the historical and archaeological record.

Some societies seek to diffuse power by enabling citizens to participate and enjoy the benefits of society widely. This approach to power I call "diffusing authority." Other societies seek to concentrate power for the benefit of a relatively small elite typically located in a capital or nodal city. This approach I call "centralizing authority." Still other societies may aim to expand the range of power geographically to benefit corporate entities or a sizable elite which may be located primarily in key regional capitals. This approach is "globalizing authority" (Table 5.1).

In each of these kinds of societies, religious authority and philosophy generally support the system of power. Cultural values develop to reinforce ways of behaving and to strengthen systems of authority (Lukes 1974; Gross 1980). All three approaches may yield evidence of charismatic leadership, hereditary leadership, or even electoral rule. Strong military authority commonly appears in association with centralizing and globalizing approaches, but less frequently with diffusing approaches where community members implicitly or explicitly consent to the established order.

Attitudes towards land vary markedly with these different approaches. Diffusing systems typically link land to identity and economic productivity. Land may be held communally, or may be distributed according to accepted principles related to issues of equity or merit. Centralizing and globalizing systems see land as something to control for strategic purposes and from which to wrest value. Centralizing systems tightly control land to serve the needs and power of central authorities. In globalizing systems, land provides the resources that fuel economic growth and expansion.

Before proceeding to apply this typology to civilizations in the historical record, I should first address the use of the term "egalitarian" which has already appeared in the discussion, though not as a label in the framework for analysis. While some may argue that what I have called a "diffusing" approach could be rendered as "egalitarian," I specifically avoid the term in talking about power or authority. The word "egalitarian" asserts a belief in equality, but its meaning can be quite varied. In the context of the relationship (if any) between social systems and built form, we could, for example, use the term to refer to a wide range of phenomena. By "egalitarian" do we mean equal benefits derived from society (including access to food, shelter, health care, and quality of life)? Do we refer to equal participation in society (in which case we must deal with issues of gender, class, age, race, bondage, and personal motivation)? Do we signify equal opportunity (to education, employment, or land)? In terms of "egalitarian" built form we could ask, do we mean platting of land into blocks of equal size, or the generation of individual building or farm lots of equal size, or the ability to gain ready access to all spaces for ease of control? Lacking precision, the word "egalitarian" often becomes a positively charged term attached to the political system or built form of one's affection. Its use in association with discussions of the grid and the kinds of authority systems that may use the grid may thus become problematic.

Applying the Framework to the Historical Record

With the framework in hand, I examined the historical record to find societies that used the grid extensively. I analyzed and categorized societies to determine their approach to authority and to identify similarities and differences among them. The examples discussed here, which because of space limitations are not comprehensive, are summarized in Table 5.2 and described in the following sections.

Table 5.2 Possible examples of approaches to the grid

Diffusing authority	Centralizing authority	Globalizing authority
Harappan (Indus Valley)	Ancient Egypt	Greek, 8th to 6th centuries BCE
Greek, 5th century BCE	Babylon, 7th century BCE	Wari and Inca
Teotihuacan	Alexandria	Japan, castle towns
United States	China	European colonies
Utopian communes	Japan, early capitals	National and corporate expansion, 19th century CE
	Tenotchtitlan	

The Grid in Societies of Globalizing Authority

When ruling interests seek to expand into ever-larger territories, and as economic interests organize more effectively to exploit the resources of empire, societies may move towards globalizing authority. With the growth of empire, controlling distant territories by establishing urban centers throughout the land becomes a useful strategy. The grid allows rapid reproduction of an ideal form and a reasonably fair means of distributing land to new residents. As Mumford (1961) and Galantay (1975) note, the grid was a distinctive feature of colonial towns throughout history. Some well-known examples of states using the grid in this way appear below.

Globalizing societies establish colonial settlements in new territories to secure control over land and resources. In many of the examples presented here, military or governmental authorities established a standard pattern and applied it vigorously to occupied territory. Many of these planned settlements had closed grids defined by defensive walls, at least until military technology rendered such walls useless.[1] Wealth in these empires continued to be funnelled to pivotal cities while also allowing growing concentration of influence in commercial sectors and in regional centers. Although inequality grew great in such societies, the built form often underplayed any hierarchy. As Castagnoli (1971) notes, equality of size and form among residential blocks appeared first in Greek cities during a period of tyrannical government.

---

[1] Marcuse (1987) argues that in the American context the pre-capitalist grid was closed, while in capitalist economies it is open. The historical record elsewhere does not confirm this hypothesis. Closed grids occur in contemporary gated communities within capitalist societies, while pre-capitalist communities like Teotihuacan featured open grids. More relevant factors to consider in whether the grid is open or closed are the likelihood and technology of security, warfare and taxation, and the rate of population growth.

Greeks, Eighth to Sixth Century BCE

The earliest period of classical Greek history involved considerable colonial expansion. The largest old cities, such as Athens and Sparta, did not follow a grid layout but were enhanced with fine buildings, sculptures, and palaces for rulers. As they moved into new territories, the Greeks forced out indigenous occupants and established new towns for their own people. Colonial cities in the west and north imposed the grid even on quite rough terrain, as the rationality of mathematics and science triumphed over topography (Castagnoli 1971; Owens 1991). Wide avenues and narrow streets created long insulae in the early cities, although regular square blocks appeared later. These blocks were not equally divided within; land was distributed according to rank and means. The new cities added walls as needed and included open spaces for temples, business and social activity. Many scholars argue that the ancient Greeks were the first to use town planning as a key tool for establishing and controlling empires in new regions (Ward-Perkins 1974; Morris 1994; Kostof 1995).

Romans

From the first century BCE to the fourth century CE, the Romans built and expanded cities through much of Europe, West Asia, and Africa, according to a rigid codex (Fig. 5.1). Based on the model of the military camp and reflecting its discipline, the Roman colonial town shows a square or rectangular grid derived from two central axes often oriented to the cardinal directions (Castagnoli 1971, Owens, 1991). Central public spaces, such as the forum, and public amenities, such as baths and amphitheatres, attempted to bring a taste of Roman culture to the provinces. Subjugated peoples in the colonies were often moved into the towns, both for control and for assimilation. Walls surrounded the towns where defense was required. While wealth and resources were funnelled to Rome and regional capitals, the colonial towns helped to disseminate Roman culture and integrate distant lands into the empire. The grid plan, rigorously executed from Africa to Britain, made the global authority of Rome physically manifest (Rykwert, 1988; Stambaugh 1988; Owens 1991).

Wari and Inca

In my original paper, I discussed only the Inca empire here. Further reading, however, confirms that in many ways—including settlement planning—the Inca drew on earlier traditions and building sites established by the Wari empire (sixth to eleventh century CE) before them (McEwan 2009; Schreiber 2009). Through conquered districts, the Wari established settlements such as Pikillacta based on a rigid grid layout; in subsequent centuries, the Inca reoccupied some Wari sites (McEwan 2009). Beginning in the twelfth century, and lasting until the Spanish arrived in the early sixteenth, the Inca led a theocratic state that united much of western and

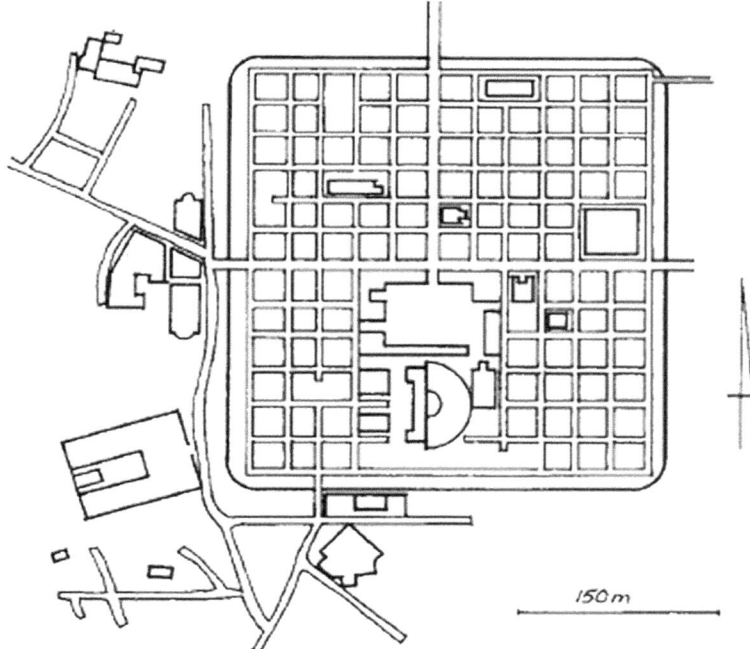

Fig. 5.1 Roman society masked its inherent hierarchy as its army planted "egalitarian" grids through the empire (as in this example of Timgad in Africa)

north-western South America. The capital city of Cuzco followed a rough grid with a magnificent central palace and square. Gridded regional cities appeared throughout the empire to consolidate control (Hardoy 1968). The Inca ruler travelled along the highways linking the cities to reinforce the global reach of the realm. To facilitate control within an area that spanned thousands of kilometers, the Inca moved conquered peoples to these planned settlements through the empire (Von Hagen 1961).

Japan

With the Tokugawa military reunification of Japan in the late sixteenth century CE, the military ruler (*shogun*) commissioned regional lords (*daimyo*) to build castle towns (Fig. 5.2) to ensure the control of territory (Hall 1955). Castle towns were conceptually modelled after the imperial capital, Kyoto, laid out in the tenth century in a centralizing model based on Chinese capital plans (see below). The castle, home to the *daimyo*, generally lay to the north of the town, in a strategic location. Fortifications and moats protected it from attack. Around it (especially to the east or south) stood the warrior samurai quarters, on generous lots within another wall or

Fig. 5.2 As the shogunate sought to consolidate its hold over a reunited Japan, it planned castle towns (like this one in Nagoya) where the size and position of blocks reflected the inhabitants' positions in society

moat. Outside that lay districts for lower ranked samurai and then to the south the lesser quarters for merchants and artisans, on an open grid of narrow lanes and streets. Although Kyoto remained the nominal capital, considerable wealth funnelled to the administrative center at Edo (Tokyo) and the commercial hub at Osaka (Karan 1997; Shelton 1999; Sorenson 2004).

European Colonies

The era of European exploration and discovery led to the development of colonies on several continents during the sixteenth to nineteenth centuries and to the expansion of new nations in the nineteenth and twentieth centuries. Many of those colonies and new nations relied on the grid for rapid development of settlements. I have space here to discuss only a few examples from North America and Australia. Eager to control territory, these nations used land as a way of attracting settlers to areas being taken from indigenous inhabitants. With military forces and commercial corporations establishing a foothold in new regions, the grid was an expeditious mechanism for preparing land for settlement. The Spanish under Philip II in 1573 developed an explicit code, the Laws of the Indies, to guide planners in setting out wide streets, public squares, and sites for churches and town buildings (Stanislawski 1947; Reps 1965). Other European nations took similar notions and carried them around the world to expand their spheres of influence (Galantay 1975).

At Louisbourg in eastern Canada, the French built a town for a population of 4000 in a square grid, heavily fortified. The British preferred rectangular grids aligned with a baseline along the harbor: they included a central parade square around which they built public buildings and churches (Wolfe 1994). Early settlements had palisades but, as hostilities with the French ended, the open grid came to dominate.[2] As settlers pressed westward, Dominion authorities switched to a square grid, applying it across the prairies as an efficient means of surveying and equitable way of distributing land (Wolfe 1994; Hodge and Gordon 2014).

In the nineteenth century, the British sought to attract settlers to Australia. Under the direction of Colonel William Light, the state of South Australia planned a system of settlements (Hutchings and Bunker 1986). The largest, Adelaide, featured interlocking and facing street grids reminiscent of the pattern of early Philadelphia (with five squares and rectangular blocks). All the towns had planned parks, a commercial core, and residential districts surrounded by a green belt. Settlers received farm lots outside the towns (Hutchings and Bunker 1986).

The grid provided a ready mechanism for rapid expansion and control of occupied territory not only in colonies around the world but also for new nations like the United States. Through the nineteenth century, as the U.S. expanded westward, the grid lost its earlier associations (as a land distribution mechanism associated with liberty and suffrage for able-bodied men—see below) and instead became a means for turning land into a commodity for speculation (Reps 1965; Marcuse 1987; Ward 1998). Aligned with the cardinal directions, the survey grid was rigorously applied to property boundaries, regardless of terrain. Western cities like Chicago grew rapidly along streets marching vigorously to the cardinal directions in an open grid (Cronon 1991). A form that may have begun alongside an egalitarian or communitarian ideology had by the nineteenth century become a technique for the disposition of a valued commodity to settlers who would facilitate state control of a landscape wrested from its indigenous inhabitants (Reps 1965; Hurtt 1983).

Civilizations pursuing a globalizing approach to authority are expansionist in their intentions, at least in key stages of development. Most rely on military might and economic prowess for their dominance. Some, such as the Inca, the Japanese, and the Romans, employed religious precepts suggesting divine origins for their rulers as ideological justification for the hierarchy they imposed on people and landscapes. The societies described here all used the grid as a template for rapid dissemination of an idea of the city, encapsulating and promulgating the ideology of

---

[2] In some cities, the street system reverted to an organic pattern outside the early core, while in other cases surveyors laid out new grid sections to accommodate growth.

the regime. All developed a system of settlements designed to facilitate the exploitation of the resources of empire for the interests of an elite located in important settlements throughout the system. Similarly, in the nineteenth century some countries offered land and other incentives to land development or railway corporations to develop vital national infrastructure and to plant service towns along transportation networks. The resulting towns—such as 33 communities built by the Illinois Central railway in the 1880s (Galantay 1975)—often faithfully reproduced grid layouts across North America and Australia (Reps 1965; Hutchings and Bunker 1986).

The Grid in Societies of Centralizing Authority

The creation of many of the greatest cities and monuments in human history appears linked to societies engaged in centralizing authority. Some societies devoted enormous wealth to the enhancement of nodal capital cities for the glory of the ruler and a small elite. In these traditions, rulers controlled the empire by and from the capital city, with the resources of the land channelled into the center. Formal central spaces at the core of the city usually included imperial palaces or religious precincts off-limits to the masses. The cities were often closed grids, walled or isolated (as on an island) to control access. Strong military control and religious ideology provided key underpinnings to maintaining authority.

Egypt

During the Middle and New Kingdoms in ancient Egypt (around 2060–1070 BCE), the great empire of the Nile River Valley built several settlements using grid plans. Each king or pharaoh chose a new location for his funerary monument and built a town there for his administrators and builders (Kostof 1995). Egyptian towns and cities were often ephemeral, abandoned once their revered creators passed away. The town at Kahun (Fig. 5.3) from the nineteenth century BCE featured mass-produced worker housing in a segregated grid layout, as did the worker's compound at the new capital built at Tel el Amarna in the fourteenth century BCE (Fairman 1949; Kemp 1977; Morris 1994). Such hierarchical, closed grids were bounded by walls, perhaps to facilitate surveillance and control (Kostof 1995).

Babylon

Early civilizations in Mesopotamia relied on winding street patterns, but the grid gradually gained in importance, particularly in Babylon. In 604 BCE, Nebuchadnezzar established a new kingdom headquartered in a rebuilt Babylon. With a high tower and palace and laid out in a formal grid, the city stood at the height of urbanity in its time and drew on the resources of a vast region (Chiera 1938). Hanging gardens and

Fig. 5.3 The closed grid for Kahun, Egypt, illustrates hierarchy and segregation

a great wall mounted with magnificent gates made the city famous. Nebuchadnezzar centralized elite populations and wealth in Babylon, rather than exporting his urban model to other parts of regions conquered. As his empire expanded, the king brought captured peoples from across the region to the city for assimilation. Described in the Biblical chronicles of the captive Judaeans, Babylon became a cultural and religious metaphor for luxury, iniquity, and oppression (Sagg 1962; Macqueen 1965; Girouard 1985).

Alexandria

The classical Greek era came to an end with the successes of Philip of Macedon and his son, Alexander, in the fourth century BCE. Conquering much of the Mediterranean and Asia Minor, Alexander planted as many as 70 cities to spread Hellenistic civilization and facilitate trade: whether he deployed the grid prior to the building of Alexandria in Egypt in 332 BCE is unclear (Hammond 1998).[3] Planned by Deinocrates, Alexandria featured a grand central axial road more than 30 meters wide and a grid of streets linking harbors on two sides of an isthmus. Alexandria had great buildings, parks, temples and a palace intended to reap the benefits of the

---

[3] If evidence exists that suggests other cities planted by Alexander used the grid, then I would reclassify Alexandrian planning to the globalizing category.

Fig. 5.4 In cities like Changa'an the hiercharical grid of the built form reflects structural inequalities within the civilization

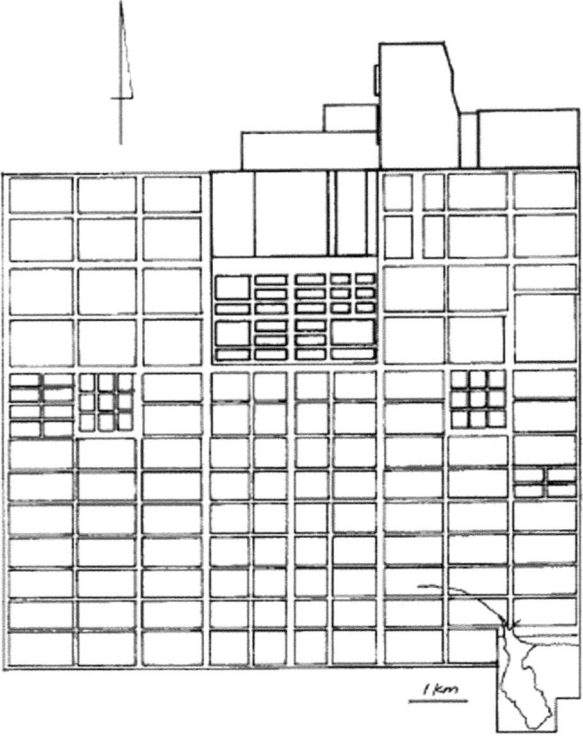

growing empire. However, Alexander's early death and a fight for succession meant that Alexandria did not become the nodal city of the vast empire he sought to create. Instead, under the Ptolemies, the Alexandrian grid served a centralizing function as plan for the capital of a more modest Egyptian kingdom (Benevolo 1980; Morris 1994).

China

From the first to the tenth century CE, a succession of Chinese dynasties established capital cities from which they ruled their empires (Wu 1986). The Han and Wei Dynasties ruled from Luoyang, capital from the first to the sixth centuries (Wu 1986). Its successor, Chang'an (seventh to tenth centuries), also followed a grid linked to the cardinal directions with a clear hierarchy of space (Fig. 5.4). In the north were the walled palace and administrative quarters. A wide avenue led north from the main gate in the earthen city wall. A million residents lived in cramped quarters in walled districts within Chang'an; as many as a million more may have lived outside the walls in the city's suburbs (Wright 1967). The only real public spaces were the markets and roads. At the end of the Silk Road, the Chinese capital was the business heart of a growing empire (Wright 1967; Morris 1994). While provincial capitals often emulated the model of the heavenly city, the design was infrequently adopted for the design of less important towns.

Japan

Inspired by the Chinese, Japan's imperial rulers established similar capitals to control the landscape from the eighth century CE onward. Nara (in the eighth century) and Kyoto (from the ninth century) also featured palaces and administrative districts to the north and a broad central avenue leading from the southern main gate (Nara National Cultural Properties n.d.). Unlike the Chinese capitals, however, the Japanese cities did not fill out according to plan and parts of the grid were abandoned as the economic center of the cities moved eastward (Hall 1970). With no real threat of attack in the early decades of empire, the rulers of Japan did not complete the earthen walls, allowing the grid to open and extend as required. As in the Chinese cities, markets, roads, and bridges provided the essential public spaces for the population and a religious ideology which held the emperor as divine provided the justification for spatial and economic hierarchy (Hall 1970; Shelton 1999). In the period when Japan adopted centralizing grid plans for its capital city, rulers in Korea and other parts of East Asia were similarly applying hierarchical grids for their capitals (Galantay 1975).

Tenotchtitlan

From their base in what is now Mexico City, the Aztecs ruled a vast military empire that controlled much of Central America during the fourteenth to sixteenth centuries CE. Tenotchtitlan exemplified and monopolized the wealth of the empire, with grand temple and palace at the center of an axial grid layout. Located on islands in a shallow lake, the capital amazed the conquering Spanish with its size and sophistication. Drawing on examples from the ruins in the Valley of Mexico, the Aztecs imagined their capital to emulate the grid, monuments, and great squares of earlier civilizations (Bernal 1967). As Smith (2008) notes, though, the Aztec did not use orthogonal planning for their regional capitals. Moreover, the grid in Tenotchtitlan resulted not from the planning of streets but as the legacy of agricultural practices: rectangular *chinampas* (raised farm beds) eventually became residential building platforms that produced a grid (Smith 2007, 2008). The grid never served a globalizing purpose for the Aztecs, but certainly played a centralizing function.

The capital cities of centralizing societies show several features in common. The wealth of a vast region funnels into the nodal capital city to reinforce and concretize the authority and luxury of those in power. In many cases, these societies feature strong military forces and a religious ideology which deifies the hereditary leadership (royalty). The building and rebuilding of these cities symbolizes the aggrandizement of those in power. Within the hierarchical grid of the city are privileged areas for rulers, administrators, and religious authorities. These are typically off-limits to the masses and may be walled to exclude them. Thus, the order of society is reified through the spatial structure of the nodal city. While other urban centers may form or be created, they are clearly secondary to the capital and need not emulate its form.

The Grid in Societies of Diffusing Authority

The gross disparities of urban wealth and privilege that appear in centralizing and globalizing systems are missing from societies that diffuse authority. Societies where rulers seek to diffuse authority and share power are uncommon in the historical record of cities. History suggests that cities are more typically associated with the accumulation and concentration of wealth and power in the hands of elites. Nonetheless, we do find potential examples of societies that have attempted to distribute or downplay power while developing an urban system using the grid. The examples that follow are those I discussed in the original paper. At that time, I believed that they showed a pattern of encouraging citizenship and political participation of a substantial proportion of members of the communities. I acknowledged then that we needed to remember that many people in these societies were precluded from active participation because of gender, age, race, or caste. As new data have emerged and as I have read further about some of these systems, my original optimism that they represented examples of the benign use of the grid have sometimes been shaken, as noted below.

The built form of towns and cities associated with diffusing authority often show central spaces for public use. These may include commons, squares, religious areas, recreational facilities, granaries, or workshops. Amenities such as water supplies and sewerage may take advantage of the planned streets of the grid for service delivery. The religious and political ideologies of these societies tend to diminish or under-play hierarchy and may promulgate egalitarian ideals. In some cases, land may be held communally or segmented into portions of roughly equal size for building and farming.

Harappan Cities

The earliest use of the grid in human history occurs in a civilization which some sources suggest shows evidence of diffusing authority and middle-class prosperity (Wheeler 1966; Meadow 1991). From about 2500 to 1900 BCE, a system of cities prospered in the Indus Valley of Southwest Asia. Home to approximately 40,000 people each, cities such as Mohenjo-Daro and Harappa enjoyed a wide range of amenities: water supply, sewer drains, wells, granaries, and workshops. Most homes had bathing platforms and latrines, providing a high standard of living (Kenoyer 1998). While some sources deny the existence of hierarchy because they find no sculptural or artistic evidence of powerful rulers or elaborate religious organizations (Wheeler 1966), other scholars (Allchin and Allchin 1982; Possehl 1990, 1997) note variations in dwelling sizes and artifacts, and argue that some classes of workers would have spent their days laboring to empty cess pits and free sewer drains of clogs. Burials show different patterns of grave goods (suggesting status hierarchies) and high levels of violence experienced by those in lower status burials (Robbins Schug et al. 2012; Robbins Schug et al. 2013). Authority may have been much less diffused than Meadow (1991) and Wheeler (1966) suggested. Since major processional avenues divide the cities, and residential areas have a network of lanes running off the avenue, some sources describe Indus Valley sites as having grid layouts (Wheeler 1966): however, Jansen doubts even the premise of a formal grid-iron plan, noting that over hundreds of years of re-building the orientation of structures in Mohenjo-Daro shifted from roughly north to north-northeast and the jumble of building layers complicates exposure of the original pattern (Jansen 1989, 1993).

Greek Cities, Fifth Century BCE

After several centuries of colonial expansion, some ancient Greek city states, like Athens, developed a democratic ideology that encouraged male citizens to participate in political decision-making. Despite the egalitarian ideology of some city-states in the period, the realities of colonization, slavery, and gender discrimination limited full participation to less than 10% of the population. Some cities built or rebuilt during this period, like Miletos (Fig. 5.5), Thourioi, Rhodes, and Olynthos, not only show large central public spaces and facilities like temples, baths, and schools, but reveal a regular grid of residential areas of similar size and shape (Owens 1991; Morris 1994). Communities were well-defined but of limited size. Women, children, and slaves lived in modest housing while male citizens enjoyed the beautiful public buildings and spaces (Owens 1991). The Greeks built gridded cities as a means of colonizing newly acquired territory, forcing out indigenous inhabitants and imposing their own rational urban forms on the landscape. Although the Greeks empowered an element of their own population, they did so at the expense of many more. While the built form of a settlement like Miletos may appear "egalitarian" in its uniform street grid, it required considerable central control to implement and maintain (Ward-Perkins 1974).

Teotihuacan

From the first through the seventh centuries CE, a large city dominated the Valley of Mexico. The ruins of Teotihuacan reveal a monumental open grid layout with 2000 planned apartment compounds to house as many as 100,000 residents (Hardoy 1968; Cowgill 1997, 2015). A grand processional avenue bisects the city from north to south, flanked by pyramids and temples. In the original paper, I drew heavily on Ester Pasztory's (1997) book on Teotihuacan. She argues that Teotihuacan was

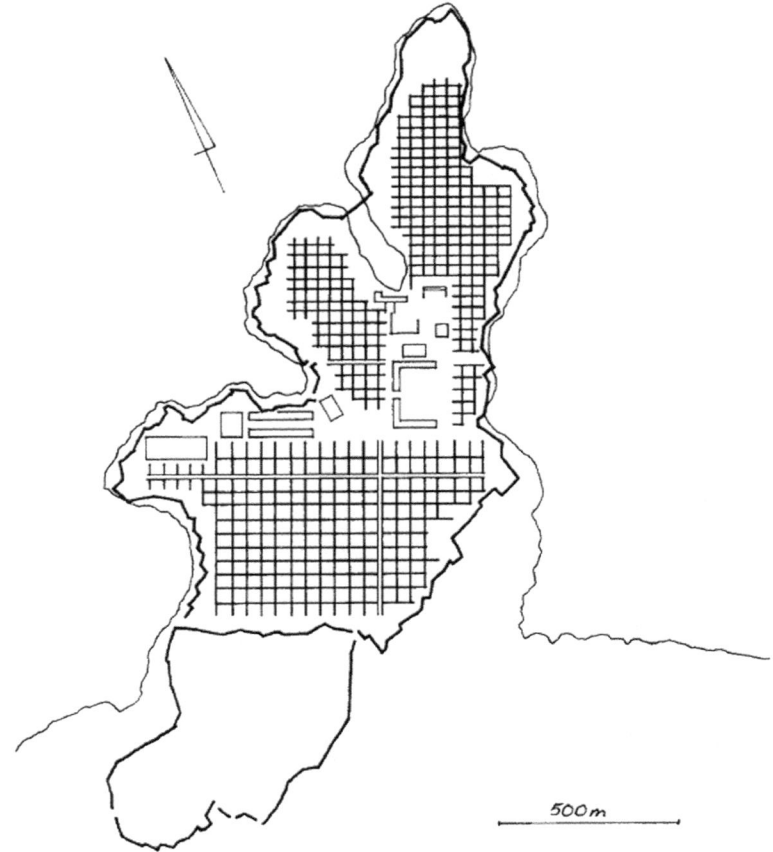

Fig. 5.5 The ancient Greek city of Miletos (in modern Turkey) featured a comprehensive grid of equal-sized blocks

organized as a communal society with administrators making decisions on behalf of the people: hence, I included the city in the category of using the grid while diffusing authority. Other scholars, however, debate Pasztory's analysis. Cowgill (1997) argues that Teotihuacan was not peaceful, and local elites served their own interests in building the city. Elite quarters are larger than most and have high quality murals decorating the walls (Cowgill 2015). Although the ruins of Teotihuacan do not illustrate the exploits of specific rulers, we cannot take that absence as evidence that elites did not control the city. Perhaps their art forms specifically avoided such references. Spence et al. (2004) and White et al. (2002) describe the sacrifice of more than 200 people (many of them local in origin) at the Feathered Serpent Pyramid in the city: an extreme exercise of power and social control that may increase skepticism about the extent of authority diffused in the city.

Early America

During the seventeenth and eighteenth centuries, the American colonies and nation relied increasingly on the grid to pattern their towns (Goodman and Freund 1968). As Hurtt (1983, 32) notes, the Continental Congress of 1785 entrenched the grid as a "reassuring symbol of settlement, safety and civilization." Early settlers belonging to dissenting religious groups committed to equality and liberty used the distribution of land as a way of conferring suffrage on male members of the community; each white male settler received enough land to gain rights. The town, Hurtt (1983) says, codified the ideal social order. The nine-square plan included a central square or common to provide space for meeting hall, church, and green, with home lots on the surrounding streets of the open grid (Rae 2005). Early cities like Philadelphia (1681) and Savannah (1733), with their strong grid interrupted with open squares (Fig. 5.6), became models for further urban development (Bacon 1967; Reps 1965; Benevolo 1980). By using equal-sized sections for surveying the nation, the continental grid reinforced the links between property and liberty that fuelled the revolution. While British and later other European settlers benefited from development through the grid, indigenous communities found themselves displaced from the land and persons of color enjoyed few rights or amenities.

Utopian Communes

In the nineteenth century, philanthropists and religious organizations established model communities and Utopian communes to give physical form and growing space to social objectives (Creese 1966; Benevolo 1967). Some of these settlements, like New Harmony, Indiana, employed a simple and closed grid with common spaces around a central square or green (Creese 1966). Common ownership of the land and shared facilities reflected the socialist and communitarian ideals of many of the movements behind the new communities. Most of these settlements were quite small and lasted only a few years or decades.

Urban traditions using the grid in a way that may diffuse authority share the notion that urban space should be designed to meet the needs and improve the lives of residents. They have used the grid as a mechanism for standardizing the pattern and distribution of space with such social objectives in mind. Hierarchy that may appear in the grid in these settlements favors public spaces intended for common use, which are often centrally located or made easily accessible. Leaders or administrators selected by members of the community governed some of these settlements, although we have no way of knowing how leaders arose in the Indus Valley or Teotihuacan.

Despite the democratic or communitarian ideology, which may have characterized some of the traditions discussed here, not everyone in these communities shared the benefits of urban life equally. Many of the societies—even the nominally democratic ones—with grids that may diffuse authority show evidence of bondage or caste systems which relegated many to a life of servitude. Women did not share

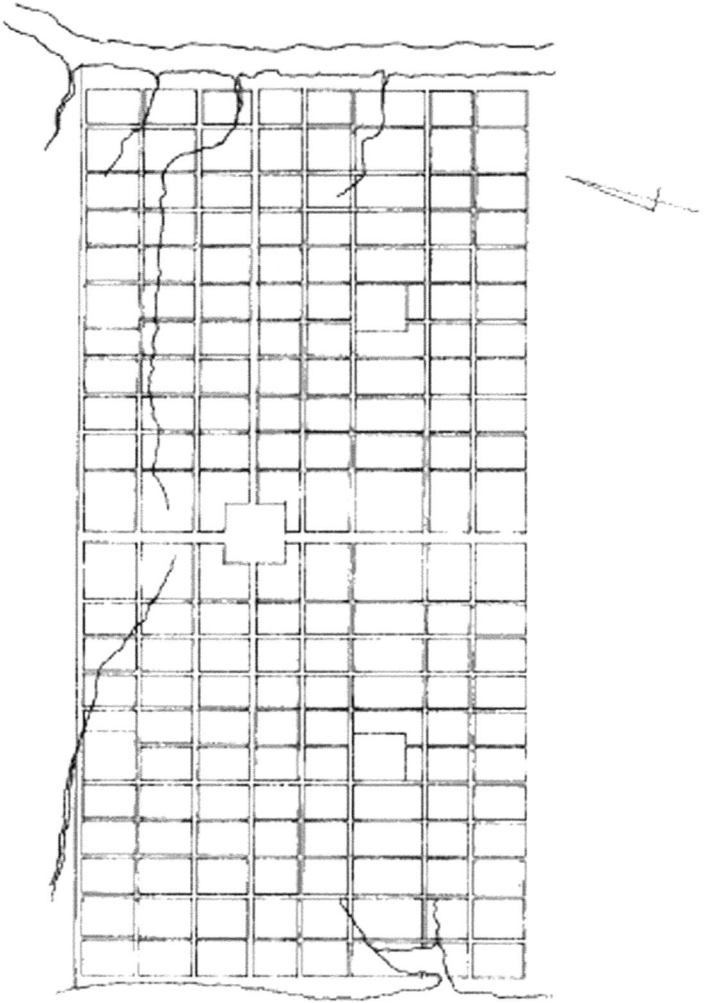

Fig. 5.6 Philadelphia, with its axial avenues and straight-forward grid, became something of a model for American urban form

equally in decision-making. Some residents were enslaved. Indigenous inhabitants of landscapes were often forced from the land, assimilated or enslaved by newcomers. Although a society that sees an element of power-sharing as its guiding philosophy may be drawn to an egalitarian grid as a formal spatial representation of its ideology, a grid of equal proportions and common access does not necessarily imply an egalitarian society. With access to additional research and analysis, I can no longer conclude that these examples constitute persuasive evidence that the grid is often used to diffuse authority. We more commonly find urban societies that central-ize or even globalize authority employing the grid to develop new communities.

Contrasting Patterns

Hurtt (1983, 37) suggests that the grid represses hierarchy: "The street, in its grid form, is anathema to closure, dominance and hierarchy and is the antagonist to locus and place." But appearances can be deceiving. Form and function are not inextrica-bly linked. Grids that differ in residential block size and access to desirable ameni-ties appear hierarchal. Urban grids with common proportions look egalitarian, but consistent block sizes or patterns do not necessarily signal regimes that are diffusing authority. As was the case for the Romans, a globalizing authority eager to accumu-late wealth and monopolize power can deploy grids that some may call egalitarian in form. Other globalizing regimes—as in Tokugawa Japan—prefer hierarchical grids and do not hesitate to enclose sections of the city to control access. Centralizing authority regimes frequently use hierarchical urban grids with blocks of different sizes and other elements of urban form to reinforce symbolic power and facilitate systems of exclusion.

What factors make a grid appear "egalitarian" or "hierarchical"? The street pat-tern is obviously pivotal. Avenues leading to key spaces and streets of varying dimensions signify order and, in some cases, hierarchy. Street layout may create blocks of equal or of varying size. Blocks of differing size are often linked to pat-terns of wealth as shown in the archaeological record: that is, the larger blocks are typically the domains of the more affluent (although they could have different func-tions, such as commercial or industrial uses). We cannot reasonably conclude, how-ever, that equal-sized blocks reflected equitable living standards throughout the city. In many of the cities described, the affluent dominated some neighbourhoods, enjoying much larger lots and better-appointed homes than did ordinary residents, even in "egalitarian grids." Block pattern may not reflect social conditions and lev-els of hierarchy and inequality within society, especially where social classes are not spatially segregated. Where democracy and egalitarian principles prevail, land may be distributed widely. In some settlements, all households may receive equal-sized parcels of land, or parcels sized to the number of members of the household. Over time, however, with generational and economic change, patterns change quickly and even what began as an egalitarian grid may well become spatially and socially segregated.

The Contemporary Grid

By the time that the modern town planning movement developed in the early twentieth century, the urban grid that dominated colonial and North American urban design had fallen out of favor, criticized as monotonous, rigid, old-fashioned, and unattractive (Bacon 1967; Benevolo 1967; Creese 1966). Winding, organic street patterns became popular and came to characterize broad areas of urban development for much of the twentieth century (Marshall 2005). By the late twentieth century, though, the grid (or modified versions of it) began a comeback. Inspired by the ideas of Jane Jacobs (1961), Peter Calthorpe (1993), and the team of Andres Duany and Elizabeth Plater-Zyberk (1992, 1996), many planners began to describe the grid of the old towns and cities as preferable to suburban sprawl. The search for community, vitality, and sustainability in the urban and suburban environment led many to argue that such attributes were readily associated with the grid. Developers seeking an edge in competitive suburban markets began experimenting with modified grids in projects like Seaside, FL, Celebration, FL, and McKenzie Towne (Calgary, AB). New Urbanism was born, not with the monolithic grids of earlier planned traditions, but using relatively small-scale plats with public squares, commons, and greens that simultaneously convey an impression of quality and character (Fig. 5.7).

New Urbanists argue that settlements need a mix of housing types to provide homes for all sectors of society; they seek a mix of uses, so that people can live without cars, by walking or taking transit to work or shop; they want to enhance sociability and participation in society. However, the reality of the New Urbanist projects built to date belies any rhetoric of diffusing authority. These projects are essentially upscale, suburban enclaves providing bedroom communities for the affluent (McCann 1995; Grant 2006). Even in a community like Celebration, FL, where the "modified grid" provides lots of similar size throughout town, significant differences in wealth obtain and are reflected in housing and other consumer goods; there are few places for the working poor to rent (Ross 1999). Rather than diffusing authority, such developments reinforce economic hierarchy. They are the creatures of a globalizing neoliberal culture that mutes uncomfortable truths through attractive design codes (Horne 1986; Brenner and Theodore 2002).

Those who advocate the grid today—and there are many—suggest that it offers the best form to ensure connectivity, walkability, efficient servicing, legibility, and ease of navigation. Movements such as smart growth and complete streets share allegiance to the grid.[4] Urban planners have overwhelmingly converted to encouraging grid layouts, and some North American plans effectively require grids. It is rare now—in an era where we worry about divided or dual cities of rich and poor (Marcuse 1989)—to hear planners suggest that grids are egalitarian, though they are quick to say the urban form promises more equitable access. The grid has become

---

[4] For instance, explore these web sites: http://www.newurbanism.org/newurbanism/principles.html
http://completestreetsforcanada.ca/element-5-encourages-connectivity
    https://www.epa.gov/smartgrowth/smart-location-mapping

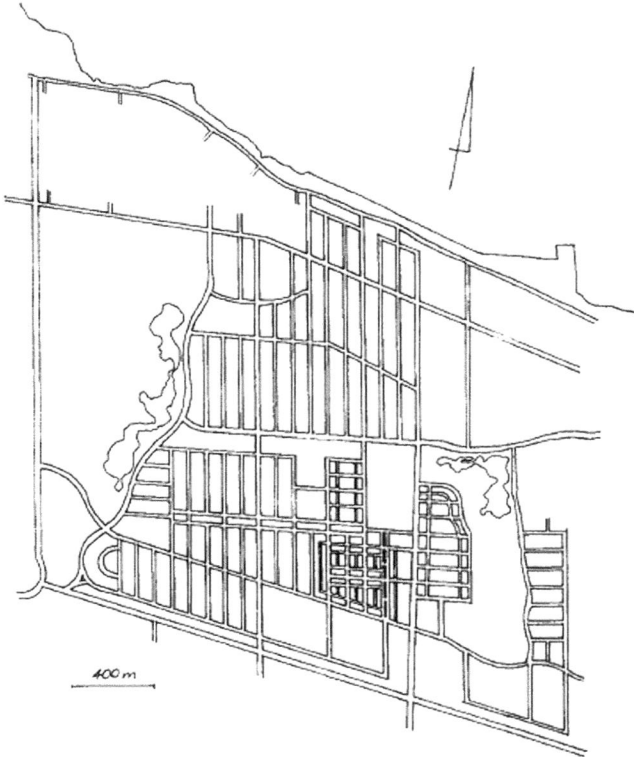

Fig 5.7 With the rise of New Urbanism, some suburbs, like this one in East Riverside, Windsor (Canada), show growth along grid layouts

embedded within a system of real estate financing and marketing that employs it to quickly commodify land. As was the case for the Greeks, the Romans, and colonizing Europeans, the grid has become fashionable and can be filled with the values important to those who deploy it. When the openness of the grid presents a problem, however, in that it may facilitate access for unwanted parties or may affect perceived property values, authorities may permit the closure or privatization of streets, or the erection of barricades (Grant and Curran 2007; Tedong et al. 2014). That many planned projects are also gated for security reasons exposes the egalitarian myths of public culture for what they can be: a mask for denying difference and globalizing power (Horne 1986; Low 2003).

Conclusion

This brief review of the grid in history finds no simple correlation between physical form and social objectives. The grid appears in many kinds of society serving divergent purposes. Hierarchical grids typically reflect and reinforce stratified social orders, but the meaning conveyed by non-hierarchical grids can differ widely. In every instance, however, the grid clearly signifies that planners were at work. It denies spontaneity and indigenous urban or landscape traditions. It imposes a rational conceptual order that transcends time, and proclaims the control and power of central authorities to shape space.

As Marcuse (1987, 307) says, "the grid is neither always as bad a plan as it has been painted in the recent planning literature, nor as 'good' a plan as its international and long-lasting adoption would suggest." The grid's usefulness as a ready template for urbanization ensures its attractiveness for colonial and expansionary societies. The form is not, however, without its warts. In some societies, the grid may have been associated with attempts to enfranchise some members of society, while in other societies the grid provided mass-produced accommodations for a life of servitude. The historical record illustrates that the grid has been associated with centralizing or globalizing societies for most of urban history. Large-scale societies promoting egalitarian philosophies prove rare; indeed, hierarchy seems intrinsically linked to urbanism, even in societies that may initially seek to diffuse authority. Thus, the grid has a dark side in as much as it has served so frequently as a tool and symbol of dominance and repression (Yiftachel 1998).

Planners' preferences for the grid plan reminds me of a saying: "if the only tool I have is a hammer, everything looks like a nail." The grid is the quintessential mark that a planner was at work. But if, as planners, we intend to argue that the grid is the best solution to contemporary dilemmas, then we have a responsibility to understand its history as we assess its potential. The grid is not inherently evil, but its strong historical association with colonization, centralization, and globalization gives pause for thought. What messages do designers convey by promoting the grid? While planners may justly critique the winding patterns of twentieth-century suburbia as confusing and monotonous, we must also recognize that such landscapes created the contexts within which millions of people generated meaningful social environments and achieved a standard of living to which others aspire. Is it these urban forms and landscape patterns which generated the problems we now seek to solve, such as lack of affordable housing, loss of farmland, over-use of the automobile, search for community? Or are we continuing to look for simplistic physical solutions to social and economic problems that derive from the structure of our society? Whether the grid is the appropriate solution to the problems of contemporary urbanization remains debatable. In the discussion of suitable planning approaches, planners should recognize the varied history of the forms we promote. We have a responsibility to be skeptical of simplistic solutions to complex problems.

Acknowledgements   This chapter was originally published as: Grant, J. (2001). "The Dark Side of the Grid: Power and Urban Design." *Planning Perspectives*, 16(3): 219-241. I owe a debt of gratitude to Anthony Sutcliffe, who was editor of the journal when I submitted the paper. Tony sent me materials, pointed me to sources, and pushed me to refine what began as a less ambitious offering. Thanks also to Michael E. Smith (Arizona State University) who addresses similar concerns about urban form in history from the archaeological side of the question: Mike challenged me on some details and pointed me to alternative data and interpretations that have proven illuminating. Thanks to Darrell Joudrey for preparing the original maps.

References

Allchin, B., & Allchin, R. (1982). *The rise of civilization in India and Pakistan*. Cambridge: Cambridge University Press.

Bacon, E. (1967). *Design of cities*. London: Thames and Hudson.

Benevolo, L. (1967). *The origins of modern town planning*. London: Routledge and Kegan Paul.

Benevolo, L. (1980). *The history of the city*. Cambridge: MIT Press.

Bernal, I. (1967). Mexico–Tenochtitlan. In A. Toynbee (Ed.), *Cities of destiny* (pp. 203–209). London: Thames and Hudson.

Brenner, N., & Theodore, N. (2002). Cities and the geographies of 'actually existing neoliberalism. *Antipode, 34*(3), 349–379.

Calthorpe, P. (1993). *The next American metropolis*. New York: Princeton Architectural Press.

Castagnoli, F. (1971). *Orthogonal town planning in antiquity*. Cambridge, MA: MIT Press.

Chiera, E. (1938). *They wrote on clay*. Chicago: University of Chicago Press.

Cowgill, G. (2015). *Ancient Teotihuacan: Early urbanism in Central Mexico*. New York: Cambridge University Press.

Creese, W. (1966). *The search for environment: The garden city before and after*. Baltimore: Johns Hopkins University Press.

Cronon, W. (1991). *Nature's metropolis: Chicago and the great west*. New York: W.W. Norton &.

Duany, A., & Plater-Zyberk, E. (1992). The second coming of the American small town. *Plan Canada, 32*(3), 6–13.

Duany, A., & Plater-Zyberk, E. (1996). Neighborhoods and suburbs. *Design Quarterly, 164*, 10–23.

Fairman, H. (1949). Town planning in pharaonic Egypt. *Town Planning Review, 20*(1), 33–52.

Galantay, E. (1975). *New towns: Antiquity to the present*. New York: George Braziller.

Girouard, M. (1985). *Cities and people*. New Haven: Yale University Press.

Goodman, W., & Freund, E. (1968). *Principles and practice of urban planning*. Washington: International City Managers Association.

Grant, J. (2001). The dark side of the grid: Power and urban design. *Planning Perspectives, 16*(3), 219–241.

Grant, J. (2006). *Planning the good community: New urbanism in theory and practice*. London/ New York: Routledge.

Grant, J., & Curran, A. (2007). Privatised suburbia: The planning implications of private roads. *Environment and Planning B: Planning and Design, 34*(4), 740–754.

Gross, B. (1980). *Friendly fascism: The new face of power in America*. Montreal: Black Rose Books.

Hall, J. (1955). The castle town and Japan's modern urbanization. *Far Eastern Quarterly, 15*(1), 37–56.

Hall, J. (1970). *Japan: From prehistory to modern times*. Tokyo: Charles E. Tuttle.

Hammond, N. (1998). Alexander's newly-founded cities. *Greek, Roman, and Byzantine Studies, 39*(3), 243–269.

Hardoy, J. (1968). *Urban planning in pre-Colombian America*. London: Studio Vista.

Hodge, G., & Gordon, D. (2014). *Planning Canadian communities: An introduction to the principles, practice and participants* (sixth ed.). Toronto: Nelson Canada.

Horne, D. (1986). *The public culture: The triumph of industrialism*. London: Pluto Press.

Hurtt, S. (1983). The American continental grid: Form and meaning. *Threshold, 2*, 32–40.

Hutchings, A., & Bunker, R. (1986). *With conscious purpose: A history of town planning in South Australia*. Netley, Australia: Wakefield Press.

Jacobs, J. (1961). *The death and life of great American cities*. New York: Vintage Books.

Jansen, M. (1989). Water supply and sewage disposal at Mohenjo-Daro. *World Archaeology, 21*(2), 177–192.

Jansen, M. (1993). Mohenjo-Daro: Type site of the earliest urbanization process in South Asia. In H. Spodek & D. Srinivasen (Eds.), *Urban form and meaning in South Asia* (pp. 35–51). Washington: National Gallery of Art.

Karan, P. (1997). The city in Japan. In P. Karan & K. Stapleton (Eds.), *The Japanese city* (pp. 12–39). Lexington, KY: University of Kentucky Press.

Kemp, B. (1977). The city of el-Amarna as a source for the study of urban society in ancient Egypt. *World Archaeology, 9*(2), 123–139.

Kenoyer, J. (1998). *Ancient cities of the Indus Valley civilization*. Oxford: Oxford University Press.

Kostof, S. (1995). *A history of architecture*. New York: Oxford University Press.

Krieger, A. (1991). *Andres Duany and Elizabeth Plater-Zyberk: Towns and town making principles*. Cambridge: Harvard Graduate School of Design.

Low, S. (2003). *Behind the gates: Life, security and the pursuit of happiness in fortress America*. New York: Routledge.

Lukes, S. (1974). *Power: A radical view*. London: Macmillan.

Macqueen, J. (1965). *Babylon*. New York: Frederick Praeger Publishers.

Marcuse, P. (1987). The grid as city plan: New York City and laissez-faire planning in the nineteenth century. *Planning Perspectives, 2*(3), 287–310.

Marcuse, P. (1989). Dual city: A muddy metaphor for a quartered city. *International Journal of Urban and Regional Research, 13*(4), 697–708.

Marshall, S. (2005). *Streets and patterns*. London: Spon.

McCann, E. (1995). Neotraditional developments: The anatomy of a new urban form. *Urban Geography, 16*(3), 210–233.

McEwan, G. (2009). *Pikillacta: The Wari empire in Cuzco*. Iowa City: University of Iowa Press.

Meadow, R. (Ed.). (1991). *Harappan excavations 1986–1990: A multidisciplinary approach to third millennium urbanism*. Madison: Prehistory Press.

Morris, A. (1994). *History of urban form before the industrial revolutions*. Harlow: Longman Scientific and Technical.

Mumford, L. (1961). *The city in history: Its origins, its transformations and its prospects*. New York: Harcourt, Brace and World.

Nara National Cultural Properties. (n.d.). *Nara Imperial Palace Site Museum*. Nara, Japan, Nara National Cultural Properties Research Institute.

Owens, E. (1991). *The city in the Greek and Roman world*. London: Routledge.

Pasztory, E. (1997). *Teotihuacan: An experiment in living*. Norman: University of Oklahoma Press.

Possehl, G. (1990). Revolution in the urban revolution: The emergence of Indus urbanization. *Annual Review Anthropology, 19*, 261–282.

Possehl, G. (1997). The transformation of the Indus civilization. *Journal of World Prehistory, 11*(4): 425–472.

Rae, D. (2005). *City: Urbanism and its end*. New Haven: Yale University Press.

Reps, J. (1965). *The making of urban America: A history of city planning in the United States*. Princeton: Princeton University Press.

Robbins Schug, G., Gray, K., Mushrif-Tripathy, V., & Sankhyan, A. (2012). A peaceful realm? Trauma and social differentiation at Harappa. *International Journal of Paleopathology, 2*(2–3), 136–147.

Robbins Schug, G., Blevins, K., Cox, B., Gray, K., and Mushrif-Tripathy, V. (2013). Infection, disease, and biosocial processes at the end of the Indus civilization. *PLOS One, 8*(12): e84814 (20 pp.)

Ross, A. (1999). *The celebration chronicles: Life, liberty and the pursuit of property values in Disney's new town*. New York: Ballantine Books.

Rykwert, J. (1988). *The idea of a town: The anthropology of urban form in Rome, Italy and the ancient world*. Cambridge, MA: MIT Press.

Sagg, H. W. F. (1962). *The greatness that was Babylon*. New York: Hawthorn Books.

Schreiber, K. (2009). The Wari empire of middle horizon Peru: The epistemological challenge of documenting an empire without documentary evidence. In S. Alcock, T. D'Altroy, K. Morrison, & C. Sinopoli (Eds.), *Empires: Perspectives from archaeology and history* (pp. 70–92). Cambridge: Cambridge University Press.

Shelton, B. (1999). *Learning from the Japanese city: West meets east in urban design*. London: E&FN Spon.

Smith, M. (2007). Form and meaning in the earliest cities: A new approach to ancient urban planning. *Journal of Planning History, 6*(1), 3–47.

Smith, M. (2008). Aztec city planning. In H. Selin (Ed.), *Encyclopaedia of the history of science, technology, and medicine in non-western cultures* (second ed., pp. 577–587). New York: Springer.

Sorenson, A. (2004). *The making of urban Japan: Cities and planning from Edo to the twenty-first century*. London: Routledge.

Spence, M., White, C., Longstaff, F., & Law, K. (2004). Victims of the victims: Human trophies worn by sacrificed soldiers from the feathered serpent pyramid, Teotihuacan. *Ancient Mesoamerica, 15*(1), 1–15.

Stambaugh, J. (1988). *The ancient Roman city*. Baltimore: Johns Hopkins University Press.

Stanislawski, D. (1947). Early Spanish town planning in the New World. *Geographical Review, 37*(1), 94–105.

Tedong, P., Grant, J., & Aziz, W. (2014). The social and spatial implications of community action to enclose space: Guarded neighbourhoods in Selangor, Malaysia. *Cities, 41*(A), 30–37.

Von Hagen, V. (1961). *Realm of the Incas*. New York: New American Library.

Ward, S. (1998). *Selling places: The marketing and promotion of towns and cities 1850–2000*. London: E&FN Spon.

Ward-Perkins, J. (1974). *Cities of Ancient Greece and Italy: Planning in classical antiquity*. New York: George Braziller.

Wheeler, M. (1966). *Civilizations of the Indus Valley and beyond*. London: Thames and Hudson.

White, C., Spence, M., Longstaffe, F., & Stuart-Williams, H. (2002). Geographic identities of the sacrificial victims from the feathered serpent pyramid, Teotihuacan: Implications for the nature of state power. *Latin American Antiquity, 13*(2), 217–236.

Wolfe, J. (1994). Our common past: An interpretation of Canadian planning history. *Plan Canada, 34*(4.) (75th anniversary edition)), 12–34.

Wright, A. (1967). Changan. In A. Toynbee (Ed.), *Cities of destiny* (pp. 138–149). London: Thames and Hudson.

Wu, L. (1986). *A brief history of ancient chinese city planning. (Urbs et Regio Series 38, Kasseler Schriften zur Geographie und Planung)*. Kassel: Gesamthochschulbibliothek.

Yiftachel, O. (1998). Planning and social control: Exploring the dark side. *Journal of Planning Literature, 12*(4), 395–406.

Chapter 6
Plan and Constitution: Aristotle's Hippodamus: Towards an "Ostensive" Definition of Spatial Planning

Luigi Mazza

Abstract This chapter examines the relationship between planning and citizenship by focusing on two passages from Aristotle's *Politics*. The first indicates that Hippodamus was a political philosopher and a planner and suggests that he cannot be considered the "inventor" of the orthogonal grid, but rather may be regarded as the first to theorize about the division of population and land within the city and to establish the connection between plan and constitution—that is, between the grid plan and various forms of citizenship. In the second passage, two models of spatial plan are set against each other as expressions of innovation and tradition, and Aristotle discusses the difference between functional and aesthetic aims and prudence, i.e., technical rationality and political reason. On this basis the chapter introduces the spatial inclusion/exclusion pairing as "a concept of planning" and discusses some notes on rules, customs, and tastes which may be helpful in designing a theory of a spatial plan.

Keywords Aristotle · Hippodamus of Miletus · Grid plan · Politics · Constitution · Citizenship · Spatial planning

This chapter, written by a planner, is particularly addressed to planners; since the author's motives are not those of an antiquarian nor an amateur historian, to take an interest in Hippodamus 25 centuries after his appearance on the stage of the Greek city may seem odd. The fact is that the subject of Hippodamus can be a starting point for an "ostensive" definition of spatial planning, in other words a definition obtained by working back from historical examples of planning in order to address

This chapter was originally published as Mazza, L. (2009). "Plan and Constitution: Aristotle's Hippodamus: Toward an 'Ostensive' Definition of Spatial Planning." *Town Planning Review*, 80(2): 113–141. Copyright © 2009 by Liverpool University Press. Reproduced with permission of Liverpool University Press.

L. Mazza (✉)
Politecnico di Milano, Milano, MI, Italy
e-mail: luigi.mazza@polimi.it

© Springer International Publishing AG, part of Springer Nature 2018
R. Rose-Redwood, L. Bigon (eds.), *Gridded Worlds: An Urban Anthology*,
https://doi.org/10.1007/978-3-319-76490-0_6

101

the general problem of whether a theoretical consideration of planning practices is possible. Hippodamus of Miletus is the first town planner of whom a literary trace remains, even if indirect, and the first town planner who reasoned about the space of the *polis* in the dual meaning of the Greek word: city-state and physical city. Hippodamus' proposals are cited by Aristotle in two brief passages in his *Politics*, where Hippodamus is presented as a political philosopher and planner. Many writers on Hippodamus tend to overlook his twofold activity and to consider him only or above all as a planner, whereas the association of constitution and plan may be the key to the Aristotelian passage.

In the following pages, it will be argued that the interpretation of Aristotle's text has been obstructed by the persistent idea among scholars that town planning is purely an instrument for spatial ordering and has no specific links to politics. This idea is not untenable, but it does not help us to explore the essence of planning. Well before anyone else, when discussing Hippodamus Aristotle establishes an association between social control and spatial control: from this perspective planning is not only the art of building cities, it is an instrument of governance, and the spatial arrangement produced by planning is presented as an instrument of social control. The name of Hippodamus is associated with a chessboard plan, the so-called "Hippodamian grid." Hippodamus was not the inventor of the grid, which was in use many centuries before him, but he could be considered as the inventor of planning if defined as an instrument of social control through spatial control.

Hippodamus' invention is to be found in his proposal for a constitution, which envisages a distribution of profits from land uses that is functional to the organization of social classes. The different allocation to the various social groups is interwoven with an isonomic grid in a pattern that is anything but linear. The purpose of this study on Hippodamus is to emphasize the association between grid and constitution, and to identify the political nature of planning practices, stemming from causes more radical than those normally recognized. It is also an attempt to think about the criteria governing planning actions, and to identify the characteristic features of these actions before condensing them into an autonomous concept of planning that is not, however, removed from the logic of politics. The study concludes with some notes for a theory of a spatial plan.

Political Philosopher and Town Planner

According to Vernant (2001, 210), the advent of the Greek city "is marked first of all by a transformation of urban space, or rather, the town plan." Our information about the planning and design of the cities of antiquity is not extensive (Liverani 1986, 1988; Owens 1991); the first literary reference to planning is a passage in *Politics*, where Aristotle introduces Hippodamus of Miletus as a political philosopher and planner. The passage is part of a discourse on forms of constitution and

Hippodamus makes his appearance as "the first man not engaged in politics who attempted to speak on the subject of the best form of constitution":

> Hippodamus son of Euryphon, a Milesian (who invented the division of cities into blocks and cut up Piraeus, and who also became somewhat eccentric in his general mode of life owing to a desire for distinction, so that some people thought that he lived too fussily, with a quantity of hair and expensive ornaments, and also a quantity of cheap yet warm clothes not only in winter but also in the summer periods, and who wished to be a man of learning in natural science generally), was the first man not engaged in politics who attempted to speak on the subject of the best form of constitution. His system was for a city with a population of ten thousand, divided into three classes; for he made one class of artisans, one of farmers, and the third the class that fought for the state in war and was the armed class. He divided the land into three parts, one sacred, one public and one private: sacred land to supply the customary offerings to the gods, common land to provide the warrior class with food, and private land to be owned by the farmers. (Aristotle, *Politics*, 1267b, 22)

Aristotle cites Hippodamus when discussing constitutions but he does not dwell only on the political philosopher: he also emphasizes his activity as a planner. Hippodamus, therefore, interests Aristotle in both capacities; and this is not entirely surprising given that, in his proposed constitution, Hippodamus relates the division of society into classes to the division of land and its profits. Population and land are both divided into three classes, but there is no symmetrical correspondence between the classes; moreover, it is not clear whether all land is involved, including urban areas, or only agricultural land, and it appears that no profits from the land are envisaged for the artisan class.

Aristotle talks about Hippodamus again in his discourse on the ideal constitution, when he dwells briefly on the location and fortification of cities, and this time with specific reference to his "modern conceptions" of how physically to arrange urban space:

> The arrangement of the private dwellings is thought to be more agreeable and more convenient for general purposes if they are laid out in straight streets, after the modern fashion, that is, the one introduced by Hippodamus; but it is more suitable for security in war if it is on the contrary plan, as cities used to be in ancient times; for that arrangement is difficult for foreign troops to enter and to find their way about in when attacking. Hence it is well to combine the advantages of both plans (for this is possible if the houses are laid out in the way which among the farmers some people call "on the slant" in the case of vines), and not to lay out the whole city in straight streets, but only certain parts and districts, for in this way it will combine security with beauty. (Aristotle, *Politics*, 1330b, 23)

Unfortunately there are no surviving writings by Hippodamus to help us understand how to interpret—and how, or whether, he himself interpreted—the double role assigned to him by Aristotle. Information about Hippodamus is not extensive, and details about his life and works are scarce (Burns 1976; Benvenuti Falcial 1982; Greco 1999). The dates of Hippodamus' birth and death are merely conjectures. As regards his works, the plan for Piraeus, cited by Aristotle, is attributed to him, while there is some controversy about the plan for the founding of Thurii (444–443 BC) and the plan for Rhodes (408–407 BC). Almost all authors who have studied Hippodamus have addressed the issue of the chronology of his work, which is still quite difficult to establish convincingly. The problem of attributions is bound up with the problem of Hippodamus' life span, since his date of birth is linked to and made dependent on the dating of the works attributed to him.

Early studies by Hermann and Erdmann in the nineteenth century were followed by studies by Wiegand and von Gerkan (1924); in 1924 the latter drew a hypothetical plan of Miletus, assigning Hippodamus an important role in the reconstruction of the city in 479 BC, after its destruction by the Persians. According to Owens (1991, 52), the city was destroyed during the Ionian revolt, at least fifteen years before its final defeat by the Persians. More recent studies have shown that it is improbable that Hippodamus was involved in drawing up the plan for Miletus. His birth is dateable to around 480 BC (Burns 1976, 415), although von Gerkan (1924) puts it earlier in 500 BC, and Lana (1949) even suggests that Hippodamus lived from around 510–505 BC to 415 BC. The issue of Miletus has been the subject of much debate, but it is nowadays thought that the grid of 479 BC traces that of the pre-existing city, even though there is no hard evidence that the plan really was a grid, because so far only the public buildings have been excavated. Besides, von Gerkan (1924) himself had presented his reconstruction of the plan of Miletus as hypothetical and from the works of Bendt, published at the end of the 1960s, Longo (1999, 196) noted that it is "possible to understand how von Gerkan's reconstruction was based solely on the modules found in the public buildings of the Hellenistic-Roman city." In short, according to Longo (1999, 199), the "topography of Mileto still raises many questions that do not allow the city's urban form in archaic and classical times to be given any clear definition that is not the fruit of theoretical constructions alone."

Nevertheless, the studies of von Gerkan have influenced the literature on Hippodamus for almost a century; Vernant (2001) also speaks of Hippodamus as the author of the plan for the reconstruction of Miletus. This confusion is understandable if one considers, as Castagnoli (1956, 10) did, that one of the greatest difficulties of these studies is "caused by the scarce knowledge of city plans. Temples and tombs are excavated: it is more rare for urban settlements to be excavated or at least for their layouts to be explored through appropriate test units." In conclusion, Owens is not wrong when he writes that "Hippodamos of Miletos not only dominates the history of classical town planning but, as the first recorded town planner of antiquity, he is a source of endless debates and confusion. Despite his reputation, Hippodamos remains an elusive and controversial figure" (1991, 51).

Despite such an uncertain framework, Aristotle's text is particularly interesting in terms of planning culture because the opening sentence of the first passage, describing Hippodamus as a Milesian "who invented the division of cities into blocks and cut up Piraeus," proposes an association between constitution and grid that throws a new light on planning, traditionally seen as the art of constructing cities. The first part of the phrase, την των πολεων διαιρεσιν ευρε, poses two problems of interpretation. The term ευρε, "he invented," raises the problem of establishing whether Hippodamus really "invented" something and, if so, the second problem is to establish what he invented. Since the invention in question is the "division of cities," the problem is to understand what this division is, and whether it is meant as a physical or social division. On this point scholars are not in agreement since, as has been observed, the meaning of the term διαιρεσιν, "division," is open to various interpretations (Burns 1976; Gorman 1995, 2001). Scholars have fallen into two groups: a larger group interprets "division" as a physical division, the other as a social division. In fact, there is a third group which avoids the issue and restricts itself to a literal translation of the text.

The first group of scholars defines Hippodamus' contribution as being, if not the invention, then at least the theorizing and popularization of the Hippodamian grid. These scholars assume that the geometric ordering of cities is the main theme of town planning and focus on the question of the "regular" city, an issue referred to in the second passage by Aristotle: "[t]he arrangement of the private dwellings is thought to be more agreeable and more convenient for general purposes if they are laid out in straight streets, after the modern fashion, that is, the one introduced by Hippodamus." From this perspective, the "division of cities" is the physical division, an interpretation that they believe is confirmed by the following words: "and cut up Piraeus." According to these scholars, the meaning of Aristotle's words is that Hippodamus invented the division of cities based on the grid and applied the grid in the division of Piraeus. To state their point of view and render the text more understandable, they translate "division of cities" with periphrases that refer to the division of Piraeus. It can be observed that for this second type of division Aristotle uses another term, κατετεμεν, but the observation in itself cannot be considered to resolve the issue. The main consequence of this line of interpretation is that Hippodamus is considered above all as a town planner and attention is deflected from what, as already mentioned, seems to be the most interesting aspect of the text, namely, the association between political philosopher and planner, between constitution and plan.

The second group of scholars interprets the "division of cities" as a division into social classes; for these scholars Hippodamus' "invention" lies in having divided the city into social classes and in having allocated three different types of land to three different social functions. The plan is thus functional to the political organization defined by the constitution and in the division of the city into three social classes and into three types of land, the association between constitution and grid seems to be visible in Piraeus. For these scholars Hippodamus remains above all a planner, to whom can be attributed the "invention" of the zoning technique: the division of territory into zones (the three types of land), and the allocation of different functions to different zones.

The "Physical" and the "Social" Division of Cities

The first cities with an orthogonal grid pattern that we know of are those of Harrapa, built in 2150 BC in the Indus Valley in the west of India. According to the information available to us, Babylon had a grid pattern, as did Kahun, a small settlement dating back more than four thousand years and formed in order to accommodate the builders of a pyramid in Egypt; moreover, according to traditional literature, cities and colonies older than Miletus had a regular or grid pattern. The grid layout was typical of cities founded by the Greeks and Romans and the position of temples and public areas was not random, but tended to respect the grid, as appears, for example, from the maps of Olynthus and Priene. The criteria for deciding the site of public spaces and buildings are a matter of pure conjecture; it is probable that the criteria changed over time and space according to changing forms of political and religious organization and the demands of political and military control over space (Zanker 1993). Zoning schemes, in other words the allocation of specific uses to specific spaces, as well as building regulations, have been discovered in very ancient cities such as Ur, but to date there are no sources available to tell us about the criteria and planning rules adopted by communities that settled before 500 BC.

If "division of cities" is translated as a physical division, the first problem of interpretation is easily solved because it is certain that Hippodamus did not "invent" the orthogonal grid (Bell and Bell 1969; Ward-Perkins 1974; Boyd 1981; Owens 1991; Morris 1994). Hippodamus cannot be considered the "inventor" of something that had already been in use for some time but, if anything, its theorizer and popularizer, as Gerkan (1924) was already arguing. In this way, the second problem is also solved, because if nothing was invented, there can be no issue about what was invented. The conclusion at which we have rapidly arrived is not surprising if we consider that Aristotle never wrote that Hippodamus invented the grid, but rather that Hippodamus "invented the division of cities." For this very reason it is not easy to explain why, when faced with the phrase την των πολεων διαιρεσιν ευρε, most scholars have not kept to the letter of the text, tending to add words attributed to Aristotle but of their own invention (Castagnoli 1956; Lavedan and Hugueney 1966; Benvenuti and Falcial 1982; for an interpretation somewhere in between, see Stewart 1968). For example, Burns (1976, 416) cites the imaginative periphrasis used in 1913 by Haverfield who, to explain the text, adds information perhaps referring to the hypothetical plan of Miletus and writes that Hippodamus "introduced the principle of straight wide streets, and first of all architects, made provision for the proper grouping of dwelling-houses and also paid special heed to the combination of the different parts of town in a harmonious whole, centred around the market place."

In Vernant (2001, 212), the theme of the city being organized around a central square resurfaces:

> [it] is he who is charged with rebuilding Miletus after the destruction of the city; and he rebuilds it according to an overall plan, which indicates a desire to rationalise urban space: instead of a city of the archaic type, comparable to medieval cities, with a maze of streets that run steeply and untidily down the slopes of a hill, he chooses a wide-open space, traces the streets with a measuring cord, so that they intersect at a right angle, and creates a chessboard city, entirely centred around the square of the agora.

But, as Burns observes, Aristotle makes no reference to the market square or agora; and it can be observed that the hypothetical plan of Miletus shows, rather than a city "entirely centred" around the agora, a very large L-shaped area of public buildings and spaces that separates three residential areas.

More numerous are those authors who expand the phrase. Newman (1950, 295), for example, writes of "the division of cities into streets or quarters"; Rackham (1950, 121) has "the division of cities into blocks." Other translations resort to the expression "regular division," taking this definition from the second passage in which Aristotle cites the Hippodamian layout. Poete (1958, 219) writes of he who "came up with the regular division of cities … new distribution which he applied to Piraeus," and of he who was the inventor "'of the division of the city into streets' as Aristotle states" (1958, 275); Benevolo (1975, 207) uses the expression "regular division of the city"; Giuliano (1966, 94) writes that: "he came up with the regular division of the city, and applied it to Piraeus."

Some scholars (Jowett 1885; Gorman 1995, 391) avoid the term "division" and write that Hippodamus invented "the art of planning cities" or, like Aubonnet (1989, 73), "the geometric layout of cities." Two recent Italian translations (Laurenti 1993, 50; Viano 2006, 117), perhaps influenced by Castagnoli (see below), state that "he came up with a town-planning scheme for cities." Benvenuti Falcial (1982, 33, n. 8) surprisingly writes that: "Significantly Aristotle says of Hippodamus την των πολεων διαιρεσιν ευρε, highlighting, with his usual pithiness and effectiveness, the speculative basis and theoretical component of the Milesian's activity," and she adds that the phrase "is structured in two parallel statements that illustrate the two aspects of Hippodamus' activity as an architect: the systematization of his theories on town planning and the more famous practical application of his art" (1982, 55). Choay (1986, 31–32), after writing that "he invented the geometric layout for cities," does not merely ignore the association between constitution and plan, but denies it: "he has left nothing but political writings on a plan for a constitution whose 'radical departure from [his] work as a builder and town planner has been rightly emphasised'"; but it is not clear who it was that "rightly emphasized." Lastly, Castagnoli (1956, 61) avoids tackling Aristotle's phrase directly, writing that Hippodamus "dedicated himself to the study of the constitution, proposing a division of the population into classes."

In contrast to traditional literature, which presents Hippodamus as the codifier if not the inventor of the urban grid plan, there is one suggested interpretation of Aristotle's text that seems more convincing. Burns (1976), to whom we owe a review of the studies available up to the early 1970s, begins by emphasizing that the two passages by Aristotle remain the most extensive and probably most reliable information about Hippodamus. He then goes on to argue that Hippodamus is interpreted as being the inventor of an urban grid plan because of a misunderstanding. According to Burns (1976, 417), the misunderstanding arises because no attention is paid to the fact that the meaning of διαιρεσιν, with reference to cities, is clarified in subsequent passages, where the same term is always used to refer to the division of cities into social classes and three types of land, whereas Aristotle uses a different verb to describe the physical division of Piraeus (yet, see Leveque and Vidal-Naquet 1973).

It has since been noted by Vanessa Gorman (1995, 391) that in 1803 Millon had already translated την των πολεων διαιρεσιν ευρε with "la division des Etats par ordres de citoyens." One hundred and fifty years later Martin (1956, 16) does not cite Millon, but uses the same translation and observes that, when Aristotle affirms that Hippodamus invented "the division of cities," it is not clear whether he is referring to the carving of territory into zones or the division of the city between social classes, concluding that the reference to Piraeus does not seem to him a good enough reason to argue for the interpretation of division into zones. Gorman (2001, 158–9) has recently taken up and developed Burns's reasoning in order to argue on contextual, structural, and historical grounds that Aristotle does not say that Hippodamus invented the division of cities into blocks, but that he was the first to theorize about the division of population and land within the city. According to Gorman (2001), Hippodamus was the first to link spatial ordering to political and social organization, and to divide space in order to allocate different social groups to specific areas, which, after all, is what Aristotle writes in the last sentence of the first passage cited above (yet, see Greco 1999). In conclusion, there is no revelation in the argument that Hippodamus was actually the inventor not of the grid, seen as a technical form of spatial ordering, but of the division of the territory into zones characterized by different functions (Greaves 2003; also, see Martin 1956; Ward-Perkins 1974).

Thus Hippodamus was the first to establish and explicitly express the connection between plan and constitution, that is, between plan and various forms of citizenship. The interpretation of "division of cities" is reflected in thought on the relationships that can be established between plan and constitution. Aristotle seems to emphasize the fact that one and the same person is interested in writing a constitution and dividing urban space. Those authors who interpret the "division of cities" as a physical division seem to be guided by a prejudice about the nature of town planning, which they consider solely as the activity, unrelated to politics, of physically constructing the city, and hence they overlook the role of Hippodamus as a political philosopher. Those authors who correctly interpret the "division of cities" as a division into social classes do not go on to establish a necessary link between constitution and plan, because their conviction is so strong that the only role of town planning is to divide the city physically that it leads them to overlook other ideas of planning that associate it with politics. For example, Martin believes that the term διαρεσιν, used in the phrase, is more applicable to political considerations than to geometry since, to indicate the division of a site and the layout of a plan, it would be more appropriate to use terms such as νεμησις, διανεηειν, κατατεηνειν (Greaves 2003, 105). Therefore, he leans towards the correct interpretation of the division of cities into social classes; but he goes no further than this and does not establish any particular link between constitution and plan. However, Benvenuti Falcial (1982, 33), for example, when commenting on the entries on Hippodamus in Hesychius and Photius, and recalling Aristotle's phrase, believes that the noun νεμησις, like the verbs used to explain it, διαιρεω and διανεμω, leads us back to the area of town planning, namely a theoretical action, more than a practical one: "to divide," "to order" here clearly indicate the action of drawing the plan of Piraeus and, at the drawing board, deciding where, how and according to what criteria to build, divide it into various zones to be developed differently, and to identify and trace the streets and the city's main poles of interest.

Castagnoli (1971) and Burns (1976) dwell considerably, and perhaps too long, on the fact that Hippodamus was the first to propose not only a town plan, but one with the features of an actual land use plan. The insistence of both on what they believe to be Hippodamus' contribution to the development of planning ends up overshadowing the link between political philosopher and planner. It is surprising, in an author as scrupulous as Castagnoli, to find such bold statements as the following:

> Hippodamian city planning is a unique chapter in the history of urban planning not only for the concept of a master plan to control all future growth and development, but also for its rational organic qualities. To recapitulate, these are summarized as follows: The street grid is regularly subdivided into wide parallel strips by a very few (usually three or four) major longitudinal arteries. At right angles to these run other streets, a few of which are major communication roads but most of which are narrow alleyways whose only purpose is to create blocks for buildings. The blocks thus formed are usually long and narrow. Buildings and plazas fall within the grid. There is no central intersection of major axes (as distinguished from the Roman axial grid) ... Aside from a strictly rational and geometric form, the grid exemplified certain criteria of absolute equality among the residential blocks. (1971, 129)

It is not easy to understand what Castagnoli means by organic qualities and on what grounds he attributes to Hippodamus the merit of theorizing about and applying a master plan that is so exacting on account of its resolution to forecast and control. Perhaps the reference is to Piraeus, but one gets the impression that Hippodamus' proposal is saddled with an idea of planning that is primarily Castagnoli's, as, moreover, happens in the case of Martin (1956) too. Taking Castagnoli's lead, Burns (1976, 420–1) goes on to say that "the salient factor seems to be that he originated the concept of land-allocation and city design according to a master plan prepared with all aspects of community life in mind," in order to conclude that "he initiated a system by which land was allocated in advance on the basis of political, social and economic considerations." Burns adds that "Hyppodamos' importance lies in a new theoretical approach expressed in his writings which consisted in a total planning concept" (1976, 427–8).

Some scholars believe that Hippodamus not only theorized and systematized the use of the orthogonal grid, but that he also introduced zoning practices. Others, such as Owens (1991), note that zoning practices were in use before Hippodamus and that the contribution made by Hippodamus lay more in his attention to scenic and monumental elements, particularly evident in the case of Rhodes, than in the application of the grid and zoning. These different opinions are explained by the different meanings attributed to the term "zoning." If zoning means the division of urban territory into zones earmarked for two main uses, public and private, with a consequent spatial distribution of religious, governmental, and residential functions, there is no doubt that zoning practices had always been in use, well before Hippodamus.

Hippodamus' innovation is thus a zoning plan in which there is a *partial match* between the political organization of the city (division into classes) and spatial plan (division into zones). Earlier zoning plans could also have had a political objective, and not just a functional purpose, but Hippodamus' innovation was, perhaps, to render the political objective explicit and to make the division of space functional to it. In other words, zoning plans before Hippodamus undoubtedly had political consequences, to some extent deriving from the forms of spatial plan, while the Hippodamian zoning plan is functional to a specifically prescribed form of constitution and, in the relationship between constitution and plan, the plan is subordinate to the political objectives of the constitution: the three types of land match three different functions, serving the different social classes.

The different relationship between constitution and plan in the Hippodamian zoning plan as opposed to previous zoning plans does not seem to have been grasped by scholars, because even those who correctly translate the "division of cities" do not believe that they can identify a particular relationship between constitution and plan. Martin (1956), for example, considers the meaning of "division of cities" as a matter of interpretation that has no further implications, and it is probable that he arrives at this conclusion because he does not believe it possible to establish any significant connection between politics and planning; on the contrary, he believes that planning should be a separate activity and not inspired or, worse still, determined by political considerations. Traina (1994, 117) adopts a position somewhere in between, describing Hippodamus' zoning as the selective distribution of population and activities for the explicit purposes of social control: "to segregate artisans and the attendant inconveniences within their own districts: noise, bad smells and uprisings." The lack of agreement among scholars about how to interpret "the division of cities" highlights the fact that, for most of them, ordering and control of space are directed above all at the construction and transformation of physical space, even if it is recognized that these cannot be achieved without reference to the political circumstances and framework. It is significant that even those scholars who recognize the connection between plan and constitution do not therefore establish a link between politics and planning, even though it is to some extent suggested in the passage by Aristotle, which presents constitution and plan as objects of interest to one and the same person.

Land, *Nomos* and Citizenship

The association between drafting a constitution and dividing space is not surprising if one recognizes there to be symmetry in the relationship: a constitution is a shape for a society that does not yet exist, just as a Hippodamian grid is a shape for a city that does not yet exist. But this is not all. In the case of Hippodamus the two actions of writing a constitution and tracing a grid are not only symmetrical ones characterized by the Pythagorean tripartition of social classes and types of land; the two actions have in common the act of "dividing," which is also the key word in the Aristotelean passage: to divide classes, to divide land. Schmitt (2006, 45) has indicated that to divide space is to establish law:

because appropriating land and founding cities always is associated with an initial measurement and distribution of usable soil, which produces a primary criterion embodying all subsequent criteria. It remains discernible as long as the structure remains recognizably the same. All subsequent legal relations to the soil, originally divided among the appropriating tribe or people, and all institutions of the walled city or of a new colony are determined by this primary criterion.

And again:

the earth is bound to law in three ways. She contains law within herself, as a reward of labor; she manifests law upon herself, as fixed boundaries; and she sustains law above herself, as *a public sign of order*. (2006, 42, my emphasis)

Rereading Aristotle in light of Schmitt, it may not be stretching a point to assume that there is a relationship between the political action of "constituting" and the technical action of "dividing," between the establishment of law and the division of space. In other words, if constitution and plan are linked by the nexus of dividing land, Hippodamus' association of the two actions no longer appears casual, but necessary. According to Schmitt (2006, 49), land appropriation "constitutes the original spatial order, the source of all further concrete order and all further law. It is the reproductive root in the normative order of history."

This key allows Hippodamus to be considered not as the inventor of a technique that already existed, but as the first person to realize the links between land and law, links that introduce the connections between political/social control and spatial ordering, and, as already mentioned, between plan and citizenship. The relationship between constitution and grid, if acknowledged, establishes a circularity between politics and plan in which planning is advanced not only as an activity that is political, because it entrusts decisions to political rationale and judgment, but, in a more profound sense, as an activity that has above all a political end: a (re)designing of citizenship that welds strategies of social and spatial control into a single process. If the spatial plan is functional to social control, planning decisions contribute to the (re)definition of forms of citizenship or, more precisely, the (re)designing of citizenship is, wittingly or unwittingly, the true aim of the plan, while functional, economic, or aesthetic objectives, normally regarded as objectives of the plan and pursued as such, are in fact means of pursuing the political objective of redesigning citizenship (Schmitt 2006, 42).

Spatial Control and Social Control

In his study on the changing cult of Hestia, Vernant (2001, 216–7) has shown how "the advent of the city, public debate, and the social 'model' of a human community formed by 'equals' allowed thought to become rational, to be receptive to a new concept of space, which is expressed on a whole range of levels at the same time: in political life, in the organization of urban space, in cosmology and in astronomy." In this process of transformation the decisive change is the reform introduced by

Cleisthenes with the aim of creating an institutional system in which traditional forms of tribal membership are superseded and "the territorial principle [ranks higher than] the principle of clan in the organization of the *polis*: the city is designed on the basis of a spatial plan; tribes, *trittyes*, and demes are drawn on the ground, like just as many realities that can be recorded on paper" (Vernant 2001, 246; also, see Gaeta 2004).

According to Vernant (2001), it is the new ideal of ισονομια—isonomy, equality before the law—that implies a geometric vision of the city, the new political rationality implying a new spatial plan. This theme is taken up by various writers who identify in the Hippodamian grid a spatial representation of the isonomic plan (Lana 1949). But Vernant (2001, 257) shows us that it is not as simple as that and that in fact "Cleisthenes" centered civic space aimed to integrate without distinction all the citizens of the *polis*, whereas Hippodamus' political space and urban space share a fundamental characteristic: differentiation. The same line is taken by Leveque and Vidal-Naquet (1973), who add that Cleisthenes did not have a concept of town planning, whereas Hippodamus may represent an attempt to create an urban space that reflects political space. Nonetheless, according to Vernant, Cleisthenes' solution represents one of the extreme poles of political space, since it aspires to create a homogeneous civic space that emulates the ideal of an egalitarian society.

Hippodamus' solution implies a differentiated social, spatial, and to some extent hierarchical organization, without this involving hierarchy in the political system. According to Aristotle, Hippodamus discerns three classes within society, each confined to its specific function—warrior, artisan, and farmer—and he divides territory into three zones: a sacred one reserved for religious rites, a shared or public one reserved for warriors, and a private one assigned to farmers. However, as already noted, all three classes are assembled within a single *demos*, which elects its magistrates on an egalitarian basis. Based on Vernant's premise, Hippodamus' proposed constitution relates social organization to spatial plan and differentiation into classes and zones is achieved through a geometric form of space that is isonomic: the grid. In other words, the grid as a technical form of dividing territory—regionalization or districting—becomes planning when the division of the three zones or types of land—sacred, public, and private—refers to social typologies. In this way, the grid is invested with functions that are not only more aesthetic, but economic and moral (redistributive).

In Hippodamus' political program two different political strategies can therefore be traced: one pursues differentiation through constitutional tripartition and the differentiated allocation of profits from land uses; the other pursues equality through the isonomy of the grid. The two political strategies that intersect in space represent two different political and scientific cultures. Hippodamus appears as an original theoretician who manages to fuse differentiation and equality by loading onto an isonomic geometry the relationships that connect social groups to types of land.

We are faced with two possibilities: to take Vernant's lead and explain the two political strategies as the result of the cultural hesitancy of the author, who is caught between two political and scientific paradigms, or to understand them as a form of political adaptability that produces a structured model of a town plan, without this preventing the basic allocations from being egalitarian. In both cases the two political strategies are expressed by a single spatial strategy, the grid, and both are achieved through land and establish rights: the social groups have different rights to the agricultural products from the land and an equal right to vote and, perhaps, to urban use of the land. The differentiation between social classes implies a form of hierarchy. The pattern of citizenship, simultaneously hierarchical and isonomic, pursued by Hippodamus' constitutional proposal, is translated into the forms of spatial control that the two strategies aspire to affirm. The forms of citizenship are defined and expressed through spatial forms.

The equality of the spatial rights produced through the grid involves the creation of a geometrically homogeneous space. Geometric regularity and hypothetical equality of building rights determine the isonomic character of the grid and the symbolic representation of the democratic order: one citizen one vote, each block equal to the others. If the two strategies are applied to different spatial environments, agricultural and urban respectively, it is possible to avoid significant interference between them. If the two strategies are applied simultaneously to a single urban environment, on top of the egalitarian pattern there unfolds a pattern that allocates in different ways to different social classes the spaces and urban profits defined by the first scheme. But the isonomic strategy, which seems to find its complete spatial projection in the grid, is bound to clash with the differentiation present in space, where, even within a homogeneous geometry, the position of the different spatial units renders them relatively different: each point in space is different from all the others. A plan designed to achieve strict spatial equality is bound to fail, even if a strictly isonomic plan still has the merit of rendering the differentiation process more transparent and controllable, and of limiting the inegalitarian aspects. The grid is therefore the spatial projection of two political strategies that simultaneously pursue different physical, aesthetic, economic, and moral objectives. As such, the grid proves to be a true technical form open to more than one representation and determination of spatial control, since its ability to carve up land and establish rights does not prevent it from serving various strategies. Therefore, the relationship between spatial control and social control is not linear; it is always open-ended and, in order to be defined, requires further closures than those offered by the spatial order constructed by the grid.

Innovation and Tradition

In the second passage cited at the beginning of this chapter, Aristotle, without referring to Hippodamus' political proposal, compares the grid model with the traditional type of town plan. Although appreciating the aesthetic and other advantages of the grid, Aristotle suggests a combination of innovation and tradition. Aristotle believes that the traditional winding streets, produced by a combination of buildings and open spaces, are more convenient because they confuse possible assailants—"for that arrangement is difficult for foreign troops to enter and to find their way about in when attacking"—and, it could be added, make them more vulnerable to ambushes by the defenders of the city. The comparison indicates how the rules governing the geometry of urban space differ according to the various strategies pursued—defense or aesthetic planning of the dwellings—and how spatial forms may not be unimportant to the pursuit of urban activities.

According to Strauss (1964, 21–22), one of the few commentators on Aristotle to reflect on Hippodamus, Aristotle discusses Hippodamus because he allows him to highlight the difference between the arts and *nomos*. Hippodamus proposes that those who have invented something useful for the city should be honored adequately, but Aristotle observes that Hippodamus has not grasped the different value of innovation for the arts and for *nomos*: Hippodamus does not grasp the possible tension between the need for political stability and technological change. This is another key that may explain why Aristotle also looks at Hippodamus' activity as a planner.

The orthogonal grid that Hippodamus does not invent, but codifies, is an example of innovation that can be appreciated from an aesthetic point of view, but not from the perspective of defending a city. For politics, defense of the city may be more important than its beauty. The opportunities for disorientating assailants and leading them into an ambush clash with the functional and aesthetic rationality of the grid. In more general terms, the traditional labyrinthine layout and the orthogonal grid propose two different forms of rationality: the rationality of nature and history (and exchange), and the (technical) rationality of the arts. The first is superior to the second because it is the expression of prudence, of practical wisdom. The tension between political reason and technical rationality that manifests itself in Hippodamus is an opportunity to emphasize the subordination of the second to the first. Subordination establishes an interrelationship, even if asymmetrical.

The decision on how to order space may spring from technical rationality, which has functional and aesthetic aims, but it must be subordinate to the prudence that governs politics, since "the true nature of public affairs often defies reason." From a planning perspective, it can be added that, in any case, however strong technical rationality may be its enforcement depends on political will, authority, and the legitimacy that a political decision confers upon it. The solution of integrating labyrinthine layout and orthogonal layout, as proposed by Aristotle, is apparently worthy of Solomon, while it is actually a way of expressing the conviction that planning and spatial control cannot be the product of an independent technique, but must be based on (the practical sound judgment of) politics.

Aristotle's final suggestion is not to build the whole city in accordance with Hippodamus' teachings, but to fuse the two models of spatial plan. It is not easy to decide what the reasons for this conclusion may be—whether security is the real reason for at least partially rejecting the grid or whether the rigidity of the grid is the real obstacle, since to some extent it appears to be incompatible with the flexibility of politics and the strata that history has deposited on the land; or, yet again, whether Aristotle is transferring his negative opinion of Hippodamus' constitution to the grid too, regarding it as the spatial projection of that constitutional plan which is too simple not to be dangerous and which is conducive to confusion.

The question is not simple and lends itself to two interpretations of the traditional labyrinthine model, which can be considered as an exemplary form of "spontaneous" order or as a form of disorder that must be eliminated. In the first interpretation, the winding and irregular labyrinthine streets are the expression of the slow and difficult formation of the community in space, its gradual and negotiated coming-together, a "spontaneous" order that is challenged by the grid as an artificial, regular form, indifferent to the irregularities and diversities of the planned territory; the aesthetics of irregularity are opposed by the aesthetics of regularity. But it should not be forgotten that the uniformity and indifference of the grid are not only functional to an aesthetic objective; they are revealed as functional to the spatial projection of a political objective: isonomy.

In the second interpretation, the labyrinthine streets can be considered, and to some extent are, the spatial projection of the tribal and hierarchical system that preceded the democratic system (e.g., Benvenuti Falcial 1982). As the geometric representation of the intended equality of citizens before the law—the three social classes constitute a single *demos* and contribute equally to the election of magistrates—the grid becomes the spatial projection of the democratic system, and in order that the democratic order can expand in space, the labyrinthine model must be cancelled. The grid as a form of democratic and modern spatial plan challenges an authoritarian and archaic spatial plan. In both cases, the two models are functional to a political design and express it through different spatial forms. The rules governing the ordering of space are functional to the political strategies that determine them; the source of the rules is therefore politics, and the effects of redefining citizenship by applying the rules are also political, since the rules that order space order the ways in which populations inhabit space.

Rules, Customs, and Tastes: Notes for a Theory of a Spatial Plan

Grid, Customs, and Tastes

It has already been observed that the grid is a technical form amenable to representing the spatial projection of different political strategies, pursuing different political, aesthetic, economic, and moral objectives. The grid may satisfy, and generally does satisfy, functional and aesthetic criteria, but it remains open to the inflections suggested by various, even contradictory, political and spatial strategies and thus to more than one spatial representation and determination of social control. The grid is receptive in two ways, politically and physically, and it is precisely to this that its autonomy and technical flexibility can be attributed—an autonomy that does not exclude the grid from subordination to politics, but renders it more amenable to it. Even if it can be considered as the spatial projection of an isonomic principle, the grid does not express a clear-cut political design for a spatial plan, and can support various structured forms of citizenship. Political determination can be conferred upon the grid only by the distinctions between inclusion and exclusion expressed by a constitutional plan. Secondly, the grid is not sufficient to define the forms of physical space. It tells us nothing about the shape of the temple located in the center of the city, or of the house that Hippodamus seems to have owned in Piraeus—it is a two-dimensional form open to several structures in the third dimension.

According to Aristotle, the grid arranges dwellings so as to make the city uniform and attractive; the innovative aesthetic result derives from the spatial order introduced by the grid, because the dwellings would have been built in the traditional manner—one- or two-storey buildings with internal courtyards almost entirely filling each block—without any substantial differences between the labyrinthine arrangement and the Hippodamian grid, in terms of the form and quality of the dwellings. Thus, at the origin of the new spatial order there is not only the grid, but also traditional building practice to establish how much and in what way to build along the traces of the grid. The physical form of the city results from a division of space combined with customs that are not defined by a constitution, or only in part: where necessary, the constitution can define how much to build, but only very partially how to build, the features still being entrusted to the customs and taste of the inhabitants and builders. Therefore, the rules determining social order and spatial order are not the same ones governing their symbolic representation since in this case it is not a question of rules but, in many respects, of customs and traditions; issues not of law but of taste.

Ideal Models of Grid

Up to this point the two terms "grid" and "plan" have been used without any special clarifications; in fact, they have different meanings. The Hippodamian grid is a technical form of spatial plan characterized by orthogonality and regular dimensions. Obviously, it is not the only possible type of grid; the main alternative is the radial-concentric grid, where the ideal form is an irregular pattern contained between radial axes and concentric rings. The main difference between the two grids does not spring from their different structures but from the different ways, extroverted and introverted, in which they project themselves into space and arrange it. The orthogonal grid has a quality that we might define as extrovert in so much as its regularity allows it to expand to infinity in each direction, because the abstract concept of space that supports it is limitless. The lack of a central reference point makes it identical in every point of space, just as the "blocks" are identical, and the orthogonal axes that define them. If the axes are always aligned in the same direction, they can be reproduced and extended into space without encountering any obstacles, even if they start from different points far apart: we can imagine the globe being crossed in two directions, north to south and east to west, solely by parallel lines crossing at right angles at every point.

On the other hand, the radial-concentric grid has by definition a center from which, and towards which, the radial axes originate and converge; and it is the existence of a center that determines its introverted nature, which manifests itself in the strain to contain space within the perimeter of the last concentric ring. In the case of the globe, extension of the radial axes—the meridians—leads to two opposite centers in the North and South poles. The maximum extension is defined by the last ring—the equator—from which it is still possible to converge towards the pole, in other words the ring beyond which the attraction of the other pole begins to operate. If, in the space considered, there are numerous centers, a moment comes when the outer rings of various grids come close to one another without the possibility of connecting; in that instant, the introverted and limited character of the radial-concentric grid is manifest.

I am not aware of an archetypal radial-concentric grid comparable with the Hippodamian archetype; in any event the two grids can be considered two ideal models alongside which the labyrinthine grid can be laid as a third model. The large number of grids found in history can be considered the result of distorting and mixing of the three main models. While the labyrinthine grid can be taken as the product of customs and practices, a product unrelated to the convergence of an explicit form of constitution with a defined spatial plan, the other two grids are the explicit and defined expression of a voluntary convergence of a constitution and a division of space.

Dilution of the ideal models of grid in the actual construction and transformation of cities increases the ability of the grids to adapt themselves to various types of political program and spatial control. This ability should not be mistaken for indifference: adulteration of the ideal models merely makes it more difficult to interpret a grid's capacity for spatial and, indirectly, social determination, without this meaning that the ability has been lost or weakened.

Grids and the Spatial Plan

The grid, a technical form that is both politically and physically open, should not be confused with a plan; the grid is only a component of the plan, even though it is the central element for the division of space. A plan is produced when the grid is loaded with political decisions and social control and spatial control converge to produce a spatial plan. A spatial plan means the linking of the envisaged forms of social control with a division of the land according to use; where the division of the land may or may not include a definition of its physical morphology in terms of quantity and quality. In both cases the plan is open to the defining contribution of taste, meaning both social and individual forms of representation, produced by traditional customs and practice, and innovative forms produced and used by emerging social groups to represent themselves in space.

Customs and taste are elements in the processes of urban transformation, regardless of the plan, and do not necessarily converge with the objectives of the plan.

Customs and taste can ensure that spatial, functional, and symbolic forms are still used, even when no longer consistent with the objectives of the plan. The role that customs and taste play in the processes of urban transformation reveal that the plan's ability to produce a city that is (as Lefebvre puts it) like an *oeuvre*, a work of art, is limited. This limit is to some extent reassuring when the knowledge and power spread by custom blunt the authoritarian nature of the plan, but it also emphasizes the authoritarian nature of the plan when it allows taste to be determined by the social groups holding the greatest power of social and spatial representation.

The overall capacity for governing the urban form therefore depends on convergence between the political objectives of those who decide the plan and the ability to translate these objectives aesthetically and represent them symbolically through customs and taste. However, it would be a mistake to reduce the power of aesthetic and symbolic determination to taste and customs, for the grid too shares part of this power; as Aristotle's account indicates, the division of land is an inseparable and sometimes vital part of the aesthetic result, regardless of building practices. Different forms of grid not only propose different forms of social control, but invite or provoke different aesthetic solutions and different symbolic representations; to understand the relationships between forms of grid and the aesthetic and symbolic features of the physical form is a theme that planners have not yet explored in great depth (yet, see Cerdà 1968).

Spatial Plans and Citizenship

A plan emerges when political decisions to include and exclude converge with technical choices about the division of land, expressed by a grid; the political decisions and technical choices both contribute to the definition of a spatial plan, whose objective and result is to design forms of citizenship. The grid by itself does not produce citizenship, but orders and gives spatial substance to the forms of citizenship decided by a constitutional design. Constitution and grid both contribute through the plan to the political and spatial definition of citizenship and, despite the circular relationship by which they are linked, preserve their own independence, defined by the different times and different duration of political and spatial decisions. The common aim of citizenship shows how the reciprocal autonomy of political decisions and technical choices does not prevent the latter from being subordinate to the former. The design of the grid opens it in two directions: towards political decisions about social control and towards choices of taste and custom that contribute to the qualitative determination of spatial control. The link between political decisions and taste is created by the technical form assigned to the grid, which, from a technical perspective, is the strong point of the plan. Nevertheless, the plan generally has a limited capacity to determine the aesthetic and symbolic features of the planned reality. In the episode of Hippodamus, it is therefore possible to grasp the rudiments of a theory of a plan centered around the idea of dividing, expressed conceptually by the distinction between inclusion and exclusion and by the design of the grid, which acquires the value of an archetypal spatial plan.

References

Aubonnet, J. (1989). *[Aristotle's] Politique, Livres I et II*. Paris: Les Belles Lettres.
Bell, C., & Bell, R. (1969). *City fathers: The early history of town planning in Britain*. London: The Cresset Press.
Benevolo, L. (1975). *Storia della città*. Bari: Laterza.
Benvenuti Falcial, P. (1982). *Ippodamo di Mileto, architetto e filosofo. Una ricostruzione filologica della personalità*. Florence: Università degli studi di Firenze.
Boyd, T. (1981). Halieis: A fourth planned city in classical Greece. *Town Planning Review, 52*(2), 143–156.
Burns, A. (1976). Hippodamus and the planned city. *Historia, 25*(4), 414–428.
Castagnoli, F. (1956). *Ippodamo di Mileto e l'urbanistica a pianta ortogonale*. Rome: De Luca.
Castagnoli, F. (1971). *Orthogonal town planning in antiquity*. Cambridge, MA: MIT Press.
Cerdà, I. (1968). *Teoria general de la urbanizacion y applicacion de sus principios y doctrinas a la reforma y ensanche de Barcelona*. Barcelona: Instituto de Estudios Fiscales.
Choay, F. (1986). *La regola e il modello. Sulla teoria dell'architettura e dell'urbanistica*. Rome: Officina Edizioni.
Gaeta, L. (2004). Athenian democracy and the political foundation of space. *Planning Theory & Practice, 5*, 471–484.
Gerkan, A. (1924). *Griechische stadteanlagen: Untersuchungen zur entwicklung des Stadtebaues im Altertum*. Berlin: Walter de Gruyter.
Giuliano, A. (1966). *Urbanistica delle città greche*. Milan: il Saggiatore.
Gorman, V. (1995). Aristotle's Hippodamos (*Politics 2.1267b 22–30*). *Historia, XLIV*, 385–395.
Gorman, V. (2001). *Miletos, the ornament of Ionia: A history of the city to 400 B.C.E.* Ann Arbor: University of Michigan Press.
Greaves, A. (2003). *Miletos: A history*. London: Routledge.
Greco, E. (Ed.). (1999). *La città greca. Istituzioni, società e forme urbane*. Rome: Donzelli.
Jowett, B. (1885). *The politics of Aristotle, with an introduction and notes* (Vol. II). Oxford: Clarendon Press.
Lana, I. (1949). L'utopia di Ippodamo di Mileto. *Rivista di Filosofia, XL*, 125–151.
Laurenti, R. (1993). *[Aristotle's] Politica*. Laterza: Rome and Bari.
Lavedan, P., & Hugueney, J. (1966). *Histoire de l'urbanisme. Antiquité*. Paris: Henry Laurens.
Leveque, P., & Vidal-Naquet, P. (1973). *Clisthene l'Athenien*. Paris: Les Belles Lettres.
Liverani, M. (1986). *L'origine delle città*. Rome: Editori Riuniti.
Liverani, M. (1988). *Uruk la prima città*. Bari: Laterza.
Longo, F. (1999). Mileto. In E. Greco (Ed.), *La città greca* (pp. 183–204). Rome: Donzelli.
Martin, R. (1956). *L'urbanisme dans la Grèce Antique*. Paris: Picard & Cie.
Morris, A. (1994). *History of urban form: Before the industrial revolutions*. Essex: Longman.
Newman, W. (1950). *The politics of Aristotle. With an introduction, two prefatory essays and notes critical and explanatory*. Oxford: Clarendon Press.
Owens, E. (1991). *The city in the Greek and Roman world*. London: Routledge.
Poete, M. (1958). *Introduzione all'urbanistica: la città antica*. Turin: Einaudi.
Rackham, H. (1950 [1932]). [Aristotle's] *Politics*. Cambridge: Loeb Classical Library.
Schmitt, C. (2006). *The nomos of the earth, in the international law of the jus Publicum Europaeum*. New York: Tele Press Publishing.
Stewart, C. (1968). *A prospect of cities: Being studies towards a history of town planning*. London: Longman.

Strauss, L. (1964). *The city and man*. Chicago: University of Chicago Press.
Traina, G. (1994). *La tecnica in Grecia e a Roma*. Bari: Laterza.
Vernant, J. (2001). *Mito e pensiero presso i Greci. Studi di psicologia storica*. Turin: Einaudi.
Viano, C. (2006). *[Aristotle's] Politica*. Turin: Utet.
Ward-Perkins, J. (1974). *Cities of ancient Greece and Italy: Planning in classical antiquity*. New York: Braziller.
Zanker, P. (1993). *Pompei*. Turin: Einaudi.

Chapter 7
City Plan as Ideology: Reading the Configuration of Beijing in Ming-Qing China

Jianfei Zhu

Abstract This chapter examines the political ideology of the grid plan through a historical case study of imperial Beijing. In its centric and symmetrical layout, Beijing is the symbolic embodiment of Confucian ideas of a sacred emperor residing at the center of the universe, coordinating the ways of "heaven" with that of humans on earth. Beijing clearly inherited a classical grid model formulated in the Han dynasty, which prescribed a grand, centric, Confucian order. The author argues in this chapter that the grid layout of Beijing was based upon the adoption of neo-Confucian ideas of imperial rule developed in the Song and the early Ming dynasties. This is reflected in a reinforced emphasis on the need to combine *wangdao* (sage rulership) and *badao* (powerful rulership) in the consolidation of a symbolic layout of urban imperial space.

Keywords Chinese urbanism · Urban planning · Political authority · Grid · Cosmology · Ceremonious design · Ideology

Introduction

As a result of the political unification of China, Chinese cities have been largely state-oriented and characteristically administrative since at least the third century BCE. This has had three manifestations. Firstly, cities in China were geographically connected with postal routes linking them to the imperial capital, and most cities were administrative nodes in a hierarchical and extensive network of state rule, with counties at the lowest level and imperial capitals at the top. Secondly, Chinese cities

This chapter is a revised version of Zhu, J. (2004). "City Plan as Ideology." In J. Zhu, *Chinese Spatial Strategies: Imperial Beijing, 1420–1911* (pp. 28–44). London: RoutledgeCurzon. Copyright © 2004 by Jianfei Zhu. Reproduced with permission of Taylor & Francis Group.

J. Zhu (✉)
University of Melbourne, Parkville, VIC, Australia
e-mail: jianfz@unimelb.edu.au

© Springer International Publishing AG, part of Springer Nature 2018   121
R. Rose-Redwood, L. Bigon (eds.), *Gridded Worlds: An Urban Anthology*,
https://doi.org/10.1007/978-3-319-76490-0_7

were planned with a formal and symmetrical plan whenever possible and especially for higher-level capitals, where government venues including offices, schools, and temples were typically placed at the center. There were also organically-developed market-towns, and hybrids of the planned and unplanned, yet centralized spatial planning with a geometrical formality to represent state rule remains a central characteristic of city building in pre-modern China. Thirdly, for every new dynasty, the court often had to build a new capital or significantly rebuild an old one. In doing so, the ruling regime imposed a formal and centralized layout for the city, with a large and coordinated labor force to deliver the construction, and with a fast pace of building using timber structures for the main palatial projects. In this sense, Chinese cities were *designed* and *planned* in a top-down fashion as "state" cities, rather than organic city-states as we find in Europe (Zhu 2014a, b, 2016).

In developing the tradition of imperial city planning in pre-modern China, the last three dynasties—Yuan (1271–1368 CE), Ming (1368–1644 CE), and Qing (1644–1911 CE)—were particularly important. The Yuan dynasty, a Mongol power under Kublai Kahn (r. 1260–1294 CE), built its capital Dade in 1274, following closely an ancient Chinese planning model based upon the centrality of the city plan, concentricity of city walls, dominance of a north-south axis, a gridded street plan, and a square-shaped plan for the whole city. This was remodelled with new constructions under the Ming dynasty, finalizing the Beijing that we know today in 1420 and 1553. By contrast, the Qing dynasty did not alter the overall plan and instead added various resort palaces outside. This chapter focuses on the formation of Beijing in early Ming dynasty. After describing the historical process of the rise of Beijing, the chapter moves on to read the plan, to find out how—by adopting a layout with embedded ideas—it acted as a vast script of the thought of state authority, a figure of imperial ideology (Zhu 2004).

Building Beijing as the Capital of China

When the Ming forces sacked Dadu in 1368, general Xu Da measured and repaired parts of the old city wall. He abandoned a northern portion of the city by building a new wall some five *li* (1/3 miles) south of the old northern wall. This reduced the exposure of the wall to the north and helped strengthen his defense (Guo 1997). Xu Da soon moved on to confront the Mongols in the north and west, and left to his subordinate general Hua Yuanlong the task of defending and rebuilding the city. In the following years, Hua modified the Yuan palace and turned it into a new residence for Zhu Di. In 1403, when the city was named "Beijing," preparation for massive construction started. From 1416 onwards, the building of the palace complex and suburban altars was directed by the court eunuch Cheng Gui and the chief builder Ruan An, with emperor Zhu Di himself overlooking the project closely (Farmer 1976; Chan 1988; Guo 1997). Centering on the same axis of Yuan Dadu, but modelled on the design of Ming Nanjing, the new palace complex was more organized in a symmetrical manner, and was larger, with extensions towards north, east, and south. The southern city wall was extended one *li* for a longer approach to the palace on an axial way. Two large suburban altars were constructed to the south of the city, on the two sides of the axis.

Although these projects were completed in 1420 and the city formally assumed the status and the functioning of a capital, significant construction work continued. A few months after the initial use, a fire destroyed three audience halls in the palace complex, and a debate soon followed on the merit of the city as a capital. The issue was not settled until 1436, when Emperor Zhengtong (Zhu Qizhen) decided to adhere to Zhu Di's original intention (Farmer 1976; Chan 1988; Chen 1991). That year, he delegated Ruan An and ministers Wu Zhong and Shen Qing to the task of rebuilding the entire city wall, which included the addition of gate towers and corner towers. After that, they rebuilt the three audience halls, and two residential palaces behind, in 1440 and 1441 (which were titled *fengtian, huagai, jinshen, qianqing,* and *kunning* respectively). On November 14, 1441, Emperor Zhengtong declared Beijing the permanent capital.

About a century later, under Emperor Jiajing (Zhu Houcong), new additions were made. After a court debate on the importance of discrete sacrifices to Heaven, the Earth, the Sun, and the Moon, the emperor ordered to offer separate worship to the gods, and three new suburban altars were constructed in 1530 (Meyer 1991; Guo 1997). They were the Altar of the Earth, the Son, and the Moon, located to the north, east, and west of the city respectively, a pattern which added a new layer of formality and symbolic significance to the whole city plan. Jiajing also added other structures, including a new building, Daxiang Dian, "temple of the greatest offering," inside the Altar of Heaven complex, which was later rebuilt in the Qing dynasty by Emperor Qianlong (r. 1736–95) and renamed Qinian Dian, "temple for yearly harvest." In the face of increasing threat from the Mongols, new sections of the Great Wall west of Beijing were constructed in the 1540s and 1550s (Waldron 1983; Mote 1988b). A new city wall, encircling Beijing, was proposed. This was not materialized due to the lack of funds and labor force. Instead, only a section of the wall was built in 1553, encircling the southern outskirts of Beijing, which had by then developed into a densely populated area with streets of busy commercial life. This new southern city, now called the Outer City, also included in its territory the two large altar complexes built before. At this point, Beijing reached its final form. The rest of Ming and Qing emperors in the following 350 years made numerous contributions on individual buildings, but offered no significant change to the layout of the city as a whole.

What emerged from the effort of Emperor Yongle (Zhu Di), Zhengtong, and Jiajing, from 1420 to 1553, was one of the largest and a most rigidly planned capital city in Chinese history. It was also the last attempt to build such a city in imperial China. In the resurgence of a vigorous Ming China in the late fourteen and early fifteenth century, the city layout reflected a grand and ambitious design, and a renewal of a classical tradition originated from antiquity.

Beijing displays a centrality and a symmetry in its overall composition (Boyd 1962; Liu 1980; Editorial Group 1983). A 7500 meter-long axis, running from north to south through the city, is the strongest organizing element of the whole plan (Fig. 7.1). An east-west axis intersects this main axis, defining the center of Beijing. This center is further defined locally by a rigidly symmetrical layout of palaces and,

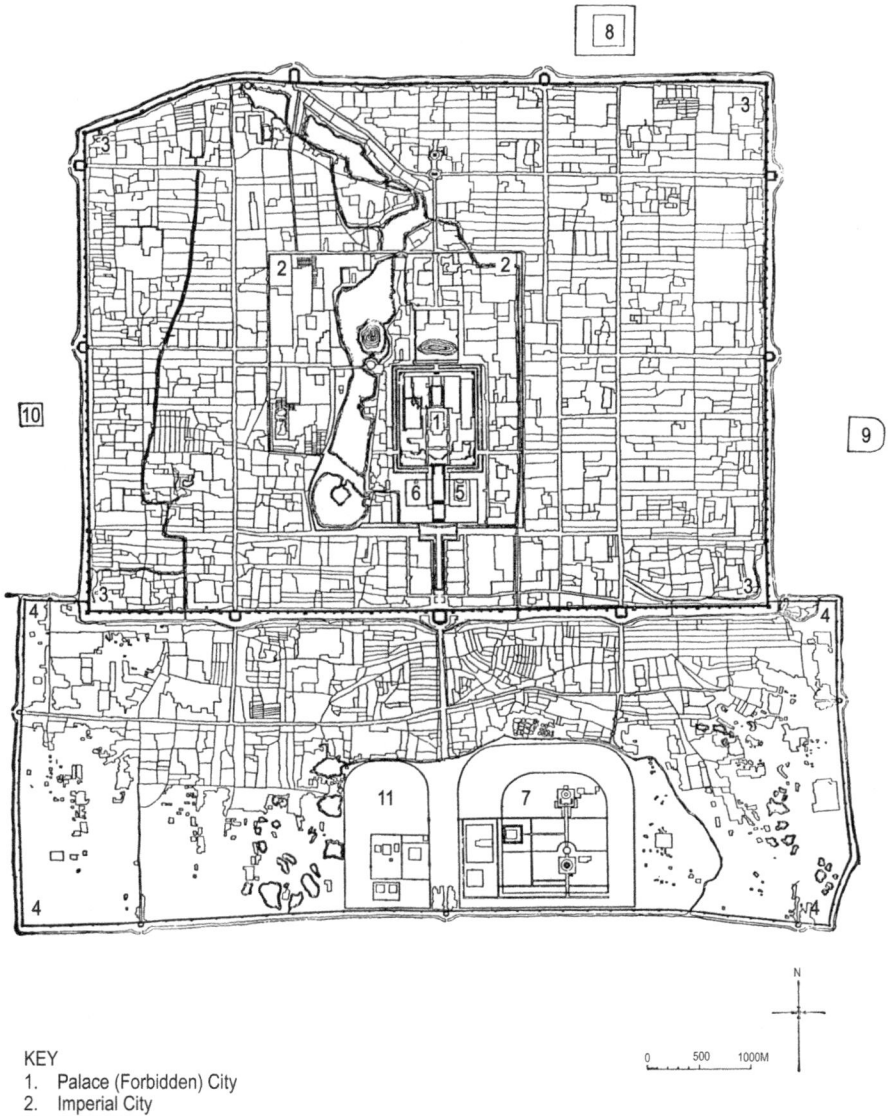

KEY
1. Palace (Forbidden) City
2. Imperial City
3. Capital City
4. Outer City
5. Temple of Ancestors
6. Altar of Land and Grain
7. Altar of Heaven
8. Altar of the Earth
9. Altar of the Sun
10. Altar of the Moon
11. Altar of Agriculture

Fig 7.1 Plan of Beijing in the Ming and Qing dynasties (1553-1750) (Adapted from Dunzhen, L. [1980]. *Zhongguo Gudai Jianzhushi*. Beijing: Zhongguo Jianzhu Gongye Chubanshe, p. 280)

at a larger scale, by a concentric layout of orthogonal "cities" of Beijing. They were, from inside out, Palace City (or Purple Forbidden City), Imperial City, and Capital City (i.e., *gongcheng* or *zijincheng*, *huangcheng*, and *ducheng*). The first was a city of palaces for the emperor and the royal family. The second was an extension of the first, and included royal gardens, altars, palaces for princes, eunuch offices, workshops, and warehouses. The third, the largest enclosure in a square shape, measuring 5350 by 6650 meters, was the capital city proper. It enclosed government ministries, residences of royal nobles and high officials, and all other urban population and urban functions. Attached to the southern wall of the Capital City was the Outer City, which enclosed a most vibrant commercial area of the capital, with a large population of merchants and artisans.

Spaces reserved for the emperor, the court, and the government dominated the city and together defined a symmetrical pattern of key structures. The large palace ensemble, included in the Palace and Imperial City, claimed not only the center of the city, but also its southern, frontal areas, extending its axial way to the central gate of the Capital City (Figs. 7.1 and 7.2). Sacrificial sites for the imperial court included, on the two sides of the axis in southern Imperial City, a Temple of Ancestors (*taimiao*) to the east and an Altar of Land and Grain (*shejitan*) to the west. Following the axis southward, in the Outer City, there were to the east and west two large sacrificial enclosures, Altar of Heaven (*tiantan*) and Altar of Mountains and Rivers (*shanchuantan*, which was later changed to Altar of Agriculture, *xiannongtan*). Other sacrificial sites, added by Emperor Jiajing, as mentioned, were the Altar of the Earth, the Son, and the Moon, to the north, east, and west of the Capital City. Most government offices, including the ministries and major boards and bureaus, were located on the two sides of the axis in the southern-central areas in the Capital City. There were, however, more such state offices in the east. These government offices were kept close to, although outside, the Palace and Imperial City.

Representing a Classical Tradition

Scholars in Chinese planning history have pointed out that this grand construction in early Ming China was an attempt, for the last time in history, to continue a long planning tradition, which was based on a classical cosmology and a symbolic layout outlined in *Zhou Li*, "the rites of Zhou dynasty" (Wright 1977; He 1985). Although the origin of this classic text is still unclear, it is generally agreed that the text as we know it now was rediscovered and rearranged in the late Western Han dynasty (202 BCE-9 CE) (He 1985; Kramers 1986). Since the content of the book was in full support of a new Confucian ideology developed by the Han emperors and scholars, one can look at the text in its re-structured form as a Han synthesis of earlier

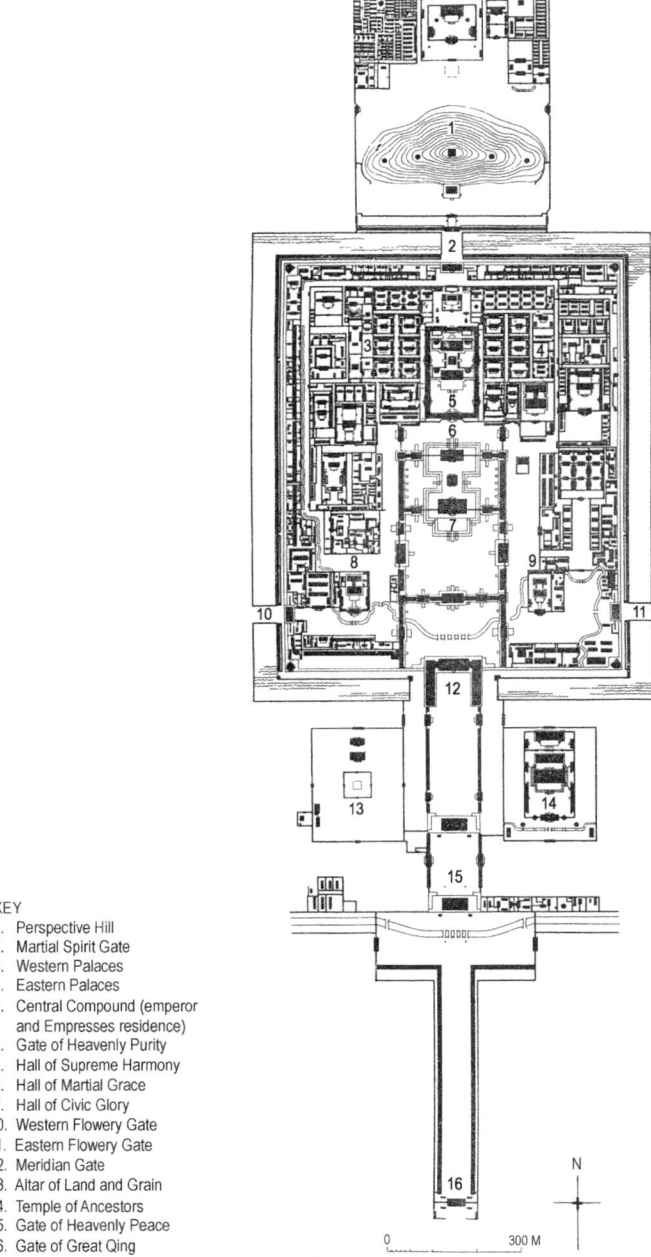

KEY
1. Perspective Hill
2. Martial Spirit Gate
3. Western Palaces
4. Eastern Palaces
5. Central Compound (emperor
   and Empresses residence)
6. Gate of Heavenly Purity
7. Hall of Supreme Harmony
8. Hall of Martial Grace
9. Hall of Civic Glory
10. Western Flowery Gate
11. Eastern Flowery Gate
12. Meridian Gate
13. Altar of Land and Grain
14. Temple of Ancestors
15. Gate of Heavenly Peace
16. Gate of Great Qing

Fig 7.2 Plan of the Forbidden City and its immediate surroundings (Adapted from Dunzhen, L. [1980]. *Zhongguo Gudai Jianzhushi.* Beijing: Zhongguo Jianzhu Gongye Chubanshe, pp. 282-3)

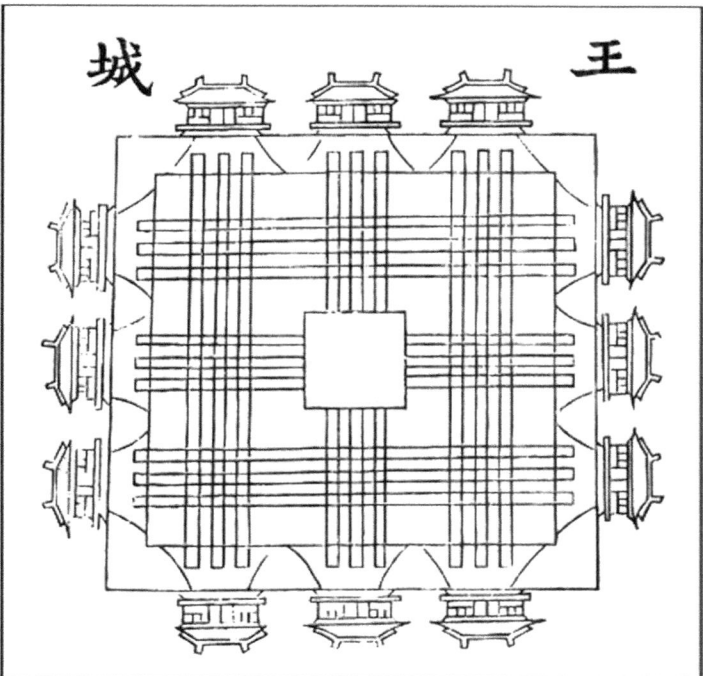

Fig 7.3 Planning scheme for an imperial capital according to *Kaogongji* (*Kaogongji*, collected in *Zhou Li* [202 BCE-9 CE at latest])

traditions.[1] In other words, *Zhou Li* can be analyzed, for its ideological content, as a product of the intellectual endeavor of the Han dynasty.

The section of *Zhou Li* that architectural historians have all referred to is *Kaogongji*, "records of construction," in which one finds the earliest articulation of a city planning theory in the Chinese classical treadition (Fig. 7.3). It says:

> The capital city shall be a square with each side nine li long and containing three gates. In the city, there shall be nine north-south and nine east-west streets. The north-south streets shall accommodate nine chariot-ways. Together they form a chessboard street pattern. On the left (east) of the city there shall be a Temple of Ancestors and on the right (west) an Altar of Land and Grain. In the front (south) there shall stand the emperor's audience halls and government ministries, in the rear (north) markets shall be located.[2]

---

[1] Obviously this is not a historical but an ideological approach to the text. The question we are asking here is not the origin of the text (in the mist of the antiquity and controversies) but the theoretical work it offered at a time of cultural and ideological construction, and its impact on subsequent dynasties. Wright (1977) clearly indicated and explored this approach.

[2] I have consulted various sources in making this English translation (Chen 1976; Wright 1977; Steinhardt 1990; Sit 1995).

There are debates concerning how much actual capital cities were influenced by this theory.[3] Some read and analyze the text closely, offer detailed geometrical plans, and argue that capital cities did follow the description. Others have disagreed, pointing out discrepancies between this model and the real cities, and suggesting that in reality new capital cities were built on specific land and social conditions, without dogmatic application of the ancient model. Although both offer valuable insights to the problem, the question of how close the cities were to the exact descriptions of this text seems misleading. Similarity and difference is a relative issue and the argument may not lead much further. A new approach is needed which views the text in terms of: (1) an abstract and relational pattern of disposition and configuration, not a precise, metrical, numerical, and positional geometry; and (2) intentions in an ideological and historical context. If one adopts this approach, the model appears indeed pertinent. In this intentional configuration, the square-ness, the numerical series based on number three, the orthogonal structure in relation to the four cardinal points, the implied domination of the north-south over the east-west orientation, the relative positioning regarding front and back as well as left and right, the importance of the southern front for the emperor's position, the implied two axes, and the suggested but not specified center, are the basic elements of an abstract pattern of this model. Other descriptions appear changeable and secondary, including: the length of the wall, the exact number of gates on each side, the number of streets in either direction, the width of the streets, the layers of walls, the disposition of zones and enclosures, and the specific position of certain functions, such as the market in relation to the palace.

Beijing, although not following all the specific descriptions, does follow the abstract and relational configuration of the model. The square-ness, the three gates on the southern front of the Capital City and the symmetrical positioning of the gates and courtyards in this frontal area, the assertive orthogonal structure in relation to the four cardinal points, the use of axes, the domination of the north-south axis, the articulation of the center, and the elaboration of the southern front of the center, were prominent in Beijing. The positioning of sacrificial sites for Ancestors, and for Land and Grain, were the only specific prescription closely followed in Beijing, and in fact in most other capital cities.[4] It represented a close application of one aspect of the ancient model. However, it was the abstract ordering of spatial relations of the city that projected the classical tradition in a totality.[5]

---

[3] A recent discussion on this issue can be found in Guo (1996). While Guo is skeptical of the dominant impact of this model in real practice, He (1985) maintains that there had indeed been major influences of the model in terms of specific and geometric arrangement. For recent research that has also placed importance on this model, see Steinhardt (1990).

[4] The paramount importance of the sacrifices to "Ancestors" and "Land and Grain" since antiquity (Zhou dynasty, c. 11th-third century BCE), the profound symbolic meaning of left and right, as well as East and West, being associated with the two gods, and the adjacency of the sites to the palace which facilitated an easier implementation in construction, seem to be some of the major reasons behind this consistent application of the classical prescription.

[5] I am suggesting here that despite the numerous interpretations of Beijing's symbolism, this overall disposition, in relation to *Zhou Li* and Han cosmological Confucianism, represented the essen-

A new reading of *Kaogongji* should also consider intentions behind this configuration. This necessitates a search beyond the descriptions in that paragraph, to look for an underlying ideology and its relation to the configuration of the city plan. Elsewhere, *Zhou Li* says:

> It is the sovereign alone who establishes the states of the empire, gives to the four quarters their proper positions, gives to the capital its form and to the fields their proper divisions. He creates the offices and apportions their functions in order to form a centre to which people may look.[6]

In other words, the emperor is the architect who shapes the human world in the form of an empire and an imperial system, and defines a spatial order with the four cardinal axes and a hierarchy of the offices, the capital, and the fields—that is, a hierarchy of center and periphery and, ultimately, the absolute center. This is a spatial, physical design of the city and the land, which represents and sustains a social and political order. But, beyond that, it also attains a cosmological meaning. *Zhou Li* also says:

> Here, where Heaven and Earth are in perfect accord, where the four seasons come together, where the winds and the rains gather, where the forces of Yin and Yang are harmonized, one builds a royal capital.

In other worlds, the capital of the empire is not only a social and political center but also a pivotal point that mediates and unifies the cosmos and the human world, sustaining a grand harmony of an entire universe. *Zhou Li* therefore offers not only a description of what a capital city should be, but also an ideology of kingship with a spatial diagram of the center, the capital, the empire, and the cosmos. Behind these ideas, if we pursue further, is a Confucian theory that, as imperial ideology, was promoted at the Han court.[7]

Based on a synthesis of earlier philosophies, ideologues of the Han court (202 BCE-9 CE) developed a theory of the universe, and of positions of heaven, humans, and the Chinese imperial system within it. This was developed largely by a court academician Dong Zhongshu (c. 179–104 BCE), an expert on early

---

tial ideas of its symbolic universe. The five agencies (wood, fire, earth, metal, water), four seasons and directions (blue dragon/East, red phoenix/South, white tiger/West, black turtle/North), three groups of stars (the middle of which is for heaven, corresponding to the palace on Earth for the king), two poles (Yin and Yang), elaborated this symbolic universe (rather heterogeneously) and were represented in the positioning, naming, and numerical specifications of major structures of the city and the palace (Jiang 1991). Local mythology (references to the figure Ne Zha) and prescriptions of fengshui (northern flows as negative forces) have also been claimed as influential in determining formal aspects of the city (Meyer 1991).

[6] This and the following translations are based on Wright (1977).

[7] On the ideology of Chinese planning theory, Wright's (1977) work remains the most pertinent. His reading of *Zhou Li* as part of Han Confucian ideology reflects a proper and insightful understanding of pre-Qin theories and Han synthesis in the history of Chinese philosophy. Guo's (1996) work also offered right intuition on this. Chinese planning theory and city symbolism should be understood in the context of Han Confucianism and subsequent development of imperial ideology. In the following paragraphs, I will expand Wright's (1977) work and explore the relations between ideology, diagram, and spatial construction.

Confucian classics such as the *Chunqiu* (*Spring and Autumn Annals*), and whose work was supported and promoted by Emperor Wudi (r. 141–87 BCE) (Fung 1953; Kung-chuan 1979; Kramers 1986). Articulated in his book, *Chunqiu Fanlu* or *Luxuriant Dew of the Spring and Autumn Annals*, Dong's theory was a synthesis of Yin-Yang cosmology and Confucianism, a universalist theory of nature and a moralist theory of human conduct and humanity: a synthesis based on an assumption of an interactive harmony between humans and nature. In this theory, *tian* (heaven, cosmos, nature) contains *yin* and *yang* forces, the interaction of which produces five agencies that are successively affirmative and negative: wood, fire, earth, metal, and water. Yin-Yang interaction and the continuous alternation of the five agencies produce a circulating temporal and spatial order (the four seasons, the four orientations, and the center), and all other events and entities of the universe. The endless flow of nature gives birth to and nurture humans. Humans are part of nature and follow, in a fundamental sense, the ways (*dao*) of heaven. As suggested by early Confucian teaching, these ways of heaven in humanity include: *ren* (love and humane-ness), *yi* (moral imperative and righteousness), *li* (ritual and culture), and *yue* (musical harmony).

Human nature contains basic goodness, but that doesn't bring about good conduct and a good society in itself. Cultivation and education are therefore important, and the king is there to ensure this, to fulfil the natural goodness and the ways of heaven. Dong says:

> Heaven has established mankind with natures containing basic goodness but unable to be good in themselves. Therefore it has established kingship to make them good. This is heaven's intention. (Fung 1953, 46)

Heaven therefore passes his mandate to the king to rule humans:

> King respectively carries forward the purpose of heaven above, and conforms to its decree and mandate. (Fung 1953, 49)

With this the king also models himself on the ways and principles of heaven. The king governs humans just like heaven coordinates the universe. The king's imperial system resembles the cosmos, and his centrality on Earth mirrors that of heaven above. He uses four approaches (beneficence, rewards, punishments, and executions) just like heaven's deployment of fours seasons and four orientations. His social world is composed of Yin-Yang differentiation manifested in the three archetypal hierarchies, that of king-minister, husband-wife, father-son. His moral order is based on five agencies, as reflected in the five ways of human virtues: *ren* (humaneness), *yi* (righteousness), *li* (ritual and culture), *zhi* (wisdom), and *xin* (faith). (Human virtues had been articulated in many different ways, although *ren* is always the central theme).

When *Zhou Li* and Dong Zhongshu's Confucian philosophy are read together as one theoretical development of the Han dynasty, one can identify a number of key characteristics. First, this Han theory represents *a holistic worldview* of man and nature in their mutual interaction. With this interaction, the theory of a good human society attains an organic, naturalist, and cosmological basis. Secondly, this theory is based upon a universal *moralism* which sanctions a moral rightness for the king-ship and the hierarchical order that the king establishes. Thirdly, following this way of theorization, the holistic worldview gives rise to a sense of totality of everything, including that of the imperial system: in other words, it leads to a form of political *absolutism*. Fourthly, there is a *centralism* in this theory of the throne, the capital, and the empire. The monarch not only resides and rules at the center, he establishes and embodies the center: he is the center, the ultimate contact point between humans and nature, the earth and heaven. Fifthly, this ideological centralism is then embod-ied in *a spatial centralism*, a spatial hierarchical order based on an articulated cen-trality, marked and constructed in the form of the palace and the capital city. Sixthly, this theory is embodied in a spatial construction as a *theoretical diagram*, which plays a pivotal role. In abstract terms, the theory already involves a diagram, a conceptual-spatial disposition of heaven, the Earth, and humans, with the sovereign as the center. In mapping this onto a geographical surface, a clearer configuration arises. The center, the two axes, the four quarters, and the hierarchical order, emerge as basic constitutive elements of the archetypal configuration, the core of the ideal city described in *Kaogongji*.

Translating the Confucian ideology into the form of a capital city, this theoretical diagram implies *three totalities*. The holistic world is the first totality. Under one sovereign, the human social world, in the form of the imperial system, is another totality. When humans are following the ways of the universe, the first totality necessitates the second. There is then a third totality: the form of the city. As the seat of the sovereign at the center of the empire, who builds the total imperial system under the totality of heaven, the spatial form of the capital also requires a grand and complete totality. "Heaven," "Earth," and the sovereign's capital city: their orders naturally accord to each other, and the totalitarian composition of one implies that of the other. A Chinese capital city therefore should adopt a thorough and complete spatial order, with one center and one hierarchical disposition.

As later history testifies, Han Confucian theory was followed closely and became the predominant imperial ideology of all subsequent dynasties. Their capitals, although different from each other in specific form and in positioning of certain functions, shared an underlying configuration, which can be traced to the theoretical diagram of Han Confucianism. In the early fifteenth century, amidst the resurgence of political power and a revival of classical culture, the Ming court built a new Chinese empire amongst the development of a Neo-Confucianism initiated in the Song dynasty. The Ming orthodox ideology, consciously developed by Emperor Yongle (Zhu Di), followed closely a rationalist development of Confucian learning (Chan 1988). Beijing, in this historical context, assumes not only a representation of the classical tradition, but also a new layer of ideological discourse.

Adding a Layer of Neo-Confucianism

Initiated by scholars in the late Tang dynasty (618–906 CE) and thoroughly developed in the Song (960–1279 CE), Neo-Confucianism combined disparate philosophical traditions including yin-yang cosmology and Buddhism into Confucian learning, and developed a metaphysical theory of ethics, human nature, and personal cultivation. The concrete and eminent result of the new learning was a promotion of four ancient texts as Confucian classics (the Four Books, including *Great Learning*, *Doctrine of the Mean*, *Analects of Confucius*, and *Works of Mancuis*), and a development of comprehensive commentaries on them. Zhu Xi (1130–1200) was the main figure that contributed most to this and was revered as the intellectual authority of the new Confucian learning.

Since the Han dynasty, the promotion of Confucianism as imperial ideology and moral orthodoxy involved a nomination of Confucian texts as the basis of a nationwide examination for recruiting officials, and as primary material for education at schools. Following this tradition, the Yuan court (1260–1368) in 1313 canonized Zhu Xi's compilation of the Four Books as standard texts for the examination (Theodore de Bary 1981; Feng 1985). In the same vein, the first Ming emperor Zhu Yuanzhang in 1384 restored the examination system and the status of Zhu Xi's Four Books (Theodore de Bary 1981; Wan 1991).

The next emperor Zhu Di was more active in promoting Neo-Confucianism. An ambitious emperor who altered the geo-political map of the empire, Zhu Di was also concerned with his role and image as a Confucian ruler, and a patron and teacher of Confucian learning. In the twenty busy years of his reign, between many of his grand projects including the building of Beijing, Zhu Di actively promoted Song Confucianism as orthodox ideology (Chan 1988; Franke 1988; Mao 1991). He prescribed the commentaries of Zhu Xi and other Song scholars as standard texts for the examination in 1404. He wrote in 1409 a famous essay *Shengxue Xinfa* ("on the cultivation of mind-heart in the sage's learning"), articulating his vision of a sage ruler and of moral cultivation for all his subjects. In 1414, he ordered the compilation of Zhu Xi and other Song scholars' commentaries and writings on human nature, which was published in 1417 as *Wujing Sishu Daquan* (great compendium of the five classics and the four books) and *Xingli Daquan* (great compendium of the philosophy of human nature). To secure his position as a Confucian ruler who concerns scholarship, he had also ordered many large-scale compilations, which resulted in the production of some largest books in Chinese history, such as the eminent *Yongle Dadian* (great literary encyclopaedia of the Yongle reign), as completed in 1470.

As "author" of all these projects in the two critical decades of his reign, Zhu Di inserted his intention and personal character in these projects. There was above all an ambitious vision of a new and restored Chinese empire. There was a resolute determination, and a dynamic approach that coordinated resources, to materialize these grand projects. Underlying all that, there was also a rigor and a rationalism in political affairs and in the ideas promoted in theoretical and moral discourses. One can identify two sides of his overall effort: an "external" work in strategic expansion, geopolitical repositioning and bureaucratic centralization; and an "internal" work in cultivating an intellectual culture and an imperial ideology in his own writings and the compilation of classics, Song treatises, and encyclopaedias. The political rationalism of the first and the rigorous moralist Confucian values promoted in the second were mutually supportive and correlated each other. They represented the vision of the emperor and an overall outlook in the historical and intellectual framework of the early fifteenth century.

As one of Zhu Di's products, Beijing stood in between the "external" political work and the "internal" ideological effort. Being a complex product, it exists simultaneously in several of the emperor's endeavors. It was part of the geopolitical effort, part of the centralist state institution, and, in terms of formal, symbolic representation, part of the ideological effort. All these, in turn, were reflected and accommodated in the capital city.

This overall imperial system, political as well as theoretical, developed in the early Ming dynasty and crystallized in Beijing in 1420 (with some additions up to 1553) and was maintained for the rest of the imperial history until 1911. Song Neo-Confucianism was always upheld as imperial orthodoxy for moral teaching and theoretical discourse (Fairbank 1973a, b; Mote 1988a). In fact, Zhu Xi's commentaries were enshrined as standard texts for examinations for the entire history in late imperial China, from 1313 to 1905 (Feng 1985). At the same time, parallel to this ideological stability was the stability of state institution, patterns of social life, and the spatial form of Beijing. And, over such a long historical time, the relations between them must have grown stronger, forming a consolidated web that strengthened the overall fabric of the city.

The argument is that Neo-Confucianism, a new form of imperial ideology upheld by the founding emperor of Beijing, and by all the subsequent emperors of the Ming and Qing dynasties, must have left significant traces in the form and the use of Beijing.[8] Before looking more closely at the interrelationship between ideology and the layout of Beijing, let us review briefly this ideology first. The word "Neo-Confucianism" is in fact a modern Western invention. It refers broadly to the whole orthodox intellectual development of late imperial China, but also specifically the initial and central stream of this development, the Learning of the Way or *Daoxue* as it was originated from the Song. *Daoxue* concerned itself with a comprehensive and systematic reinterpretation of classical Confucian moral philosophy as in the works of Confucius, Mencius, and other masters.[9] Its major work was a metaphysical theorization of Mencius' idealist interpretation of human nature. The metaphysical notions in Neo-Confucianism, on the other hand, were derived from the classical Yin-Yang cosmology and Confucian scholars' interpretations attached to the book

[8] The relationship between the development of Neo-Confucianism and the making of Beijing was insightfully though briefly suggested by Wright (1977). Such a significant relationship, however, is hardly explored in the existing scholarship on Beijing and on Chinese cities.

[9] The following introduction on Neo-Confucianism and relevant streams of Chinese thought are based on Fung (1952), Feng (1985), and Peterson (1998).

Yi Jing (the Book of Changes), which offered ideas of universal principle and notions of reason. Neo-Confucianism was also influenced by Mahayana Buddhism and its Midyamika and Chan (Zen) schools, bringing into the new learning a rich stream of notions on "mind" and "nature," and ways of metaphysical abstraction. Neo-Confucianism's relation with Dong Zhongshu's work at the Han court is not clear: without borrowing directly from Dong Zhongshu, it nevertheless redeveloped a cosmological ethics that supported the position of the sage ruler in a more sophisticated form of articulation. Neo-Confucianism inherited the essentials of moral teachings of Confucius and Mencius, and Dong's ethical political theory, although its framework was more broadly based, and its conceptualization more subtle and abstract.

Early Confucian scholars have used notions of *dao* (the way) in expanding the principles displayed in the diagrams of Yin-Yang cosmology in the book, *Yi Jing*. Referring to a rational and nameable principle in natural and human realities, this Confucian *dao* is different from that in Daoism in the works of Laozi and Zhuangzi (who employed this word for an unnameable oneness and nothingness). In the Confucian tradition, rectification of name, that is, assuring correct behavior according to one's position is essential. To rectify morality and conduct is to insure the Confucian way be properly established and followed. In the late Tang dynasty, scholars complained the loss of the Tradition of the Way (*daotong*) and called for a new study of Confucianism, a new Learning of the Way or *Daoxue*. In the following Song dynasty, *Daoxue* finally achieved a substantial development in the works of Chen Hao (1032–85) and Chen Yi (1033–1108), who each respectively initiated an idealist and a rationalist line of thought in the following centuries.

Along the idealist line, Chen Hou developed the crucial Confucian notion *ren* (love and humane-ness) into a metaphysical concept, suggesting that *ren* is a union of man with the universe, which also implies that there is a humane-ness in all things in the universe. This was followed by Lu Jiuyuan's (1139–93) proposition that the universe is my mind and my mind is the universe. In the late Ming dynasty, Wang Shouren (Wang Yangming, 1473–1529) arrived at an extreme point of this line of thinking, in his thesis that mind is nature and reason, and in his summary of the whole teaching of human cultivation (for the person, the family, the state, and the world as expressed in the classic, *Great Learning*), in terms of "reaching the inner moral conscientiousness" (*zhi liang zhi*), which exists in all individuals.

On the rationalist line, Chen Yi worked on the notion of *dao* as laws and principles of the universe, and developed the notion of *li* as metaphysical reason or principle, at an abstract level above matter and substance of all things. Zhu Xi, following Chen Yi's concept of *li*, established a comprehensive interpretation of Confucian moral philosophy and offered substantial commentaries on Confucian classics. In the late Song dynasty, it was the Chen-Zhu school of thought that was most influential in the academic circle, which was promoted in the following Yuan, Ming, and Qing dynasties as imperial orthodoxy (known as *Chen Zhu Lixue* or *Song Ming Lixue*). In the late Ming, when Zhu Xi's rationalist school was firmly established in the official circle, the idealist and intuitive thought of Wang Shouren became influential among scholars, who often used this as a basis to critique the rationalist orthodoxy. However, for the imperial court and the standard examination, the position of Zhu Xi remained unchallenged.

Zhu Xi's central concept is *li*, translated often as "principle" and "reason" (Fung 1953; Feng 1985). *Li* is metaphysical, above the world of matter. *Li* is also concrete, existing in all specific things and events. The totality of *li* is a "supreme ultimate" (*taiji*), which is also an "ultimate nothingness" (*wuji*). *Li* or reason exists in all things in their concrete form, but also exists in the supreme ultimate, just like the moon exists in all infinite reflections in lakes, rivers, and oceans but also exists out there in itself (*yuyin wanchuan*). *Li* as reason is also referred to as *dao* (in the Confucian sense). While there is *li* in the metaphysical world, there is also *qi* (air, either, energy, flow) in the physical world. While *li* informs the metaphysical world with *xing* (nature, properties), *qi* informs the physical world with concrete shapes and forms. The relationship between *li* and *qi*, between abstract principle and material flow, is a focus of attention and debate. Zhu Xi emphasized the interdependence between the two: one cannot exist without the other. On the process of cosmogony, Zhu Xi says that active principles inform active material flow which creates Yang, while passive principles inform passive flow which creates Yin. Yin and Yang interact and create Five Agencies which in turn produce ten thousand things.

On human nature, Zhu Xi says there is also *li* (principle) and *xing* (nature and properties) in human beings. Human nature, or *li* and *xing* within humans, is fundamentally good. The endowment of *qi* (air, flow, material qualities), however, is different, which makes difference in character and conduct in actual persons. The sage is one that has pure endowment which reveals inner *xing* and the fundamental good. The unwise and unkind are those that have impure endowment which covers the inner good. This inner *xing*, as the fundamental and metaphysical good, is *ren*, love, kindness, and humane-ness, the central concept of Confucian teaching. In saying that *li* and *xing* in humanity is *ren*, Zhu Xi's theory reaches an absolute definition of his outlook: human nature is kindness, is humane-ness.

On political theory, Zhu Xi says that there is also *li* in governing the state. This is *li* of the sage ruler, the Way of the Sage Ruler, which is rulership based on the inner good, humane-ness, and benevolence. Zhu Xi here follows Mencius' moral idealism on the inner good, and on separation between the Way of the Sage Ruler and that of the Powerful Ruler, between *wangdao* and *badao*. Mencius says that the former uses virtue to exercise kindness whereas the later uses power to exercise false kindness. Song scholars including Zhu Xi all suggested that, during their time, the Way of the Sage Ruler was lost, and gone was the tradition of the Confucian Way, and, it was time to re-establish the tradition. What Zhu Xi and other Song scholars had done in effect was a metaphysical and ontological articulation of Mencius' classical thesis.

The consequence of this argument, for theory of human nature and that of political philosophy, is an approach to cultivation for everyone and for the emperor. In Zhu Xi's system, cultivation is a process of purifying *qi* (air and material qualities), to reveal the inner good and humane-ness, so as to become a sage, whether as an ordinary person or as an emperor. Zhu Xi advocates two inseparable paths of cultivation: "investigation of things" and "exercise of reverence," the first for knowing reasons and principles of things, the second for an enlightenment to see inner nature as good and humane. With them, human being shall be able to see the supreme ultimate, the rational, and the humane. For the emperor, this is the way of cultivation that will enable him to become a sage ruler.

Moral idealism in Zhu Xi's Neo-Confucian theory, for sage's rulership at the court, had a certain difficulty in conceptual articulation as well as in practical reality. This difficulty centered on a tension between moral idealism and political realism, between the aspiration to uphold the ideal of humane-ness and the need to use resources and power in reality. In Chinese philosophical terms, it was a question of a relationship between *li* (principle) and *shi* (propensity in the flow of reality), which was regarded as an extension of the relationship between *li* (principle) and *qi* (material flow). Later Neo-Confucian scholars such as Wang Fuzhi (1619–90) offered a subtle and complex articulation on inextricable relations between *li* and *shi*, between moral idealism and political realism (McMorran 1975). In Zhu Xi's theory, the *li-qi* dialectic already opened a path to this later development. In reality, and in political practice of the imperial court especially, this was always a problem and had been dealt with in a difficult synthesis of the two approaches, as manifested in the simultaneous use of Confucianism and Legalism, an expressive moral idealism and a latent theory of power practice.

How is this theory, as imperial ideology, related to the spatial arrangement and formal layout of Beijing? Two aspects can be identified: an intentional projection of the ideal of a sage rulership (*wangdao*) on the formal plan of the city; and a synthesis of sage and powerful rulership (*wangdao* and *badao*), of *li* and *shi*, of a formal representation and an actual spatial practice.

(1) *A formal representation of wangdao.* That the emperor should be a sage ruler, and all humans should follow him and follow ways of Heaven and cultivate themselves as sages, was the core content of Han and Song Confucianism. Its implications for Beijing were pervasive in all spheres of social life in real space and ideological discourse in formal representation. For social practice in space, the most eminent systems included the nation-wide examination based on Confucian classics. A twice-monthly reciting of Sacred Edicts on Confucian ethics in all cities, towns, and villages was another significant practice for imparting orthodox values to the population. The formation of the neighbourhood-unit across the cities and countryside, for moral supervision and practical control, was another prominent system. For the emperor, there was also an institutionalization of Confucian values at the court, which helped cultivate an ideal sage ruler in every emperor. The complex rules and codes at the court imposed a frame of correct behavior of all including the emperor himself. His daily life was closely observed and recorded, and systematically compiled in the imperial archive (*qijuzhu*). There was a system of remonstration by officials and scholars to the emperor (*jinjian*) as well as a program of regular lectures on Confucian classics delivered by scholars to the emperor. The emperors themselves, on the other hand, participated in these discursive practices. They were, at least superficially, active in cultivating their own role and image as a Confucian sage ruler, through their own Imperial Edits and other writings, as well as their own studies. Qing emperor Kangxi is often revered as a sage ruler. He is

certainly among the most eminent in pursuing a disciplined self-cultivation and in his life-long enquiry on Song Confucianism (Spence 1974; Metzger 1977; Chan 1988; Gao 1995).

These practices, however, were already programmed into social institutions. They were no longer ideology in an internal or semantic sense. Their spatial patterns were also scattered and dispersed. A direct relationship between ideology and the city resides most directly and clearly, as explored above, in a symbolic representation on the plan of the city as a whole. As noted, Beijing, as a product of the early Ming emperors, represented the core values of Confucian ideology developed from the Han, in the intellectual milieu of Neo-Confucian discourse strongly promoted by the emperors. The new and the old Confucian ideologies overlapped closely at this juncture, on the layout of the city. Zhu Di's projection of Neo-Confucian ideas was in the frame of the classical planning model. However, beyond that, elements developed in the new historical context were also added. The new contribution resides, one could argue, in the particular articulation of the Chen-Zhu school of Song Confucianism. Ideas of universal reason, and a rigorous rationalism in moral cultivation and political governance, lend a particular emphasis on a total and totalitarian composition of the whole city. If this tendency was already there in the classical tradition, then in the ideological climate of the early fifteenth century, it was pushed much further. A stronger determination to project the sacred position of the sage ruler, and a total domination of this position in the city, were very obvious on the city plan, and was carried out to the extreme point unseen before in Chinese history. The large complex at the center, the uncompromising assertion of the axis over almost the entire city, and, in association with that, the relentless projection of an imposing image of a gate and a palace along the axial way, testify to this rather clearly. The ideal image of the sage ruler, sacred and dignified, is well represented and embodied in this symbolic form (Figs. 7.1 and 7.2).

(2) *A synthesis of wangdao and badao, of li and shi, of a formal representation and a spatial practice.* Zhu Di in his *Shengxue Xinfa* made it clear that as he was to follow strict disciplines of moral cultivation as a sage ruler, his ministers were also expected to follow and assist the emperor loyally, and all his subjects were to follow the Confucian teaching of proper conduct according to their proper position (Chan 1988). In making himself a sage ruler, Zhu Di was asserting a perfect hierarchy where he was, and ought to be, at the top, which affirmed the totalitarian and authoritarian system of the state. Moral idealism offered a rationalization of the state, which leads to a political realism. Further, the idea of *li* as principle and reason, lent a spirit and attitude of rigor to all things carried out by the imperial court, which added a quality of severity to the exercise of authority, as best manifested in the first Ming emperor Hongwu (Zhu Yuanzhang) and the Qing Emperor Yongzheng and Qianlong.

In this process, the idealistic theory of Confucianism came to be associated with the realistic theory of power and authority in Legalism, a situation which required the imperial court to follow both Confucianism and Legalism, in order to maintain and operate the imperial system. On the one hand, there was a need to uphold the Confucian ideal of the good and the humane and the justified hierarchy of the imperial system. On the other hand, there was a need to operate the system and to exercise power and authority as advised in Legalism. The difficulty in this synthesis was fully appreciated and reflected upon by Wang Fuzhi, the Neo-Confucian scholar in the late Ming and early Qing dynasties. Wang contemplated the problem in terms of the relationship between *li* and *shi*, between moral reason and political propensity. He strove to maintain a balance and synthesis between them, and suggested that there is no moral reason above reality and no political superiority without moral reason (McMorran 1975; Jullien 1995). Wang was dealing with a real problem facing the imperial court, and his contrived argument reflects a deep and acute reading of the problem amongst the elite and officials in late imperial China.

In relation to that, and probably under the influence of these debates and conscious efforts as well, there was a new historical development that integrated the two principles more closely. A latent thread in both Neo-Confucian moralism and Legalist realism became more apparent. Since the opening of the Ming court in the late fourteenth century, the two approaches came to relate more closely in the rise of a generic rationalism in all aspects of life and work of the court. The abolishing of prime ministership in 1380 by the first Ming emperor Hongwu (Zhu Yuanzhang), which provided the emperor with direct and absolute power over the entire bureaucracy, and the subsequent strengthening of central authority in the reign of Yongle (Zhu Di) in the Ming and of Yongzheng in the Qing, were the key moments of this development. The ongoing Legalist practice, the rise of rationalist thought in Zhu Xi's Neo-Confucianism, and the ascendancy of absolutism in the structure of imperial authority in Ming Qing China were inevitably related and became aspects of one development.

In formal and spatial embodiment, this extension from *li* to *shi*, from Confucian moral theory to the operation of power, leads us to consider political functioning of the sage ruler at the center of the capital, above the government and the empire. It leads us to consider not only the symbolic representation of Confucian ideals, but also the functional exercise of Legalist principles. Beijing has to be examined both as a symbolic form and a functional space, as a representation of *li* and as an accommodation of the exercise of *shi*. Conceiving Beijing as a form of sage leadership (*wangdao*) and a space of political domination (*badao*), a central argument in this research can be outlined. While the formal layout of the whole city plan represented the idealist Confucian ideology, the actual space in reality, centering on the palace and extending outward to the city and the provinces of the empire, acted as a latent and constitutive realm for the exercise of imperial power and domination. Corresponding to the duality of *li* and *shi*, *wangdao* and *badao*, Confucianism and Legalism, is that of symbolic representation and functional practice, of a formal plan and an actual space.

References

Boyd, A. (1962). *Chinese architecture and town planning, 1500 BC-AD 1911*. London: Alec Tiranti.

Chan, H. (1988). The Chien-wen, Yung-lo, Hung-his, and Hsuan-te reigns. In F. Mote & D. Twitchett (Eds.), *The Cambridge history of China, The Ming dynasty, 1368–1644, Part 1* (Vol. 7, pp. 182–304). Cambridge: Cambridge University Press.

Chen, C. (1976). The growth of Peiching. *Ekistics, 253*, 377–383.

Chen, J. (1991). Yingzhong rui huangdi Zhu Qizhen (the emperor Zhu Qizhen). In X. Daling & W. Tianyou (Eds.), *Mingchao shiliu di (the sixteen emperors of the Ming dynasty)* (pp. 117–136). Beijing: Zijincheng Chubanshe.

Editorial Group. (1983). *Zhongguo Jianzhushi (a history of Chinese architecture)*. Beijing: Zhongguo Jianzhu Gongye Chubanshe.

Fairbank, J. (1973a). State and society under the Ming. In J. Fairbank, E. Reischauer, & A. Craig (Eds.), *East Asia: Tradition and transformation* (pp. 188–193). London: George Allen & Unwin.

Fairbank, J. (1973b). Traditional China at its height under the Ch'ing. In J. Fairbank, E. Reischauer, & A. Craig (Eds.), *East Asia: Tradition and transformation* (pp. 228–234). London: George Allen & Unwin.

Farmer, E. (1976). *Early Ming government: The evolution of dual capitals*. Cambridge: Harvard University Press.

Feng, Y. (1985). *Zhongguo zhexue jianshi (a short history of Chinese philosophy)*. Beijing: Beijingdaxue Chubanshe.

Franke, W. (1988). Historical writing during the Ming. In F. Mote & D. Twitchett (Eds.), *The Cambridge history of China, The Ming dynasty, 1368–1644, Part 1* (Vol. 7, pp. 726–782). Cambridge: Cambridge University Press.

Fung, Y. (1952). *A history of Chinese philosophy, Vol. 1* (trans: D. Bodde). Princeton: Princeton University Press.

Fung, Y. (1953). A history of Chinese philosophy, *Vol. 2, The period of classical learning* (trans: D. Bodde). London: George Allen & Unwin.

Gao, X. (1995). *Kangyongqian Sandi Tongzhi Sixiang Yanjiu (a study on the thought of rulership of the three emperors: Kangxi, Yongzheng, and Qianlong)*. Beijing: Zhongguo Remin Daxue Chubanshe.

Guo, H. (1996). Guanyu Zhongguo gudai chengshishi de tanhua (on the history of Chinese traditional cities: An interview). *Jianzhushi (architect), 70*, 62–68.

Guo, H. (1997). Ming Qing Beijing (Beijing in the Ming and Qing dynasties). *Jianzhushi (architect), 78*, 76–81.

He, Y. (1985). *Kaogongji Yingguo Zhidu Yanjiu (a study of the planning system of Kaogongji)*. Beijing: Zhongguo Jianzhu Gongye Chubanshe.

Jiang, S. (1991). Wuxing, sixiang, sanyuan, liangji: Zijincheng (five agencies, four quarters, three constellations, two poles: The forbidden city). In Y. G. Qingdai (Ed.), *Qingdai Gongshi Tanwei (studies on the history of the Qing court)* (pp. 251–260). Beijing: Zijincheng Chubanshe.

Jullien, F. (1995). *The propensity of things: Towards a history of efficacy in China* (trans: Janet Lloyd). Cambridge: MIT Press.

Kramers, R. (1986). The development of the Confusian schools. In D. Twitchett & M. Loewe (Eds.), *The Cambridge history of China, The Chi'in and Han empires, 221- BC-AD 220* (Vol. 1, pp. 747–765). Cambridge: Cambridge University Press.

Kung-chuan, H. (1979). *A history of Chinese political thought, Vol. 1* (trans: Janet Lloyd). Princeton: Princeton University Press.

Liu, D. (1980). *Zhongguo gudai jianzhushi (a history of traditional Chinese architecture)*. Beijing: Zhongguo Jianzhu Gongye Chubanshe.

Mao, P. (1991). Chengzu wen huangdi Zhu Di (the emperor Zhu Di). In D. Xu & T. Wang (Eds.), *Mingchao Shiliu Di (the sixteen emperors of the Ming dynasty)* (pp. 55–89). Beijing: Zijincheng Chubanshe.

McMorran, I. (1975). Wang Fu-chih and the neo-Confucian tradition. In W. Theodore de Bary (Ed.), *The unfolding of neo-Confucianism* (pp. 413–467). New York: Columbia University Press.

Metzger, T. (1977). *Escape from predicament: Neo-Confucianism and China's evolving political culture*. New York: Columbia University Press.

Meyer, J. (1991). *The dragons of Tiananmen: Beijing as a sacred city*. Columbia: University of South Carolina Press.

Mote, F. (1988a). Introduction. In F. Mote & D. Twitchett (Eds.), *The Cambridge history of China, The Ming dynasty, 1368–1644, Part 1* (Vol. 7, pp. 1–10). Cambridge: Cambridge University Press.

Mote, F. (1988b). The Ch'eng-hua and Hung-Chih reigns, 1465–1505. In F. Mote & D. Twitchett (Eds.), *The Cambridge history of China, The Ming dynasty, 1368–1644, part 1* (Vol. 7, pp. 343–402). Cambridge: Cambridge University Press.

Peterson, W. (1998). Confucian learning in late Ming thought. In D. Twitchett & F. Mote (Eds.), *The Cambridge history of China, The Ming dynasty, 1368–1644, Part 2* (Vol. 8, pp. 708–788). Cambridge: Cambridge University Press.

Qingdai, G. (Ed.). (n.d.). *Qingdai gongshi tanwei (studies on the history of the Qing court)*. Beijing: Zijincheng Chubanshe.

Sit, V. (1995). *Beijing: The nature and planning of a Chinese capital city*. Chichester: John Wiley & Sons.

Spence, J. (1974). *Emperor of China: Self-portrait of Kang-his*. New York: Alfred A. Knopf.

Steinhardt, N. (1990). *Chinese imperial city planning*. Honolulu: University of Hawaii Press.

Theodore de Bary, W. (1981). *Neo-Confucian orthodoxy and the learning of the mind-and-heart*. New York: Columbia University Press.

Waldron, A. (1983). The problem of the Great Wall of China. *Harvard Journal of Asiatic Studies, 43*(2), 643–663.

Wan, M. (1991). Kaiguo huangdi Zhu Yanzhang (the founding emperor Zhu Yuanzhang). In D. Xu & T. Wang (Eds.), *Mingchao Shiliu Di (the sixteen emperors of the Ming dynasty)* (pp. 5–40). Beijing: Zijincheng Chubanshe.

Wright, A. (1977). The cosmology of the Chinese city. In G. William Skinner (Ed.), *The city in late imperial China* (pp. 33–73). Stanford: Stanford University Press.

Zhu, J. (2004). *Chinese spatial strategies: Imperial Beijing, 1420–1911*. London: Routledge Curzon.

Zhu, J. (2014a). Empire of signs of empire: Scale and statehood in Chinese culture. *Harvard Design Magazine, 38*, 74–79.

Zhu, J. (2014b). Political and epistemological scales in Chinese urbanism. *Harvard Design Magazine, 37*, 132–141.

Zhu, J. (2016). Ten thousand things: Notes on a construct of largeness, multiplicity, and moral statehood. In C. Lee (Ed.), *Common frameworks: Rethinking the developmental city in China* (pp. 34–45). Cambridge: Harvard University Graduate School of Design.

Chapter 8
Military Considerations and Colonial Town Planning: France and New France in the Seventeenth Century

Gilbert A. Stelter

Abstract This chapter provides a historical account of the grid-pattern design of the French *bastide* towns as the most significant model for France's New World expansion during the seventeenth century. Endowed with both political and agricultural functions by making agricultural expansion possible through the political process of colonization, the author considers the classical roots of this urban model during the European Renaissance and then examines its use in France and New France as a military strategy of fortified urban design. The chapter concludes with a discussion of the territorial conflicts between France and England during the mid-eighteenth century, which had disastrous effects for France's colonial settlements in North America.

Keywords France · New France · *Bastides* · Plantation towns · Grid · Agro-villes · Colonization · Fortifications

Towns played a key role in the imperial expansion of France, both in Europe and in the New World. In one respect, France's colonial towns were peripheral outposts of an urbanization process that changed the structural character of the European urban system in the early modern era. In another, the way in which these towns were used as agencies of territorial occupation and settlement in the New World was largely

This chapter was originally published as Stelter, G. (1993). "Military Considerations and Colonial Town Planning: France and New France in the Seventeenth Century." In R. Bennett (Ed.), *Settlements in the Americas: Cross-Cultural Perspectives* (pp. 210–237). Copyright © 1993 by the Associated University Presses. Reproduced with permission of Associated University Presses.

G. A. Stelter (✉)
University of Guelph, Guelph, ON, Canada
e-mail: gstelter@uoguelph.ca

© Springer International Publishing AG, part of Springer Nature 2018
R. Rose-Redwood, L. Bigon (eds.), *Gridded Worlds: An Urban Anthology*,
https://doi.org/10.1007/978-3-319-76490-0_8

141

derived from the practice that European states such as France developed in securing and expanding their homelands.

The term *urbanization* is used here to describe urban change that was a product of *structural* changes in the system. This differs from the most widely used demographic concept of urbanization, that of population concentration, the growth of numbers of urban places, and especially the rise in the percentage of urban residents to the total population. Instead the structural aspects of urbanization will be examined here in which change was reflected in the redistribution of population among cities in a developing hierarchy. This change was the product of decision-making of various kinds, such as those of the controllers of capital and their investment behavior, or, what is particularly significant, that of the state and its political decisions. The thrust of these political decisions in Europe was the growth of the nation-state and the control of new empires. The implications for the developing urban system were threefold: first, larger cities grew enormously if they were the main administrative centers—Paris, London, Amsterdam, and Madrid. Second, those places that were ports serving the colonies became more important. At the same time, hundreds of smaller European places declined, for other factors of growth were weak. Inland trading, ecclesiastical, and manufacturing centers did not cash in on the boom created by government and overseas trade. Third, hundreds of new towns were planted to consolidate contiguous frontiers and a smaller number were created overseas as agents of imperial expansion (de Vries 1984).

An important element of the state's role in the structural aspects of urbanization was the use of its military arm in determining the pattern of settlement. Decision makers in Western Europe were well aware of this tradition in the histories of the countries for the physical evidence still surrounded them in many communities. For example, the Roman army had created many of the still existing towns and cities. In some cases these had originated as colonies of discharged veterans and were designed to be showcases of Roman urban life—equated with civilized life—as at Colchester in England, Lyon in France, and Merida in Spain. Or they began as legionary fortresses, such as Chester and York in England and Strasbourg, Bonn, and Cologne in the Rhineland (Kain and Norris 1982; Watkins 1983). This military tradition in town building was maintained through the medieval period and into the early modern era in France and England.

This military tradition had a major bearing on the nature of early Canadian settlement. While Canadians like to picture themselves as a peaceful people and their country as the product of gradual evolution rather than of violent revolution,[1] Canadian communities were created in what could be called the Second Hundred Years War between France and England in the seventeenth and eighteenth centuries. Decisions about where a town would be located, what its function would be, how it would be shaped, and what kind of people would live in it were often made in the context of military considerations. The decision-makers were usually military

---

[1] For example, Northrup Frye suggests that the Canadian tradition "might well be called a quest for the peaceable kingdom," and historian William Kilbourn (1970) used this concept as the title of his guide to the history and culture of the country.

officers and surveyors, and commercial and colonization potential was regarded as an adjunct, albeit and important adjunct, of an empire's strategic needs.

The French had no overseas experience in town building prior to their colonization efforts in the New World in the seventeenth century. But the latter pattern of conquest and colonization was similar to the process used to pacify the homeland itself. As in Spain, where the medieval struggle to win the country from the Moors led to the founding of strong urban enclaves that then provided the model for the New World (Hardoy 1978), the French colonial practice was established by centuries of experience of consolidating the nation-state. In some respects the old Gallo-Roman system continued to be the basis for town life in the medieval period, for Gaul had been the most urbanized of Rome's provinces. Early medieval *civitates* and *burgi*, like Limoges, Tours, and Dijon, evolved around a nucleus of church and castle or with competing nuclei, eventually surrounded by a common wall. By the eleventh and twelfth centuries, *villes nueves* were used by lords and bishops to open new territory and to extend settlement. Places like Saint-Denis remained unfortified for a time and emphasized their functions as weekly and annual markets. The form was a simple agglomeration with two streets informally focusing on the abbey's precincts (Gutkind 1980).

The most significant models for New World expansion—the bastides of the twelfth and thirteenth centuries—combined the notion of compact settlements and fortifications. The term *bastide* is the Gascon word for a planted town, derived from the verb meaning "to build"; the builders of new towns thus were *bastidors* (Beresford 1967, 8–9). These plantation towns were common throughout Europe, as lords, kings, and emperors sought to expand or retain their territory from the Spanish Christian princes' use of them in the reconquest, to frontier expansion in eastern Europe, and the defensive function in eastern Russia or China. Several characteristics of these places in France are particularly relevant for later overseas colonial use. The political function was crucial. In southern France where most were built, they were used in the territorial struggle between the king and the counts of Toulouse. This included Montauban, Aigues-Mortes, and Carcassonne. The lord was responsible for the walls that were built by the labor of the residents of the town and area. These towns usually were not feudal, but their purposes were political and territorial. The settlers were freemen, attracted to the place by promises of land, building materials, and especially exemption from feudal obligations.

Directly related to the first function was the agricultural function, for these were to be protected places making agricultural expansion possible. The planning of the *bastide* sometimes included the division of land into three zones: the town itself, with lots of equal size; garden lots surrounding the town, with enough allotments for one garden lot per family; beyond the garden lots were the farm lots, presumably to be cultivated by the same families. This combination of urban and rural functions was to have a long life in colonial expansion in the New World, so it must have worked out reasonably well in practice.

The plans of these *bastides* were generally more regular than most medieval towns, where houses, not streets, were the primary elements of composition. In fact, plans became more stereotyped as the thirteenth century progressed, with rectangular grids becoming the norm. The plans directly reflected the functions. First the walls determined the shape, with planning from the periphery to the interior. The gates of the walls determined the basic layout of the principal streets; the streets then became the organizing features, not the houses. The extent to which the fortifications set the tone for the physical internal layout was a precursor to much of the practice of colonial town planning during the Renaissance and baroque periods (Beresford 1967; Vance 1977; Cherville et al. 1980).

The Roman principles of symmetry, regularity, and organized composition had not been abandoned during the medieval age, although scholars have tended to emphasize that aspect of urban development that could be characterized as spontaneous growth by accretion. By the early sixteenth century, the Italian Renaissance notions of regularity and rationality in town planning entered France through the monarch, François I, perhaps because of his travels in Italy. For example, François I chose an Italian, Girolamo Marini, to design a fortified Renaissance-type town, Vitry-le-François, in 1545, to control an important passage against the Holy Roman emperor, Charles V. The square fortifications determined the interior organization, with two major streets crossing at the huge central square. The square, large even by today's traffic requirements, was designed primarily for the assembling of troops. As in the *bastide* towns that it resembled, incentives were offered to prospective settlers. The surrounding fortifications represent the latest in Italian concepts, for medieval-type fortresses had been dramatically shown to be ineffective against artillery with gunpowder. The projecting, arrowhead plan of the bastions illustrates the new approach, as they represent a system with each bastion defended by other bastions (Cherville et al. 1980; Gutkind 1980).

French interest in the New World was partly a response to the growing colonial empires of the Spanish and Portuguese. For example, the king commissioned and sent Jacques Cartier of St. Malo to explore the area north of the Spanish territory in 1534, in order to find a passage to Asia and to find gold as the Spanish had in Mexico. His voyages failed to establish a colony and interest in the area was maintained only by fishermen from French ports who also became involved in trading fur with the natives.

Hints of a new order were continued after the devastating wars of religion by Henry IV in the 1590s. The defense and attack of towns and cities was a crucial aspect of Henry's rise to power and in his eventual centralization of monarchial control. As the leader of the Protestant Huguenots, he had operated from his fortified base at La Rochelle, a medieval port strengthened with the building of a modern defense system (Pearson 1963; de Levis-Mirepoix 1971). French expansion overseas was not a major effort during this period although it was spurred on after the turn of the century by rivalry with two other maritime powers—the Netherlands and England. The initiative was largely private and commercial. Henry IV appointed Pierre de Gua, Sieur de Monts, as lieutenant-general of the vast and vaguely known regions of Acadia and the St. Lawrence, and granted him a ten-year monopoly of the fur trade. This led to his association with a lieutenant destined to become the first colonizer and town planner in Canada, Samuel de Champlain.

Champlain was trained as a painter and draftsman and he served in Henry IV's army as a quartermaster where he seems to have participated in Henry IV's sieges and attacks on various French towns. Also interested in navigation, he traveled to the Spanish West Indies, although the published narrative of this voyage is of questionable authenticity (Trudel 1963, 1966a, b). He helped choose the site for the first settlement, a small island in the St. Croix River (now the boundary between Canada and the United States), "having found no place more suitable" (Biggar 1922, vol. I, 91–202). Champlain later wrote that de Monts "proceeded to get the workmen to build houses for our residence, and allowed me to draw up the plan of our settlement" (Biggar 1922, vol. I, 274). For what would be the first planned settlement in Canada, Champlain designed what vaguely resembled a Spanish town surrounding a central square. But this elaborately planned settlement had too many basic flaws in terms of location. Its exposed character and the difficulties of provisioning the place from the mainland made it unsuitable as either a trading post or as an agency of colonization.

After a first winter the site was abandoned in favor of a move to a new location across the Bay of Fundy at Port Royal. In contrast to the open character of St. Croix, the plan chosen was that of a compact trading-post fortress, resembling the layout of a medieval, fortified abbey. The enclosed quadrilateral of buildings provided defense against the weather as well as against intruders. The defensive features included loopholes and even projecting cannon platforms on the corners facing the river.

After withdrawing from Acadian because of a lost monopoly, de Monts and Champlain turned their attention to the St. Lawrence area in 1608. The primary motive in founding a new place was not to form a *settlement*, despite Champlain's use of the term. The approximate site of what would be Quebec, was that of Stadacona, the Indian village where Cartier had wintered in 1535. Here the St. Lawrence narrowed sufficiently for cannon to command the river. A great cliff dominates the river at this point, making it one of the best natural strongholds on the continent. Whoever controlled this spot controlled access to the interior of a vast potential empire. Champlain's first building, a "habitation," was located on a narrow strand, a low-lying bank at the base of the great cliff. The habitation was a more elaborate version of that at Port Royal and incorporated three two-story buildings—a residence, and mercantile and supply stores. The defensive features resembled those of a late medieval castle, with a fifteen-foot moat and a surrounding stockade of stakes (Biggar 1922, vol. II, 24–56).

In emphasizing the defensive characteristics, Champlain had several enemies in mind. Foremost, perhaps, were other French and European fur traders. The English and Dutch privateers might also be a problem. But the native population, the source of the sought-after furs, involved a complex system of alliances and opponents. Champlain very early allied himself with the local Algonquin tribes of the Northwest, which made him an enemy of the Iroquois to the South. The subsequent history of French colonization was based on this arrangement, with the Iroquois later closely tied to the rival interests of the English. In 1620, Champlain began construction of

Fort St. Louis on the top edge of the cliff overlooking the habitation. Its medieval structure included a double *enceinte* (defensive perimeter) of walls and bastions.

Champlain's motives in founding and strengthening Quebec slowly evolved into an impressive colonization scheme based on trade rather than agriculture. In Champlain's view, France did not require additional agricultural production from a colony, but rather, French greatness would be better served by a colony that actively promoted trade with the Orient. In 1618, Champlain put forward an elaborate proposal to the king concerning a colonization scheme whereby the colony would act as a major agency in collecting customs on Asian trade. In practice, this seems to have meant the strengthening of two existing places, Quebec and Tadoussac, and the building of two new towns, for he suggested that if the king provided the necessary funds, in fifteen years, "no human force need be feared in the four towns built along the said St. Lawrence ..." (Biggar 1922, vol. I, 336). In Champlain's view, these towns would be made up of military personnel, religious orders, and colonists. A town was to be built at Quebec, presumably where the St. Charles River enters the St. Lawrence. There would be located "a town almost as large as St. Denis, which shall be called, if it please God and the King, Ludovico, in the centre of which will be built a fair temple ... called the Church of the Redeemer." A monastery with fifteen Recollet friars was to be erected near the church. A fort with five bastions would be constructed beside the new town, commanding it and the narrows of the river (presumably the St. Lawrence). Another fort of the same dimensions would be built directly across the river "in order to bar completely the passage of the said river, as being the gateway of the said country" (Biggar 1922, vol. I, 332).

The allusion to Saint-Denis as a model for the proposed town may be somewhat surprising in that new towns of the early seventeenth century in France were no longer based on religious foundations such as an abbey or church. Probably the reference was meant to impress the king with Champlain's piety, but even more with his loyalty to the monarchy, for St. Denis had become a symbol of fidelity to the monarchy and the kings were traditionally buried in the cathedral. The Ludovico project and others were not realized during Champlain's time in the colony. His death in 1635 meant that he did not witness renewed French efforts by the government and a new company to create towns and settlements.

Two trends in early seventeenth-century France were to have a major impact on the character of settlement in New France: the monarchy's increased military power, and the Counter-Reformation. Both were embodied in the personality of Cardinal Richelieu who became first minister of France in the 1620s. An example was Richelieu's moves against the Huguenots whose one hundred and fifty strongholds presented, in his view, a state within a state. In 1629, he was able to reduce La Rochelle, the Huguenot center, after a year's siege. Paris itself became a kind of second Rome, a vanguard of the Counter-Reformation, with a great many new convents and churches (Bussman 1984).

These French trends were mirrored in New France when Richelieu established a new company more interested in populating the colony. A new governor, Montmagny, and the surveyor Jean Bourdon were soon described as having "drawn the plans of a city, in order that all building hereafter shall be done systematically" (Father

Lejeune 1636, as cited in Thwaites 1959, 132). This appears to have included projects for strengthening the defenses of the original trading post site, the regularizing of the place, which became known as Lower Town, and the creation of a new town above the cliff, Upper Town, focused on Champlain's original Fort St. Louis. There were no plans at this stage to build a wall around the town. Rather, each of the religious institutions in Upper Town were actually a series of *reduits*—minor fortifications.[2]

The religious enthusiasm and missionary zeal represented by the establishment of the order in Quebec led directly to the founding of a mission post to the west— Montreal. A group of extremely devout laymen and clerics formed the Société de Notre Dame de Montreal in 1640, and were granted the island of Montreal by the Company of New France. The society chose a young army officer, Paul de Chomodey, Sieur de Maisonneuve, to lead the project. He was joined by about seventy men who agreed to serve a three-year term. A palisade of stakes was quickly erected and the post, name Ville Marie, built. A plan drawn about five years later by Jean Bourdon indicates a community organized around a central *place d'armes*, and including a chapel, the store, the kitchen, the bakehouse, living quarters for the civil and religious leaders, a rudimentary fort wall with four bastions, and several cannon placed strategically.[3]

A new age in town planning and building in France and the French colonies was ushered in when the young Louis XIV took over the reign of government in the 1660s. His chief minister, Jean-Baptiste Colbert, reorganized the economy on an imperial basis. Elements of his overall scheme included challenging the Dutch position in maritime trade and making the colonies an integral part of a mercantile system by having them provide raw materials and purchase French manufactured goods (Priestly 1939; Erlanger 1965; Wolf 1968).[4]

Louis XIV had moved his administration to Versailles from Paris because he distrusted the city ever since the rebellion of the nobility known as the Fronde. But Paris was transformed during his reign, probably because Colbert insisted that the greatness of the monarchy had to be manifested in the grandeur and beauty of France's central city. In 1676, Louis decreed that "future construction undertaken in the city be regulated by a specific plan" and this control was extended to architectural design in an effort to create a national French style, distinct from the Italian baroque. Some of the major projects included massive additions to the Louvre in the classical style and Le Notre's Jardin des Tuileries, extending west in a new avenue, the Champs-Elysées. And in sharp contrast to capital cities elsewhere on the

---

[2] Montmagny's plan has never been found. For an excellent analysis of what it may have looked like, see Charbonneau et al. (1983).

[3] The literature on the founding of Montreal is excellent. Among the most useful are Adair (1942), Lanctot (1969), and Dechêne (1974).

[4] For an excellent brief analysis of Colbert's mercantilism, see Betts (1968). Betts makes the point that mercantilism was an economic policy with political objectives. It was based on the assumption that since the amount of the world's resources was limited, any addition to a state's economic growth required a subtraction from that of another state. Economic development was therefore a crucial aspect of an interest in political power.

continent in the seventeenth century, Louis had the city's walls torn down, and replaced on the Right Bank with a semicircle of tree-lined alleys, the Boulevards—a term used to describe part of a rampart (Heron de Villefosse 1939; Clebert 1958; Chartier et al. 1981).

This dramatic gesture of an open city was only possible because of the degree to which Louis had established his control internally in France, and especially to the degree that the frontiers had been secured by his armies and frontier towns fortified by the great military engineer, Sébastian Vauban. Part of Vauban's importance within the French military and political hierarchy stemmed from his success in organizing sieges and taking towns. But his name also became synonymous with the design and construction of fortifications, and innumerable commentators since then have described his supposed "three systems" of fortifications. If these existed in reality, Vauban did not clarify the issue. More important for our purposes was the designed relationship between the fortifications and the town. Rather than being dogmatic in the application of any system, Vauban appears to have adapted some of the currently fashionable theoretical models in solving the problems of particular places (Blomfield 1938; Parent and Verroust 1971; Gutkind 1980; Charbonneau et al. 1983; Fry 1984).[5] Two types of solutions emerged, each the product of specific situations. The first and most common was the construction of a citadel next to an already existing town of considerable size. Vauban's first experience with this situation stemmed from the French occupation of Flanders in the 1660s and the necessity of holding towns like Lille and Arras. The citadels he built at these places became classic examples of bastioned defensive systems. At Arras, a citadel based on a pentagon was placed on a slight ridge, with one point facing the town. The intent was obviously to intimidate the town as well as protect it. Arras had evolved during the medieval period from two nuclei, one dependent on the kings of France, the other on the country of Flanders. As a former Spanish possession with a Flemish population, its loyalty to France probably remained in doubt.

Much the same situation was the case with Basançon, the traditional controlling point of the passage between the Jura plateau and the Vosges Mountains near the Swiss border. Besançon had been a free imperial city for over six hundred years before coming under French control in 1678. Vauban strengthened its defensive wall and particularly added to a citadel overlooking the town.

The other major type of fortification designed and built by Vauban involved the building of a completely new town for defensive purposes. The possibilities of creating an ideal town of this kind had inspired a number of Renaissance theoreticians and had led to some actual towns such as Palma Nova, built in 1593 by Vincenzo Scammonzi as a regional defensive site for Venice. A number of French theoretical writers included Jacques Perret, who published an important folio of ideal, fortified towns *(Des fortifications et artifices, architecture et perspective* [1594]). These

---

[5] My description of Vauban's fortified towns also depends on my study of the models of these places, which were made in the late seventeenth and early eighteenth centuries and are housed in the Musée de Plans—Reliefs, part of the Army Museum at the Hotel des Invalides in Paris, and on-site visits in May, 1985.

ideal types offered the possibility of either a radical interior plan, in which the town's shape is subjugated to the requirement of quick access from the central *place d'armes* to the peripheral walls, or an orthogonal design, with rectangular or square blocks. For his new towns Vauban emphasized the orthogonal arrangements, as at Hunique, Saar-Louis, and Longwy, and especially at Neuf-Brisach, his last and most highly regarded work, built from 1697 to 1708. Vauban's use of this arrangement had a significant bearing on the internal spatial organization of Neuf-Brisach for the *place d'armes* now became a central square, not the site of barracks and supplies requiring rapid access to the walls. Instead, buildings such as barracks and other military service buildings were placed parallel to and next to the walls on a rampart road that surrounded the residential portion of the town (Halter et al. 1972).

The moves to centralize royal authority during Louis XIV's reign had a significant impact on the settlement of the colonies as well. In Colbert's schemes, the colonies were to play a more important role in the French economic system and he took steps to establish direct royal control of New France in the 1660s. The main threat to the colony was not the English or Dutch, in the opinion of royal officials, but the Iroquois confederacy of five Indian nations that continually assaulted settlements, especially very small places. The Iroquois could put two thousand eight hundred warriors into the field, making them the largest military force in North America. They were attempting to become the middlemen in the western fur trade by diverting the fur traffic from the northern and western tribes to the English at Albany, rather than to the French at Montreal. The official Colbert sent to New France, the intendant, Jean Talon, attempted to concentrate the scattered rural population into centers that would be more defensible against the Iroquois. The three villages established to the north of Quebec were designed according to a radial plan, but the scheme did not become more widespread because colonists appear to have resisted the increased official control the system seemed to imply (Eccles 1964, 1959, 1969; Harris 1968).

Despite Colbert's wishes, succeeding colonial administrators followed an expansionist policy, pushing New France's borders to the northwest and southwest in pursuit of the fur trade and, incidentally, to cut off English expansion westward. Colonial officials called on Vauban for advice about defending the colony in 1684 and took considerable interest in the colony after that. In his numerous memos, he emphasized his belief that colonial posts such as Fort Frontenac should be fortified with embanked palisades and bastions; apparently he sent plans to Canada although these have not been found. He also concerned himself with the process of settlement via fortified boroughs that might become proper towns. In a memorandum written in 1699 (while Neuf-Brisach was being built), he described a Roman type of system that depended initially for population on companies of soldiers. An engineer would make the crucial decisions about the site's physical suitability and its commercial potential. Presumably government officials would plan the land and streets and build the first houses, the church, storehouses, the hospital, and mills (from France's Archives Nationales [hereafter AN] 1699).

These principles seem to have been adopted in some of the new town buildings that took place at the turn of the century. French officials approved La Mothe

Cadillac's proposal to found a settlement at Detroit in 1701 partly because it seemed to be a move at consolidating several dispersed places. Like the earlier builders of bastides in his native Gascony, Cadillac claimed his settlement would have military, commercial, and agricultural functions. It would hold the territory for France by restraining the Iroquois and by preventing further English expansion and it would attract traders and farmers. The fortifications of this compact, rectangular grid were a far cry from the elaborate Vauban-style system and seem designed only as a protection against Indians, not English attack. Slightly more elaborate was the plan for Mobile, founded in 1702 by Pierre le Moyne, Sieur d'Iberville. This settlement near the mouth of the Mississippi was the product of Louis XIV's decision to stymie any possible English advance in this area. Here the design included a rectangular grid without a surrounding fortification. Defense was supplied by a small fort located in a *place d'armes* between the grid and the Mobile River (Zoltvany 1965; Reps 1969).

The concern for fortifications and regularity also affected the older towns of New France. In the 1660s, Colbert hoped to make Quebec into a fortress capable of resisting a siege by a European power (AN 1667). But when Governor Frontenac argued for permission and funds to begin the operation in the 1670s, France was embroiled in European problems. Colbert concluded that the North American threat was from the Indians and the solution was the centralization of the rural population into defensible villages (AN 1673 and 1674). Frontenac was therefore forced to lower his ambitions and concentrate instead on rebuilding the old Fort St. Louis. Two minor attempts at building walls floundered for lack of funds. In reality, Quebec remained an unfortified town, incapable of mounting a defense against a siege from the landward side, on what was known as the Plains of Abraham (Charbonneau et al. 1983).

The second-ranking town, Montreal, slowly evolved into a fur trading town from its original purpose as a mission post. The religious society that founded the community became plagued by debts and was forced to give up its seigneurial rights to the island to the Sulpicians in 1663. The superior of the Sulpicians, Dollier de Casson, laid out the first formal plan of the town in 1672, thirty years after the founding of Ville Marie. Using the existing St. Paul Street, which had informally developed parallel to the river, as the basis for a grid, he laid out a new parallel street, Notre Dame, farther up the gently rising bank of the St. Lawrence, and also planned the necessary connecting streets (de Casson 1927; Marsan 1951). The town's first wall, basically a wooden palisade, was built about fifteen years later under the direction of colonial officials. A large amount of area was enclosed in relation to the population since landowners such as the religious order had large properties they used as gardens.

It was in the existing smaller places that royal officials could more closely approximate their notions of ideal fortifications. The major figure in this process was Jacques Lavasseur de Neré, the royal engineer of the colony in 1694, who had served in some fortified French towns and had been with Vauban in several sieges. In response to royal instructions, Lavasseur drew up proposals for at least four towns and boroughs in 1704. For Trois Rivières, for example, on the St. Lawrence halfway between Quebec and Montreal, he planned a bastioned wall made of embanked palisades around the substantial existing town with its established street layout, dating back at least to 1650. The new wall enclosed a large amount of garden and open space, allowing for future expansion. At the smaller sites of Chambly, Prairie de la Madeleine, and Sorel simple embanked palisades with rather primitive towers or square redoubts surrounded these rather haphazard collection of buildings. Thus even in the smallest concentrations of population, the royal presence was strongly apparent in the form of fortifications and in small contingents of troops (AN 1705).

By the end of the seventeenth century, the French world's urban system was well established at home and abroad. The position of Paris at the head of this pyramid-like structure was unchallenged, even though Louis XIV had made Versailles the symbol of his grand style. A series of fortified towns had extended and consolidated France's boundaries and the western ports of La Rochelle and Bordeaux were thriving with the colonial trade of the West Indies and New France. A rudimentary urban system had been established along the St. Lawrence in New France, headed by Quebec as the administrative, religious, military, and cultural center of the colony. Quebec's population had expanded under royal government control from 547 in 1666, to about 2000 in 1700. Together with Montreal, about half as large, the two towns represented about 20 percent of the colony's population.

The sporadic worldwide conflict between France and England in the seventeenth century erupted into a major war in the eighteenth century, which resulted in the loss of most of France's North American possessions. The early part of the century had witnessed a great intensification of town buildings by France. New frontier towns such as St. Louis and New Orleans were founded on the Mississippi. The fortifications of Quebec and Montreal became more sophisticated and these towns evolved into major urban centers. But the epitome of French colonial town building was Louisbourg, planned in 1713 as a major Atlantic fortress. Royal engineers who were disciples of Vauban built a massive fortification, which dictated the town's internal organization. As in some Vauban projects, the king's bastion at Louisbourg was designed to protect imperial officials from the town as well as from any potential imperial threat.

The final struggle between France and England during the Seven Years War (or the French and Indian War) had disastrous consequences for France's colonial settlements. Louisbourg fell for the second time in 1758 after a siege; its walls were blown up and its population was dispersed. Quebec fell in 1759 after a lengthy siege and bombardment, which destroyed much of one of the finest cities on the continent. Montreal surrendered the following year. The future of these communities was to be played out under the flag of the old enemy, Britain, in what would eventually become Canada.

References

Adair, E. (1942). The evolution of Montreal under the French regime. *Canadian Historical Association Report, X*, 20–41.

Beresford, M. (1967). *New towns of the middle ages*. New York: Butterworth.

Betts, R. (1968). *Europe overseas, phases of imperialism*. New York: Basic Books.

Biggar, H. (1922). *The works of Samuel de Champlain* (6 Vols.) Toronto: Champlain Society.

Blomfield, R. (1938). *Sébastien le prestre de Vauban, 1633–1707*. New York: Metheun.

Bussman, K. (1984). *Paris and the Ile de France: Art, architecture, history*. Paris: Tabori.

Charbonneau, A., Desloges, Y., & Lafrance, M. (1983). *Québec, the fortified city: From the 17th to the 19th century*. Ottawa: Parles Camona.

Chartier, R., et al. (Eds.). (1981). *La ville classique, histoire de la France urbaine*. Paris: Seuil.

Cherville, A., Le Goff, J., & Rossiaud, J. (1980). *La ville medieval. Histoire de la France urbaine*. Paris: Editions du Seuil.

Clebert, J. (1958). *Les rues de Paris*. Paris: Dumont.

de Casson, F. D. (1927). *A history of Montreal, 1640–1672*. Montréal: Senecal.

de Levis-Mirepoix, D. A. (1971). *Henri IV, roi de France et de Navarre*. Paris: Librairie Académique Perrin.

de Vries, J. (1984). *European urbanization: 1500–1800*. Cambridge: Harvard University Press.

Dechêne, L. (1974). *Habitants et marchands de Montréal au XVIIe siècle*. Paris: Plan.

Eccles, W. J. (1959). *Frontenac: The courtier governor*. Toronto: McClelland and Stewart.

Eccles, W. J. (1964). *Canada under Louis XIV* (pp. 1633–1701). McClelland and Stewart: Toronto.

Eccles, W. J. (1969). *The Canadian frontier* (pp. 1534–1760). New York: Holt and Winston.

Erlanger, P. (1965). *Louis XIV*. Paris: Fayard.

Fry, B. (1984). *An appearance of strength: The fortifications of Louisbourg*. Ottawa: Parks Camona.

Gutkind, E. (1980). *Urban development in Western Europe: France and Belgium*. New York: Free Press.

Halter, A., Herrscher, R., & Roth, J. (1972). *Neuf-Brisach*. Sydney: Colman.

Hardoy, J. (1978). European urban forms in the fifteenth to seventeenth centuries and their utilization in Latin America. In R. Schaedel, J. Hardoy, & N. Kinzer (Eds.), *Urbanization in American from its beginnings to the present* (pp. 215–248). The Hague: Manton.

Harris, R. (1968). *The seigneurial system in early Canada*. Madison: University of Wisconsin Press.

Heron de Villefosse, R. (1939). *Construction de Paris*. Paris: Massol.

Kain, R., & Norris, H. (1982). Military influence on European town planning. *History Today, 32*, 10–15.

Kilbourn, W. (1970). *Canada: A guide to the peaceable kingdom*. Toronto: Macmillan.

Lanctot, G. (1969). *Montreal under Masionneuve*. Toronto: Clark Irwin.

Marsan, J. (1951). *Montreal in evolution*. Montreal: Fides.

Parent, M., & Verroust, J. (1971). *Vauban*. Paris: J. Freal.

Pearson, H. (1963). *Henry of Navarre: His life*. London: n.p.

Priestly, H. (1939). *France overseas, through the old regime: A study of European expansion*. New York: Appleton Century.

Reps, J. (1969). *Town planning in frontier America*. Princeton: Princeton University Press.

Thwaites, R. (1959). *Jesuit relations*. New York: Pageant.

Trudel, M. (1963). *Histoire de la Nouvelle-France, les vaines tentatives, 1524–1603*. Montréal: Fides.

Trudel, M. (1966a). *Histoire de la Nouvelle-France, le comptoire* (pp. 1604–1627). Ottawa: University of Ottawa Press.

Trudel, M. (1966b). Samuel de Champlain. In *Dictionary of Canadian biography* (Vol. I, pp. 186–199). Toronto: University of Toronto Press.

Vance, J. (1977). *This scene of man: The role and structure of the city in the geography of Western civilization*. New York: Harper and Row.

Watkins, T. (1983). Roman legionary fortresses and the cities of modern Europe. *Military Affairs, The Journal of Military History, 47*, 15–24.

Wolf, J. B. (1968). *Louis XIV*. London: Cassel.

Zoltvany, W. F. (1965). New France and the West (1701–1713). *Canadian Historical Review, 66*, 301–322.

France's National Archives, Paris [AN] (1667). Colonies, C11A, 2:295, Colbert to Talon, 5 April 1667.

France's National Archives, Paris [AN] (1673). Colonies, C11A, 2:295, Frontenac to Colbert, 13 November 1673.

France's National Archives, Paris [AN] (1699). Colonies C11A, 5:365v, Memorandum from Governor Denonville to Vauban; Vauban to Maurepas, 21 January 1699.

France's National Archives, Paris [AN] (1705a). Colonies, C11A, 22:348, Lavasseur de Neré to Minister, 18 October 1705.

France's National Archives, Paris [AN] (1705b). Section Outre-Mer, Dépôt des fortifications des Colonies, Amérique sptentrionale, no. D'ordre 460, Lavasseur de Neré, 15 November 1705, Concerning Trois-Rivières.

Chapter 9
Indigenous Architecture and the Spanish American Plaza in Mesoamerica and the Caribbean

Setha M. Low

Abstract Plazas are often important spatial representations of society and social hierarchy. The grid-plan plazas built in Mesoamerica and the Caribbean under the direction of the Spanish have been interpreted as architectural representations of colonial control and oppression. Underlying these interpretations is the tacit assumption that plaza-centered gridded urban design was of solely European derivation, in spite of considerable evidence of pre-Columbian contributions. This chapter argues that the correspondence between indigenous forms and Spanish reconstruction—both modelled on the grid layout—is so well documented that the denial of its significance is startling. In fact, the ethnohistorical and archaeological evidence suggests that the colonial plaza evolved from both indigenous and Spanish influences and models that created a new urban design form. Consequently, cultural tensions of conquest and resistance are embedded in this urban design and accompanied architecture.

Keywords Colonial Hispanic culture · Indigenous Mexican cultures · Urban grid · Plaza · Heritage studies · Politics of historical preservation

Introduction

Any spatial form, contemporary monument, or town plan is a product generated by conflicting sociopolitical forces (Harvey 1985). Yet the seemingly unchallengeable hegemonic interpretation of architecture and urban design often obscures subtexts of meanings. Political implications lie at the root of all aesthetic sensibilities, and

This chapter is an abridged version of Low, S. (1995). "Indigenous Architecture and the Spanish American Plaza in Mesoamerica and the Caribbean." *American Anthropologist*, 97(4): 748–762. Copyright © 1995 by the American Anthropological Association. Reproduced with permission of American Anthropological Association.

S. M. Low (✉)
City University of New York, New York, NY, USA
e-mail: SLow@gc.cuny.edu

© Springer International Publishing AG, part of Springer Nature 2018
R. Rose-Redwood, L. Bigon (eds.), *Gridded Worlds: An Urban Anthology*,
https://doi.org/10.1007/978-3-319-76490-0_9

certainly the design of an urban space reflects the political agency of the state. In this sense, architecture and urban design contribute to the dominance of one group over others and function as mechanisms for coding their reciprocal relationships at the level of the surveillance and control of bodily movement (Foucault 1975; Rabinow 1989). Physical space is ordered by and reflects the power structures to which the community is subordinated; the community may contest this subordination through local interpretation and use of space. Examining the origins and use of spatial forms provides insight into the discourse of power relations.

The symbolic importance of the built environment is found in its interpretation as an expression of culturally shared mental structures and embodied processes. By their configuration, content, and associations, the spatial or physical attributes establish a system of relationships that represent aspects of social life. Symbolic theory approaches built forms as tangible evidence for describing and explaining often intangible features of expressive cultural processes (Lawrence and Low 1990, 466). The examination of the built environment, then, can provide insights into meanings, values, and processes that might not be uncovered through other observations.

Further, the assumption that the Nahua and Maya peoples were passive recipients of colonial Hispanic culture has been thoroughly refuted within anthropology (Weeks 1988; Jones 1989). Although widely accepted, this insight is still analytically significant, particularly in those domains where the ascendancy and control of the Spanish colonizers remains unquestioned. Contemporary debate concerning the allocation of space and rights of excavation in the *zocalo*, the historic *plaza mayor* of Mexico City, highlights these themes. The tensions between Spanish colonial and indigenous Mexican cultures and their spatial and architectural representations can be seen in the struggle for the restoration and preservation of the remaining architecture and archaeological materials. The archaeological excavation of the Templo Mayor of Tenochtitlán stages one through six (Cortés destroyed the seventh stage to build the current colonial plaza and buildings), together with the building of the new Museo del Templo Mayor, has caused considerable concern among architectural historians and other scholars interested in the history and architecture of the colonial period. A number of important colonial buildings were torn down to excavate the site and make room for the new museum that interprets the archaeological remains. Further, the excavations disturbed the foundations of many of the remaining colonial buildings on the zocalo, including the cathedral and the National Palace, causing serious damage to the facades of some. The archaeological site itself is rising, apparently due to the removal of the weight of the colonial buildings and the expansion of the spongy soil of the original lake bed. Colonial historians and architects worry that continued excavation will cause even more damage. Some would like to stop or at least slow down plans for additional archaeological projects in the area.

Although this preservation dilemma provides insight into the sociopolitical struggle for representational control of space in the symbolic center of Mexico City, the most interesting part of the story is that the contemporary conflict recapitulates the colonial struggles of almost 500 years ago. The emergence of the Templo Mayor has created considerable cultural capital for the indigenous Indian representation of Mexican identity (Lomnitz Adler 1992). In response, historians and architects involved in the cultural conservation of the Spanish colonial past and the preservation of colonial symbols of Mexican identity are attempting to reappropriate the zocalo, the most sacred and political of Mexican spaces. The irony is that Cortés attempted to erase the indigenous past when he tore down the seventh stage of the Templo Mayor, only to have the temple's reemergence become a vindication of the submerged indigenous culture. The plaza remains a contested terrain where the ongoing dialectic between the indigenous presence and Spanish aspiration continues to be played out. Other dissenting groups, not tied to an indigenous ideology, also appropriate this space to oppose the state. These struggles illustrate how important these symbolic spaces are for the formation and maintenance of cultural identity, and how meanings from the past are encoded in the built environment and manipulated through spatial representations and architecture to create the sociopolitical present.

The Paradox of the Plaza in the New World

The grid-plan town with a central plaza, built under the direction of the Spanish throughout their colonial domain, has been interpreted as an architectural representation of colonial control and oppression. This urban form is thought to be based on Renaissance rules of rationality rather than being a traditional cultural expression in the colonizing country (Foster 1960). Valerie Fraser even suggests that "it is as if the Spanish colonists were drawing on some sort of cultural memory, an inherited, almost instinctive knowledge. Under the special circumstances of America the sense of what was right and proper in architecture and town planning comes to the surface to be transformed into physical reality" (1990, 7). The central square of space and its surrounding structures—the cathedral, administration buildings, arsenal, customs house, and later the residences of the social elite—represented the double hierarchy of church and state, and were "conceived and executed as propaganda vehicles, symbolizing and incarnating civilization" (Crouch et al. 1982, xx). The plaza "was, and in many places still is, a manifestation of the local social order, [of] the relationship between citizens and citizens and the authority of the state" (Jackson 1984, 18). In the colonial city, this relationship was one of social and racial domination (King 1980; Gutierrez 1983).

These interpretations are based on a tacit assumption that the plaza-centered urban design was of solely European derivation, in spite of considerable evidence of pre-Columbian contributions to plaza form. More tenuously, researchers suggest that the 1573 "Laws of the Indies" or the writings of the Italian Renaissance were the main sources of New World plaza design, even though some were published many years after the establishment of the first Spanish American towns. As for early Renaissance European cities themselves, their medieval design lacked the characteristic organization of pre-Columbian cities, which integrated the plazas into the overall urban grid plan (Low 1993). In fact, it is likely that the redesign of cities in Spain under Philip II was partly stimulated by the urban design experiments of the New World. Nonetheless, the hegemonic discourse that privileges the European sources of architectural influence over pre-Columbian sources has gone unrecognized, resulting in an architectural history that has remained unchanged for the past 40 years (Ricard 1947; Stanislawski 1947; Palm 1955, 1968; Benevolo 1969; Borah 1972; Zawiska 1972; Hardoy 1973; Borah et al. 1980; Crouch et al. 1982; Hardoy and Hardoy 1978; Kubler 1978; Morse 1987; Schaedel et al. 1978).

Cities such as Tenochtitlán (Clendinnen 1991a) and Cuzco (Hyslop 1990) were large, centered on ceremonial plazas surrounded by major temples and residences of the ruling elite. Upon their arrival, the Spaniards admired these exceptional models of urban design and wrote about the grandeur, order, and urbanity of these newly discovered cities. Though the lowland urban form lacked the straight streets that characterized cities of the valley of Mexico, a hierarchy of central plazas and temples appeared in most Mesoamerican cities. The ceremonial and commercial uses of these plazas, as well as their sacred and civil meanings and regular form, also inform the subsequent colonial plazas built after the Conquest. In fact, the correspondence between the indigenous plaza forms and Spanish reconstruction is so well documented that the denial of its significance is startling.

Fraser, in *The Architecture of Conquest* (1990), is unclear about the role of the indigenous urban design influences while at the same time providing archaeological and ethnohistorical evidence that many, if not most, Spanish American towns were built directly on top of or otherwise utilized the existing settlement patterns and buildings. She also agrees that the indigenous towns and architecture were greeted with admiration and an appreciation of the skill and knowledge that it took to design and build such magnificent urban centers:

> Many early travellers in South America were impressed by indigenous towns and indigenous architecture, but this seems not to have weakened their confidence in the superiority of their own culture .... As the Spanish colonies are consolidated, so this cultural confidence is in fact strengthened rather than weakened. Once the Indian towns have been appropriated and recognizably Europeanized then there is less evidence of a non-European urban society to upset this confidence. The unsettling possibility that a completely different, non-European people might also have developed a form of town based on straight streets, square blocks and a central plaza surrounded by important political religious buildings could be set aside, to be dealt with by later historians. (Fraser 1990, 80)

Although she provides a plausible psychological interpretation of why the Spanish did not acknowledge the contribution of indigenous architecture and planning, she still argues that the new town forms were basically European, coming from an almost subconscious impulse to create a particular cultural order. Thus, the historical literature on the origin of the plaza continues to be Eurocentric.

The question of the origin of the plaza urban design has implications for the cultural interpretation of the meaning of the plaza complex. The case of Tenochtitlán provides a revealing example. David Carrasco (1990a) states that for the Mexica, the ideal city type was a sacred space oriented around a quintessentially sacred center, and that the design of the city replicates cosmological space. Eduardo Matos Moctezuma reiterates the cultural significance of the sacred center:

> The Mexica's first act upon settling in this place was to build a small shrine to Huitzilopochtli. They thus established their "center," the navel of the world, the sacred space from which would emerge the four fundamental divisions of the city. Within this supremely sacred space they attempted to reproduce architecturally the entire cosmic order. (1990, 56)

Further, a symbolic relationship existed between nature and architecture such that the main pyramid was considered a sacred mountain (Matos Moctezuma 1992; Townsend 1992). This correspondence between architectural sites and natural and supernatural places is also evident at Quirigua, Guatemala, where a stela erected in the main ceremonial plaza specifies the spot as "Black Water Sky Place" (Gube et al. 1991). This suggests that place names refer to supernatural and natural locations, and that the Maya—as well as the Mexica—constructed their cities to replicate the supernatural world.

If the central plaza and Great Temple of Tenochtitlán constituted the sacred space of the Mexica world, what happens when Cortés decides to rebuild the city on the ruins of the space, re-presenting (re-creating) the Mexica ceremonial plaza and Great Temple in the form of a new Spanish American plaza and cathedral? Can it be argued that each time an indigenous plaza is reconstituted or rebuilt in a way that maintains some aspects of its original spatial form and integrity, the new form retains some of the original cultural meanings? Are the new uses of these plazas so different from what they were before? Why has the plaza not been treated as a representation in which the forms and cultural meanings merge the two traditions?

To answer these questions it is important to consider temporal scale, since, as Michael Smith (1992) points out, there is often a confusion between ethnographic and archaeological time. Similarly, there is often confusion when architectural historians lump two centuries of colonial life into one period. The study of the built environment and its cultural meanings is best achieved as Inga Clendinnen (1991b) did when she broke down the temporal scale, chronicling the year-by-year decisions and movements of Cortés and his soldiers in order to interpret his actions and their consequences. In the case of the origins of the Spanish American plaza, this is often difficult to do because the data are incomplete and rudimentary. A start can be made, even so, by examining what data are available, city by city and site by site.

There are multiple cultural sources and architectural models for plaza design. Ethnohistorical research during the past ten years has reinforced the perspective that the origins of any cultural artifact are based on a complex set of influences (Todorov 1984; Gillespie 1989; Williams and Lewis 1993). Studies in the social production of built form suggest that many of these forces are latent rather than manifest and must be teased out of the data, or may be found in tangential sources (King 1980). Issues such as the role of the indigenous laborers who built these new towns, the models the Spanish found in their new environment, and the influence of these models on form and style have not been adequately researched (Matos Moctezuma 1990). The evidence suggests that there were differing forces affecting the building of plazas in each city and town, including chronology, local materials, geographical site, history, environmental context, and particular individuals. By examining a number of sites, the interplay of forces becomes clearer and questions can be answered based on the history of a particular place.

Architectural and Urban Design Traditions

Many researchers have argued that "the design of colonial capital cities has nothing to do with local traditions, or with persistence of pre-Columbian town planning concepts" (Gasparini 1978, 274). Others, however, argue that hidden in the space and concepts of urban design are physical and ideological elements of pre-Columbian cultural practices (Gracia Zambrano 1992). Indigenous cultures were already employing domestic and/or ceremonial urban designs that the Spanish would have seen whether in living towns and cities or in the ruins they encountered. In order to balance the Eurocentric view of plaza design and to set the stage for a discussion of the Spanish American plaza as a new form, neither solely European nor solely indigenous, the evidence from Mesoamerica needs to be reviewed.

Much of the ethnohistorical evidence is based on firsthand Spanish accounts that have been criticized for representing native peoples in terms of models and myths from Spain and Europe (León-Portilla 1992; Williams and Lewis 1993). These critiques have been helpful in clarifying and deconstructing the European image of the New World. Nonetheless, a recent review found that most of these Spanish accounts show interest and respect for the native (Delgado-Gómez 1993). The accuracy of the physical descriptions of cities, towns, and ruins has not been directly challenged, although Clendinnen (1991b) comments that Cortés chose strategically to dwell on the wealth and grandeur of Tenochtitlán.

As a monumental urban center of 150,000 to 300,000 inhabitants, Tenochtitlán is probably the clearest source of evidence for indigenous influence on architecture and urban design. Firsthand accounts suggest that the Spanish were impressed by the straight causeways that ran directly into the main ceremonial plaza, and by the regular plan and urban design of the city in general (Diaz del Castillo 1963). Other Indian towns were also planned with a grid centered on a fortified temple enclosure with a plaza that stood at the intersection of social thoroughfares. According to Motolinia, "In the whole land we find that the Indians had a large square court in the best part of the town; about a crossbowshot from corner to corner, in the large cities and provincial capitals; and in the smaller towns, about a bowshot" (Hardoy 1973, 178–9).

One of the explanations for the central design of Mexica ceremonial sites is the use of the four cardinal points in much of Mexica cosmology (Toussaint et al. 1938). The cosmos was re-created in the architectural structure of the Great Temple, which "was the place, real and symbolic, where Mexica power was centered" (Matos Moctezuma 1987, 25). The twin shrines that faced the plaza were dedicated to the two great deities: Tlaloc, god of rain, water, and agricultural production, and Huitzilopochtli, god of war, conquest, and tribute. They represented the economic structure of the Mexica state, whose income came from agricultural production and tribute paid by subject communities.

The Mexica were developing principles of city planning in order to achieve an efficient urban organization (Hardoy 1973). Their towns were roughly rectangular, a plan that evolved from the division of land among the clans. The central plaza served as a center for communal gatherings and as a marketplace, and simultaneously functioned as the courtyard of the central temple. This pattern is not unlike that of the representational and functional uses of the Spanish American plaza that replaced it.

Both Paul Zucker (1959) and Edward Calnek (1978) have suggested that social status among the Mexica was reflected in the architectural markers and the distance of houses from the plaza, with the highest status locations being those on the perimeter and surrounding blocks of the central plaza. A similar organization of social status was later employed by Cortés in his plan for Mexico City. William Schell (1986) argues that with the exception of the Yucatec Maya, Mesoamerican culture and economic structure resembled that of Iberia in many ways, including landholding systems, governance by city-states, and market laws, and that this explains some of the ease with which Cortés was able to conquer and govern, and some of the spatial congruity that arose.

Pre-Classic and Classic Maya sites were less rectangular in their plan and in the placement of their ceremonial plazas than those of the Mexica. However, though the ceremonial sites were not organized in a grid, lowland Maya house sites were grouped around plazas (Ashmore 1981). Moreover, the social status of house sites was determined by their proximity to the plaza (Becker 1982). Plazas were the focus of community life and pivotal gathering places, whether adjoined by temples or houses. Excavations at a number of sites reveal that the earliest form of the ceremonial center consisted of "a single small plaza and its associated structures" (Andrews 1975, 11). The Maya plaza was an open space, cleared of trees and artificially leveled and paved. This architectural statement became an essential aspect of Maya cities.

In Yucatan, late Classic and post-Classic Maya sites show a cosmopolitan mix of influences, evident in the material culture, that may account for the design of main plazas such as those at the site of Chichen Itza. The town of Izamal illustrates how the Spaniards built their church and monastery next to a massive Maya ceremonial platform topped with a pyramid. The Maya site of Tipu also illustrates the building of a colonial church and plaza near post-Classic temples. At the Belizean site of Lamanai, the first church was superposed directly on a post-Classic temple platform (Pendergast 1986; Graham et al. 1989).

Descriptions from firsthand accounts throughout the Maya region suggest that the Spanish were aware of the design and grandeur of abandoned indigenous sites. In a description of Guatemala dated March 8, 1576, Diego Garcia de Palacio described the plaza in the ruins of Copán:

> Near here, on the road to the city of San Pedro, in the first town within the province of Honduras called Copán, are certain ruins and vestiges of a great population and of superb edifices, of such skill, that it appears they could never have been built by a people as rude

as the natives of that province .... Near this, is a well built plaza or square, with steps or grades, which from the description, resemble those of the Coliseum at Romes [sic]. In some places it has eighty steps, paved, and made in part at least of fine stones, well-worked. In this square are six great statues. (Parry and Keith 1984, 546)

Wendy Ashmore presents a partial rationale for the site planning and plaza organization of Copán and other pre-Columbian Maya centers (1987a, b, 1989). She argues that Copán was designed on the basis of principles deriving from Maya cosmology, and she suggests a site-planning template for testing this idea (Ashmore 1991b). Maya cities were laid out as microcosms that equated the architectural center of civic power with the center of the universe. Architectural meaning was determined by the spatial relationship between the supernatural and the hierarchy of the state (Coggins 1980). This sacred geography may account for the striking regularities found in these sites. Places such as Quiriguá copied the Copán civic layout, with its monumental plaza and Acropolis, in some cases making them even larger than their original model (Ashmore 1991a). The centralization and hierarchical arrangement of plazas at Tenam Rosario, in Chiapas, also show evidence of master planning in the repetition of architectural elements found at other Maya sites (Agrinier 1983; De Montmollin 1989).

Although the Maya evidence is not as clear as that of the Mexica tradition, research suggests that there was a Maya site-planning tradition replicated throughout the region. Although the impact of the Maya architectural and site-planning traditions is not clearly documented in the ethnohistorical and archaeological record, Spanish references to existing sites and indigenous architecture in letters and travel accounts suggest that the Spanish were aware of these design traditions.

Evidence on the Taino of the West Indies comes from the writings of Las Casas (1951) and Oviedo y Valdés (1959), and from archaeological sites. There were plazas, situated in front of cacique houses, where ball playing and in some cases ancestor worship took place. The majority of these excavated plazas are reported for Puerto Rico; Stahl describes them as quadrilateral or rectangular, enclosed by flat stones standing on end (Loven 1935). Some plazas were very large, up to 258 yards long by 96 yards wide, but their relationship to settlement patterns is not always clear (Wilson 1990).

In his description of Taino villages, Las Casas (1951) states that the house of the king or gentleman of the town was in the best location, fronting on a large plaza that was very level and well swept for ball playing. There were other houses near this plaza, and if it was a very large town there would be other plazas for smaller ball games (Loven 1935). Las Casas's writings have recently been labeled as revisionist history, written to empower the native populations (Arias 1993) and present a counterdiscourse to depictions of native peoples written by their conquerors (Merrim 1993). In any event, from these descriptions it seems that Taino plazas had become formalized as places for ball playing, while retaining their sociospatial and hierarchical meanings.

Based on a review of ethnohistorical and archaeological sources, Irving Rouse (1992) states that the cacique's house was presumably a temple that faced a plaza where dances and ceremonies were held. Archaeologists have identified enclosures (recorded as "dance grounds") that the Taino built for these activities (Rouse 1992), which included an annual homage to the chief and other rituals commemorating a battle, marriage, death, or tribute to the ancestors. It would appear, then, that there were plazas in the Taino villages of the West Indies, where Spaniards first arrived, and not only among the urban Mexica and Maya.

Archaeological and Ethnohistorical Case Studies

Three cities and one archaeological site have been selected to demonstrate how different combinations of cultural models and influences were important at different sites. Tipu is one of the few excavated examples of a site exhibiting continuous occupation from the post-Classic into the historic period. Lamanai in Belize was also continuously occupied, but it differs from Tipu in the degree and form of colonial impact and is discussed only to provide a context for the Tipu material (Pendergast 1991). Santo Domingo and Tenochtitlán/Mexico City are the earliest well-documented cities in the Caribbean and Mesoamerican region; a third, Mérida, although poorly documented, is reported to have been built on indigenous ruins of Tihoo in the Maya Yucatan. These cases illustrate how each plaza evolved in its own historical moment and within distinct sociopolitical and cultural contexts.

Tipu, Belize

The site of colonial Tipu, known in Belize today as Negroman, provides an opportunity to combine ethnohistorical and archaeological evidence to study Maya and Spanish influences on a colonial frontier town (Graham et al. 1985; Graham et al. 1989; and Graham 1991). Spanish documents used to locate small churches (*visitas*) built in the region under Spanish direction, led investigators to Tipu's general locus. Anomalous mound configurations, very different from nearby Classic and post-Classic features, helped investigators pinpoint the site (Graham et al. 1989).

The reconstruction of the colonial encounter at Tipu reveals a long period of resistance by the native population to Spanish control, marked by bloody rebellions (Jones 1989). The documentary, architectural, and ceramic evidence suggests that the Spaniards established nominal colonial rule in 1544 and modified existing structures for their use (Graham et al. 1989; Jones 1989). Spanish pottery was recovered from the core of church walls, and the church itself was erected over the corner of a pre-Columbian building, the remaining portion of which was modified and used in historic times. It was not until the pacification of the rebellions of 1567–68 that a major reorganization of the community took place, "represented by the laying out of a European-style, ground-level plaza around which the church and other buildings, entirely colonial in style, were arranged" (Graham et al. 1989, 1256).

By 1638, Tipu joined in a widespread rebellion that expelled the Spaniards from most of Belize until 1695 (Jones 1989). During this rebellion a platform of pre-Columbian style was built in the nave of the church, apparently for the purpose of carrying out rituals (Graham et al. 1989). After the violent conquest of the Maya at nearby Dzuluinicob, Spanish interest in Tipu waned and after 1707 it was no longer an occupied town. However, the pre-Columbian style of the pottery found in the debris of abandoned buildings indicates that some pre-Conquest habits persisted (Graham et al. 1989).

Spanish power was reflected mostly in community planning and construction techniques (Graham et al. 1989). Traditional groups of inward-facing structures were replaced in part by a single central plaza surrounded by the most important buildings. The style of masonry also changed during the colonial period. However, based on observations of other aspects of material culture such as pottery, stone, and shell, Spanish material culture formed a relatively small part of the artifact inventory, and indigenous preferences, materials, and styles predominated (Graham et al. 1989; Pendergast 1993).

Evidence from excavations at both Tipu and Lamanai shows that local Maya continued to be concerned with pre-Columbian rituals and, by extension, pre-Columbian beliefs. At Lamanai, an animal effigy (bat or jaguar) was placed in the stairside of a platform incorporated within the first Christian church, and a late post-Classic-style effigy pendant and marine shell were placed in a cache in the foundation of a building constructed during the historic period at Tipu (Graham et al. 1989; Pendergast 1993). Similar evidence has been cited from archaeological excavations at the Great Temple in Mexico City, where carvings of Mexica deities were incorporated in the foundation of the colonial church and plaza. Matos Moctezuma (1990) suggests that the Mexica were concerned that their old gods be appeased even in the colonial context.

Tipu provides a documented example of a continuously active colonial population living in the shadow of post-Classic temples that stood "only a stone's throw away from the Historic central plaza" (Jones et al. 1986, 43). Spanish olive jar sherds were found in platform debris along with late post-Classic-style censer fragments, indicating that one of these temples, by then partly in ruins, was the site of some pre-Columbian-style ritual activity (Jones et al. 1986). From an architectural perspective, we may be witnessing an amalgam of Maya and Spanish traditions rather than any dominance of one tradition over the other. The portable material culture recovered from excavation is more equivocal, and the documentary evidence sheds little light here because the Spaniards "were least interested in recording those things that loom largest in the archaeological record: the components of Maya material culture" (Graham 1991, 332).

At Lamanai, the first church was built over a destroyed Maya temple (Pendergast and Graham 1993). "Superposition had the eminently practical aim of perpetuating precontact patterns of activity while supplanting one form of religious practice with another" (Pendergast 1991, 343). At both Lamanai and Tipu, the frontier situation meant that European buildings were interpreted within a Maya architectonic tradition as they were built by Maya masons with little guidance from infrequently visiting priests (Pendergast 1993).

The combined ethnohistorical and archaeological study of these sites presents some interesting insights into Maya-Spanish interaction. It suggests that the Spaniards utilized Maya buildings until they could construct their own, and that even when some architectural changes were made by the Spanish, Maya workers incorporated these buildings into their own religious system. Further, it seems that the building of the church and plaza on the edges and foundation of the pre-Columbian Maya settlement at Tipu, or superposed on the ceremonial platform at Lamanai, served only to add another cultural dimension rather than to eradicate existing Maya ritual and belief.

Santo Domingo, on the Island of Hispaniola

In December of 1492, Christopher Columbus built a crude fortress known as La Navidad from the timbers of the wrecked Santa Maria on the northern coast of Hispaniola (Columbus 1493). This first military outpost of Europeans in the New World did not survive, and it was not until 1496 that Bartolome Colon founded Santo Domingo on the southern side of the island (Reps 1969).

Columbus and his crew found a number of indigenous Taino towns on the island, and it appears from the account of Las Casas that they attained a size that can be explained only by the enormous amount of good land suitable for cultivation. The streets were generally straight, with plazas for ceremonial use. Las Casas describes a definite design for building, beginning with the felling of trees to clear a place for the plaza and continuing with the opening of four streets in the form of a cross. However, not all of the towns were large enough to have real plazas laid out, and many houses aside from those of the cacique were built in an irregular pattern without streets (Loven 1935). Many early chroniclers reported seeing these plazas and house sites (Wagner 1942; Oviedo y Valdés 1959; Parry and Keith 1984; Wilson 1990).

The failure to establish a permanent settlement and a bungled administration on the island prompted the crown to send Fray Nicolas de Ovando as governor in 1501. King Ferdinand's instructions to Ovando give little in the way of guidance:

> As it is necessary in the island of Española to make settlements and from here it is not possible to give precise instructions, investigate the possible sites, and in conformity with the quality of the land and sites as well as with the present population outside present settlements establish settlements in the numbers and in the places that seem proper to you. (Stanislawski 1947, 95)

Ovando arrived in 1502 with 2500 settlers. When a hurricane destroyed his capital after two months, he re-sited it on the right bank of the Ozama. He developed a geometric layout as the model for a master scheme of a network of towns on Hispaniola, for which he "coordinated selected urban sites, controlled municipal appointments and determined the disposition of lots around the plazas" (Morse 1987, 171). Ovando's experiences with the implementation of this scheme informed the crown's 1513 instructions to Pedrarias Davila, which directed him to choose healthy places with good water and air, to divide plots for houses according to the status of the individuals, and to arrange the houses in relation to the plaza, church, and pattern of streets. These instructions have been interpreted to imply a grid plan (Stanislawski 1947).

Gonzalo Fernandez de Oviedo y Valdés described Santo Domingo as superior even to Barcelona, and to all the other Old World cities he had seen. Myers (1993) has noted that Oviedo uses the first person so that the reader is allowed to see through his eyes, creating a visual epistemology that justifies his representation of New World phenomena. This literary technique is particularly convincing in his descriptions of cities and towns, but they should also be read as descriptions written for the king and therefore politically motivated: "Since the city was founded in our own time, there was opportunity to plan the whole thing from the beginning. It was laid out with ruler and compass, with all the streets being carefully measured. Because of this, Santo Domingo is better planned then any town I have seen" (Oviedo y Valdés 1959, 11). The earliest plan of the first permanent city in the New World reveals that the impressive settlement described by Oviedo centered around its plaza and cathedral (Bigges 1588). Straight, wide streets divide the town into rectangular blocks containing the homes of the settlers, warehouses, barracks, and buildings for religious orders. In the engraving, the plaza's relationship to the cathedral is as a side yard. It resembles the Patio de las Naranjas side yard of the Mezquita in Cordoba and the church-plaza relationship of the *bastides* and Santa Fé in Granada more than the front-facing cathedral and plaza design of later Spanish American cities (Low 1993).

The colonists' relationship to the native population must also be considered in an interpretation of the origins of the plaza in the Santo Domingo design. Rouse's (1992) overview of ethnohistorical and archaeological research on the Taino documents the abuse, violent subjugation, and mass killing by Ovando and other colonists in their attempts to use the native peoples as laborers. In this first encounter, the indigenous population and their cultural traditions did not survive. The enduring influence of Taino architecture and planning was limited by the devastating impact of Spanish domination and control. Thus Santo Domingo's plaza appears mostly derived from a Spanish-Islamic model, primarily the design of a mosque/cathedral side yard, with some possible reference to the indigenous Taino cultural pattern of placing a plaza in front of the cacique's house. Santo Domingo was a frequent way station for travelers to the New World, so that there were opportunities for voyagers to compare the open plazas of pre-Columbian cities with the marketplaces and parvis (an irregular open space in front of a cathedral) of medieval European cities. It is particularly frustrating that there is no direct evidence for the derivation of the Santo Domingo plaza, because it provides one of the earliest models for later Spanish American cities.

Tenochtitlán/Mexico City

The Mexica capital, Tenochtitlán, was first entered by Cortés and his men in 1519, when they were given temporary quarters by Moctezuma II. At that time it was probably the largest city in the world. The descriptions of chroniclers emphasized the size and grandeur of the city, as well as the design and importance of the main plazas. Bernal Diaz del Castillo marveled at the scale and order of the plaza in memoirs written many years after the Conquest: "Some of our soldiers who have been in many parts of the world, in Constantinople, in Rome, and all over Italy, said that they have never seen a market (plaza) so well laid out, so large, so orderly, and so filled with people" (1963, 235). The Anonymous Conqueror wrote,

> There are in the city Temistitan (Tenochtitlan), Mexico, very large and beautiful plazas where they sell all of the things which the natives use. There was especially the great plaza which they call the Tutelula (Tlatelolco) which may be three times the size of the square of Salamanca. All around it are porticos where every day from twenty to twenty-five thousand people come to buy and sell. (Saville 1917, 65)

Cortés was also impressed by the city, writing to the king as follows:

> The city itself is as big as Seville or Cordoba. The main streets are very wide and very straight; some of these are on the land, but the rest and all the smaller ones are half on land, half canals where they paddle their canoes .... This city has many squares where trading is done and markets are held continuously. There is also one square twice as big as that of Salamanca, with arcades all around. (Cortés 1986, 102-3)

Clendinnen (1991b) notes that the reader must interpret the glowing commentaries of the Spanish about the "planned" nature of Tenochtitlán in the context of the Spaniards' experience of cities as places filled with organic clutter and filth. The Mexica city grandeur was planned in scale and orientation in a way that was unknown among Spanish and most European cities of that time.

The conquest of Tenochtitlán and the siege of 75 days left the city destroyed. Clendinnen (1991a) argues that Cortés did not want to destroy the city but rather wanted to present it to the king. Having failed at this, he first wanted to build a new city on a better site, but then he changed his mind: "As the city was so renowned and was so important it seemed well to us to rebuild it" (Kubler 1948, 70). In the process of rebuilding Tenochtitlán, the Spaniards changed its appearance and identified themselves with the space of the prior political and governmental center (Kubler 1948). The religious, administrative, and civic importance of Tenochtitlán's central buildings was maintained: colonial plazas replaced the markets, the cathedral was built next to the Templo Mayor, and the National Palace covered the destroyed houses of Moctezuma II (Matos Moctezuma 1987). This kind of successive dominion over core-central space became a crucial part of the Spanish strategy of conquest and was repeated throughout the Mesoamerican region.

There is also some dispute about the master plan of Mexico City. Toussaint states that Alonso Gracia Bravo was the author of the plan following his expedition with Pedrarias Davila. He modified the Mexica plan by opening up new streets, widening others, and bringing in new streets at right angles (Toussaint et al. 1938; Boyer

1980). Kubler (1948), however, points out that the surveyor, Gracia Bravo, was not called in until 1524 in order to discuss municipal land titles, and that by the time the master plan was drawn (1523–1524) the cardinal thoroughfares had already been laid out and a year of building had taken place. Thus, the original Mexica plan rather than the Spanish master plan must have guided the earliest phase of urban development.

During the next hundred years, Mexico City grew in importance and size to become a city visited by travelers whose accounts give a detailed description of its physical and social character. Thomas Gage's account described the plaza during this period:

> The chief place in the City is the Market place, which though it be not as spacious as in *Montezuma* his time, yet is at this day very fair and wide, built all with Arches on the one side where people may walke dry in time of rain, and there are shops of Merchants furnished with all sorts of stuffes and silks, and before them sit women selling all manner of fruits and herbes. (1655, 59)

To this day, Mexico City maintains the central plaza and cathedral in its sacred ceremonial center.

Mérida, Yucatan

Built on the ruins of the Maya town of Tihoo near the Mayan sites of Uxmal, Chichen Itza, and Tulum, Mérida was and still remains the principal city of post-Conquest Yucatan. According to the *Relaciones Geograficas* (1890–1900), the peninsula was first reported in 1517 by Hernández de Córdoba, who saw fine cities of masonry houses, abundant populations, plantations, and gold (Wagner 1942). Next came Juan de Grijalva in 1518, and Hernán Cortés passed through in 1519 on his way to Tenochtitlán. Finally, Fernando de Montejo was sent to settle the region in 1527. In Peter Martyr's account of the discovery of the Yucatan he noted, "The Spaniards discovered a fortified town on the shore of such importance that they named it Cairo after the capital of Egypt. It possesses houses with towers, magnificent temples, regular streets, squares and marketplaces" (Wagner 1942, 33).

This description has been associated with the site of Tulum. Other nearby sites also had a rectangular ceremonial plaza, with straight causeways leading to it. Chichen Itza, a post-Classic site, is even more regular in plan, but while Tulum still functioned as a trading center, both Uxmal and Chichen Itza had been abandoned and so appeared in Spanish accounts only as ruins.

Although there are few early plans for Mérida, there is rich textual material concerning its founding and development. The Maya resisted Spanish invasion and resettlement throughout Yucatan (Jones 1989), and the city of Mérida was not founded until 1541. Diego López de Cogolludo, in his 1688 *Historia de Yucathan Compuesta*, described the founding of Mérida as following a great battle at Tihoo, in which 60,000 Maya warriors were defeated (López de Cogolludo 1688). The

Spaniards replaced the leadership of these people and built their own city on the same site, so that people would know that their success would be permanent (López de Cogolludo 1688). This superposition appears to have been undertaken with the same strategic intent as at Mexico City, rather than because of the practical considerations that were followed in the frontier area of Lamanai (Pendergast 1991).

In 1548 Fray Lorenzo de Bienvenida described the site of Mérida as follows:

> After the beautiful buildings [Tihoo] contains: in all the discoveries in the Indies none so fine has been found. Buildings of big and well-carved stones—there is no record of who built them. It seems to us they were built before Christ, because the trees on top of the buildings were as high as the ones around them. Amongst these buildings, we, monks of the Order of St. Francis, settled. (Bienvenida, as quoted in Hammond 1982, 33–4)

The center of the new city was the plaza, which was the main stage for social display and verbal exchanges. Organized around the plaza were the cathedral to the east and royal and municipal government buildings to the north, with the latter alongside a mansion built for Montejo (Clendinnen 1987). Today, residents still pass the day exchanging news and commentary on the plaza benches. It is possible that the plaza of Mérida/Tihoo, much like those of Tipu and Lamanai, reflects a confluence of Maya ceremonial center and Spanish colonial design in which Maya cultural practices were maintained even as the new plaza was constructed from the stones of pre-Columbian ruins.

These four cases—Tipu, Santo Domingo, Mexico City, and Mérida—illustrate the complexity of determining the architectural and cultural influences on the development of the Spanish American plaza. Tipu was a continuously occupied town that flourished in the period prior to the Conquest, although it did not have the number of masonry buildings or architectural density of the other three sites. It demonstrates in greater detail the interrelationships of Maya and Spanish architecture. Further, Tipu reaffirms my earlier contention that even though Spaniards built a new plaza near the original post-Classic temple (and superposed a church on a ceremonial platform in Lamanai), this did not necessarily represent a break with earlier traditions. The Maya continued to practice their own religion even while building for Spanish priests.

Santo Domingo's plan most closely resembles the Spanish bastide-like garrison town of Santa Fé in Granada, and the plaza itself is reminiscent of the side yard of the mosque/cathedral in Cordoba (Low 1993). There is some suggestion that the knowledge of indigenous Taino towns may have suggested the inclusion of a plaza, or that voyagers provided descriptions of the open plazas of pre-Columbian cities on the mainland, but there is no direct evidence for this.

The plan of Mexico City, influenced by Cortés and executed by Alonso Garcia Bravo, is derived from the structure and foundations of the Mexica city of Tenochtitlán. The zocalo and the surrounding buildings retain a close relationship to the original order of indigenous governmental and religious architecture. The pattern of successive core-central space domination is appropriated by the Spanish and repeated throughout the region.

Mérida is another city built on top of or close to an indigenous town, in this case Tihoo, but there is no evidence as to the details of the indigenous town plan, whether from descriptions or from archaeological excavations. There were nearby Maya sites with large ceremonial plazas, but by 1541 there were also a number of examples of Spanish American town plans and skilled surveyors available. The design of the plaza at Mérida, like that at Tipu, most likely reflects elements from both indigenous and Spanish architectural and planning traditions.

It seems apparent that the central plaza design of Spanish America must be interpreted in terms of both indigenous and Spanish architectural and urban design traditions. Unfortunately, we have only limited evidence about the process by which this synthesis took place and few texts that discuss the process of spatial appropriation beyond the naming and establishment of towns (Seed 1993). It could be argued, especially for Mexico City and for archaeological sites like Tipu and Lamanai, that the spatial relationships maintained by building on ruins, using the same stones and foundations, allowed elements of the indigenous politico-religious system to remain. These latent meanings were not necessarily acted upon publicly, but they may have been useful in reinforcing aspects of indigenous identity, self-esteem, and spiritual power that helped to preserve indigenous folkways, beliefs, and practices. There remains the question as to what such designs mean when they were used in areas where there were no corresponding indigenous architectural forms.

Ashmore (1987a) has suggested that there are three patterns of archaeological site growth in which social evolution may be detected. Her original purpose was to systematize observations of site growth regularities in order to analyze pre-Columbian architecture in southeastern Mesoamerica, but the patterns also seem workable for the examination of the architectural evolution of contemporary plazas and city centers. They are as follows:

1. *Simple expansion*: the evolution of a civic center in which the original plan is essentially preserved or modified gradually through time. This usually occurs when there is linear growth and continuous occupation of a center by the same society (Ashmore 1987a, 3).
2. *Engulfment*: the development of a center in which an early structure or structure group is preserved unmodified while the surrounding structures and groups develop through simple expansion. Her example is taken from Quiriguá, Guatemala, where "Group 1B-1 includes engulfment of a single structure within growth of a single group" (Ashmore 1987a, 4).
3. *Lateral displacement*: the establishment of new focal civic groups adjacent to but without direct spatial association with antecedent construction. The older center seems to be recognized and may allude to even more ancient power but is not included in the newer development (Ashmore, personal communication, 1994; also, see Helms 1988). The cases of Izamal or Tipu could be considered examples of lateral displacement. On a larger scale, Santo Domingo is a new town and plaza center that displaces any former Taino organization or settlement hierarchy.

A fourth possible category, not elaborated by Ashmore, is the "establishment of a new center after destruction of the old—but this is much less immediately recognizable archaeologically" (Ashmore 1987a, 3). It could be argued that the two remaining examples, Mexico City and Mérida, fall into this fourth category. But recent archaeological excavations reveal that in some ways, Mexico City/Tenochtitlán might represent a particular kind of lateral displacement. Even though the Mexica Great Temple (or its outermost layer) and ceremonial plaza were destroyed, there are extensive archaeological remains under the colonial overlay. The lateral displacement and establishment of a new center architecturally represent examples of colonization or the incorporation of outside influences in order to maintain local control (Ashmore 1989).

Conclusion

Returning to the larger project of the relationship of space and power and the symbolism of the built environment, I would like to conclude by pointing out how little we know about the meaning of these plazas. I am no longer comfortable with simply stating that the colonial plaza was an instrument of colonial domination and control. We must uncover how it was designed and built, by whom, and for what purposes. The meanings of indigenous and colonial plazas need to be found through the study of their use. Many of these plazas became the sites of executions, particularly of the indigenous residents, while others became markets, or places solely designated for the mestizo and Spanish elites. More needs to be known about the significance of the sacred spaces that were built upon by a colonizing people. Does the reemergence of the Great Temple in Mexico City mean that Mexica meanings were always there, just waiting to be uncovered? Does architecture obscure, as well as highlight, what is happening in other cultural realms? At Tipu the architecture changed, but judging from other aspects of material culture, beliefs and everyday practices went on just as before. What relationship does the built environment have to the experience of everyday life—and how do our analyses, constrained by our own biases and fragmentary visions, distort our interpretation of those environments?

These questions have been partially answered in this exploration of the Mesoamerican and Caribbean influences on the design of the plaza. The ethnohistorical and archaeological evidence suggests that the colonial plaza evolved from both indigenous and Spanish influences and models that created a new urban design form. This new form, the Spanish American plaza, retains architectural, spatial, and physical elements from both traditions, such that the cultural tensions of conquest and resistance are symbolically encoded in its architecture. The plaza remains a contested terrain of cultural meaning, providing an example of how cultural meanings of the past are represented and re-presented in the built environment. Spatial representations of the dominant culture do in fact obscure the representations of less powerful cultures. However, this obfuscation can be at least partially remedied by the investigation of specific examples, utilizing historical, ethnological, and archaeological research.

The juxtaposition of colonial and contemporary struggles, and the reemergence of indigenous built form against the backdrop of the modern city, provide intriguing evidence that can best be understood within a multidisciplinary framework. Cultural anthropological, architectural, archaeological, and ethnohistorical theory and method can be integrated in new and productive ways.

References

Agrinier, P. (1983). Tenam rosaro: una posible relocalización del clásico Maya terminal desde el Usumacinta. In L. Ochoa & T. Lee (Eds.), *Antropologia e historia de los Mixe-zoques y Mayas* (pp. 243–253). Mexico: Universidad Nacional Autonoma de Mexico.

Andrews, G. (1975). *Maya cities: Placemaking and urbanization*. Norman: University of Oklahoma Press.

Arias, S. (1993). Empowerment through the writing of history: Bartolomé de las Casas's representation of the other. In J. Williams & R. Lewis (Eds.), *Early images of the Americas* (pp. 63–183). Tucson: University of Arizona Press.

Ashmore, W. (1981). *Lowland Maya settlement patterns*. Albuquerque: University of New Mexico Press.

Ashmore, W. (1987a). Architectural expression and social complexity in the southeast Mesoamerican periphery. Paper presented at the 86th Annual Meeting of the American Anthropological Association, Chicago.

Ashmore, W. (1987b). Cobble crossroads: Gualjaquito architecture and external elite ties. In E. Robinson (Ed.), *Interaction on the Southeast Mesoamerican frontier* (pp. 28–48). Oxford: BAR International Series 327.

Ashmore, W. (1989). Construction and cosmology: Politics and ideology in Lowland Maya settlement patterns. In W. Hanks & D. Rice (Eds.), *Word and image in Maya culture* (pp. 272–286). Salt Lake City: University of Utah Press.

Ashmore, W. (1991a). Of catherwood and cauac sky. Paper presented at the Annual Meeting of the Society for American Archaeology, New Orleans.

Ashmore, W. (1991b). Site planning and concepts of directionality among the ancient Maya. *Latin American Antiquity, 2*(3), 199–226.

Becker, M. (1982). Ancient Maya houses and their identification. *Revista Española de Antropologia Americana, 12*, 110–129.

Benevolo, L. (1969). Las nuevas ciudades fundadas en el siglo XVI in América Latina. *Boletín Centro de Investigaciones Historicas y Estéticas, 9*, 117–136.

Bigges, W. (1588). *Expedito francisci draki*. London.

Borah, W. (1972). European cultural influence in the formation of the first plan for urban centers that has lasted to our time. In R. Schaedel, J. Hardoy, & N. Kinzer (Eds.), *Urbanización proceso social in América* (pp. 35–54). Lima: Instituto de Estudios Peruanos.

Borah, W., Hardoy, J., & Stelter, G. (1980). *Urbanization in the Americas*. Ottawa: National Museum.

Boyer, R. (1980). La ciudad de México en 1628. *Historia Mexicana, 115*(XXIX(3)), 447–471.

Calnek, E. (1978). The internal structure of cities in America: Pre-Columbian cities: The case of Tenochtitlan. In R. Schaedel, J. Hardoy, & N. Kinzer (Eds.), *Urbanization in the Americas from its beginnings to the present* (pp. 315–326). The Hague: Mouton.

Carrasco, D. (1990a). Myth, cosmic terror and the templo mayor. In J. Broda, D. Carrasco, & E. Moctezuma (Eds.), *The creat temple of Tenochtitlan* (pp. 124–162). Berkeley: University of California Press.

Carrasco, D. (1990b). *Religions of Mesoamerica: Cosmovision and ceremonial centers*. New York: Harper-Collins Publications.

Clendinnen, I. (1987). *Ambivalent conquests: Maya and Spaniard in Yucatan, 1517–1570*. Cambridge: Cambridge University Press.

Clendinnen, I. (1991a). *Aztecs*. Cambridge: Cambridge University Press.

Clendinnen, I. (1991b). Fierce and unnatural cruelty: Cortés and the conquest of Mexico. *Representations, 33*, 65–100.

Coggins, C. (1980). The shape of time: Some political implications of a four-part figure. *American Antiquity, 45*(4), 727–741.

Columbus, C. (1493). *De insulis inventis*. Basel.

Cortés, H. (1986). *Hernán Cortés: Letters from Mexico* (trans: A. Pagdan). New Haven: Yale University Press.

Crouch, D., Daniel, P., Garr, J., & Mundigo, A. (1982). *Spanish city planning in North America*. Cambridge, MA: MIT Press.

De Montmollin, O. (1989). *The archaeology of political structure*. Cambridge: Cambridge University Press.

Delgado-Gómez, A. (1993). The earliest European views of the New World natives. In J. Williams & R. Lewis (Eds.), *Early images of the Americas* (pp. 3–20). Tucson: University of Arizona.

Diaz del Castillo, B. (1963). *The conquest of New Spain*. Harmondsworth: Penguin.

Foster, G. (1960). *Culture and conquest: The American Spanish heritage*. New York: Viking Fund Publications in Anthropology.

Foucault, M. (1975). *Discipline and punish*. New York: Random House.

Fraser, V. (1990). *The Architecture of conquest: Building in the viceroyalty of Peru*. Cambridge: Cambridge University Press.

Gage, T. (1655). *A new survey of the West Indies*. London: E. Cates.

Gasparini, G. (1978). The colonial city as a center for the spread of architectural and pictorial schools. In R. Schaedel, J. Hardoy, & N. Kinzer (Eds.), *Urbanization in the Americas from its beginnings to the present* (pp. 269–281). The Hague: Mouton.

Gillespie, S. (1989). *The Aztec kings*. Tucson: University of Arizona Press.

Gracia Zambrano, A. (1992). El Poblamiento de México en la época del contacto, 1520-1540. *Mesoamérica, 224*, 239–296.

Graham, E. (1991). Archaeological insights into colonial period: Maya life at Tipu, Belize. In D. H. Thomas (Ed.), *Columbian consequences, The Spanish borderlands in Pan-American perspective* (Vol. 3, pp. 319–335). Washington, DC: Smithsonian Institution Press.

Graham, E., Jones, G., & Kautz, R. (1985). Archaeology and ethnohistory on a Spanish colonial frontier: An interim report on the Macal-Tipu project in the Western Belize. In A. Chase & P. Rice (Eds.), *The lowland Maya postclassic* (pp. 206–214). Austin: University of Texas Press.

Graham, E., David, A., Pendergast, M., & Jones, G. (1989). On the fringes of the conquest: Maya-Spanish contact in colonial Belize. *Science, 246*, 1254–1259.

Gube, N., Schele, L., & Fahsen, F. (1991). Odds and ends from the inscriptions of Quiriqua. *Mexicon, 13*(6), 106–112.

Gutierrez, R. (1983). *Arquitecturay urbanismo in Iberoamerica*. Madrid: Ediciones Cáedra, S.A.

Hammond, N. (1982). *Ancient Maya civilization*. New Brunswick: Rutgers University Press.

Hardoy, J. (1973). *Pre-Columbian cities*. New York: Walker and Company.

Hardoy, J., & Hardoy, A. (1978). The plaza in Latin America: From Teotihuacan to Recife. *Culturas, 5*, 59–92.

Harvey, D. (1985). *Consciousness and the urban experience*. Baltimore: Johns Hopkins University Press.

Helms, M. (1988). *Ulysses' sail*. Princeton: Princeton University Press.

Hyslop, J. (1990). *Inka settlement planning*. Austin: University of Texas Press.

Jackson, J. B. (1984). *Discovering the vernacular landscape*. New Haven: Yale University Press.

Jones, G. (1989). *Maya resistance to Spanish rule: Time and history on a colonial frontier*. Albuquerque: University of New Mexico Press.

Jones, G., Kautz, R., & Graham, E. (1986). Tipu: A Maya town on the Spanish colonial frontier. *Archaeology, 39*, 40–47.

King, A. (1980). *Buildings and society*. London: Routledge and Kegan.

Kubler, G. (1948). *Mexican architecture in the sixteenth century*. New Haven: Yale University Press.

Kubler, G. (1978). Open-grid town plans in Europe and America. In R. Schaedel, J. Hardoy, & N. Kinzer (Eds.), *Urbanization in the Americas from its beginnings to the present* (pp. 327–342). Mouton: The Hague.

Las Casas, F. (1951). *Historia de las Indias* (Vol. 3). Mexico City: Fondo de Cultura Económica.

Lawrence, D., & Low, S. (1990). The built environment and spatial form. *Annual Review of Anthropology, 19*, 453–505.

León-Portilla, M. (1992). *The Aztec image of self and society: An introduction to Nahua culture*. Salt Lake City: University of Utah Press.

Lomnitz Adler, C. (1992). *Exits from the labyrinth*. Berkeley: University of California Press.

López de Cogolludo, D. (1688). *Historia de Yucathan compuesta*. Madrid: Juan Garcia Infanzon.

Loven, S. (1935). *Origins of the Tainan culture, West Indies*. Göteborg: Elanders Bokfryckeri Akfiebolag.

Low, S. (1993). The cultural meaning of the plaza: The history of the Spanish American gridplan-plaza urban design. In R. Rotenberg & G. McDonogh (Eds.), *The cultural meaning of urban space* (pp. 75–94). Westport: Bergen and Garvey.

Matos Moctezuma, E. (1987). The templo mayor of Tenochtitlan: History and interpretation. In J. Broda, D. Carrasco, & E. Matos Moctezuma (Eds.), *The great temple of Tenochtitlan* (pp. 15–60). Berkeley: University of California Press.

Matos Moctezuma, E. (1990). *The great temple*. Mexico City: National Institute of Anthropology and History.

Matos Moctezuma, E. (1992). The Aztec main pyramid: Ritual architecture at Tenochtitlan. In R. Townsend (Ed.), *The ancient Americas: Art from sacred landscapes* (pp. 187–196). Prestel Verlag: Munich.

Merrim, S. (1993). The counter-discourse of Bartolomé de las Casas. In J. Williams & R. Lewis (Eds.), *Early images of the Americas* (pp. 149–162). Tucson: University of Arizona Press.

Morse, R. (1987). Urban development. In L. Bethell (Ed.), *Colonial Spanish America* (pp. 165–202). Cambridge: Cambridge University Press.

Myers, K. (1993). The representation of New World phenomenae visual epistemology and Gonzalo Fernandez de Oviedo's illustrations. In J. Williams & R. Lewis (Eds.), *Early images of the Americas* (pp. 183–214). Tucson: University of Arizona Press.

Oviedo y Valdés, G. (1959). In J. de Tudela Bueso (Ed.), *Historia general y natural de las Indias (1535–1547)*. Ediciones Atlas: Madrid.

Palm, E. (1955). *Los monumentos arquitectónicos de la Española*. Ciudad Trujillo: Republica Dominicana.

Palm, E. (1968). La ville espagnole au nouveau monde dans la première moitié du XVI siècle. In *La découverte de l'Amérique*. Paris: 10 Stage International d'Études Humanistes.

Parry, J., & Keith, R. (1984). *New Iberian World* (Vol. 3). New York: Hector and Rose.

Pendergast, D. (1986). Stability through change: Lamanai, Belize, from the ninth to the seventeenth century. In J. Sabloff & E. Wyllys Andrews V (Eds.), *Late lowland Maya civilization* (pp. 223–250). Albuquerque: University of New Mexico Press.

Pendergast, D. (1991). The southern Maya lowlands contact experience: The view from Lamanae, Belize. In D. Thomas (Ed.), *Columbian consequences, The Spanish borderlands in Pan-American perspective* (Vol. 3, pp. 337–353). Washington, DC: Smithsonian Institution Press.

Pendergast, D. (1993). Worlds in collusion: The Maya/Spanish encounter in sixteenth and seventeenth century Belize. *Proceedings of the British Academy, 81*, 105–143.

Pendergast, D., & Graham, E. (1993). La Mezclade arqueologia y etnohistoriae el estudio del periodo hispanico en los sitios de Tipu y Lamanai, Belice. In M. Ponce de León & F. Ligorred Perramon (Eds.), *Perspectivas antropológicas en el mundo Maya* (pp. 331–353). Madrid: Sociedad Española de Estudios Mayas.

Rabinow, P. (1989). *French modern*. Cambridge, MA: MIT Press.

Relaciones Geograficas. (1890–1900). Relaciones de Yucatán. In *Colección de documentos inéditos relativo de descubrimiento, conquista y organización de la antiquas posesiones españolas de Ultramar*, 2nd ser., vols. 11, 13.

Reps, J. (1969). *Town planning in frontier America*. Princeton: Princeton University Press.

Ricard, R. (1947). La plaza mayor en espagne et en Amérique espagnole. *Annales, Economic-Sociétés-Civilisations, 2*(4), 433–438.

Rouse, I. (1992). *The tainos: Rise and decline of the people who greeted Columbus*. New Haven: Yale University Press.

Saville, M. (1917). *Narrative of some things of New Spain ... by the anonymous conqueror, A companion of Hernán Cortés*. New York.

Schaedel, R., Jorge, P., Hardoy, E., & Kinzer, N. (Eds.). (1978). *Urbanization in the Americas from its beginnings to the present*. The Hague: Mouton.

Schell, W. (1986). *Medieval Iberian tradition and the development of the Mexican hacienda*. Syracuse: Foreign and Comparative Studies, Latin American Series, 8.

Seed, P. (1993). Taking possession and reading texts. In J. Williams & R. Lewis (Eds.), *Early images of the Americas: Transfer and invention* (pp. 111–148). Tucson: University of Arizona Press.

Smith, M. (1992). Braudels temporal rhythms and chronology theory in archaeology. In A. Knapp (Ed.), *Archaeology, annales and ethnohistory* (pp. 25–36). Cambridge: Cambridge University Press.

Stanislawski, D. (1947). Early spanish town planning in the New World. *Geographical Review, 37*, 94–105.

Todorov, T. (1984). *The conquest of America: The question of the other* (trans: R. Howard). New York: Harper and Row.

Toussaint, M., Gomez de Orozco, F., & Fernandez, J. (1938). *Planos de la ciudad de Mexico. Siglos XVI y XVII. Estudio historico, urbanistico y bibliografico*. Mexico: XVI Congreso Internacional de Planificación y del a Habitación.

Townsend, R. (1992). The renewal of nature at the temple of Tlaloc. In R. Townsend (Ed.), *The ancient Americas* (pp. 171–186). Munich: Prestel Verlag.

Wagner, H. (1942). *The discovery of Yucatan by Francisco Hernández de Córdoba*. Berkeley: Cortes Society.

Weeks, J. (1988). Residential and local group organization in the Maya lowland of southwestern Campeche, Mexico. In R. Wilk & W. Ashmore (Eds.), *Household and community in the Mesoamerican past* (pp. 73–96). Albuquerque: University of New Mexico Press.

Williams, J., & Lewis, R. (Eds.). (1993). *Early images of the Americas*. Tucson: University of Arizona Press.

Wilson, S. (1990). *Hispaniola: Caribbean chiefdoms in the age of Columbus*. Tuscaloosa: University of Alabama Press.

Zawiska, L. (1972). Fundación de las ciudades hispano-americanas. *Boletín Centro de Investigaciones Historicas y Estéticas, 13*, 88–128.

Zucker, P. (1959). *Town and square*. Cambridge, MA: MIT Press.

Chapter 10
Beneath the City's Grid: Vernacular and (Post)colonial Planning Interactions in Dakar, Senegal

Liora Bigon and Thomas Hart

Abstract This chapter traces the history of the indigenous grid-pattern settlement in Senegal and the Western Sudan, drawing significant contrasts with the uses of the grid plan as a tool of European colonial rule in Africa. The authors maintain that while the search for a unitary "origin" of the grid is historically refutable, questions about the grid's origins are still sensitive in African Studies. By providing qualitative insights into the grid-*pènç* relations, particularly in Dakar from its colonial creation to the present time, this chapter demonstrates that indigenous and occidental planning cultures became intimately entangled. Moreover, indigenous spatial practices have still survived in the most Westernized parts of Dakar and the region. The authors' focus on the Lebou enclaves beneath the grids of the oldest colonial quarters of Dakar also balances current research tendencies, which are preoccupied with Lebou Islamic practices in Dakar's suburbs.

Keywords Senegal · Dakar · Lebou settlement-design · *Pènç* · Grid · French colonial planning · Touba · Spatial production · Bubonic plague

Introduction

This chapter examines the dynamism of spatial interactions between indigenous and Western planning cultures in an African city from the pre- and early colonial period up to the present. The French colonial grid plan of Dakar, Senegal, is discussed

A version of this chapter will also be published as Bigon, L. and Hart, T. (2018). "Beneath the City's Grid: Vernacular and (Post)colonial Planning Interactions in Dakar, Senegal." *Journal of Historical Geography*, 59: 52–67. Copyright © 2018 by Elsevier. Reproduced with permission of Elsevier.

L. Bigon (✉)
Holon Institute of Technology, Holon, Israel

T. Hart
Independent Scholar, Paris, France

against the vernacular Lebou traditions of settlement design, showing the changing character of their intimate entanglement across the period. Conceptually, this is an integral part of the urban history literature on the colonial and post-colonial periods in Africa which has revealed the multiplicity of hybrid forms of urban space.[1] This chapter is also in line with some important studies of French colonial politics in Senegal, showing that the colonial authorities were constantly obliged to engage with vernacular political forms and social practices. Hybridity was thus a consequence of the multiple "paths of accommodation" that were embraced by the French colonial regime due to certain inherent weaknesses in the colonial project in Sub-Saharan Africa (Johnson 1971; Conklin 1997; Diouf 2000; Robinson 2000). The unique contribution of this chapter is derived, however, from the perspective of urban planning literature on the specific yet global configuration of the grid plan.

Globally, the history of the urban grid embraces both multiple regions and time periods (Stanislawski 1946; Rose-Redwood 2008). It is also connected with a variety of forms of political, economic, and social organization, ranging from egalitarian to more centralized and authoritarian regimes (Grant 2001). Since the ancient city of Mohenjo-Daro in present-day Pakistan and Egypt's Middle Kingdom pyramid town of Kahun, both dated to the third millennium BCE, grid plans have been implemented by the Assyrians, Greeks, and Romans as well as in Renaissance Italy, Germany, China, the French bastide towns, and in late medieval England (Kostof 2001). Yet, in almost all the historical studies regarding the modern colonial period, grid-plan designs have been associated exclusively with the exercise of European power overseas and with the occidental rationalist tradition. Colonial cities—normally laid out on the grid plan but also on other designs—have therefore been perceived in the urban planning literature as a direct continuation of European modes of planning beyond Europe. This is true concerning the Portuguese, Spanish, and French colonization of the New World, the later westward movement of settlement across North America, and other colonized places in Asia and Africa (e.g., Foster 1960; King 1976; Marcuse 1987; Fraser 1990; Pinon 1996; Reps 1997; Njoh 2007).

As a result, it seems that the urban planning literature has absolved itself of having to deal with non-Western planning cultures in these regions, or with their possible long-term interactions with colonial Western ones. The introduction of the grid plan in colonized countries has been described in this literature as an act exercised on a spatial *tabula rasa*. Thus baptized, colonized regions globally were "whitened" and could enter the mainstream of urban history. This Eurocentric view has persisted in some classic planning history textbooks regarding the many decades that followed the implementation of the grid plan in colonial urban sites. Nothing is said in these textbooks about Native American, Indian, and African planning concepts and their possible interactions with the colonial grid following the laying out of New York, New Delhi, or Abidjan. This epistemological gap applies broadly to

---

[1] For only a partial list of book-length studies on urban Africa, see Wright (1991), Çelik (1997), Myers (2003), Coquery-Vidrovitch (2005), Freund (2007), de Boeck and Plissart (2014), and Bigon (2016c). Also, for the literature beyond Africa, see Jacobs (1996), Yeoh (1996), Topalov (2002), Kusno (2010), and Simone (2010).

urban history in colonial and post-colonial North America, South-East Asia, and Sub-Saharan Africa.[2]

Ironically, not only were the vernacular traditions of settlement design erased from the historiography of urban grid plans in colonial contexts, but even where gridded configurations are an integral part of indigenous heritage, this has gone unacknowledged. For instance, in the case of the grid plan town with the central plaza in Spanish America, archaeological research shows considerable correspondence with the pre-colonial vernacular gridded-plaza design, and that the Spanish colonial endeavor amounted to a reconfiguration of the indigenous design (Gasparini 1993). Yet, as Setha Low notes, "the hegemonic discourse that privileges the European sources of architectural influence over pre-Colombian sources has gone unrecognized, resulting in an architectural history that has remained unchanged for the past 40 years" (1995, 749). A similar situation was clearly noted by the urban geographer Eric Ross, a leading authority on settlement configurations of the Mouride Way and of other Islamic-Sufi Ways in Senegal.[3] While lecturing on the holy city of Touba, with its converging avenues and straight crossing streets, one of his colleagues remarked that the "Haussmannian" influence of French urban planning was clearly evident there.[4] Yet Touba's gridded configuration reflects autochthonous urban ideas that do not have a colonial origin and can be traced back to the laying out of the royal capitals of the Wolof-speaking hinterland in the twelfth century (Ross 2006, 2015).

This chapter focuses on Dakar. The city on Cap Vert first served as the capital of the federation of French West Africa (AOF) between 1902 and 1960, and then as the capital of post-independence Senegal. Since the French took command in the second half of the nineteenth century, Dakar has been considered in both academic and popular discourse to be the most Westernized city in West Africa. What follows challenges these views of the city and its gridded configuration. It draws particular attention to the city center: the commercial and administrative nerve center since the former colonial project. We begin our exploration of Dakar's urban design by studying its pre-colonial settlements. We then trace the continuous and multifaceted rela-

---

[2] For some such "classical" textbooks, see Kolson (1996), Reps (1997), Pinon, Lambert-Bresson, and Térade (2014), and Njoh (2016).

[3] "Way" (literally from *tarîqa* in Arabic, sometimes translated as "order" or "brotherhood"/*confrérie*) means a path, which, in the Sufi tradition, is connected to an idealistic search for ultimate truth. The Senegalese Mouridiyyah is a Sufi "Way" established by Cheikh Amadou Bamba (1853–1927), with its name derived from the word *murîd* in Arabic (literally "one who desires")—a term designating a disciple of a spiritual guide. Other dominant Sufi Ways in Senegal are the North Africa originated Tijânîyah, and the Layenne that is derived from the legacy of Seydina Limamou Laye (1845–1909), who is believed by the predominantly Lebou members to be a messianic leader. Today, the Layenne has become an influential institution especially in Cape Vert. Several key spatial principles that appear in Touba, including the gridiron plan, are echoed in its settlements of Yoff-Layène and Cambérène (Laborde 1995; Ross 2006).

[4] With a resident population of more than 850,000 (2013 census), rapidly-growing Touba is the second largest city in Senegal after the capital of Dakar, with its more than three million inhabitants. Touba is a holy Mouride city, established by Cheikh Amadou Bamba. For a note on Ross' lecture, see Ross (2002).

tionship between these endogamous (Lebou) settlement traditions and the exogamous (French) ones they had to accommodate. These continuous interactions, which moved dynamically as new challenges were met, are examined over a relatively long period of time—from the nineteenth to the twenty first centuries— using qualitative research methods including archives, visual evidence, in-situ observations, historic and satellite mapping, field interviews, and oral history.

This study of indigenous vernacular planning cultures interacting with Western ones in a colonized place aims to contribute to the broadening of urban planning historiography. In particular, this chapter adds to the less-researched urban history and heritage of the Global South, and to the burgeoning study of European planning cultures beyond Europe. In doing so, we highlight the agency of a "receiving" planning culture in its interactions with an "introduced" culture. This contrasts with much of the current Eurocentric historiography of planning. While French colonial planning practices in Dakar have been extensively studied, those of the Lebou—a small community whose importance lies in being indigenous to the Cap Vert peninsula—are far less well researched.[5] When there have been studies of the Lebou, they have focused on Dakar's margins rather than the old city center, with the assumption being that this "Western" place would leave little room for their vernacular spatial practices. It is true that far from the center, in Lebou ex-villages like Ngor, Yoff, Yoff-Layène, and Cambérène (now semi-independent villages on the northern periphery of Cap Vert), the authorities' disciplinary touch has always been relatively light. This has permitted clearer expressions of the vernacular spatial traditions (Gallais 1954; Ross 2006). Furthermore, most research on urbanized Lebou communities has not focused on settlement design, but rather on more "striking" cultural expressions such as the cult of spirit-possession and related socio-religious Islamic practices (Zempleni 1966; Dumez and Kâ 2000; Ndoye 2010).

Therefore, this study contributes by revealing the persistence of African modes of planning beneath the lines of the occidental grid in Dakar's city center throughout the pre-colonial, colonial, and post-colonial periods. A further contribution is a demonstration of the importance of place names as a usable tool for tracing the African past throughout the periods discussed. This can invigorate the current wave of critical toponymic research, which has been overly preoccupied with nationalist politics in Europe and North America.[6]

Based on a rich set of variegated sources and work in-situ, this chapter consists of three parts. The first part elaborates on the early encounter between the Lebou and the French on Cap Vert in terms of their respective planning cultures. It details the origins of the gridiron master-plan of colonial Dakar and its consequences, laid atop the Lebou settlement of Ndakarou which already occupied the site. A prominent feature in the organization of the pre-colonial settlement, as we shall see, had

---

[5] The number of the Lebou in Senegal is estimated to be approximately 100,000 (Agence Nationale de la Statistique et de la Démographie du Sénégal 2013). Most of them live in Cap Vert peninsula/ metropolitan Dakar (total population of 3,137,000 in 2013), yet they can be found all along Senegal's littoral.

[6] For a critical review of place name studies historiography, see Bigon (2016b).

been the *pènç* or public square (in Wolof, pronounced as "pench," hereafter *pénc*). From this point, the French and Lebou spatial histories became intimately tangled, though, as implied by the context of the colonial situation, not always harmoniously. The second part examines the competing interaction between the imposed colonial layer of Dakar's master-plan and the colonized layer of the *pénc*-centered design. Dakar's gridiron lines were drawn over Ndakarou. It was designated for European expatriates and therefore envisioned the suppression of the Lebou presence. Intensified by early twentieth-century disease outbreaks, this suppression resulted in the imposition of a second grid on the city, this time designated for Africans. However, the obstinate and vivid persistence of traditional Lebou settlement forms and toponyms beneath the orthogonal lines of the colonial system is remarkable, and the initial tension between the exogamous and endogenous planning cultures gradually turned into absorption and coexistence. This process became noticeable especially during the post-colonial period—the subject of the third part. This shows the symbiosis, on a less compulsory basis, between the two planning cultures, taking the form of ancient vernacular designs woven into the grid of the very city center with its high rises, modern architecture, and the celebrated image of Senegal's capital as the most Westernized city of West Africa.

The Planning Cultures of Ndakarou and Dakar: Early Encounters

The Lebou population of Cap Vert was estimated at around ten thousand in the early nineteenth century. Being indigenous to the peninsula, they are not an "ethnic" group per se, but rather a consolidated community in terms of social and political identity, and in the observance of strict endogamy. Composed of peoples that immigrated in small groups from the hinterland, some practices, settlement modalities, and linguistic features were introduced amongst them when passing through areas of the Wolof and Sérère, with whom they are sometimes associated (Dumez and Kâ 2000). Lebou oral traditions link the geographic origins of this group to Fouta Toro, a valley north of the middle Senegal River. By 1700, they had moved southwards, especially toward the Wolof areas of Djolof and Cayor, and thus were influenced by Wolof culture. But upon the establishment of their fishing and agricultural communities on Cap Vert at the edge of Cayor, they embraced a more egalitarian society based on Islamic principles, in comparison to the contemporary Wolof autocratic organization supported by a class of slave-warriors. Subjected to the Damel (Wolof ruler) of Cayor by the end of the eighteenth century, several Lebou leaders started a two-decade long struggle for independence from the Wolof. While Dial Diop was proclaimed their *Grand Sérigne* (*sëriñ*)—the paramount head of the Lebou polity who based his rule on Islamic law—political rule was administered in practice by several chiefs, cadis, and household heads (Charles 1977; Diouf 1990). Of this traditional organization, pursued to this day by the Lebou in parallel to the modern state and municipal administration, two central functions need to be stressed: the *Grand Djaraaf*, that is, the head of a village community; and the *Ndeye Ji Rew*, who is responsible for relations amongst the Lebou communities (Dumez and Kâ 2000).

Referred to by the Lebou as "Ndakarou," their Cap Vert settlement included eleven villages, each of which encompassed several hundred inhabitants organized by patriarchal households. The round-hut complexes, made of straw, were typically arranged around the *pénc*, comprising a central square for communal activities, one or several large trees, and a small mosque made of temporary materials (Gallais 1954; Gamble 1957). The centrality of the *pénc* in Ndakarou fully conformed with the spatial configuration of other Islamic settlements in the wider region. For instance, the principal organizational element of the city of Touba is the Great Mosque, which stands in a large public square facing towards Mecca. This orientation creates the city's dominant axis. The spacious sandy square is surrounded by the large plots (*këur-*s, also "houses" in Wolof) of the compounds of close associates in the Mouride administration and other relevant institutions. Converging avenues then cross the city from several directions connecting it to a network of other Mouride settlements, mostly designed as gridded residential spaces (Ross 2002, 2006).

Indeed, the persistence over several centuries of the central public square as a principle of settlement design in the Wolof-speaking hinterland is remarkable. The term *pénc* means both a public assembly and the site where such an assembly is held. It also refers to a small settlement or village whose community is identified with a particular founding father or lineage. In physical terms, the *pénc* is focused on the mosque and can house other common facilities such as a quranic school, mortuary, and public wells, with the compounds of the town's founding family in its immediate vicinity. As demonstrated by Ross (2006), in pre-Islamic Senegal and the wider region a large tree (usually mbul, kapok, acacia, or baobab) stood at the center of the *pénc* and served as both a social and political institution and a symbolic civic monument. While not considered "sacred" and seldom used for any religious activity, it operated as a "palaver tree," under which communal meetings and decisions were taken. With the Islamization of the region, the *pénc* did not disappear as an institution but rather consolidated: the Great Mosque took the place of the tree in the middle of the square, but normally one or several large trees also stand alongside it. In this way, large trees continue to play a major role in the urban configuration of the region, being connected with the Wolof as well as with other ethnic groups (Mandinka, Serrer, Lebou), and with the Mouride as well as with other Sufi Ways (Ross 2006).

Against the historiographic background of the erasure of the colonized built heritage—especially when the colonial grid has been enforced right over the indigenous grid as in Latin America—it might be interesting to ask whether Ndakarou itself was gridded. This question is also relevant viewing the prevalence of the grid pattern around the *péncs* in the Wolof and other neighboring Islamic settlements of the region in the pre-colonial period; and viewing its prevalence in some of the Lebou settlements in the northern part of Cap Vert, such as Yoff-Layène. There is, however, no clear evidence whether Ndakarou's villages were essentially organized in a gridded pattern. One scholar even indicated that their village roads were never allowed to be straight, since evil spirits were believed to be able to move only in straight lines (Gamble 1957). In the absence of written and other forms of documentation in many parts of pre-colonial Sub-Saharan Africa, Africanist historians tend, traditionally, to look for answers by criss-crossing data from a variety of fields.

Lebou oral epics, for instance, reveal the central role of the *pénc* in the history of Ndakarou. These epics are rich in symbolic and practical socio-cultural details, including accounts of the key role assigned to various trees, *péncs*, and settlements (Gueye 2010; Ndoye 2010). For instance, in the *céét* genre—songs that accompany the bride to the bridegroom's household—the name "Daqaar" is often mentioned, signifying both a tamarind tree and its fruit, used at important ceremonies. The *céét* often narrates the night journey of the bride, who, together with her female friends, sings and walks from one *pénc* to another, sitting under their great trees and asking for rest and water from the households' heads (Ndione 1993). Yet it is hard to draw conclusions about a supposed gridded organization of Ndakarou from an examination of the Lebou epics, or from other oral sources. For instance, upon the alignment of one of the first streets by the French, that is, the straight and wide "Rue Vincens" that traversed the village of Kaye at its north, this street was referred to by the Lebou as "la grand'rue."[7] This might imply the rather exceptional phenomenon of the straight street from the local perspective, though such appellations probably became irrelevant and gradually disappeared following the introduction of more straight streets, avenues, and boulevards of the colonial grid plan by the French authorities.

Similarly, it is also hard to draw conclusions about a supposed alignment of Ndakarou along straight lines from the series of early colonial maps of Cap Vert, consulted at the Archives Nationales du Sénégal in Dakar (ANS) and at the Archives Nationales d'Outre-Mer in Aix-en-Provence (ANOM). This includes the 1853 map of Louis Faidherbe, the then Head of the Corps of Engineers and from the following year governor of Senegal. In Faidherbe's map, the exact name and location of each of the eleven Lebou villages is demarcated by its general spatial limits and not by hut arrangement (Fig. 10.1).[8] While this map does not confirm the gridded alignment of pre-colonial Ndakarou, its value in documenting the original names and locations of Ndakarou's villages is significant because many of these villages were transferred further inland, sometimes several times, in order to expand colonial Dakar as a model space designated for Europeans.

The names of the eleven Lebou villages that were identified by Faidherbe (with their current transcription in parentheses, unless unidentified) are: Alonga, Sainba Dionni (Soumbédioune), Kamen, Thédem (Thiéudeme), M'botte (Mbott), N'grave (Ngaraf), Kaye (Kaye), Kaye Toute, Sintia (Santiaba, Sinthiaba), M'bor (Mbor), and Tanne (Thann). While many of these names are still in use in the old colonial quarters of downtown Dakar, not all of these names necessarily refer to their original locations as indicated by Faidherbe due to the transfer of the villages by the

---

[7] According to A. Diouf, an old Lebou resident in Dakar-proper, as interviewed in the 1970s by I. Mbaye Diend (David 1978).

[8] Plan des villages de Dakar, 1853, Archives Nationales d'Outre-Mer. Aix-en-Provence [hereafter ANOM], FM SG SEN/XII/13.

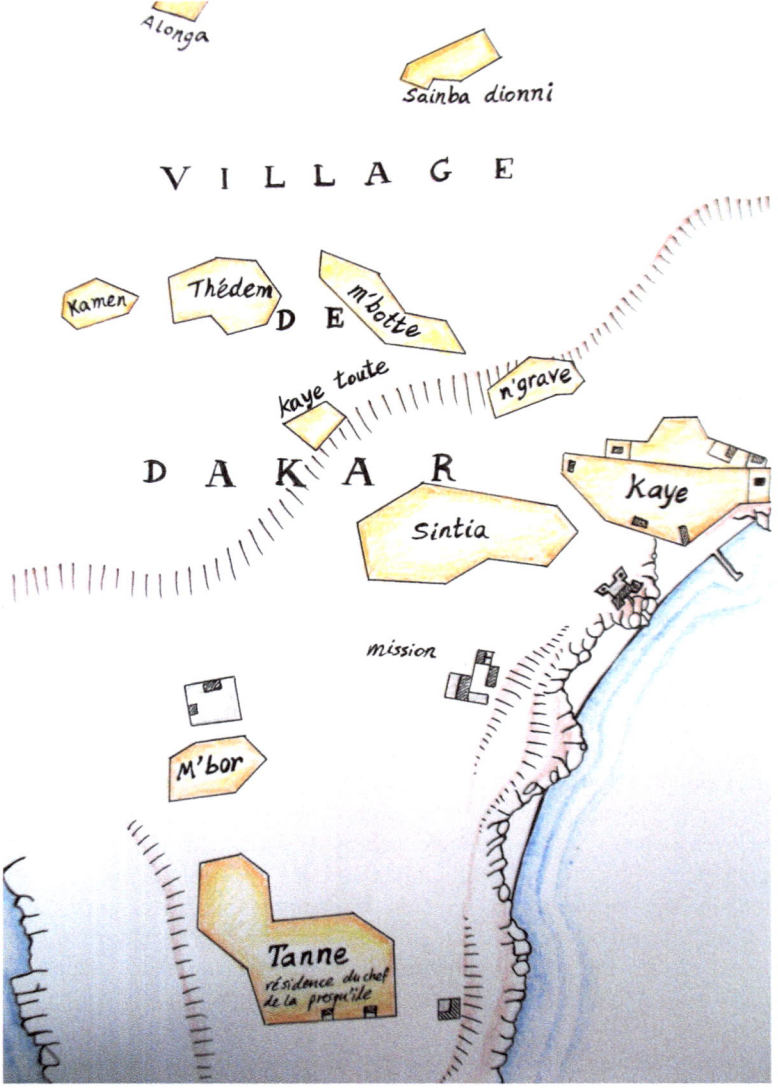

Fig 10.1 Faidherbe's map of pre-colonial Ndakarou in 1853 entitled "The village of Dakar" (redrawn by the authors according to the original held in ANOM)

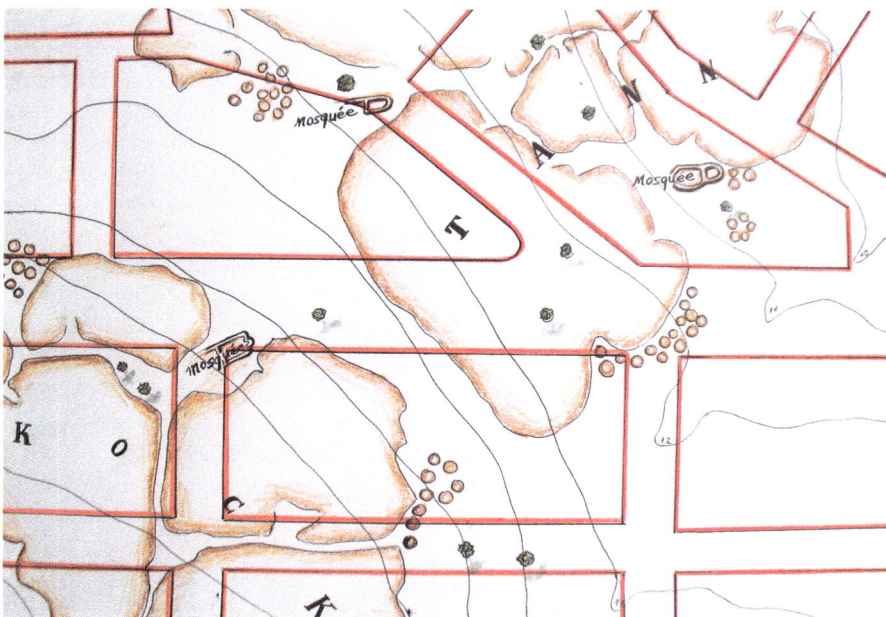

Fig 10.2 Part of the 1863 version of Pinet-Laprade's master-plan for Dakar (redrawn by the authors according the original held in ANOM)

French. The village of "Tanne," for instance, shown on the lower part of Faidherbe's map and mentioned there as the residence of the *Grand Sérigne* of Ndakarouis only as a memory of its original location, signified by "Rue de Thann" near Kermel Market in the heart of modern Dakar.[9]

In trying to read early colonial planning documents against the grain, the first master-plan of Dakar is remarkable. Drawn up by Jean Marie Emile Pinet-Laprade, then head of the local Corps of Engineers, this map exists in several versions made to different scales, the largest of them, dated to 27 July 1863, is 3.6 meters long.[10] It shows the spatial limits of most of the Lebou villages just beneath the thick red quadrilateral lines Laprade drew right over them. While the location of some straw huts is indicated, it is still impossible to conclude whether the Lebou villages were necessarily gridded. What is clear is that the original location of the Lebou *péncs* is strongly implied in this map, particularly through the location of large trees and mud mosques (Fig. 10.2).

---

[9] "Le grand Sérigne" or the "Président de la République lébou" (termed "republic" because of its aforementioned egalitarian organization) resided in the village of Thiérigne, whose toponym means "at the *sëriñ*'s" (Seck 1970, 129). Since Faidherbe did not mention Thiérigne (which was close to Thann) but rather Thann as the residence of the *sëriñ*, it is possible that he considered both villages (which are also close in their pronunciation) as "Thann."

[10] Plan des alignements de la ville de Dakar, 27 juillet 1863, ANOM, FM SG SEN/XII/12.

The gridded design of Dakar, therefore, was an exogamous colonialist creation, but one which was far from being implemented on a *tabula rasa*. The Cap Vert peninsula, sparsely populated by Lebou villagers in the mid-nineteenth century, became a strategic site for the French following the Crimean War and within the scramble for Africa. The *tricouleur* presented by Léopold Prôtet, the Commander-in-Chief of the area, in May 1857 for local chiefs to raise over their straw huts, symbolized an occupation in which the Lebou assisted in refitting a small European complex as a strategic stronghold. The subsequent gridiron master-plan for the city exemplified an essentially occidental and rationalistic vision conceived in 1862 by Pinet-Laprade, within the first five years of the French occupation (Charpy 1958) (Fig. 10.3).

In terms of orthogonal street layout and organization of plots and central squares, Pinet-Laprade's master-plan was similar to other contemporary plans for overseas colonial settlements made by French military engineers. Examples range from 1830s Algeria to older settlements such as Fort de France in Martinique (1681), Kourou in Guyana (1763) and Saint Louis in Senegal (1659), the last constituting an exceptional example of an early European settlement in West Africa (Malverti and Picard 1991; Sinou 1993; Pinon 1996). In the colonial context, the orthogonal plan represented an attempt to discipline a newly conquered territory through the fixing and definition of space within legislative boundaries. It also conveyed the symbolic dimension of "domestication" in a land always imagined as "terre des fièvres et de la barbarie" by carving out a "civilized" urban space intended for European expatriates within a savage *terra incognita* (Said 1978, 35–50).

Although the French historian Roger Pasquier has described the creation of embryonic Dakar as "nothing but a dead city, a chessboard yet to be occupied" (Pasquier, 1960, 406), Dakar's plan was not rigidly orthogonal. There was some accommodation to the topographical features of the site, such as breaking the right angles in an easterly direction to fit the curved edge of the peninsula. With the building impetus following the initiation of the Dakar-Saint Louis railway line in 1885, the inauguration of the city as the capital of the French West Africa federation, and the accompanied demographic growth, Dakar rapidly grew from its embryonic state. In fact, the area covered by Pinet-Laprade's plan, which became known in Dakar as in other French colonial cities in Sub-Saharan Africa and beyond by the generic name "Plateau," was not designated for expatriate habitation only. It was also designed as the focal point for political management, economic institutions, and transportation. Today this prestigious area is still officially designated as the "Plateau" by the municipal authorities, aside from several unofficial names such as "downtown," the "city center" (in spite of the decentralization of the modern metropolitan area), the "old city" (*la vieille ville*, recalling the initial colonial establishment), or the "real city" (*la vraie ville*, referring to its dominant occidental atmosphere versus the informality prevalent in the expanding periphery).

Among the most prominent features of the master-plan, three should be highlighted. First, the plan is crowned by a central square named "Place Prôtet," encom-

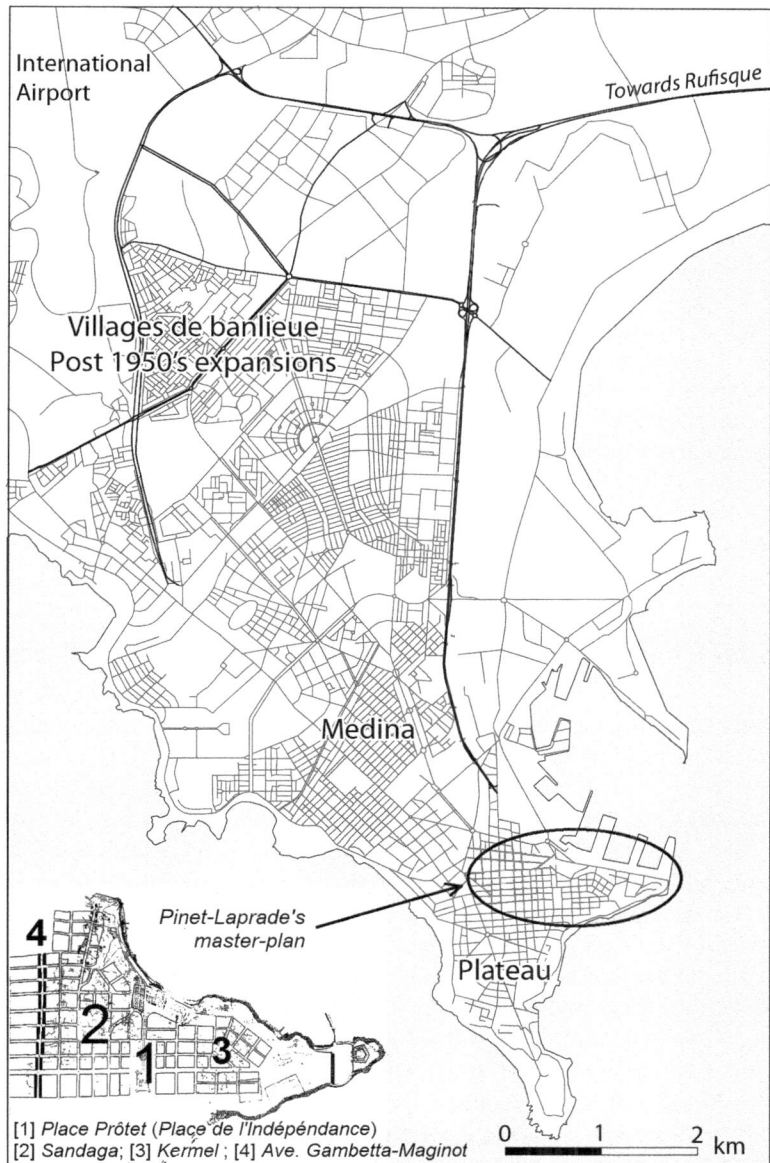

Fig 10.3 Metropolitan Dakar with a focus on the Plateau and Médina quarters against the background of Dakar's first master-plan (map made by authors)

passing a fort and a cathedral. Constituting the heart of the colonial city, it is known today as "Place de l'Indépéndance" and still stands as the state's political, administrative, and commercial hub. Two other market squares were planned on either side of "Place Prôtet," Kermel and Sandaga—and these have retained their function and names today.[11] Second, on the symbolic level, an explicitly Eurocentric street-naming system was offered by Pinet-Laprade for the city's grid within a few years of the official occupation of Cap Vert. This toponymic system underwent only a few changes during colonial and postcolonial times and is still dominant today (Bigon 2008). Finally, the master-plan's gridded plots were aligned right over most of the Lebou villages and their round straw huts. This exemplifies the approach of the "founder" of Dakar to its pre-colonial spatiality: the latter was not only conceived as *terra incognita* (an unknown land), but also as *terra nullius* (an empty land). This approach perfectly reflected the contemporary French colonial doctrine of "assimilation," under which subjugated indigenous cultures were considered waiting to be enlightened and lifted up by Western practices, modes of living, and thought (Betts 1961; Lewis 1970). Yet, as will be shown, the colonialist governmental project of creating the European city through enforcing the grid could not erase the Lebou presence and spatial practices from central Dakar.

Colonial Challenges: Top-Down Grids and Bottom-Up *Péncs*

In the immediate decades following the realization of the master-plan and the laying out of its first main avenues, an occasional and unsystematic process of moving several of the Lebou villages from their original location was initiated. The villages of Thann and Kaye were the first to be removed, followed by Ngaraf, Thiérigne, and Hock. They were relocated from the eastern coast of the peninsula to its western coast, around Rue Vincens. In 1900, a yellow fever epidemic outbreak accelerated further displacements, with Kaye and Hock relocated again further west. In fact, by 1908 most of the Lebou villages found themselves at the very western edges of Pinet-Laprade's plan. They were still encapsulated within its gridiron lines, such as around Rue Vincens and beyond the north-south artery of Avenue Gambetta-Maginot (today's Avenue du Président Lamine Gueye) (Fig. 10.4). Among the relocated villages, aside from the aforementioned ones, were Santiaba, Yakhadieuf, Tiédème, Mbott, Bakanda (hereafter Mbakeunda), and Kaye Ousmane Diène (Seck 1970). Prior to the 1862 master-plan, only two villages were situated to the west of the Gambetta-Maginot Avenue-to-be: Soumbédioune and Yakhadieuf. Indeed, not all of the Lebou toponyms mentioned above were on the maps of Faidherbe and Pinet-Laprade (such as Yakhadieuf or Mbakeunda), which indicate eleven villages,

---

[11] Notice that the architectural style of the structures of Kermel (neo-Moorish) and Sandaga (neo-Sudanese) is an invented colonial style which has nothing to do with the preservation of native cultures (Bigon and Sinou 2013). This is unlike the persistence of the Lebou toponymy, which occurred in spite of, and not because of, the French toponymic policy.

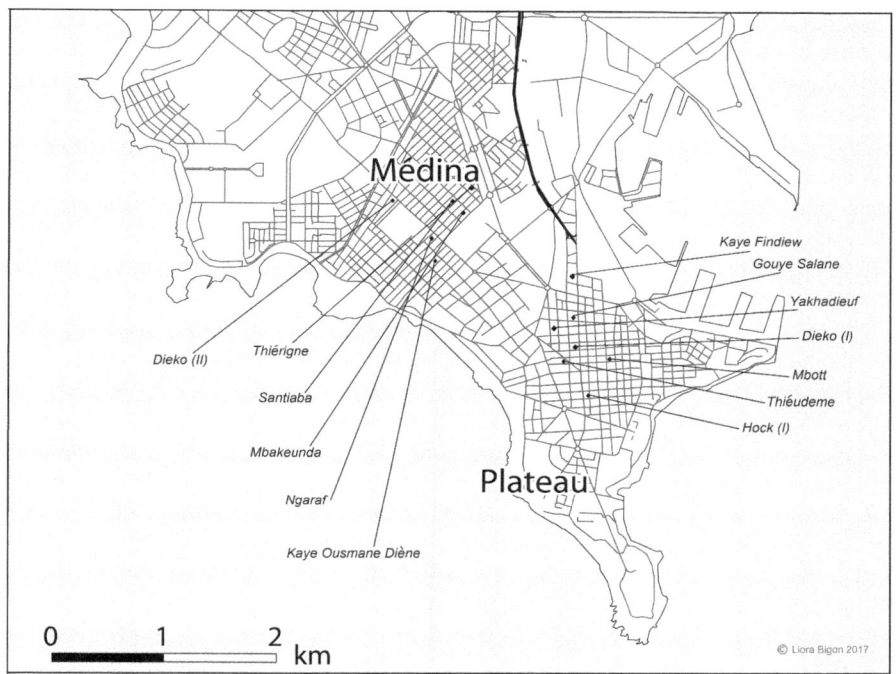

Fig 10.4 The location of the twelve Lebou *péncs* today in the old city centre (map made by authors)

while there were probably a few more.[12] There is also ambiguity given the fact that during the first relocations some villages were split or re-established under different names, such as Gouye Salane (formerly Thann) and Kaye Ousmane Diène (Kaye).

The process of displacement was realized by the colonial authorities through direct purchases of land, expropriation with or without (symbolic) compensation, or annexation by compulsory purchase. Land title and other Western ideas that arrived with the colonial grid, such as land privatization and commercialization, were then totally foreign to the Lebou. Land allocation in pre-colonial Ndakarou was carried out by the chief of each village under the supervision of the *Sérigne*. No private land ownership was acknowledged, only communal ownership by the extended family, as approved by the chief. Even today among the Lebou we cannot speak, for example, of "*këur* Alssan Njaay" (the house of Alsaane Ndiaye), for such a designation would be regarded as almost an offense against custom. Instead, we speak of "Njaayeen" (the extended family unit of the Ndiaye) (Ndione 1993, 98). Thus, in the early period of colonization, the Lebou seemed not to completely understand the

---

[12] In trying to trace the displacement of the indigenous quarters in this early period, Assane Seck confronted several discrepancies between archival evidence and oral accounts on the part of Lébou notables, particularly that of M'bor Diène (1878–1965) (Seck 1970).

meaning and consequences of European land contracts and ownership papers, nor the full implications of acts such as signatures on documents. With the growth of the city and the immense increase in land prices and speculation in the central area, there was considerable dissatisfaction, leading to claims by Lebou that they had been cheated by the administration and had received inappropriate sums of compensation, if at all.[13] Yet in the pre-1914 period, in spite of these occasional transfers, most of the Lebou villages were still relocated "dans le cadre ancien de Dakar," that is, within the limits of the gridded Plateau area and its immediate environs (Seck 1970, 129). This was not the case after 1914, when a second grid system was introduced beyond the Plateau with different aims and connotations.

At the end of the nineteenth century and during the first quarter of the twentieth, a bubonic plague epidemic spread globally by way of the maritime routes created by the European colonizing forces. Arriving from Australia, bubonic plague threatened a series of urban centers all along Africa's coast from 1900. Mortality in Dakar during the plague, which occurred between April 1914 and January 1915, was 3653 out of a total population of 26,000 (M'Bokolo 1982). The plague outbreak in the city has been researched extensively because it generated more systematic racial segregation. Even if this segregation was not fully completed, it has been considered one of the most drastic acts in the city's history (Betts 1971; M'Bokolo 1982; Salleras 1984; Echenberg 2002; Bigon 2016a). We shall therefore only stress below the introduction of the new gridded quarter (called Médina) that was designated for Africans in 1914, and its relationship to older Lebou settlement forms remaining in the Plateau-Médina area, the city center.

In the first weeks following the plague outbreak the idea of complete separation between what was to become the *quartier indigène* (Médina) and Dakar's Plateau had yet to be raised. However, harsh measures were forcefully implemented by the medical authorities, including the burning of hundreds of straw huts in the Plateau, the formation of temporary quarantine camps, and the establishment of two *cordons sanitaires*. Each a few hundred meters wide, the first *cordon* served as a barrier between the "European" gridded Plateau, and the *quartiers indigènes* to its west. The second *cordon* was intended to prevent the disease from spreading to the rest of the colony and was located close to the peninsula's bottleneck. While the second *cordon* proved useless and ceased to exist immediately after the plague, the first, which corresponded to segregationist logic, was retained as an unbuilt zone with some public functions (stadiums, race-course) during most of the colonial period, until gradually built over through land-use pressures (Echenberg 2002). However, three months after the plague outbreak, several ordinances issued by the lieutenant

---

[13] Beyond the scope of this chapter, the issue of indigenous land rights is quite complicated in Dakar as in many other colonial and postcolonial cities, including white-settler societies. For more on the reasons for Lebou disquiet, see Johnson (1971). The colonial documentation is preoccupied with land ownership on Cap Vert, including names of Lebou owners, compensation amounts, petitions, and court appeals (e.g., Procès verbal du conseil d'administration du Sénégal, 31 mars 1865, ANOM. 3E 32; Étude du conseiller général Robert Delmas membre du grand conseil concernant l'aménagement de la presqu'ile du Cap Vert, 15 avril 1948, Archives Nationales du Sénégal in Dakar [hereafter ANS] 4P 22).

governor of Senegal rigidly enforced the construction of "sanitary" houses. All thatched huts in the Plateau area had to be demolished, while permanent structures had to be fumigated.[14] For those who could not afford or did not wish to build with permanent materials, plots were offered in a newly established *ville indigène* northwest of the Plateau. There, in order to attract Africans, land-use legislation was lax in comparison with the Plateau. Exempted from the cost of compensation for re-erecting the burnt-out huts in the city center, the colonial authorities provided straw, wooden beams and bricks for the building of low-cost standard structures in the Médina, initially called the "village de segregation."[15]

The ordinances were applied quickly. The proposed new residential quarter had been defined geographically by August 1914, and within a few months several thousand Africans were transferred to the area. In this context, the grid plan of the Médina had nothing in common with the civic pride of carving out a "civilized" urban space in a savage land, as in the Plateau. The grid of the Médina rather constituted one of the first colonialist examples of systematic indigenous settlement in Senegal. It has, perhaps, an antecedent in the historic *villages de liberté,* gridded settlements subject to colonial surveillance that were built in the Upper Senegal and Niger to house "liberated" African slaves following abolition (Bouche 1968). Dakar's grid was also a tool for government security and surveillance. It facilitated recapturing deserters from forced labor and military service. And, as often recalled by a director of public works in the AOF, a single armored car placed at an intersection could control the entire length of two streets (Bugnicourt 1982) (Fig. 10.3). One should, however, distinguish between the neat orthogonal colonial creation of Dakar's Médina and the North African *médina* (meaning, in Arabic, a "town" or "dwelling place") or *casbah.* These refer to the medieval heart of the Muslim city, later engulfed by the French *villes nouvelles.*

In fact, both gridded master-plans of contemporary Dakar, in the Plateau and Médina quarters, exemplified the highly centralized orientation that characterized the French spatio-political tradition. As in the cases of early colonial Algiers and Beirut, French master-plans based on gridiron or star-like shapes were brutally implemented on top of the indigenous built environments, causing considerable damage to the pre-colonial layer (Çelik 1997; Davie 2003). Such a planning rationale fully complied with the centralist colonial doctrine of *assimilation*, under which, for instance, Algeria was considered an extension of France in 1871, and Dakar was proclaimed by the Colonial Congress of 1889 to be a distant suburb of Paris (Betts 1961; Lewis 1970). But the centralist-cum-assimilationist rationale was deeply rooted in the metropolitan arena as well. Here Haussmann's Paris obviously comes to mind, as well as the social imagery and politico-administrative relation between Paris and "provincial" France. This relationship was echoed in the colonial mind with the status of the model space of Dakar's Plateau, the capital of French West Africa, opposed to the less prominent status of the capitals of each territory within the federation (Rabinow 1989; Bigon 2008).

---

[14] Peste à Dakar, 1914, ANS, H 55; Seck (1970).

[15] l'Hygiène à Dakar, 1919–1920, rapport sur l'hygiène à Dakar de 1899 à 1920, ANS, H 55 and H 22.

However, the living conditions in the Médina were poor, especially during the first decades. Its sandy, infertile, and relatively low terrain tended to flood in the rainy season, which together with the high population density constituted a source of disease. Minimal infrastructure was introduced from the late 1920s, including most basic public amenities.[16] But by that time only eight thousand Dakarois were living there, while twenty thousand were still living in the Plateau, mostly Lebou in "sub-standard" houses.[17] While other non-native African immigrant groups (Toucouleur, Bambara, Wolof) were transferred into the Médina in the summer of 1914, the Lebou resisted displacement to the point of violent struggle. Not only were they already the main sufferers from colonial land policy in Cap Vert, but further expropriations took place when Lebou landowners of confiscated terrain in the Médina-to-be area were obliged by the colonial court to accept compensation considerably lower than that initially offered. They regarded these small amounts as a bribe, yet their appeals were dismissed as submitted "too late."[18] To this dissatisfaction were added extensive hut demolitions, and the refusal of the hated *Conseil d'hygiène* to return the bodies of the infected for burial in accordance with Muslim rites. The result was active resistance by the Lebou, moving between a boycott of selling food to the white households at Kermel Market and direct violence (Betts 1971). Moreover, the sanitary issue immediately became politicized following the outbreak of the Great War in August 1914, the major recruitment drive in West Africa for the French Army, and rising black politics under the leadership of Blaise Diagne, the first black deputy from Senegal to the French National Assembly.[19] The then governor general of French West Africa, William Ponty, stopped hut demolitions, and the transfer to the Médina was delayed. As a result, only five of the Lebou settlements, less than half, were transferred into the Médina: Santiaba, Thiérigne, Mbakeunda, Kaye Ousmane Diène, and Gouye Mariama.

Colonial rule was thus more ambivalent than imagined, with systems of control often far from absolute and subject to considerable negotiation due to the inherent weakness of the colonial state in Sub-Saharan Africa.[20] The case of the plague in

[16] Assainissement et urbanisme de Dakar, village de Médina, création de village, 1915–1919, ANS, P 190; Urbanisme à Dakar: aménagement de la Médina, plan d'extension, 1927, ANS, 4P 133; Construction d'un Marché couvert à Médina, 1940, ANS, 4P 1537; Médina, secteur 2B, plans et devis, 1940–1955, ANS, 4P 141 and 144; Résidence de Médina, 1941, ANS, 4P 512.

[17] This is also clear from aerial photos of the city taken after the Médina's establishment (see ANS, H22).

[18] ANS, P 190; Création d'un village de ségrégation, expropriation des terrains du village indigène de Médina près Dakar, 1915, ANOM, FM 1tp/95.

[19] For more details on the politization of the situation on the eve of WWI, see ANS, H55; Betts (1971). A considerable part of Echenberg's study dealing with the 1914 epidemic fully covers these critical days in Dakar, though his socio-political analysis is less focused on spatial issues (Echenberg 2002, part I; also, see Johnson 1971; Diouf 2000).

[20] In both British and French West Africa, conquest and administration were backed by only meager resources, run on shoestring budgets, and chronically underfunded and under-staffed. This situation affected the implementation of colonial urban planning schemes, and it was also significantly favorable to the interests of the indigenous populations, who occasionally canalized this weakness to their own advantage (Robinson 1990; Bigon 2016a).

Dakar and its resultant segregation demonstrate the partiality of the colonial project in terms of both politics and urban planning. It was especially in times of crisis that a gap opened to include a variety of hybrid forms, as the colonial authorities were forced to accept compromises. Evidence of such compromise is provided by a colonial document which embraces the Lebou toponymy within what was considered as "our streets and our boulevards" of the Plateau.[21] An official survey from 1920 of public hygiene in Dakar following the plague clearly identifies the Lebou *péncs* that were still left, as stated in a list prepared for the benefit of relevant European staff, such as doctors and sanitary authorities, who came in direct contact with the African residents in this quarter. The list not only indicates each of these seven villages by name, but is also invaluable in locating their *péncs* within the French gridiron system of the Plateau:

> M'bot/ Comprised within Rue Sandiniéry, Boulevard National, Avenue Gambetta, Rue Blanchot/ Occupied by Lebou; Tiédème/ Comprised within Avenue Jauréguiberry, Rue de Thiong, Rue Paul Holle/ Occupied by Lebou; Gouye-Salane/ Comprised within Rue Carnot, Rue Raffenel, Avenue de la République and Gambetta/Occupied by Lebou and African strangers; Hook/ Comprised within Boulevard National, prolonged Avenues République and Gambetta/ Occupied by Lebou; Yakhédieuf/ Comprised within Avenues Gambetta, Rue Grassland and Route de Bel-Air/ Occupied by Lebou; Dieko/ Comprised within Rue de Thiès, Rue Sandiniéry, Rue Blanchot, Avenue Gambetta/ Occupied by Lebou; N'Graff/ Comprised within Avenue Faidherbe, Rue Thiès, Rue Raffenel, Rue Blanchot/ Occupied by few Lebou and many strangers.[22]

Not only are most of these Lebou toponyms clearly identified with the ancient village names that were documented in Faidherbe's map of about seventy years earlier (the villages that were transferred to the Médina also preserved their original toponyms). The list also testifies to the fragility of colonial power by showing that a share of the Lebou villages survived segregationist attempts and remained encapsulated within the gridded Plateau and environs. Further contemporary evidence for this toponymic persistence is related not only to the original village names, but more particularly to smaller units, including names of lineages and families. Thus, the area on the Plateau where the General Hospital is located today (between the streets of Route de la corniche est. and Docteur Guillet), which was inhabited by Lebou of the village of Gouye (-Salane), was named "Gouye" by the Dakarois. One of its sub-units, named "Kay Biram Koddou" after its respective lineage, and certain family areas, were also identified by the names of their heads, such as "Bèng" and "Mbeng."[23] It is noteworthy that these indigenous toponyms survived independently, notwithstanding the official French colonial toponymic system. The latter system was all but hybrid, with street names on the Plateau essentially assimilationist in their character, while streets on the Médina were mostly numbered.[24]

---

[21] Rapport sur l'hygiène à Dakar de 1899 à 1920, ANS, H22, 384.

[22] Rapport sur l'hygiène à Dakar de 1899 à 1920, ANS, H22, 384.

[23] According to A. Diouf and A. Fatim, two old Lebou residents on the Plateau, who were interviewed by Mbaye Dieng in the 1970s (David 1978).

[24] In contrast, British official toponymy in colonial Sub-Saharan Africa reflected the softer "indirect rule" approach and encompassed indigenous toponyms (Bigon 2009).

While African movement to the Médina continued well after the plague outbreak and the First World War, it was no longer obligatory. It included in-country migration of a variety of ethnic groups from the rural north and from nearby territories, as well as those Lebou *péncs* or parts of them which had to split or leave the *cadre ancien* of the Plateau due to growing demographic pressures on their allocated gridded lots. The first of them, such as Dieko and Gouye Salane, found a place near the margins of the Médina, where the walking distance from the Plateau rendered the area in high demand, but within a short time the others had to be settled over the boundary into Médina itself. While the traditional orthogonal plan of the Médina was further enlarged during the 1940s and the 1950s toward the west and the northeast, examples of Lebou voluntary relocations into these areas included part of the village of Mbott, whose families settled beyond the Gueule-Tapée bridge and called their *pénc* "Mbott i Pom Alia Kodou" (that is, "Mbott of Alia Kodou Bridge") commemorating a great Mbott notable. The original *pénc* of Mbott remained in downtown Dakar under its established name. Another example is the village of Hock. Retaining only a small representation on the Plateau, it split into Hock-Fann and Hock-Colobane, with the respective secondary toponyms indicating the neighborhoods of their new locations.

Beyond these areas, public housing initiatives led by post-independence Senegalese officials (for instance, the quarters of OHLM, SICAP, Grand Dakar) also attempted to decolonize the French grid system, breaking with it through experimentation with other styles inspired by, for example, Scandinavian modes of planning (Bugnicourt 1982). Moreover, growing Lebou communities preferred to sell or rent their premises in the Médina to Senegalese and other African immigrants, moving themselves to the northern parts of the peninsula. In this way old and more recent Lebou suburban settlements were expanded, including Yoff, Yoff-Layène, and Cambérène (Mercier and Balandier 1952; Dumez and Kâ 2000). There, in a looser planning environment on the part of both colonial and present-day authorities, Lebou principles of settlement configuration and communal suburban design are expressed more clearly.

This spatial process is very surprising. The persistence of the most ancient Lebou toponyms throughout the colonial period enables us to trace the original mobile geographies of their *péncs* in the two oldest quarters of Dakar, the Plateau and the Médina. In fact, tracing these toponyms and geographies of movement reveals a strong continuity that stretches beyond the colonial period up until the present. This continuity constitutes much more than a lesson in history. The following section shows a historical heritage of spatial conceptions that vividly connects the past with the present. As we shall see, beneath the "top-down" screen of the occidental gridiron system and spoke patterns in the Senegalese capital, ancient "bottom-up" modes of planning such as the *pénc* remain central and noticeable. To borrow the words of the French sociologist Christian Topalov, from his introduction to a unique collective project entitled *Les divisions de la ville*, "in capturing the words for an object, one can better understand the divisions of cities. Beneath the prominent simplicity of the spatial divisions of modern administration, the traces of ancient institutions can be perceived, the placement of the past within the present, and the spatial claims of groups" (Topalov 2002, 1, authors' translation).

Postcolonial Cohabitation: Beneath the Grids of Central Dakar

Present-day Dakar, a city of more than three million people, shares with Abidjan the unofficial status of "capital" of Francophone West Africa. It is a regional and international center in terms of politics, economics, banking, business, foreign investment, communications, transportation routes, and tourism. Dakar is also a transnational center for money transfers from a composite network of Mouride small businesses from a variety of countries in Europe and North America. This fortune, also drawn on by Mouride religious associations (*dahiras*) overseas, flows mainly through Sandaga Market, operating as the main hub of Mouride business in Senegal (Diouf and Rendall 2000; Ross 2011). Dakar is also a place where transnational flows of capital earned by migrants—estimated by the Senegalese Ministry of Finance at $1.9 billion in 2016 and representing 12% of national GDP—are visible in almost every part of the city. This money is not invested in the market, but rather in household subsistence and extensive building of residential houses which are mostly extra-legal in terms of title to land and property rights (Melly 2010; Mboup 2017). These active construction projects funded by Senegalese migrants living and working in the diaspora have dramatically transformed the urban landscape. This change is most noticeable in the suburban quarters on the mainland and other quarters of the Peninsula (mostly on state land), rather than the old quarters of the city center.

On the Plateau and the Médina, pockets of privately-owned land that have been held by the Lebou since the colonial period still exist, although some of it has been sold since the 1960s, leading to intense property speculation in this prestigious area. This westernmost point in West Africa, as most of the travel guides claim with the Plateau in mind, is also Dakar's most Western-oriented point, dreary as it may sometimes be depicted. In colonial Dakar, as Emil Lengyel suggested in 1943, "if the visitor closed his eyes and forgot the heat, which was of course impossible, he could imagine himself at a corner of a Parisian suburb." It was, he said, the "Paris of the tropics" (Lengyel 1943, 30). In the bustling city center of today, every plot on the ceremonial diagonal Beaux-Arts and across the grid is occupied and commercialized, masked with a mélange of public and private facades ranging in style from run-down colonial and modernist to avant-garde. It is therefore quite unexpected that beyond the Westernized image of the city center—inhabited by expatriates, Lebanese bourgeoisie, and elite Senegalese—these pockets of ancient Lebou settlement designs such as the *pénc* have survived and thrived. But, how did indigenous cultures, especially over the long term, react to the imposition of the grid? And how did they "digest" the grid, adapt it or weave their spatial notions into it?

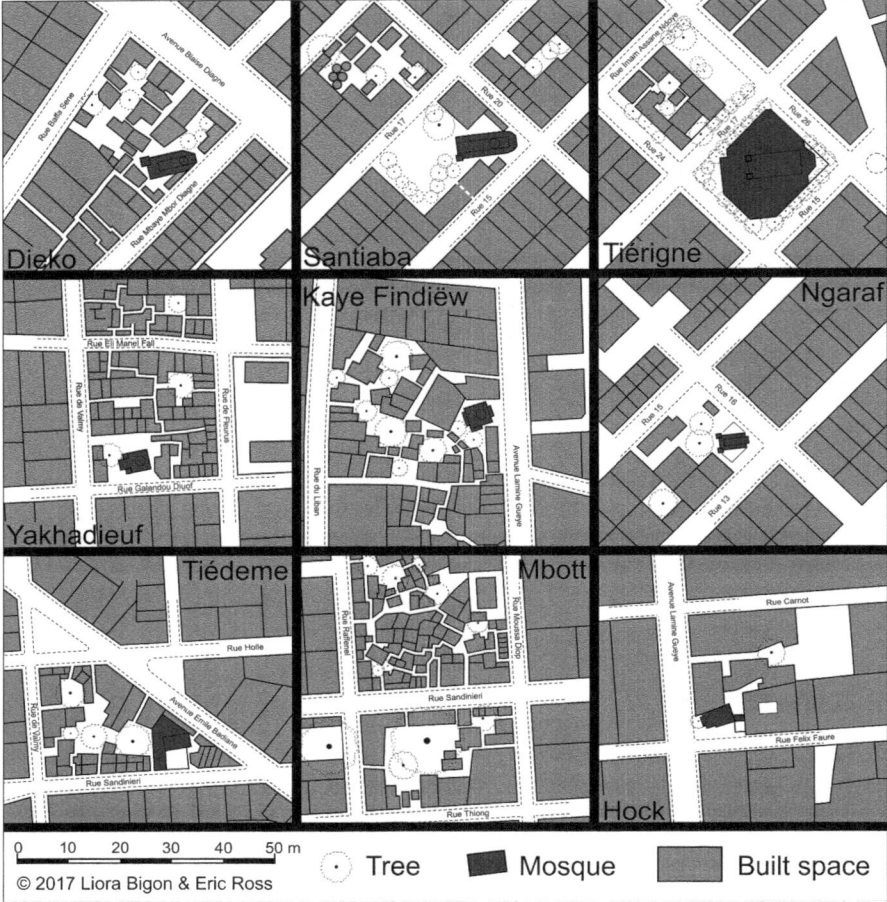

Fig 10.5 Exemplary mapping of nine of the twelve Lebou *péncs* in the Plateau-Médina area (map made by L. Bigon and E. Ross)

Our fieldwork demonstrates that most of the Lebou *péncs* continue, remarkably, to exist in the Plateau and the Médina under their ancient village names (Fig. 10.4), and that pre-colonial logics of settlement design are still distinguishable beneath the grids of these quarters. The prominence of certain open spaces in relation to mosques and large trees—the position of these trees and their species being different from occidental-style tree-lined avenues—constitutes an important indicator for *pénc* identification. A mapping of most of the Lebou *péncs* in these two quarters clearly reveals the visibility and recurrence of such spatial elements as the public square surrounded by the compounds of the community members, the large tree and the mosque. Since the latter is oriented towards Mecca, in many cases it breaks the orthogonal plan by its diagonal position within the allocated square plot (Fig. 10.5).

While the Médina is now densely populated in comparison to the Plateau, we have noticed that the Lebou communities/ *péncs* in the Médina tend to conform to the lines of the grid in terms of plot arrangement and regular alignment of structures.[25] In contrast, the Lebou built-up tapestry beneath the gridded lines of the Plateau is characterized by a multiplicity of smaller, irregular, and dense structures with narrow paths between them—an arrangement that echoes the organic patterns evident in the traditional coastal settlements of Yoff and Ngor, north of Dakar proper.[26]

What follows describes a typical selection of the dozen ex-villages of the Lebou that are located in the old city center of Dakar, starting from three of the *péncs* on the Plateau, and then proceeding to three of those that are located in the Médina. The names of the present *pénc* communities (Fig. 10.4) directly correspond with Faidherbe's 1853 map and/or the 1920 colonial sanitary survey.

Deep in the city center, embedded among the Plateau's high rises and informal markets, lies *pénc* Mbott in its pre-1914 location behind the Place de l'Indépendence. The Paye are Mbott's founding family, which takes its name from a type of tree or bush. The *Grand Djaraaf*—the ancient title for the head of a village community, which originates in Sérère culture and continues to function today—is traditionally a Paye. He, currently El Hadj Ibra Paye, occupies a house in the *pénc*, while the former public open area between the great tree, the mosque, and his residence has now been almost entirely built over. The *pénc* is roughly bounded by the Avenue Bourgi, Rue Raffanel, Rue de Thiong, and Rue Moussa Diop. There are, however, no precise or legal boundaries for a *pénc*, which describes both the central public space with the mosque and great tree, and the now privately-owned homes and shops of the *pénc's* members (*dom pènç*), often occupying several nearby blocks. The great kapok tree (fromager or *Ceiba Pentandra*) that is located at the heart of Mbott can easily be seen from the crossing of Rue Raffenel and ex-Rue Sandinieri (today Mbaye Gueye). As part of the grid, the latter street now separates the tree from the *pénc* courtyard and mosque. According to oral tradition, when *tirailleurs sénégalais* (African soldiers under French command) were sent by the French authorities to remove Mbott during the plague outbreak of 1914, they were driven off by a swarm of mystical bees that had been summoned by occult means from this very tree.[27] Although only a tiny space remains around it these days, the tree is still

---

[25] Population density is 43,580 habitants per km² (Médina) vs. 10,000 (Plateau).

[26] This is true aside from the symbolic presence of Hock (Hook, Khock) on the Plateau, originated in the village of Thann, which consists today of only a small mosque and a great tree directly on busy Avenue Lamine Gueye at Rue Felix Faure (Figs. 10.4 and 10.5). While a very few families remain around the *pènç*, most of its population has moved further out of the city center to the areas now known as Hock-Fann and Hock-Colobane. Still, one should differentiate these Lebou irregular urban "pockets" from the "urban villages" of China, for instance, where the irregular built form that is provided by the landowners for an essentially poor and transient population, is also associated with social problems. Not only has the Lebou, as indigenous to Cap Vert, still pertained special land rights. But more generally in Dakar, irregularity—which includes 40% of the population in Dakar proper and 70% in its peripheral quarters—does not necessarily means poverty, and includes middle and upper class families as well (Mboup 2017).

[27] Gaye (2002), citing the *Djaraaf* of Mbott Ibra Paye, who subsequently recounted the same event to Thomas Hart in an interview on 13 December 2015).

Fig 10.6 Mbott, the mosque entry area with its internal large tree (authors' photo)

circled seven times for the important *Ndawrabine* ceremony conducted by the *Grand Djaraaf* to mark the beginning of the rainy season for the Lebou community. The sandy surface of the *pénc* courtyard evokes the vanished Ndakarou, and is a rare unbuilt space in the very city center. The mosque area features a second great tree that is growing through the roofed-over space (Fig. 10.6), a unique situation that virtually unifies the pre-Islamic function of the "palaver tree" in Africa and the vertical shape of the minaret.

The large and lively *pénc* Thiéudeme is adjacent to, and much encroached upon, by the Sandaga Market. Indeed, the Rue El Hadj Mbaye Gueye (ex-Sandinieri), where one enters the *pénc* with its central mosque and great tree, is completely filled with street vendors and stalls. This triangular block, defined by Rue El Hadj Mamadou Paye Aassane (ex-Valmy) and Avenue Emile Badiane, also contains the residence of the Mbengue, the founding family and chiefs of Thiéudeme. The current head or *Borom Pénc*, Mapote Mbengue, fifth in the lineage, bears the name of the *pénc's* founder. The *pénc* also boasts matrilineal ancestry of the line of *Grands Sérignes* (*sëriñ*-s), since the mother of the first *Grand Sérigne*—namely Dial Diop under whom the Lebou won their independence in the 1790s—was Ngone Mbengue of Thiéudeme.[28] The name "Thieudeme" apparently derives from the jujube fruit or

---

[28] Thomas Hart's interview with the *Borom Pénc* of Thiéudeme, Mapote Mbengue, on 28 November 2015.

Fig 10.7 Kaye Findiew, an inside glance towards the *Pénc's* mosque and baobab tree, with the little empty space that was still left over (authors' photo)

bush (*deme* in Wolof, or *Ziziphus Jujuba*), although there is also a village of the same name near Lac Tanma, a Wolof area in southern Cayor close to the Sérère, from which direction the Lebou migrated. A great Kapok tree is integrated into the mosque courtyard.

Further down the major artery of Avenue Lamine Gueye, toward the new National Theatre, one finds *pénc* Kaye Findiew opposite the Direction de l'Intendance des Armées, at Rue Dodds. While the mosque and baobab tree are relatively modest, in its atmosphere Kaye Findiew is the most intimate and village-like of the downtown *péncs* (Fig. 10.7). An abundance of tiny lodgings, shops, and alleys hem in the central courtyard, reaching back to the Rue du Liban. Kaye Findiew appears to lie remarkably near the location of the village of Kaye on the Faidherbe map, and, as at Thiéudeme, has the Mbengue family as its chiefs, with the current *Borom Pénc* being Mohammad Lamine Mbengue. The word "Kaye," meaning "come" in Wolof, is a common toponym amongst the vast Wolof-speaking regions, signifying places of welcome.[29] The proudest legend of Kaye Findiew concerns its violent, and successful, resistance to the attempted displacements of 1914, led by Yousou Bamar Gueye and a thousand sons of the *pénc* (Gaye 2002).

In passing from the Plateau to the Médina, the erstwhile *cordon sanitaire* between the two grid systems is still distinguishable in its open spaces in spite of the accu-

---

[29] Hart's interview with the *Borom Pénc* of Kaye Findiew, Mohammad Lamine Mbengue, 28 November 2015.

Fig 10.8 Mbakeunda's *Pénc* Office (authors' photo)

mulated land pressures. According to oral tradition, Mbakeunda, now located in the Médina, was at an earlier date a fishing village near the present Hôtel de Ville on the Plateau, and the toponym derives from the memorable event when a great whale beached itself near the village. While Faidherbe's 1853 map places the Catholic mission at this spot, perhaps further research in the archives of the Pères du Saint-Esprit who settled there in 1848 under the protection of the Lebou chiefs might uncover mentions of the village and incident (Delcourt 1974). Mbakeunda had already been displaced by 1900 due to the Pinet-Laprade plan and an outbreak of yellow fever in an area adjacent to Kaye Findiew along Avenue Faidherbe and between Rue Raffenel and Rue Vincennes. According to the current *Borom Pénc* El Hadj Sidy Mohamed Mbaye, the *pénc* was displaced to Médina on 19 October 1914, under the leadership of his grandfather, Mapate Mbaye. Mbakeunda is perhaps the least physically impressive of all the *péncs*. No mosque was ever built there due to its proximity to the large Santiaba mosque, and the communal open space has been an income-generating office building that houses a modest *pénc* meeting room built over it (Fig. 10.8). As the meaning of *pénc* in Wolof is both a public assembly and the site where such an assembly is held, its function has been preserved even without a public square or tree. Mbakeunda therefore retains a lively sense of community identity spreading over the nine blocks bound by Rue 11 to Rue 17, and Rue 20 to Avenue Blaise Diagne. Most of this neighborhood area is inhabited by the traditional *pénc* families of Mbaye, Thiaw, and Mbow, who boast rich traditions of craftsmanship, such as shoemaking, jewellery, and leather work.

Fig 10.9 Kaye Ousmane Diène: Mosque and public square that houses a morgue, large tree and Koranic school, surrounded by buildings belonging to descendants of the *pénc*. Those with red-tile roofs date from the post-1914 displacement period (authors' photo)

By common agreement the most recent of the twelve *péncs*, Kaye Ousmane Diène, is named after its progenitor. According to oral tradition, Ousmane Diène lived to the age of 101 (1799–1901) and possessed such extraordinary occult powers that Governor Faidherbe referred to him as "the genie." As the toponym implies, Kaye Ousmane Diène was established following the early relocation of the Kaye village noted on the 1853 map. Prior to the 1914 displacements, it was located on the north side of the current Kaye Findiew. That village successfully resisted the 1914 evacuation and remains in the Plateau area. In 1914, the *Borom Pénc* was Ousmane's son, Ndiogou Diène, who re-established his community in the Médina between Rues 12–16 and Rues 9–13. The modest but prosperous-looking green-tiled central mosque, its common area, large tree, morgue, and school are located at Rue 11 (now known as Rue Ousmane Diène) between Rue 12 and Rue 16 (Fig. 10.9). According to Abdoulaye Diène, himself deputy imam of the Grand Mosque, Ndiougu Diène originally planned to have the *pénc* share the nearby Ngaraf mosque, but following disputes built his own.[30] From the roofs of the Diène family descendants, among them the current *Borom Pénc* Ibrahima Diène, one can get an idea of the early colonial settlement pattern of the Médina. Founder Ndiougu Diène's origi-

---

[30] Ngaraf is more particularly known for its Islamic religious and educational leadership within the Lebou community than for any particular profession. The quiet, shady environment of its *pènc* seems to reflect this quality, compared to the noisy workshops of Mbakeunda and street trade of Thiéudeme.

nal house, now dilapidated, was located at the center and was originally surrounded in the early twentieth century by a circle of semi-temporary dwellings for his children made with wooden beams and straw. Now these, in turn, have been replaced by concrete structures, some of them multi-storeyed, belonging to their heirs.

Dieko is unique among the *péncs* in having moved to the Médina in 1914 while still retaining a toehold in its previous location in the Plateau. There are therefore two widely separated Dieko mosques, united by a single *Borom Pénc* and a single imam. According to community leader Issa Ndir, the roots of Dieko—a toponym derived from the word for a well or spring, signifying "an ideal place"—lay in the initial Pinet-Laprade settlement zone, the downtown area between the present locations of the Kermel Market and the Hôtel de Ville.[31] By the time of the 1914 displacements, Dieko was located on Avenue Lamine Gueye between Rue Galandou Diouf and Rue Abdul Karim Bougie, where the secondary Dieko mosque can still be found. While that mosque is still active, only a few members of the Dieko community now live nearby. Ndir's ancestor Mbor Diagne is remembered as the founder of the *pénc* on the northern edge of Médina in 1914 in an open space that suited the agricultural pursuits of its inhabitants. During the subsequent decades, the *pénc* community spread as far as from Rue 25 to the Gueule-Tapée canal, and between Rue 6 and Rue 22. The *pénc* center and mosque are now situated on Rue Mbor Diagne (ex-Rue 29) between Rue 10 and Avenue Blaise Diagne, near that major artery. In fact, the growing semi-informal urbanization along widened Avenue Blaise Diagne appears to have split the *pénc* down the middle and thereby considerably interrupted its sense of community. Perhaps the most notable relic of the former site of Dieko is the original 1914-era home of founder Mbor Diagne, a well-maintained building located at the corner of Avenue Blaise Diagne and Rue Baffa Sene.

The significance of present day material expressions of the *péncs* is that these autochthonous spatial logics are variegated and innovative, responding pragmatically to gradual developments in terms of demographic pressures, social organization, and building materials. The space of the former central square, for instance, has sometimes been entirely built over by multi-storey permanent blocks (Kaye Ousmane Diène), or by compounds made from more temporary materials by lineage members (Kaye Findiew) (in Lebou memory and oral history, each of the ex-villages is identified with a particular founding father and certain lineages). Sometimes, though increasingly rare in the Plateau, the central square has been preserved unbuilt and still encompasses the peninsula's sandy dunes (Mbott). In addition, some *péncs*, and therefore the lives of their communities, have been almost randomly sliced into parcels by one or more of the gridded avenues and highways (Hock). Elsewhere, a *pénc* has been turned entirely into an institutionalized cement office block of several floors, without its tree (Mbakeunda). This means that due to the importance of the *pénc* as an institution, it has not been erased but rather changed its form. Another demonstration of the unification of historical layers of symbolism and function has also been observed in a mosque that encompasses a large tree into

---

[31] Hart's interview with Issa Ndir, 15 December 2015.

its very building. The tree grows right through the ceiling, or rather the ceiling was built around the tree (Mbott). While some of these configurations could easily be grasped through mapping based on aerial photography of the ex-villages, we have seen that other evolving physical characteristics are more noticeable on the ground.

Conclusion

In the historiography of the urban grid in colonial and post-colonial contexts, this urban form is normally presented as a representative of Western modes of planning, and the colonial city it lays out is conceptualized as an exogamous creation. As a consequence of this exclusive Eurocentric perception, urban planning literature seems to absolve itself of examining the vernacular planning traditions which prevailed on the eve of the laying out the grid plan in colonized territories. This literature is also quiet as to the variety of bottom-up spatial interactions that have occurred in the long term since the implementation of the grid.

This chapter has brought to the fore the interaction between the endogamous and exogamous traditions of settlement design in the light of the grid plan in an African city. By treating this subject, the chapter also contributes to the more specific literature on the Lebou community. In terms of planning, this literature tends to concentrate on their suburban settlements in metropolitan Dakar, where land regulations are more lax and enable relative freedom of spatial expression in comparison to the city center. Yet still, most of the literature on the Lebou community is preoccupied with the nuances of their unique Islamic practices rather than their spatial practices.

Against the background of the persistent vernacular planning practices of the Lebou community of Cap Vert, Senegal—particularly the *pénc*, or meeting place— the grid plan of Dakar was examined from its establishment by the French colonial authorities until the present. Integrating a rich variety of historical sources and methodologies, ths chapter has provided an in-depth qualitative insight as to the complexities of the grid-*pénc* relations. The relationship between the occidental French and the vernacular Lebou planning cultures changed its character during a relatively long period. In conformity with the colonial situation, the encounter between the two spatial logics was not always a positive or harmonious one, and the vernacular settlement was often subjected to attempts at erasure and marginalization by the colonizing power.

Yet the Lebou community was far from being a passive recipient of the grid plan and its accompanying attempts at regularization and surveillance, and had its own crystallized and stubbornly persistent spatial practices of settlement configuration. These practices are clearly noticeable in post-colonial Dakar and, quite unexpectedly, in its Westernized city center. The Lebou practices of settlement configuration have not therefore been placed "side by side" with the French colonial gridded quarters in downtown Dakar—as one might expect of the literature on the "dual" colonial city—but rather in dynamic involvement with them. It has been demonstrated that since the colonial encounter, the grid-*pénc* relational interactions became intimately entangled and hybridized, and eventually changed their character from challenge and competition to adaptation and cohabitation.

Acknowledgements We thank Abdou Khadre Gueye and the Lebou community of Dakar, who showed us the *péncs*, and the Truman Research Institute for the Advancement of Peace at the Hebrew University of Jerusalem for financial support. We also thank the *Journal of Historical Geography*, where this chapter has been originally published, and its editor, Professor Miles Ogborn, for his careful reading and constructive remarks.

References

Agence Nationale de la Statistique et de la Démographie du Sénégal. (2013). http://www.ansd.sn/ (visited 10 October 2017).

Betts, R. (1961). *Assimilation and association in French colonial theory, 1890–1914*. New York: Columbia University Press.

Betts, R. (1971). The establishment of the Medina in Dakar, Senegal, 1914. *Africa, 41*(2), 143–152.

Bigon, L. (2008). Names, norms and forms: French and indigenous toponyms in early colonial Dakar, Senegal. *Planning Perspectives, 23*(4), 479–501.

Bigon, L. (2009). Urban planning, colonial doctrines and street naming in French Dakar and British Lagos. *Urban History, 36*(3), 426–448.

Bigon, L. (2016a). Bubonic plague, colonial ideologies and urban planning policies: Dakar, Lagos and Kumasi. *Planning Perspectives, 31*(2), 205–226.

Bigon, L. (2016b). Introduction. In L. Bigon (Ed.), *Place names in Africa: Colonial urban legacies, entangled histories* (pp. 1–25). Cham: Springer.

Bigon, L. (2016c). *French colonial Dakar: The morphogenesis of an African regional capital*. Manchester: Manchester University Press.

Bigon, L., & Sinou, A. (2013). The quest for colonial style in French West Africa: Prefabricating Marché Kermel and Sandaga. *Urban History, 39*(4), 709–725.

Bouche, D. (1968). *Les villages de liberté en Afrique noire française, 1887–1910*. Paris, Mouton.

Bugnicourt, J. (1982). Dakar without bounds. In Aga Khan Award for Architecture (Ed.), *Reading the contemporary African city* (pp. 13–46). Concept Media: Singapore.

Çelik, Z. (1997). *Urban forms and colonial confrontations: Algiers under French rule*. Berkeley: University of California Press.

Charles, E. (1977). *Precolonial Senegal: The Jolof kingdom*. Boston: African Studies Center.

Charpy, J. (1958). *La fondation de Dakar (1845, 1857, 1869)*. Paris: Larose.

Conklin, A. (1997). *A mission to civilize: The republican idea of empire in France and West Africa, 1895–1930*. Stanford: Stanford University Press.

Coquery-Vidrovitch, C. (2005). *The history of African cities south of the Sahara: From the origins to colonization*. Princeton: Markus Wiener.

David, P. (1978). *Paysages dakarois de l'époque coloniale*. Dakar: ENDA.

Davie, M. (2003). Beirut and the Étoile area: An exclusively French project? In J. Nasr & M. Volait (Eds.), *Urbanism: Imported or exported?* (pp. 206–229). Chichester: Wiley-Academy.

de Boeck, F., & Plissart, M. (2014). *Kinshasa: Tales of the invisible city*. Leuven: Leuven University Press.

Delcourt, J. (1974). Les Anciennes églises de Dakar. *Horizons Africains, 274*, 18–21.

Diouf, M. (1990). *Le Kajoor au XIXe siècle: pouvoir ceddo et conquête colonial*. Paris: Karthala.

Diouf, M. (2000). Assimilation coloniale et identités religieuses de la civilité des originaires des Quatre Communes (Sénégal). *Canadian Journal of African Studies, 34*(3), 565–587.

Diouf, M., & Rendall, S. (2000). The Senegalese murid trade diaspora and the making of a vernacular cosmopolitanism. *Public Culture, 12*(3), 679–702.

Dumez, R., & Kâ, M. (2000). *Yoff, le territoire assiégé: un village lébou dans la banlieue de Dakar, Dossiers régions côtières et petites îles 7*. Paris: UNESCO.

Echenberg, M. (2002). *Black death, white medicine: Bubonic plague and the politics of public health in colonial Senegal, 1914–1945*. Portsmouth: James Currey.

Foster, G. (1960). *Culture and conquest: The American Spanish heritage*. Chicago: Quadrangle Books.

Fraser, V. (1990). *The architecture of conquest: Building in the viceroyalty of Peru*. Cambridge: Cambridge University Press.

Freund, B. (2007). *The African city: A history*. Cambridge: Cambridge University Press.

Gallais, J. (1954). *Dans la grande banlieue de Dakar: les villages Lébous de la presqu'île du Cap Vert*. Dakar: Institut des Hautes Études.

Gamble, D. (1957). *The wolof of Senegambia: Together with notes on the Lebu and the Sereer*. London: International African Institute.

Gasparini, G. (1993). The pre-hispanic grid system: The urban shape of conquest and territorial organization. In R. Bennet (Ed.), *Settlements in the Americas: Cross-cultural perspectives* (pp. 78–109). Newark: University of Delaware Press.

Gaye, A. K. (2002). Le Peuple Lébou a travers lès âges: repères historique. *Info Penc*, May 15, n.p.

Grant, J. (2001). The dark side of the grid: Power and urban design. *Planning Perspectives, 16*(3), 219–241.

Gueye, M. (2010). *Woyyi Céet*: Senegalese women's oral discourses on marriage and womanhood. *Research in African Literatures, 41*(4), 65–86.

Jacobs, J. (1996). *Edge of empire: Postcolonialism and the city*. London: Routledge.

Johnson, W. (1971). *The emergence of black politics in Senegal: The struggle for power in the four communes, 1900–1920*. Stanford: Stanford University Press.

King, A. (1976). *Colonial urban development: Culture, social power and environment*. London: Routledge and Kegan Paul.

Kostof, S. (2001 [1991]). *The city shaped: Urban patterns and meanings through history*. London: Thames and Hudson.

Kusno, A. (2010). *The appearances of memory: Mnemonic practices of architecture and urban form in Indonesia*. Durham Duke University Press.

Laborde, C. (1995). *La confrérie Layenne et les Lébou du Sénégal*. Bordeaux: CEAN.

Lengyel, E. (1943). *Dakar: Outpost of two hemispheres*. New York: Random House.

Lewis, M. (1970). One hundred million Frenchmen: The assimilation theory in French colonial policy. In R. Collins (Ed.), *Problems in the history of colonial Africa, 1860–1960* (pp. 165–178). Englewood Cliffs: Prentice-Hall.

Low, S. (1995). Indigenous architecture and the Spanish American plaza in Mesoamerica and the Caribbean. *American Anthropologist, 97*(4), 748–762.

M'Bokolo, E. (1982). Peste et société urbaine à Dakar: l'épidémie de 1914. *Cahiers d'Études africaines, 22*(85), 13–46.

Malverti, X., & Picard, A. (1991). Algeria: Military genius and civic design (1830–1870). *Planning Perspectives, 6*(2), 207–236.

Marcuse, P. (1987). The grid as city plan: New York City and laissez-faire planning in the nineteenth century. *Planning Perspectives, 2*(3), 287–310.

Mboup, G. (2017). Land: The hidden assets in African cities. Paper presented at the 2017 World Bank Conference on Land and Poverty, Washington DC, 20–24 March.

Melly, C. (2010). Inside-out houses: Urban belonging and imagined futures in Dakar, Senegal. *Comparative Studies in Society and History, 52*(1), 37–65.

Mercier, P., & Balandier, G. (1952). *Les pêcheurs Lébou du Sénégal*. Saint-Louis, Sénégal: IFAN.

Myers, G. (2003). *Verandahs of power: Colonialism and space in urban Africa*. Syracuse: Syracuse University Press.

Ndione, T. (1993). *Woyi Céét*: Traditional marriage songs of the Lebou. *Research in African Literatures*, 24: n.p.

Ndoye, O. (2010). *Le N'döep: transe thérapeutique chez les lébous du Sénégal*. Paris: EPHE.

Njoh, A. (2007). *Planning power: Town planning and social control in British and French colonial Africa*. London: UCL Press.

Njoh, A. (2016). *French urbanism in foreign lands*. Cham: Springer.

Pasquier, R. (1960). Villes du Sénégal aux xix siècle. *Revue française d'histoire d'outre-mer, 168-169*, 387–426.

Pinon, P. (1996). Raisons et formes de villes: approche comparée des fondations coloniales française au début du xviii siècle. In C. Coquery-Vidrovitch & O. Goerg (Eds.), *La Ville européenne outre-mers* (pp. 27–56). Paris: l'Harmattan.

Pinon, P., Lambert-Bresson, M., & Térade, A. (Eds.). (2014). *Architectures urbaines, formes et temps*. Paris: Picard.

Rabinow, P. (1989). *French modern: Norms and forms of the social environment*. Cambridge: MIT Press.

Reps, J. (1997 [1965]). *The making of urban America: A history of city planning*. Princeton: Princeton University Press.

Robinson, J. (1990). A perfect system of control? State power and 'native locations' in South Africa. *Environment and Planning D, 8*(2), 135–162.

Robinson, D. (2000). *Paths of accommodation: Muslim societies and French colonial authorities in Senegal and Mauritania, 1880–1920*. Ohio: Ohio University Press.

Rose-Redwood, R. (2008). Genealogies of the grid: Revisiting Stanislawski's search for the origin of the grid-pattern town. *Geographical Review, 98*(1), 42–58.

Ross, E. (2002). Marabout republics then and now: Configuring Muslim towns in Senegal. *Islam et sociétés au sud du Sahara, 16*, 35–65.

Ross, E. (2006). *Sufi city: Urban design and archetypes in Touba*. Rochester: Rochester University Press.

Ross, E. (2011). Globalising touba: Expatriate disciples in the world city network. *Urban Studies, 48*(14), 2929–2952.

Ross, E. (2015). The grid plan in the history of Senegalese urban design. In C. Silva (Ed.), *Urban planning in sub-Saharan Africa* (pp. 110–128). New York: Routledge.

Said, E. (1978). *Orientalism*. New York: Pantheon.

Salleras, B. (1984). *La peste à Dakar en 1914: Médina ou les enjeux complexes d'un politique sanitaire*. EHSS Paris: Ph.D. diss.

Seck, A. (1970). *Dakar, métropole ouest africaine*. Dakar: IFAN.

Simone, A. (2010). *City life from Jakarta to Dakar*. New York: Routledge.

Sinou, A. (1993). *Comptoirs et villes coloniales du Sénégal: Saint-Louis, Gorée, Dakar*. Paris: ORSTOM.

Stanislawski, D. (1946). The origin and spread of the grid-pattern town. *Geographical Review, 36*(1), 105–120.

Topalov, C. (Ed.). (2002). *Les divisions de la ville, collection "Les mots de la ville."* Paris: UNESCO.

Wright, G. (1991). *The politics of design in French colonial urbanism*. Chicago: University of Chicago Press.

Yeoh, B. (1996). *Contesting space: Power and the built environment in colonial Singapore*. Oxford: Oxford University Press.

Zempleni, A. (1966). La dimension thérapeutique du culte des Rab, Ndöp, Tuur et Samp: rites de possession chez les Lébu et les Wolof. *Psychopathologie Africaine, 2*(3), 295–439.

Chapter 11
American Cities: The Grid Plan and the Protestant Ethic

Richard Sennett

Abstract By expanding on the relation between space and culture, this chapter scrutinizes the interaction between the grid plan and the Protestant Ethic. Moving between a critique of religious philosophy and the psychology of the urban form as a social construct, the chapter exemplifies the entanglement of cultural values with the spatial order. The author argues that this entanglement and its particular realization in the very form of U.S. cities has had a powerful effect on modern vision, just as, in Max Weber's formulation, religious techniques of self-regulation continued long after religious faith had waned. The chapter suggests that the American grid plan was a sign of a peculiarly modern form of repression based upon the denial of meaning and difference through the production of abstract urban spaces of neutrality.

Keywords Grid plan · Symbolic power · U.S. cities · Capitalism · Repression · Neutrality · Max Weber · Protestant Ethic

The Making of Grids

The Egyptian hierograph which the historian Joseph Rykwert (1988, 192) believes was one of the original signs for a town is ⊕, transcribed as "nywt." This hierograph is a cross within a circle, and suggests two of the simplest, most enduring urban images. The circle is a single, unbroken closed line; it suggests enclosure, a wall or space like a town square; within this enclosure, life unfolds. The cross is the simplest form of distinct compound lines; it is perhaps the most ancient object of environmental process, as opposed to the circle, which represents the boundary defining

This chapter was originally published as Sennett, R. (1990). "American Grids: The Grid Plan and the Protestant Ethic." *International Social Science Journal*, 42(3): 269–285. Copyright © 1990 by Blackwell Publishing Ltd. Reproduced with permission of Blackwell Publishing Ltd.

R. Sennett (✉)
London School of Economics, London, UK
e-mail: r.sennett@lse.ac.uk

© Springer International Publishing AG, part of Springer Nature 2018   207
R. Rose-Redwood, L. Bigon (eds.), *Gridded Worlds: An Urban Anthology*,
https://doi.org/10.1007/978-3-319-76490-0_11

environmental size. Crossed lines represent an elemental way of making streets within the boundary, through making grids.

The Babylonians and the ancient Egyptians made cities by planning straight streets to meet at right angles, thus creating regular, repeating blocks of land on which to build. Hippodamus of Miletus is conventionally thought the first city builder to conceive of these grids as expressions of culture; the grid expressed, he believed, the rationality of civilized life. In their military conquests the Romans elaborated the contrast between the rude and formless camps of the barbarians and their own military forts, or *castra*. The Roman camps were laid out as squares or rectangles. The perimeter was at first guarded by soldiers, and then, as the camp grew into a permanent settlement, the four sides were walled in. When first established, a *castro* was divided inside into four parts by two axial streets, the *decumanus* and the *cardo*; the meeting point of these two principal streets was where the principal military tents were placed in the early stages of settlement, and later the forum was placed just to the north of the crossing. If the encampment did indeed prosper, the spaces between the perimeter and the center were gradually filled up by repeating the overall idea of axes and centers in miniature. For the Romans, the point of these rules was to create cities on the pattern of Rome itself; wherever in the world a Roman lived, he was at home.

In the subsequent history in Western urbanism, the grid has been of special use in starting new space or in renovating existing space devastated by catastrophe. All the schemes for rebuilding London after the great fire of 1666—Hooke's, Evelyn's, and Wren's—made use of the Roman grid form; these schemes influenced Americans like William Penn in conceiving the making of a city from scratch. Nineteenth-century America seems a whole nation of cities created on the principles of the Roman military camp, and the American example of "instant" cities in turn influenced the new city building in other parts of the world.

In its origins, the grid established a spiritual center. "The rite of the founding of a town touches on one of the great commonplaces of religious experience," Joseph Rykwert writes in his study of the Roman city,

> The construction of any human dwelling or communal building is in some sense always an *anamnesis*, the recalling of a divine "instituting" of a center of the world. That is why the place on which it is built cannot arbitrarily or even "rationally" be chosen by the builders, it must be "discovered" through the revelation of some divine agency. (1988, 90)

The ancient writer Hyginus Gromaticus believed that the priests inaugurating a new Roman town must find its place in the cosmos, for "boundaries are never drawn without reference to the order of the universe, for the *decunami* are set in line with the course of the sun, while the *cardines* follow the axis of the sky" (Rykwert 1988, 90–1). However, no physical design ever dictates a permanent meaning. Grids, like any design, become whatever particular societies make them represent. The Romans saw the grid as an emotionally charged design, while the Americans used it for a different purpose: to deny that complexity and difference existed in the environment. The grid has seemed in modern times a plan which neutralizes the environment.

The Roman military city was conceived to develop in time within its boundary, designed to be filled in. The modern grid was meant to be boundary-less, to extend block after block after block outward as the city grew. In contriving the grid plan of 1811 which has since determined modern Manhattan above Greenwich Village, the planning commissioners acknowledged "it may be a subject of merriment, that the Commissioners have provided space for a greater population than is collected at any spot on this side of China" (Bridges 1811, 30). But just as Americans saw the natural world around them as limitless, they saw their own powers of conquest and habitation as subject to no natural or inherent limitation.

The Romans imagined from the sense of a distinct, bounded whole how to generate a center at the intersection of the *decumanus* and the *cardo*, and then how to create centers for each neighborhood by imitating this crossing of principal axes in each subsection. The Americans tended more and more to eliminate the public center, as in the plans for Chicago devised in 1833, and San Francisco in 1849 and 1856, which provided only a handful of small public spaces within thousands of imagined blocks of building. Even when the desire for a center existed it was difficult to deduce where public places should be, and how they should work, in cities conceived like a map of limitless rectangles of land. The humane civic spaces in Colonial Philadelphia created by Penn and Holme, or at the opposite pole, the brutal slave market squares of *ante bellum* Savannah—both workable spaces for organized crowd life—faded as models during the era when vast sums were poured into urban development.

The American grids inflected, it is true, a certain intensification of value at the intersections of streets, rather than in the middle of blocks; in modern Manhattan, for instance, tall buildings in residential neighborhoods are permitted at the corners, whereas the middle of the block is kept low. But even this pattern, when repeated often enough, loses these powers of "imageability," which the urbanist Kevin Lynch sought, powers of designating the character of specific places and of their relationship to the larger city.

Perhaps the most striking grids made in this fashion were in the southern rim of settlement in America, in the cities developed under Spanish rule or influence. On 3 July 1573, Philip II of Spain laid down a set of ordinances for the creation of cities in his New World lands, the "Law of the Indies." The key provision is the decree that towns will take form symmetrically through defining their centers, a decree expressed simply and rigorously:

> The plan of the place, with its squares, streets, and building lots is to be outlined by means of measuring by cord and rule, beginning with the main square from which streets are to run to the gates and principal roads and leaving sufficient open space so that even if the town grows it can always spread out in a symmetrical manner. (Royal Ordinances Concerning the Laying Out of New Towns, cited in Reps 1965, 29)

Beginning with cities like St. Augustine, Florida, royal decree was meticulously obeyed, as it was along the entire Spanish rim during the course of nearly three centuries. An early plan for Los Angeles in 1781 would have looked familiar to Philip II or for that matter, to Julius Caesar. Then, suddenly, with the coming of

railroads and massive doses of capital looking for a home, there came a break in
towns on the Spanish rim with the principles enunciated in the "Law of the Indies."
The square ceased to be a center; it no longer was a reference point in generating
new urban space. Town squares became random dots amidst block after block of
building plots, as in a plan for Santa Monica as part of the "new" Los Angeles in
1875, and then they disappeared entirely, when the "new" Los Angeles on paper
became a fact a generation later.

The twentieth century completed both these geographic processes at work in the
making of grids, even when development occurred by building a thousand houses
along arbitrarily twisting streets which could be called "Willow Lane" and "Old
Post Road," or by digging out lumps of industrial park, office campus, and shopping
mall on the edges of highways. In the development of the modern "megalopolis," it
has become more reasonable to speak of urban "nodes" than of centers and suburbs.
The very fuzziness of the word "node" indicates the loss of a language for naming
environmental value: "center" is charged with meanings both historical and visual,
while "node" is resolutely bland.

This American pattern is in many ways the extreme toward which other forms of
new development tend; the same kind of settlement has occurred in Italy and France,
in Israel, in the Soviet Union beyond the Urals. In all of these, development lacks a
logic of its own limits and of form established within boundaries; the results of
amorphous building are places without character. The grid in particular doesn't
"cause" this blandness; neutrality has changed its form from an endless city of regularly intersecting lines to winding housing developments, shopping strips, and clots
of offices or factories. But the recent history of the grid reveals what might be called
the nastiness underlying blandness; in making an environment, as in conducting a
life, neutrality is often a weapon of passive aggression. The dull city, like the life
consecrated to routine, is a way to deny that, in the end, other people, other needs,
matter very much.

In April 1791, Pierre Charles L'Enfant was courageously engaged in combating
Thomas Jefferson's plan to create the new American capital according to a grid-iron
plan. L'Enfant wrote to President Washington:

> Such regular plans ... become at last tiresome and insipid and it [the grid] could never be in
> its origin but a mean continuance of some cool imagination wanting a sense of the real
> grand and truly beautiful. (cited in Kite 1929, 47–48)[1]

A capitol should reverberate with symbolic power, and L'Enfant imagined the regularities of the grid as empty of such reverberations. It was neutral space, in the sense
of being empty. The following century was to show, however, that these neutral
environments were perfect spaces in which to practice the denial of difference.

The American urbanists used grid planning to deny even elemental disturbances
prompted by geography. In cities like Chicago, the grids were laid over irregular

---

[1] Pierre Charles L'Enfant, "Note relative to the ground lying on the eastern branch of the river
Potomac." Undated, but necessarily written between 4 April, when President Washington for-
warded Jefferson's ideas to L'Enfant, and 10 April 1791, when Jefferson accepted L'Enfant's control of the planning of the new national capitol.

terrain; the rectangular blocks obliterated the natural environment, spreading out relentlessly no matter what hills, rivers, or forest knolls stood in the way. The natural features which could be levelled or drained were the obstacles which nature put against the grid; the irregular course of rivers or lakes was ignored by these frontier city planners, as if what could not be harnessed to this mechanical, tyrannical geometry did not exist. Often, this relentless imposition of a grid required a willful suspension of the logical faculties. In Chicago, the grid created immense problems of transport across the river cutting through the center of the city; the lines of the streets suddenly end at one river bank only to continue on the other side, as though the river were spanned by innumerable, if invisible, bridges. A visitor to the new town of Cincinnati noticed, in 1797, if the "inconvenience" of applying the grid to a similar river topography; further,

> if they had made one of their principal streets to face the river and other at the brow of the second bank … the whole town would have presented a noble appearance from the river. (Baily 1856, 226, as cited in Wade 1959, 24–25)

Cincinnati bore an ancient name but was no Greek city; these urban plans imposed arbitrarily on the land rather established an interactive, sustaining relation to it.

Though it was one of the oldest cities in America, New York's planners treated it during the era of high capitalism as if it, too, were a city on the frontier, a place required to deal with the physical world as an enemy. The planners imposed a grid at one blow in 1811 upon Manhattan from Canal Street, the edge of dense settlement, up to 155th Street, and then in a second stroke in 1870 to the northern tip. They imposed the grid more gradually in Brooklyn east from its old harbor. The settlers on the frontier, whether from fear or simple greed, treated the Indians as part of the landscape rather than as fellow human beings; on the frontier nothing existed, it was a void to be filled up. Planners could no more see life outside the grid in New York than they could in Illinois. The farms and hamlets dotting nineteenth-century Manhattan were expected to be engulfed rather than incorporated as the grid on paper became building in fact; little adaptation of the plan was made in that process, even when some more flexible arrangement of streets would make better use of a hill or better suit the vagaries of Manhattan's water table. And, inexorably, development according to the grid did abolish whatever existing settlement was encountered. In this Neoclassical age, the nineteenth-century planners could have built as Romans, or nearer at hand, like William Penn, laying out squares or establishing rules for where churches, schools, and markets were to go. The land was available, but they were not so minded. Economic development and environmental consciousness were inseparably linked in this neutralizing denial. The New York Commissioners declared that "right angled houses are the most cheap to build, and the most convenient to live in" (Bridges 1811, 25). What is unstated here is the belief that uniform units of land were also the easiest to sell. This relationship between the grid city and capitalist economics has been stated at its broadest by Lewis Mumford thus:

the resurgent capitalism of the seventeenth century treated the individual lot and the block, the street and the avenue, as abstract units for buying and selling, without respect for historic uses, for topographic conditions or for social needs. (1961, 421)

In the history of nineteenth-century New York, the matter was in fact more complicated, because the economics of selling land were very different in New York in 1870 than they were in 1811. The city at the beginning of the century was a dense cluster of buildings set in the wilderness. Land sales were of empty space. After the Civil War, they were of places which would soon fill up. To sell land profitably required a social reckoning: where people should live, where transport should most efficiently be located, where factories should go. Looking at a map which shows only blocks all the same size answers few of these questions. The grid was rational as an urban design only in an abstract, Cartesian sense. And, therefore, as was true of investments in rails and industry, the latter economic history of the grid is as much the story of disastrous investments as of large profits. Those who sought to profit from a neutral environment shared the same necessarily blank consciousness of its character as those like L'Enfant who hated it.[2]

Denial of Meaning

Whenever Americans of the era of high capitalism thought of an alternative to the grid, however, they thought of bucolic relief, a leafy park or a promenade, rather than a more arousing street, square, or center in which to experience the complex life of the city. The construction of Central Park in New York is perhaps the most bitter example of this alternative, an artfully designed natural void planned for the city's center in the expectation that the cultivated, charming territory already established around it—as bucolic and refreshing a scene as any city-dweller could wish for within a few minutes drive from his house—would be razed to the ground by the encroachments of the grid.

Its designers Olmsted and Vaux themselves wanted to obliterate the simplest reminder that Central Park was located in the midst of a thriving metropolis. This reminder would occur, for instance, in seeing or hearing the traffic crossing it. These Americans therefore built contrary to the makers of the Bois de Boulogne, who made traversing the Bois a pleasure even for those who had business which required the journey. Olmsted and Vaux hid such people away, literally; they buried the traffic routes in channels below the grade of the Park. In their own words, these roads are to:

be sunk so far below the surface ... The banks on each side will be walled up to the height of about seven feet ... and a little judicious planting on the tops or slopes of the banks above these walls will, in most cases, entirely conceal both the roads and the vehicles moving in

---

[2] The reader interested in the irrational course which was the actual process of "the logic of capitalism" might want to read Marcuse (1987).

them, from the view of those walking or driving in the park. (cited in Olmsted and Kimball 1928, 214–232)

These were the dualities of denial: to build you act as though you live in emptiness; to resist the builder's world you act as though you do not live in a city.

Some of this denial of meaning to the American city has a uniquely American source, derived from the sheer visceral impress of our natural landscape made upon all those who travelled in it, Americans and visitors alike. This natural world once was immense, unframed, boundary-less. The impress of a boundary-less world becomes clear, for instance, in comparing an American painting of wilderness, John Kensatt's "View near West Point on the Hudson" of 1863 to Corot's "A View of Volterra" of 1838, two paintings organized around roughly similar views. What we see in Kensatt's painting is limitless space, a view bursting its frame, the eye going and going and going without obstruction. All the rocks, trees, and people in the painting are deprived of substance because they are absorbed into immensity. Whereas, in Corot's painting, we feel the vivid presence of specific things in a bounded view, or, as one critic has put it, "a solid architecture of rocks and even of foliage to measure the deep space" (McCoubrey 1963, 29). It seemed that only the most arbitrary imposition could tame the American vastness; an endless, unbounded grid. This effort of will, however, rebounded: the arbitrary spoiled what it tamed, the grid seemed to render space meaningless—and so sent an eye like Olmsted's searching for a way to recover the value of nature, seemingly free of the visible presence of man.

The nineteenth-century grid was horizontal; the twentieth-century grid is vertical; it is the skyscraper, and its powers of neutrality extend beyond the American scene. In cities of skyscrapers, Hong Kong as much as New York, it is impossible to think of the vertical slices above street level as having an inherent order, like the intersection of *cardo* and *decumanus*; one cannot point to activities which particularly ought to happen on the 6th floor of buildings. Nor can one relate visually 6th floors to 22nd floors as opposed to 25th floors in a building. The vertical grid lacks definitions of both significant placement and closure. However, as historians assure us, history does not repeat itself.

By the time homes for families were built in vertical grids, their makers knew that something was wrong. In America, they felt, it is true, the echo of a peculiar past, of that nineteenth-century practice in which families used hotels as semi-permanent residences. Such families wandered from hotel to hotel, the children only occasionally allowed to run in the corridors, the families dining in the same large rooms with commercial travellers and foreigners and unknowable women. But, more broadly, planners have come to believe that the apartment house is also a vertical grid of inherently neutral character. An editorial in the New York *Independent* newspaper argued in 1902 what was coming to be felt by the Garden City planning movement in England, and by socialist planners under the sway of face-to-face community ideals in France and Germany, namely, that large apartment houses destroy "neighbourhood feeling, helpful friendships, church connections and those homely common interests which are the foundations of civic pride and duty." In

New York, this view was codified in the Multiple Dwelling House Act of 1911, which treated all apartment buildings as similar in social function to hotels; the "lack of fundamentals on which a home was founded" could be perceived, as late as 1929 in one of the first books on apartment house architecture, to derive from "a building of six, nine, or fifteen stories, where the plan of one floor is repeated exactly throughout the entire building; individuality is practically non-existent" (cited in King 1980, 181). A skyscraper is no place for Ruskin's Dream.

The common-sense view of change is that when people become conscious of an evil they react against it. A more realistic account is that people act out the evils they discover. They know what they are doing is wrong and yet they move closer and closer to making it happen, in order to see if what they think or perceive is real. Certainly this is true in our time among those who have built vertical grids for families. It was with a fear of the loss of family values in neutral, impersonal spaces that architects and planners like Robert Moses began in the 1930s to build the great housing projects in New York which would eventually realize these very fears. There are, perhaps, no devils in this story; the housing project is a reformist dream dating back to nineteenth-century efforts to build healthy homes *en masse* for workers. Only, the visual vocabulary of building betrays another set of values, one which converts old ideas about unbounded space into new forms of denial.

Housing projects meant for the poor, like those along Park Avenue in Harlem, are designed according to the principles of the unbounded, amorphous grid. Everything is graded flat; there are few trees. Little patches of lawn are protected by metal fences. The Park Avenue apartments are relatively free of crime but, according to the complaints of the residents, are a hostile environment for the conduct of family life. That hostility is built into their very functionality; they deny one is living in a place of any value. They are, in this, passive-aggressive spaces.

It is disconcerting to hear this denial given voice in the bars on the edge of a Harlem project like the one along upper Park Avenue. (There are no places to drink in public within the forest of towers itself). It is strange because the language of sociability is so broken into fragments. I used to think it was because I was present, but in these Park Avenue bars after a while people forget about a stray, balding, familiar white. These are family bars, cleaning ladies and janitors drinking beer; places which are more lively are for people living on the shadows of the underworld. The bars next to this project seldom have an actual bar; they are just rooms where someone has put bottles on a table. Here it is as though time has stopped; the day hangs in dust roused by the commuter trains shuttling in and out of a tunnel next to the buildings, the bar at night has a television turned on without sound, there is the ebb and flow of police sirens, a fan in summer. This is the space that talk filled, but I came to understand it was enough: the drops of sound made for a consciousness of presence, of living, if barely audible, *here*. These words came eventually to impress me more than the most inflamed political rhetoric: they came from the desire to make a place in which it mattered to speak, if this mattering place were constructed from no more than broken chairs and the stained plastic table shoved into an abandoned storefront which people called their bar. This construction countered the functional, neutral places made for them in which they were nowhere and no one.

Neutrality, as a space of social control, seems to explain a great divide between nineteenth-century European planning and those more modern practices which first took shape horizontally in nineteenth-century America and are now more universally deployed in the skyscraper. Baron Haussmann was engaged in remaking Paris during the era in which Central Park was created. Haussmann confronted a congested city a thousand years old whose twisted streets were a breeding ground for, in his mind, the unholy trinity of disease, crime, and revolution. He imagined a traditional means of repression in the face of these dangers. The cutting of straight streets through a congested Paris was to make it easier for people to breathe, for police, and if necessary, troops to move. The great streets of the Haussmannian era were, however, to be lined with apartments over elegant shops, in order to attract the bourgeoisie into previously working-class districts; the economy of local working class life, he hoped, would become therefore, dependent upon servicing the bourgeois who dominated the *quartier*; he imagined a kind of internal class colonization of the city. At the same time as he opened the city mass transport to the swift flow of traffic, he also hoped the working classes were to become more locally dependent. This paradox expresses perhaps the contradiction of every bourgeois, that mixed desire for progress and order. Haussmann was a man who mixed neighborhoods, who diversified, all in the name of re-establishing local bonds as though the respectable businessmen and professionals could become a new class of squires. He sought to create a Paris of steady if demanding customers, of concierge-spies, and a thousand little services.

American urbanism during its great flowering has proceeded by another path of power, one which repressed the overt definition of significant space in which domination and dependence were to occur. No building form like the Haussmannian apartment house with its courtyard of artisans. Instead, both horizontal and vertical development proceeded among us as a more modern, more abstract operation of extension. In the making of the grid cities, Americans proceeded as in their encounters with the Indians, by "erasure" of the presence of an alien Other, rather than by colonization. Instead of establishing the significance of place, control operated through consciousness of place as neutral.

Denial of Difference

Withdrawal and denial are two allied means of repressing differences. The one acknowledges that complexity exists but tries to run from it. The other tries simply to abolish its existence. In our cities homes are places of withdrawal, grids are places of denial. It was given to the greatest foreign observers of nineteenth-century America to understand how withdrawal and denial might come together. The young Alexis de Tocqueville's family were among the band of aristocrats of 1830 who refused to participate in the new regime, and made the *émigration intérieure*. He arranged his famous voyage to America as a way out of his own difficulties in taking the regime's Oath of Loyalty. His first days in New York were for him clues to what he would have to explain.

In his time, the usual way for a foreigner to journey to New York was to sail into the harbor coming up from the south, a route which afforded the voyager a sudden view of the crowd of masts along the packed wharves, behind which spread offices, homes, churches, and schools. This New World scene appeared to be a familiar European one of prosperous mercantile confusion, like Antwerp or the lower reaches of London on the Thames. Tocqueville instead approached New York from the north, coming down through Long Island Sound. His first view of Manhattan was its bucolic upper reaches, still in 1831 pure farmland dotted with a few hamlets. At first what excited him about the view of the city was the sudden eruption of a metropolis in the midst of a nearly pristine natural landscape. He felt the enthusiasm of a European coming here who imagines he can plant himself in this unspoiled landscape like a city, that it is fresh and simple and Europe is stale and complex. And then, after that fit of youthful enthusiasm passed, New York began to disturb him, as he later wrote to his mother. No one seemed to take where they lived seriously, to care about the buildings through which they hurried in and out; instead the city was treated by its citizens simply as a complicated instrument of offices and restaurants and shops for the conduct of business.

Throughout his American journey Tocqueville was struck by the bland and insubstantial character of American settlement. Houses seemed mere stage-sets rather than buildings meant to last, there seemed nothing permanent in the environment. And this physical scene has a political consequence. The very lack of physical constraints made the masses of people feel they could do whatever they wished, or so it seemed to Tocqueville in the first volume of the *Democracy*, written in the heat of his travel impressions and published in 1834.

In this first volume the young writer, reflecting upon American blandness, was still very much a child of his own past. The masses of America in which all are equal appeared to him as the mob of the Great Revolution had appeared to his noble parents. This mass, the majority, was an active body; it trampled the rights of dissent, it admitted no contrary voice to its own will, sought to impose itself, like an intolerant mob, upon the minority:

> I know of no country in which there is so little independence of mind and real freedom of discussion as in America … In America the majority raises formidable barriers around the liberty of opinion; within these barriers an author may write what he please, but woe to him if he goes beyond them … he yields at length, overcome by the daily effort which he has to make, and subsides in silence, as if he felt remorse for having spoken the truth. (Tocqueville 1945 [1850], vol. I, 273–274)

The city, as Tocqueville perceived in America, helped arouse this mob passion:

> The lower ranks which inhabit these cities constitute a rabble even more formidable than the populace of European towns … they also contain a multitude of Europeans who have been driven to the shores of the New World by their misfortunes or their misconduct; and they bring to the United States all our greatest vices. (1945 [1850], vol. I, 299)

And against the mob, the forces of order built in wood. The blandness of the American environment made it easier for mob passion to rule—nothing "out there," no stones of history or forms of ritual, will chasten the mob and hold them back.

The second volume of the *Democracy in America* was written after Tocqueville had tasted a few years of the new regime in France. It was published in 1840 and is quite different in outlook, and enters the story we have to tell. The author returned to his own society of pear-shaped men. He saw a whole generation withdraw in disgust at the competitive, cynical world epitomized by Louis Philippe's stirring appeal to his people, *"Enrichissez-vous!"*—get rich! He witnessed the *émigration intérieure* take place among his childhood friends, indeed his entire generation; they were a depressed generation, and increasingly withdrawn rather than provokingly sarcastic in their disillusion. Their depression made him rethink his own past.

His memories of America passed through the prism of the present and now he remembered America as the harbinger of this new danger in European society; across the ocean there was a country suffering in more modern ways than from mob violence restrained only by wood. In his travel notes, Tocqueville had recorded how much one place looked like another, how little variation the local economy, climate, and even topography seemed to matter in constructing a town. Tocqueville had at first explained this homogeneity in building a city as the result of unbridled commercial exploitation. Now he inclined to a more tragic view: these were the signs of a people who willed their built environment into a neutral state for the same reasons they willed their lived into this condition. The famous American "individual," rather than being an adventurer, is in reality most often a man or woman whose circle of reality is drawn no larger than family and friends. The individual has little interest, indeed, little energy, outside that circle. The American individual is a passive man, and monotonous space is what a passive society builds for itself.

Tocqueville enters our story at the point at which he conceived that denial of and withdrawal from difference might go hand in hand. The action a passive society takes is to neutralize—to sand the grain smooth. Smothering discord in toleration and understanding, like Norman Mailer with his graffiti, is a modern Tocquevillian instance. In space, the shipping strip, the endless repetition of glass and steel skyscrapers, the ribbon highway, the reduplication of the same stores selling the same goods in city after city, the reign of discrete, unobstrusive good taste, or that soft high-tech called by New Yorkers "eurotrash"—all these are modern Tocquevillian signs. A bland environment assures people that nothing disturbing or demanding is happening "out there." You build neutrality in order to legitimate withdrawal.

Tocqueville was the first of the thinkers about mass society—Ortega, Huxley, Orwell. He condemned neutrality as the invisible sign of a tired conformism rather than a rampaging mob:

> The reproach I address to the principle of equality is not that it leads men away in the pursuit of forbidden enjoyments, but that it absorbs them wholly in quest of those which are allowed. By these means a kind of virtuous materialism may ultimately be established in the world, which would corrupt, but enervate, the soul and noiselessly unbend its springs of action. (Tocqueville 1945 [1850], vol. II, 141)

But, in looking at the fatigue of his own generation, who were themselves becoming more passive, turning a more bland face to the world, he came to a further conclusion. The psychological aristocrat is really much more a brother to the American individualist than the European would like to think. They both withdraw, and they both suffer because they withdraw. Once people succeed in neutralizing the outer and withdrawing into the interior, Tocqueville believed they would gradually experience a loss of self-control. War, economic disaster, violent crime are all experiences in which a loss of control happens *to* someone. Neutrality has a different, more insidious character. Physically it is a lack of stimulus, behaviorally a lack of demanding experience; without these, people begin to feel disoriented. They then start to come apart from within. Nothing coheres in blandness.

There are bars everywhere in New York, bars devoted to heavy drinking and bars which are a mere afterthought, like the bar in the Museum of Modern Art; there are bars in discos, bank buildings, brothels as well as improvised in housing projects. The great bars are in hotels—the Oak Bar in the Plaza, the bar of the Algonquin; they are panelled and filled with large comfortable chairs, like the clubs nearby, but there is no discreet murmur of voices here. A great bar is a place where you have to shout to make yourself heard. Few New York bars though, even in the center of the city, are great. Instead they are resolutely neutral, especially in places of power, for instance in the bar of the Hotel Pierre, on Fifth Avenue just where Central Park begins. The physical contrast between this bar and the room up in Harlem with a table crowded with bottles is so extreme as to be meaningless. The Pierre bar, with its ample tables, flowers, and subdued lights, has always conveyed a peculiar discretion; people come here who need to do business without being seen to be doing it. This is evident in little details: when people recognize others here, they seldom table-hop; at most there are brief nods of recognition. The drinks at the Pierre are mostly for show. Two men will sit for an hour nursing the glasses in front of them; the waiters are trained not to hover.

It is a nervous bar with so many people paying careful attention to one another. The Pierre bar is neutral in the way a chess board is; it serves a grid for competition. And yet in this power center, among these men in their quiet, expensive clothes, sunk deep into their leather chairs, the atmosphere seems more charged by fear than entrepreneurial zeal. The men are afraid of giving away too much. "Control" is a meaningless word uptown; here it is a synonym for anxiety. If you don't pay careful attention, things will come apart.

To the ordinary New Yorker, the reality of these fears must forever be a mystery; all that the ordinary New Yorker can know is that these deals are cut in neutral surroundings, decorated in "Eurotrash" or "Olde English"—rooms whose very blandness does not distract the players from their anxieties.

The scene represented by the bar at the Hotel Pierre is a puzzling element, it must be said, in Tocqueville's story. Tocqueville imagined a mass society of equals suffering from the very acts which made them equal. The equalizing, in the sense of neutralizing of the environment, causes them to lose their bearings. He saw this lack of cohesion in the "restlessness unto death" of Americans, for instance, their inability to take seriously and to enjoy whatever part of the common life they possessed at the moment. They were, and are, always thinking about moving, even though other places might be almost the same. In modern New York, the cultural illnesses of making everything the same, or neutralizing, appear, however, in a society of deep material inequality. Tocqueville, no less than St. Augustine, taught us to take seriously how things look. Thus, if nothing coheres in blandness, the saying may be as true of making money as of suffering poverty—but the phenomenon of neutrality cannot be the same for both rich and poor.

We could pose this puzzle abstractly as a question: how can the cultural denial of difference operate in a society in which social and economic differences are becoming greater and more extreme? The leveraged-buyout specialist doing a deal at the Pierre denies that the loss of thousands of jobs in the course of financial restructuring is part of the reality in which he is involved. We can understand that his soothing physical trappings reinforce his desire to proceed as if nothing is real other than the numbers on his papers. Freud, like Tocqueville, tells us people suffer from their denials. How, eventually, is the leveraged buy-out specialist going to suffer from having denied that other lives than his own mattered? He is a realistic adult; he knows that retributive justice seldom strikes back at the rich. No one punished the New York Commissioners, either; while they were alive their work was treated as a model of progressive planning.

It may seem peculiar to turn to the history of religion again to explore how a culture denying difference persists in a society of great economic, ethnic, and racial differences. But one lingering presence of religion in modern life is to give people the faith that the worldly pains you deny *can* be denied. If religion once offered people a concrete sanctuary into which to escape, something like a smoldering religious sentiment offers another, more comforting if less material refuge: nothing "out there" is real. You can make it go away. And, by no stake of divine retribution, certainly, people who do believe they can make outside reality go away eventually do begin to come apart within.

"My Civil Wars Within"

The God-ghost who lives in the faith that you can make differences go away appears in the most prosaic fact. We remarked that American grids, unlike their Roman predecessors', lacked boundaries. The age that built churches was much occupied by the question of whether, without boundaries of all kinds, a human being can have a center. Learning the limits of human desire and the boundaries of human knowledge revealed to men and women where they stood in the divine chain of being, in the hierarchy God has established, we must take our places, Aquinas said, on God's ladder. This theology taught a psychological lesson: the modest soul, aware of its own limits, feels secure; it is the security of the Priest in Chaucer's *Canterbury Tales* who is at home in the world because he is at home in himself:

And though he hooly were and vertuous,
He was to synful men nat despitous,
Ne of his speche daungerous ne digne,
But in his techung discreet and benygne

[And yet, though he himself was holy and virtuous, he was not contemptuous of sinners
nor overbearing and proud in his talk; rather, he was discreet and kind in his teaching.]
(Chaucer 1971, original 357, translated 10)

From this inward moral centeredness a city could be made. Chaucer literally meant
to evoke a sense of place when he described the priest's virtues as those of a "good
man of the church": they were parish virtues rather than the virtues of the wandering
mystic. What would happen to the comforts of faith when Mankind no longer lived
in a bounded world?

It was this problem of Mankind unchained, the maker of its own life in a constantly shifting, materially expanding society, that the sociologist Max Weber took
up in his famous study of the "Protestant Ethic." The early Protestant, in Weber's
view, took everyday life much more seriously than his Catholic forbears, who con-
signed it to the links of the unplanned and the chaotic. The Protestant instead saw
the life of the street as a place in which competition against others meant something
about his own self-worth. But this new Christian couldn't allow himself to enjoy
what he earned; he was afraid pleasure would corrupt him. Thus he was both worldly
and ascetic, aggressive in making money and then denying its power to make him
more comfortable, fatter, elegant, or amusing. The most daring thing about Weber's
picture of this new businessman was to see him as a Christian. "Christian asceticism," Weber wrote in *The Protestant Ethic and the Spirit of Capitalism*:

at first fleeing from the world into solitude, had already ruled the world which it had
renounced from the monastery and through the Church. But it had, on the whole, left the
naturally spontaneous character of daily life in the world untouched. Now it strode into the
marketplace of life, slammed the door of the monastery behind it, and undertook to penetrate just that daily routine of life with its methodicalness, to fashion it into a life in the
world, neither of nor for this world. (as translated by, and cited in, Green 1974, 152)

Christianity thus took to the streets to find its truths; the religion lost its earlier cer-
tainty about the division of this world from the next. Perhaps people might make
gains in this world which would bear on their life in the next. Yet also, one's fate,
one's election or damnation came to seem more uncertain when it became tied to the
flux of the street.

Weber, as we know from the very title of his book, sought to connect this new
spiritual value placed on competition to the origins of modern capitalism. He did so
in the most straightforward way imaginable: the competition for wealth, immemo-
rial and universal in all societies, now became also a demonstration of virtue. It
could be so, however, only as long as it was a demonstration, only so long as it
didn't result in pleasure or the love of the things one earned. The hedonist may be
greedy, but he lacks discipline and so he is likely to lose. Thus, in a competitive
society, inequality appears to be denial. Those who are better self-deniers are more
likely to succeed.

What is subtle about Weber's analysis is that he understood that denial is a double-edged experience: you develop the strength to deny yourself immediate gratification only by denying that anything out there right now is of real value, or to be taken seriously for its own sake. Making money one does not spend, holding back—these acts we now call "delayed gratification" neutralize radically one's emotional attachments by neutralizing the value of what we desire; he-she-it wasn't worth my time. The person good at competition is good at denying the reality of anything else.

The early Protestants engaged in delayed gratification for the sake of God. God made competition a virtue, the denial of reality real. Unfortunately God was also unknowable, and one's sin was infinite. How much success and how much denial would demonstrate that one was a good person worthy of being saved? The question was unanswerable, and one felt driven to go on, to compete and succeed more, delaying gratification even longer, hoping in the future at last to find an answer which never came. The restlessness Tocqueville noted among Americans who were, puzzlingly, also so indifferent to their surroundings, Weber explained as the very last consequence of this religious stew cooked up with denial. To save and to be saved; to deny the present so as to be deserving of the future; to compete ruthlessly against others so as to prove one's worth; to deny concreteness for the sake of inner-ness; to live in a state of endless becoming. Weber had, I think, more to do with Freud than Marx here, for the mechanics of capitalist competition, as Weber understood it, was a demonstration of Freud's thesis that people suffer from their own denials.

Just before he wrote *The Protestant Ethic and the Spirit of Capitalism,* Weber travelled to America, in the age in which the Vanderbilts had dinners for seventy served by seventy powdered footmen. The luxury-loving capitalists of Weber's day seemed an aberration of the species. In time, men of power would learn to protect themselves by not flaunting their wealth. Culturally, they would seek to be just "one of the boys," as we would say, they would seek to fit in. Yet in fact they would remain adversaries to others; Weber's genius was to understand that they would feel driven to compete long after they were financially secure. The man who would treat others as a pawn was a man struggling with his own demons: its form first became visible in the Protestant movement to make consciousness of one's inner state the focus of faith. The genius of his idea was, again, to understand how people might try to resolve doubts about their inner worthiness by a certain kind of exercise of power, in which the person wins but does not enjoy the victory. This self-denial proves that someone has a strong character—stronger than others, and strong enough to stand up to the temptations of desire within himself. Weber wanted to explain what the competitive person proving to himself was proving.

To demonstrate the unhappiness underlying competition, Weber took an extreme to represent and dramatize the mean: he cited Calvinists and the small band of Puritan Protestants of the seventeenth century, particularly those refuged in America as evidence for the impact of Protestant conscience upon the world. Like Tocqueville, Weber saw the lives of these Americans as a talisman of what Europe would become.

He imagined the Puritans to be heroic neurotics, people wrecked with inner doubt by the life-long struggle to prove themselves worthy.

In one way they were hardly suitable for his story. The places in which the Puritans had lived would have been instantly recognizable to their contemporaries as traditional European villages, a nucleus of houses packed tight around a green. Beyond this traditional village, the pastures and fields extended out to the township lines. In the later seventeenth century, this traditional village pattern begins to give way, and for reasons that would be painted for the next two hundred years. Once the village nucleus was established, "in land division the settlers abandoned the conservatism which had characterized their street plans. The allotment of wilderness seemed to ridicule humble European field systems" (Garvan 1951, 52). And by the eighteenth century, these tight-knit villages had unraveled, as the bulk of the population moved out to live on the land they worked.

While they lasted, these nucleated villages were highly co-operative rather than competitive. The Salem Village Church Covenant of 1689 states, in part:

> We resolve uprightly to study what is our duty, and to make it our grief, and reckon it our shame, whereinsoever we find our selves to come short in the discharge of it, and for pardon thereof we humbly to betake our selves to the Blood of the Everlasting Covenant.
>
> And that we may keep this covenant, and all the branches of it inviolable for ever, being sensible that we can do nothing of our selves.
>
> We humbly implore the help and grace of our Mediator may be sufficient for us.
> (as cited in Rice 1874)

This covenant declares that inner distress and mutual co-operation are inseparable. "Neutrality," "indifference to others" are not the operative words of these settlements; at first, the little New England villages hardly seemed to be the environment for the social denials of the Protestant Ethic.

And yet the people in them also came to live out the drama of denial through neutrality, lived out that drama and suffered on a heroic scale because of it. The Puritan imagined himself in need of removal from the worldliness in which he was born due to the unhappy warfare within his breast. His salvation or damnation was predestined by God, who had also, with a twist of the divine Knife, made it impossible for the Puritan to know whether he would be saved or damned. He was obliged, in the words of the American Puritan, Cotton Mather, "to preach the unsearchable Riches of Christ," but he was all too human, he was a man who wanted to know his fate, in search of evidence (as cited in Silverman 1985, 24). The world's daily sins and temptations were no more within his power to control—he lacked even the Catholic belief of absolution for sin. Nothing could be known ultimately, nothing could be absolved—his god was like a sadistic Fortune. Conscience and pain became, therefore, inseparable companions.

Perhaps the most graphic expression of this inner conflict was a popular poem of the early seventeenth century by George Goodwin, which reads in part:

> I sing my self; my civil wars within;
> The victories I hourly lose and win;
> The daily duel, the continual strife,

The war that ends not, till I end my life
(as cited in Bercovitch 1975, 19)

From such misery the Puritan was tempted by the wilderness, by a place of emptiness which would make no seductive demands of its own upon him, in order that he
try to get his life under control, however forlorn that hope. Cotton Mather's father,
Increase Mather, one of the first generation of Puritans to set sail, wrote the following on the title page of his diary:

Give me a Cell
      To dwell
Where no foot hath
      A Path
There I will spend
      And End
My wearied years
      In tears (as cited in Hall 1961, 352)

The first Americans were ravaged human beings. Mundane labels like "the first
colonists" or "English adventurers" don't account for the motives that would drive
people to make hazardous voyages in order to live out their lives in a cold, mos-
quito-infested, rocky landscape. The Puritans were the first Americans to suffer the
dual need to "get away from it all" and to attempt to "get control of your life." This
duality was flight from others in the name of self-mastery.

The churches in the centers of traditional European villages and towns made it
obvious where to find God. These centers defined a space of recognition. God is
legible: he is within, within the sanctuary as within the soul. On the outside there is
only exposure, disorder, and cruelty. The Puritan "inside" was illegible, a place of
war, conscience at war with itself; this terrible business of "finding oneself" will
only become more confusing if the outside, other people, other confusions intrude.
The Spaniard came to the New World as a lord, conversion and conquest, all of a
piece; he came as a Catholic. The Puritan came as a refugee; conversion was a duty,
conquest a necessity for survival, but neither of these was his reason for coming.
The place he arrived at had to be treated like a blank canvas for the double compul-
sion to play itself out, to start again somewhere else by getting more control over
himself.

Language frequently failed to express what passed within the breasts of the people embarked on this purifying experiment; a deadly failure in which Salem was the
true witches brand: silence. But more generally in our culture the failure of words to
reveal the soul was tied to a heightened self-awareness in an immense, alien place.
Failing a language adequate to inner experience, the life of each would be more and
more locked within, impossible to declare, perhaps at best intimated by the rendering of an impression. The inner space of medieval Catholicism was physical, it was
a space people could share. The inner space of the Puritan was the space of the most
radical individualism and was impalpable. The Puritan eye could only see within
itself.

For the Puritan, emptiness therefore signified spiritually. Even in the early knots
of village houses, he was alone with the conundrum of himself. Later observers who

wondered at the relentless push westward of people who could have been richer, and more content, cultivating what they already possessed, were observing one form of the Protestant Ethic—the inability to believe that whatever is, is sufficient. Somehow, by changing, the man so moved believes he will find himself—the very hardship of the struggle seems to give it that inner value. He is competing for the sake of pain, and competing ultimately with himself.

Faith at first made the nature of this inner struggle clear: good did combat sin. The nature of that inner struggle became less and less clear as people undid the European knot and moved out on their own. In a classic American text of our Western movement, the novel *The Little House on the Prairie*, the family uproots every time another house becomes visible on the horizon, without anyone in the family being able to explain why another roof-top is an intolerable sight, and yet they all feel threatened; they keep moving. This is the beginning of the suburban story: whenever you can afford it, move farther away from other people. Density is an evil. Only in emptiness, in neutrality, only without stimulation or "interference" with others can the psyche wrestle itself. This is the duality of flight from others and the struggle for self-control.

It may seem a very American story, indeed a story bound to a small seventeenth-century sect. Yet in the way that we sometimes find an illumination in the lives of people far distant from ourselves, who never intended to mean anything to us, so this land wrestling with "civil wars within" speaks to the present. Tocqueville mistook in one way the character of individualism; he thought it was simply indifference to other people—a generous mistake, it might be said, in reading a more modern reality. In fact the code for establishing self-control, as it first developed in our country, contains a deep hostility toward the needs of other people, a resentment of their very presence. They interfere; to get in control, nothing "out there" can count. This hostility now marks the way, in many cities, in which those who are homeless or mentally disturbed are treated on the streets—resented because of the very fact that they are visibly needy and they do not go away. More, it stands behind that competition in identities which made its appearance on the graffiti-smeared subway cars of the city, which is a competition for recognition. The Puritan could answer the question, "Recognition by whom?" We lack his belief in God, and so can give no comparable answer to this question, but still we feel the Puritan need to be validated. The ancient shadow lingers. It obscured the presence of others.

In our history the relentless use of grids found its place in casting that shadow. The grid seemed to resolve the threat of environmental value by an act of geometric repression: there was nothing "out there" to account for, in laying down a grid. The cultural problems of the city are conventally taken to be its impersonality, its alienating scale, its coldness. What I am suggesting is that there is more in these charges that meets the eye. "Impersonality," "coldness," "emptiness" are essential words in the Protestant language of environment. They are words which express a certain interest in seeing; the facts of separation, exclusion, coldness are treated as reasons to look within for value. The story the Protestant Ethic tells about this interested perception is not a happy one. It is a story of value scarcity. Indeed, it is a story in which men create the very conditions and circumstances which they then feel to be cold or empty. Such is the perverse consequence of denial. A person deals neutrally with the outside and then feels empty by doing so. This perversion is as applicable to the creation of space as to the creation of capital.

As it has become built into the fabric of everyday secular life, however, this Protestant conscience of space is no longer a heroic neurosis.

In sum, the relation between grid space and the Protestant Ethic is an instance of the way, more generally, space and culture can be related. Just as Weber did not conceive religion to determine economics but rather to interact with it, so do cultural values intersect equally with the spatial order. This particular intersection has had a powerful effect on modern vision, just as, in Weber's formulation, religious techniques of self-regulation continued long after religious faith had waned. Neutrality in the planning of visual space establishes a field for competition. On this field, the players are morally withdrawn into themselves. The American grid plans were the first sign of a peculiarly modern form of repression, one which denies value to other people and specific places by building neutrality.

References

Baily, F. (1856). *Journal of a tour in unsettled parts of North America in 1796 and 1797*. London.
Bercovitch, S. (1975). *The puritan origins of the American self*. New Haven: Yale University Press.
Bridges, W. (1811). *Map of the city of New York and island of Manhattan*. New York.
Chaucer, G. (1971). *The Canterbury tales*. R. Lumiansky (Ed. and Tr.). New York: Pocket Books.
Garvan, A. (1951). *Architecture and town planning in colonial Connecticut*. New Haven: Yale University Press.
Green, M. (1974). *The Von Richthofen sisters*. New York: Basic Books.
Hall M. (Ed.) (1961). *Proceedings of the American Antiquarian Society*. LXXI.
King, A. (Ed.). (1980). *Building and society*. London: Routledge & Kegan Paul.
Kite, E. (Ed.). (1929). *L'Enfant and Washington, 1791–1792*. Baltimore: Johns Hopkins University Press.
Marcuse, P. (1987). The grid as city plan: New York City and laissez-faire planning in the nineteenth century. *Planning Perspectives, 2*(3), 287–310.
McCoubrey, J. W. (1963). *American tradition in planning*. New York: Braziller.
Mumford, L. (1961). *The city in history*. New York: Harcourt, Brace, Jovanovich.
Olmsted, F., & Kimball, T. (Eds.). (1928). *Frederick Law Olmsted*. New York: No Publisher.
Reps, J. (1965). *The making of urban America: A history of city planning in the United States*. Princeton: Princeton University Press.
Rice, C. (1874). *Proceedings at the celebration of the two hundredth anniversary of the First Parish at Salem Village*. Boston.
Rykwert, J. (1988). *The idea of a town: The anthropology of urban form in Rome, Italy, and the Ancient World*. Cambridge: MIT Press.
Silverman, K. (1985). *The life and times of Cotton Mather*. New York: Columbia University Press.
Tocqueville, A. (1945 [1850]). *Democracy in America*. F. Bowen (Ed.), H. Reeve (Tr.), II vols. New York: Vintage.
Wade, R. (1959). *The urban frontier*. Cambridge: Harvard University Press.

Chapter 12
Mythologies of the Grid in the Empire City, 1811–2011

Reuben Rose-Redwood

Abstract This chapter examines the performative dimensions of historical narration as a form of modern mythmaking by reconsidering conventional narratives on the "origins" of Manhattan's grid street plan of 1811. The historical mythology of the grid espoused in canonical readings of the Plan of 1811 relies extensively on a rearticulation of the official explanation that the grid's designers provided in a foundational text known as the "Commissioners' Remarks." The author argues that such accounts result in an extraordinarily narrow and formulaic interpretation of the utilitarian motives and intentions behind the city's grid plan, one that reinforces a form of "morphological essentialism." To support this argument, the author shifts the focus of attention beyond the "Commissioners' Remarks" in order to complicate readings of the intentionality that gave rise to the 1811 street plan. The chapter concludes by suggesting that the mythic search for the "origins" of the grid in the realm of founding intentions can most effectively be challenged by drawing attention to the proliferation of countermyths of gridded space.

Keywords Essentialism · Genealogy · Grid · Mythology · Narrative · New York City · Urban planning history

Introduction

Few city plans have captured the popular imagination more than Manhattan's gridded streets and avenues, which are commonly taken to be a quintessential symbol of the modern city (Spann 1988; Rose-Redwood 2002; Scobey 2002). Given the

This chapter was originally published as Rose-Redwood, R. (2011). "Mythologies of the Grid in the Empire City, 1811–2011." *Geographical Review*, 101(3): 396–413. Copyright © 2011 by the American Geographical Society of New York. Reproduced with permission of John Wiley & Sons, Inc.

R. Rose-Redwood (✉)
University of Victoria, Victoria, BC, Canada
e-mail: redwood@uvic.ca

© Springer International Publishing AG, part of Springer Nature 2018
R. Rose-Redwood, L. Bigon (eds.), *Gridded Worlds: An Urban Anthology*,
https://doi.org/10.1007/978-3-319-76490-0_12

central role that New York City is accorded in the history of urban planning, its famous grid plan, generally referred to as the "Commissioners' Plan of 1811," is often highlighted as marking a significant turning point in the age of modern urbanism (Adler et al. 2009). Not surprisingly, considerable scholarly attention has been devoted to uncovering the "origin" of the city's grid plan. A myth first popularized by Frederick Law Olmsted, one of the designers of New York's Central Park, perhaps best encapsulates the spirit of historical criticism over the past two centuries. "There seems to be good authority for the story," declared Olmsted and his colleague James Croes in 1877, "that the system of 1807 was hit upon by the chance occurrence of a mason's sieve near a map of the ground to be laid out. It was taken up and placed upon a map, and the question being asked, 'what do you want better than that?' no one was able to answer. This may not be the whole story of the plan, but the result is the same as if it were" (Olmsted and Croes 1971, 45).

The "story" is completely fictional, of course, but it nevertheless calls our attention to the long-standing desire to construct foundational myths that explain the intentions behind the origin of cities. Although subsequent scholarship has relied on more rigorous examinations of archival materials, I argue here that such works have constructed a mythology of their own, one which relies on the "good authority" of a foundational text that serves as the basis for reconstructing the original intentions of the grid's designers.

This article contributes to a genealogy of urban form which, as I have noted elsewhere, calls into question the belief that the "essence" of the grid or any other settlement pattern can be deciphered by uncovering its authentic origin in a distant past (Rose-Redwood 2008; see also Huxley 2010). The doctrine of what we might call "morphological essentialism" posits that the symbolic meaning of urban form is determined primarily by the original intentions or functions associated with such morphological structures at the foundational moment of their initial conception (for a recent illustration of this doctrine, see Hubbard 2009). A critical genealogy of planning history, by contrast, rejects the reductionism that underpins this theoretical position and instead seeks to broaden the conceptual horizon of landscape interpretation by acknowledging the multiplicity of meanings that are often affixed to particular spatial formations in contradictory ways to serve competing interests. Such a theoretical shift has important methodological implications, one of which is a general skepticism toward privileging the explicit intentions expressed in official planning documents as providing an authoritative foundation for interpreting the significance of urban form. This methodological issue may seem self-evident, but all too often historical commentators and planning practitioners rely on such official statements to construct canonical accounts of urban planning history.

In this study, I seek to demonstrate how the historical scholarship on Manhattan's grid street plan has constructed a mythology of the grid through the narration of urban origins. Within this context the notion of "myth" should not be taken as referring to false speculations about past events. On the contrary, I make the counterintuitive claim that the most "truthful" historical narratives, or at any rate, those accounts that remain most faithful to the archival record have the greatest capacity to produce historical mythologies. What is at issue in this conception of myth is not

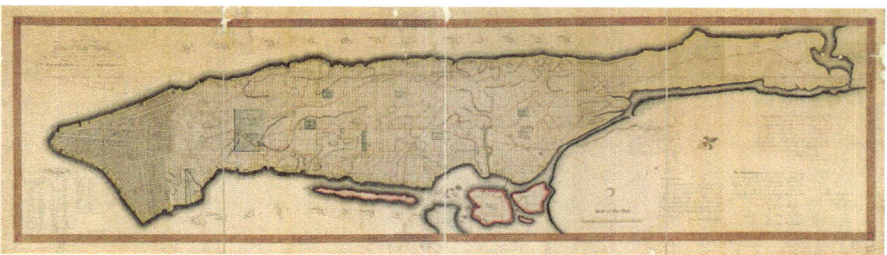

Fig 12.1 The Commissioners' Plan of 1811, surveyed by John Randel Jr. and published by William Bridges (reproduced courtesy of the Library of Congress)

so much the truth content of a historical narrative but the extent to which it becomes incorporated into a ritual of narrating historical origins. In his classic study of mythology in modern societies, Roland Barthes suggested that one of the chief characteristics of myth is that it dehistoricizes the past, resulting in what he referred to as the "miraculous evaporation of history" (1982, 141). Here I would like to make precisely the opposite argument: that modern myth rehistoricizes the geographies of the present through the performative reenactment of historical origins.

This conversion of history into myth is most apparent in the theatrical reenactment of historical events that is commonly organized during centennial celebrations (Cook 2004; Gapps 2009). Yet, as I demonstrate here, even the most erudite scholarly traditions of historical narration have played a role in constructing the mythic rituals of historical memory. Such a genealogical critique is particularly timely, for the year 2011 marks the bicentennial of the 1811 Plan, which is all the more reason to reconsider how particular historical interpretations of New York's grid plan have been incorporated into prevailing narratives of the modern city and how the city's gridded spaces may also be imagined otherwise.

The Commissioners' Plan of 1811 and the Mythology of Historical Origins

With its standardized city blocks and rectilinear street layout, New York's grid plan has come to epitomize the "ruthless utilitarianism" of economic calculation that pervaded nineteenth-century conceptions of urban life (Burrows and Wallace 1999, 420). According to most historical accounts, the Commissioners' Plan of 1811 represented a triumph of economic utility over aesthetic concerns or larger claims to national grandeur (Fig. 12.1). For instance, Alan Trachtenberg long ago maintained that Manhattan's street plan was "totally devoid of any pretension to art or beauty; it was a pure application of plane geometry. Its only intention was to subdivide the land and lay out streets.. ... The commissioners were unmoved by thoughts of national grandeur; their motive was avowedly commercial and utilitarian" (1964, 8).

Other scholars have made similar claims, suggesting that the Plan of 1811 represented "a significant shift away from earlier forms of urban design, imbued with sociopolitical and aesthetic concerns, to simpler and more utilitarian plans intended to facilitate the rapid urban development which occurred during the nineteenth century" (Spann 1988, 11). One commentator writing at the turn of the twentieth century went so far as to maintain that "of artistic effect there was not a suggestion; the thought of such a thing probably never entered the heads of the planners. Their ideas were narrow and provincial" (Flagg 1904, 253). Such attempts to decode the motives and intentions behind the 1811 Plan have typically drawn much the same conclusion: that the grid's designers privileged economic utility above all else in an attempt to promote real estate development and the most economically efficient use of urban space.

There is, of course, little doubt that the grid plan had a profound effect on the real estate economy of nineteenth-century New York (Marcuse 1987; Spann 1988; Scobey 2002). Many urban scholars have thus followed Lewis Mumford's lead in arguing that the grid "fitted nothing but a quick parcelling of the land, a quick conversion of farmsteads into real estate, and a quick sale" (1961, 421). Planners and historians alike have often lamented the strict utilitarian logic of the grid and its apparent disregard for aesthetics or local topography. Little wonder, then, that the distinguished urban planning historian John Reps maintained that Manhattan's grid plan was "a disaster whose consequences have barely been mitigated by more modern city planners" (1965, 299). In his monumental *The Making of Urban America*, Reps argued that "the commissioners ignored well-known principles of civic design that would have brought variety in street vistas and resulted in focal points for sites for important buildings and uses" (1965, 299). Instead of following the contours of the land, the prevailing historical narrative has insisted that the modern grid neutralized urban space, rendering it void of any meaning beyond the utilitarian calculation of its exchange value as commodity (Sennett 1990a, 1990b, 1994).

What is remarkable about the scholarship on New York's grid plan is not the specific arguments that various scholars have made per se but the utter consistency and predictability with which these arguments have been made over the past two centuries. If we define "historical mythology" as the formulaic rearticulation of conventional narratives concerning the historical origin of things, then the historiography on the Commissioners' Plan of 1811 offers a classic illustration of the rituals of historical myth par excellence. One of the hallmarks of historical mythology is the establishment of "foundational" texts that anchor the narration of historical origins within a seemingly coherent domain of human meaning and intentionality. As part of the sedimentation of canonical narrative traditions, foundational texts often become what Michel Callon (1986) called an "obligatory passage point" through which one must travel to gain access to the true essence of historical understanding. A degree of solemnity is generally associated with the interpretation of such texts, in large part due to the passage of time and the weight of historical orthodoxy, which has the effect of valorizing certain texts over others through scholarly rituals of historical explanation; for example, consider the manner in which specific quotations are repeated time and again as obligatory references within particular historiographic traditions.

The very act of drawing attention to such scholarly rituals qua rituals will no doubt be perceived as a heterodox tactic of iconoclasm, for it calls into question the taken-for-grantedness on which most historical sacraments depend. From the standpoint of the genealogical method, however, it is precisely such a heterodox reading of the rituals of narration that holds the greatest potential for opening up the realm of historical understanding to multiple interpretative possibilities (Foucault 2003). The genealogical approach that the French philosopher Michel Foucault developed seeks to excavate the many layers of systematized and ritualized knowledge in order to uncover those marginalized "historical contents that have been buried or masked in functional coherences or formal systematizations" (2003, 7). Below I provide a genealogical reading of the historical mythology that currently informs interpretations of New York's grid plan, which is based on the obligatory reading of a foundational text known as the "Commissioners' Remarks," submitted by the grid's designers as the official explanation and justification for the grid plan of 1811.

In their attempt to uncover the origin and meaning of Manhattan's gridded streetscape, scholars have invariably turned to the "Commissioners' Remarks," in which the state-appointed street commissioners explained that economic "convenience and utility" were the primary motives for choosing the grid plan (Bridges 1811). In fact, it is almost as if the commissioners themselves anticipated such a quest for historical origins when they remarked that, "if it should be asked, why was the present plan adopted in preference to any other? the answer is, because, after taking all circumstances into consideration, it appeared to be the best; or, in other and more proper terms, attended with the least inconvenience" (1811, 25). If there was any doubt of their true intentions, the commissioners went on to insist that because "the price of land is so uncommonly great, it seemed proper to admit the principles of economy to greater influence than might, under circumstances of a different kind, have consisted with the dictates of prudence and a sense of duty" (1811, 26). One of the most cited passages from the "Commissioners' Remarks," however, is surely the following:

> That one of the first objects which claimed their attention, was the form and manner in which the business should be conducted; that is to say, whether they should confine themselves to rectilinear and rectangular streets, or whether they should adopt some of those supposed improvements, by circles, ovals, and stars, which certainly embellish a plan, whatever may be their effects as to convenience and utility. In considering that subject, they could not but bear in mind that a city is to be composed principally of the habitations of men, and that strait sided, and right angled houses are the most cheap to build, and the most convenient to live in. The effect of these plain and simple reflections was decisive. (1811, 24)

With such a detailed explanation of these "plain and simple" historical intentions at their disposal, it is hardly surprising that urban commentators have steadfastly relied on the "Commissioners' Remarks" as a foundational text that provides readymade answers to questions concerning the grid's historical origins.

The repetitious invocation of the "Commissioners' Remarks" goes a long way in explaining why historical scholarship on New York's grid plan has so consistently interpreted the plan as a simple result of crass commercialism and utilitarian motivation. This argument was best summarized by Reps when he insisted that "one cannot avoid the conclusion that the commissioners, in fixing upon their plan, were motivated mainly by narrow considerations of economic gain" (1965, 299). Such a conclusion is unavoidable, it should be noted, only because the commissioners sought to preempt alternative explanations of their work from the very beginning and because subsequent scholars have generally accepted the planners' initial claims at face value as an authoritative statement of the utilitarian motivations behind the Plan of 1811.

This process of valorizing a foundational text in order to gain access to the "true" intentions that explain the historical origins of a city plan is the stock-in-trade of historical mythology. Viewing this tradition of scholarship on the origins of the Manhattan grid as a form of modern mythmaking does not imply that such accounts have no claim to historical truth. Quite the contrary, the myth of the grid's origins has acquired much of its performative force precisely because it is based on a canonical reading of an officially sanctioned text that has been cited innumerable times in the repetitious act of rearticulating the founding intentions of the grid's designers. The reliance on what appears to be clear-cut archival evidence bolsters the claim that one cannot avoid drawing the same historical conclusions, thereby reproducing the mythologies of the grid within the constraints imposed by the tightly scripted interpretation laid out by the historical record itself.

Rethinking the Grid Beyond the "Commissioners' Remarks"

Extricating oneself from the somber weight of historical traditions is not an easy task, particularly when specific narrative tropes have become entrenched in the scholarly and popular literature on a given subject. I must confess that, when I sat down to write this article, I found myself tempted to replicate the classic narrative on the grid plan's origins, which might read as follows:

> On April 3, 1807, the New York State Legislature appointed three prominent men, Gouverneur Morris, Simeon De Witt, and John Rutherfurd, to serve on a commission to devise a street plan for the City of New York, which was then largely confined to the southern tip of Manhattan Island. The commissioners hired the young surveyor John Randel Jr. to map out the streets and avenues of the plan, which was unveiled to the public in 1811. The so-called Commissioners' Plan consisted principally of 12 main avenues and 155 cross streets, which were overlaid on the preexisting topography and property boundaries of the island, thereby stamping the commissioners' utilitarian logic upon the landscape to establish a rationalized space of economic calculation that would serve as the basis for the city's emerging real estate economy.

Inserting a few strategic quotations from the "Commissioners' Remarks," according to custom, might then do the trick in providing a compelling account of the grid plan's historical origins. Such a narrative would certainly be informative to readers who are not acquainted with New York City's historical geography, yet the problem with this account is that it simply rehashes the same old tune that the city's commentators have repeated like a broken record for the past two centuries. My aim, then, is not so much to dismiss this classic account of Manhattan's grid plan as completely inaccurate as it is to reshuffle the music of history by excavating the traces of historical content that have been buried and masked by the systematized and ritualized narrations of historical mythology.

One strategic way to challenge a seemingly unshakable historical mythology is, quite simply, to beat it at its own game; in short, to uncover new evidence in the archives that speaks to a more complex set of human intentions and motivations associated with the historical processes under consideration. This methodological technique turns the very same tools of scholarship employed in the construction of historical mythologies against itself in an attempt to undercut the broken record of canonical narration by demonstrating how a critical engagement with archival materials allows for multiple readings of the past. The danger with this type of methodological strategy, however, is that, although it may challenge specific details of historical myths, it does not call into question the belief that the significance of history lies in the idealist search for historical origins. As a result, any compelling evidence presented in such a new account will likely be incorporated into preexisting narrative traditions without fundamentally altering the structure of historical narration itself. Before considering this latter question, I shall first strategically play the "game" of uncovering alternative historical content that has heretofore been marginalized by the dominant narrative on the grid to see how this might reshape our understanding of the Commissioners' Plan of 1811.

Although most historical accounts of the 1811 street plan have privileged the motivations that the grid's designers laid out in the "Commissioners' Remarks," virtually no scholarship has considered how the "Remarks" may relate to other texts written by the grid's original planners. This silence is especially remarkable because street commissioner Gouverneur Morris was one of the final drafters of the U.S. Constitution and Simeon De Witt, who had served as chief surveyor under George Washington during the Revolutionary War, was serving as the surveyor-general of New York State when he was appointed to the Street Commission of New York City in 1807. Moreover, both Morris and John Rutherfurd were former U.S. senators, and all three street commissioners were captivated by the spirit of "improvement" that swept through the nation at the turn of the nineteenth century. It is simply unconvincing, therefore, to dismiss the commissioners as being "motivated mainly by narrow considerations of economic gain," as Reps and others have suggested. Rather, as we shall see, the commissioners' utilitarian values were part of a broader vision of what Morris referred to as "the moral orbit of empire" (1821, 37). Let us venture beyond the "Commissioners' Remarks" for a moment, then, to consider the possibility of an alternative reading of the utilitarian rationale behind the Plan of 1811.

Shortly before his death in 1816, Morris gave an inaugural address as president of the New-York Historical Society, in which he cautioned his audience that, in the study of history,

> facts, as well as motives, are frequently misrepresented. . . . Events are attributed to causes which never existed, while the real causes remain concealed. Presumptuous writers, affecting knowledge they do not possess, undertake to instruct mankind by specious stories, founded on idle rumour and vague conjecture. Those who are well informed smile at the folly. Great minds disdain to tell their own good deeds: it seems, moreover, to those who have managed public business, almost impossible that the tittle tattle of ignorance should meet with belief. Nevertheless, such writings, though sheltered by contempt, from contemporaneous contradiction, are raked out, in a succeeding age, from the ashes of oblivion, and relied on as authority. . . . Neither is it certain that wholesome nourishment will always be extracted even from truth. Like other food, it may be so mixed and manipulated as to nauseate, or so seasoned as to give false appetite, stimulate morbid sensibility, and excite spasmodic action. (1821, 28–9)

Though skeptical of the power of historical mythmaking, Morris did believe that historical "facts" could indeed be "authenticated," thereby producing what he called the "Skeleton of History" (1821, 30). Morris was enthralled by the achievements of modern science, yet he questioned the utilitarian doctrine that "man is a rational creature." Instead, he asked, "Is that assumption just? or, rather, does not History show, and experience prove, that he is swayed from the course which reason indicates, by passion, by indolence, and even caprice? When the foundation is false, the superstructure must fall" (Morris 1821, 28). Interestingly, he insisted that "man" was, above all else, a "contradictory creature" (1821, 30), which explains how Morris himself had no qualms uniting a commitment to modern science, industry, and commerce with his faith in divine revelation.

Morris could speak in one breath, for instance, about the glories of the "culture of science" yet in another prophesize on the "final event" of the coming of Jehovah. The religious undertones behind Morris's utilitarianism are nicely illustrated in the following passage:

> Hail Columbia! child of science, parent of useful arts; dear country, hail! Be it thine to meliorate the condition of man.... Let mankind enjoy at last the consolatory spectacle of thy throne, built by industry on the basis of peace and sheltered under the wings of justice. May it be secured by a pious obedience to that divine will, which prescribes the moral orbit of empire with the same precision that his wisdom and power have displayed, in whirling millions of planets round millions of suns through the vastness of infinite space. (1821, 40)

A contemplation of the "holy writings," Morris argued, would serve as "the clue to all other history" and would therefore provide "the principle of all sound political science" (1821, 30–4). All of this talk of religion as the basis of empire and the contradictions of human life is entirely absent from the "Commissioners' Remarks," yet the utilitarianism of the latter can be read in a new light when juxtaposed with Morris's broader discourse on history.

The rhetoric of "empire" is especially noteworthy, for Morris used the term on numerous occasions to refer to the newly independent United States. For example, after comparing America to the glories of the Roman Empire, Morris exclaimed, "And grant, Oh God! that a long and late posterity, enjoying freedom in the bosom of peace, may look, with grateful exultation, at the day dawn of our empire" (1821, 37). Yet the shortsightedness of many of his contemporaries led Morris to question whether the long-term interests of empire would be sacrificed at the alter of short-term gain. "Men sore with present suffering," he warned, "have not temper to reflect on remote consequence. In the maddening moment, they are deaf even to the voice of a prophet.... Oh man! How short thy sight. To pierce the cloud which overhangs futurity, how feeble" (Morris 1821, 31 and 37). Morris uttered these words a mere five years after commissioning the city's grid plan, which placed him in the social role of "prophet" calling on his generation to lay the foundations of the Empire City in the Empire State.

The only question was, as Morris explained in a speech delivered in 1812, what should serve as "the great columns which are to support the fabric of our wealth and power?" For Morris, the answer was clear. "Am I mistaken in concluding," he rhetorically asked,

> that we should encourage husbandry, commerce, and useful arts, as the great columns which are to support the fabric of our wealth and power? That we should promote order, industry, science, and religion, not only as the guardians of social happiness, but as the outworks to the citadel of our liberty? And, finally, that we should, as the best means of effecting those objects, so arrange our concerns, as that the management of public affairs be entrusted to men of wisdom, firmness, and integrity? (1814, 148)

Morris was adamant, however, that the pursuit of wealth and power for their own sake was insufficient and that, rather, it must serve a higher purpose. In his *Inaugural Discourse* of 1816 he concluded, "There must be something more to hope than pleasure, wealth, and power. Something more to fear than poverty and pain. Something after death more terrible than death. There must be religion" (1821, 32). At this point in our excursion beyond the "Commissioners' Remarks," we have uncovered the entanglement of wealth, power, science, religion, and empire in the thought of one of the grid's designers, Gouverneur Morris, all of which complicates any account of the "intentions" he brought to bear on his service in public life. Yet, compared with Simeon De Witt, Morris admittedly had little technical training in the art and science of surveying and mapping, which played a significant role in the design of the 1811 street plan. Let us consider, then, a little known treatise on linear perspective that De Witt wrote shortly after serving as street commissioner.

In 1813, De Witt published *The Elements of Perspective*, in which he espoused a vision of how the world could be remapped to conform to the "wonderful system" of Cartesian calculability. This work may, at first glance, have the appearance of a mere technical manual on the principles of perspective drawing, but it also reveals De Witt's passionate plea for a Cartesian aesthetic of symmetry, order, and proportion, which he believed would discipline the mind and, thus, "have a wholesome influence on the morality and happiness, as well as the usefulness of men as members of society" (1813, iii). Because most historical accounts of the Plan of 1811 have assumed that questions of economic utility and aesthetics are incommensurable, scholars have generally argued that the commissioners privileged the former over the latter. Such a conclusion is indeed confirmed by the "Commissioners' Remarks," which makes no mention of aesthetic sensibilities but highlights the paramount importance of the "principles of economy." However, a careful reading of *The Elements of Perspective* leads to a quite different conclusion.

Given his training as a surveyor, De Witt was mesmerized by the power of Cartesian perspectivalism in granting access to the surface appearance of things. "Perspective drawing," De Witt maintained,

> especially that of Landscape, gives him who is made familiar with its principles and practices a new and deeper interest in THE APPEARANCE OF THINGS. By it he becomes habituated to discriminating views of their beauties, and thus they acquire a superior power of ministering to his pleasures. In the aspect of nature, where others see nothing to affect them, but look "with brute, unconscious gaze," he sees the distinct myriads of parts, wonderfully formed and put together by infinite wisdom to constitute a whole, perfect in all the varieties of proportion, shape, color, and purpose, and his sensations are absorbed and dissolve in the harmony that reigns universally among them. Delight streams into his soul from every quarter to which he turns the contemplative eye. (1813, xix)

In other words, Cartesian perspective could be used as an instrument to organize the chaos of human perception into the calculable order of gridded space. Through the proper application of the "rules of symmetry" one would achieve an appreciation of "that relish for the harmonies of proportion" (De Witt 1813, xii-iv). Or, put differently, "Besides serving those purposes of *practical utility*, Perspective drawing, as a minister of RATIONAL AMUSEMENT, holds a high station in the graduations of merit; and may almost dispute precedency with the poetic muse" (1813, xv-vi; italics in the original). Here we find De Witt aestheticizing the "appearance of things" through the construction of a "well arranged" Cartesian landscape. So much, then, for the standard line repeated ad nauseam that the grid's designers privileged utility over aesthetics: We can see here how De Witt viewed the utilitarian order of the grid itself through an aesthetics of Cartesian visuality.

As historians of philosophy are well aware, one of the foundations of Cartesian rationalism is the belief that "clear" and "distinct" ideas should form the basis of modern, scientific reason (Flage and Bonnen 1999). De Witt drew directly on this Cartesian conception of knowledge in his argument that the practice of linear perspective "creates habits of forming clear and distinct ideas of complex objects, with the relative bearings of all their parts, whether such objects have been presented to the eye, or be only creatures of the mind, and changed to every shape and position, in order to ascertain which will best answer a meditated purpose" (1813, ix). The elements of perspective, it seemed, could liberate the imagination from the "unconscious gaze" of the untrained eye. "The imagination becomes so far improved by it," argued De Witt, "that the models it forms are as complete as those made of material substances. But its most useful office is to give substance and visibility to those aerial shapes" (1813, ix) (Fig. 12.2). These abstract spatial models could then be used to remake the world in their own image. As De Witt confidently declared, "The productions of the creative mind grow under the pencil till they result in wonderful systems, endowed with powers to produce effects of incalculable benefit to man" (pp. ix-x).

But what made Cartesian perspectivalism such a powerful mode of reasoning? The answer, De Witt maintained, lies in the fact that it renders the techniques of

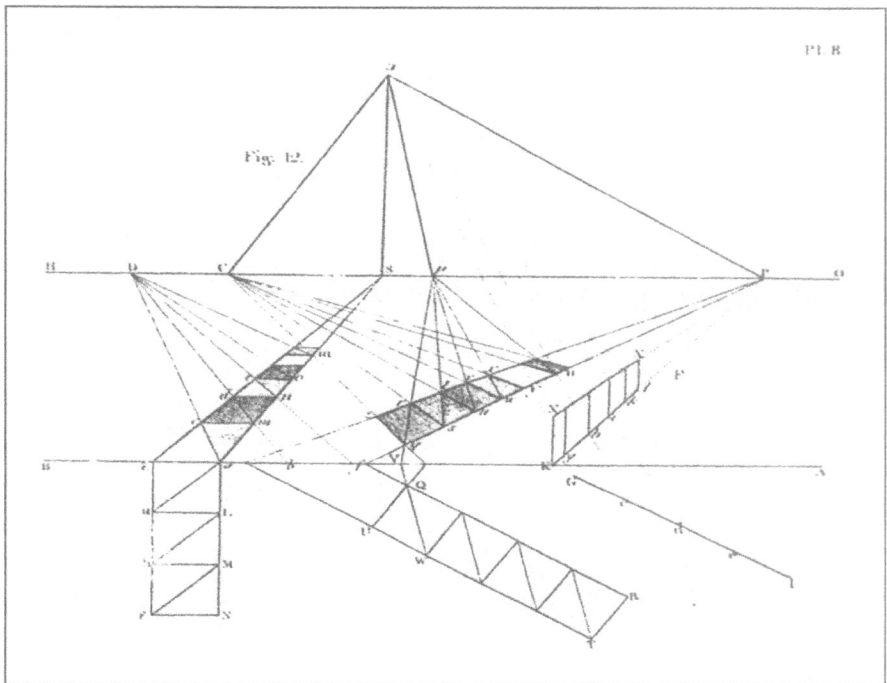

Fig 12.2 Simeon De Witt's illustration of the means by which to "give substance and visibility to those aerial shapes" produced through the lens of Cartesian linear perspective (De Witt 1813, 78)

calculation visible, because "the aid of algebraic characters... keep[s] the whole process of his reasoning continually before his eyes, and render[s] his progress to the conclusion practicable and easy" (1813, x). It is worth noting that the grid plan of 1811 was one of De Witt's "wonderful systems" composed of "algebraic characters" that literally recreate "the whole process of... reasoning continually before [one's] eyes" (Fig. 12.3). The principal benefit of cultivating a Cartesian sensibility, according to De Witt, was that it would discipline the mind through the repetitious enactment of calculative reasoning. De Witt made this connection explicit by stating that it "opens a path into which strong allurements invite the reasoning faculties. It is therefore well calculated to lead them into a cheerful submission to that extent of discipline which is held necessary for rearing them to maturity; and this consideration alone gives it a stamp of value that entitles it to more than common regard" (De Witt 1813, viii-ix; italics in the original).

The calculative rationalities of the Cartesian grid, then, were seen as a means of discipline that would serve as a remedy for what De Witt saw as the "idleness and dissipation" that often resulted from the "customs of cities," and in a later publication he suggested that "frugality, temperance and economy" were the only means by which to deal with such debauchery (1819, 35). The religious undercurrent noticeable in De Witt's aesthetic contemplations can also be detected in his understanding

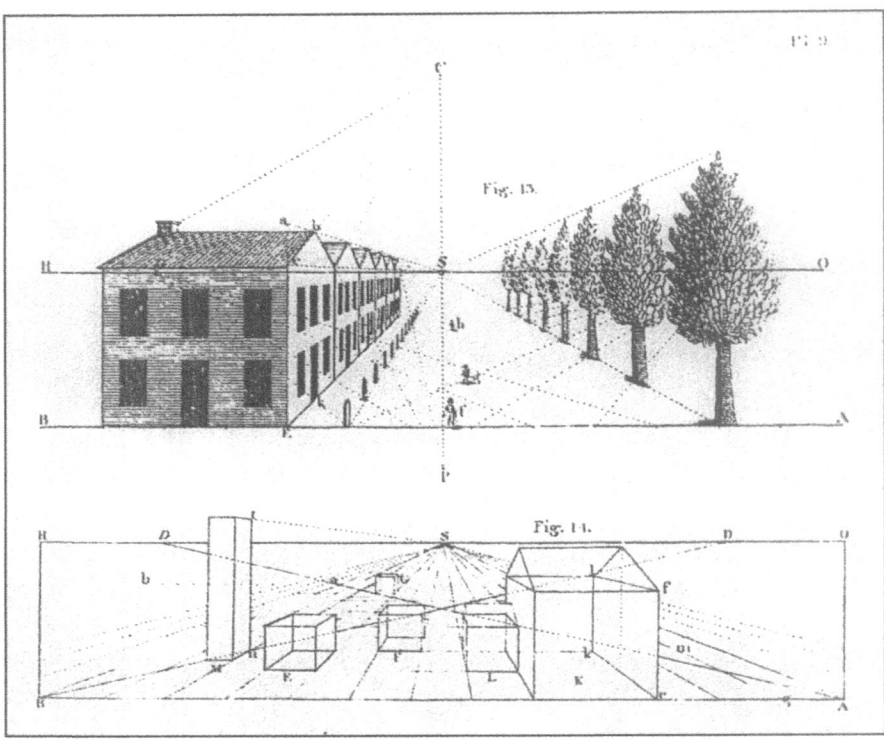

Fig 12.3 Simeon De Witt's "wonderful system" materialized, a hypothetical utilization of Cartesian perspectivalism to remodel the world (De Witt 1813, 79)

of political economy and the management of public affairs, as is evident in the following statement:

> By the infallible oracles of divine inspiration we are taught, that no man can obtain a good character as a christian, unless he denies himself, takes up his cross—cuts off a right hand, or pulls out an eye, if necessary for his advancement to perfection—Figurative expressions denoting the extremes of self-denial, fortitude and voluntary suffering. The same doctrine may, with a qualified propriety, be addressed to those who aim at distinction in any of the professions of civil life. Whatever may be the genius or natural power, there must be the labor improbus, hard labor, strong exertions, struggles against improper propensities, a rigid observance of rules, a radical extermination of evil habits, a scrupulous improvement of time, an unwavering perseverance, and a judicious exercise of a well disciplined reason in the selection of means for the attainment of the objects to be achieved. (De Witt 1819, 12–3, italics in the original)

This passage is remarkable for a number of reasons, most notably because on the surface it appears to confirm Max Weber's famous "Protestant ethic" thesis, which asserts that Protestant asceticism was the foundation from which the modern capitalist ethic of methodical self-conduct was born. According to Weber, the so-called Protestant ethic "strode into the market-place of life, slammed the door of the monastery behind it, and undertook to penetrate just that daily routine of life with its methodicalness, to fashion it into a life in the world, but neither of nor for this world" (2000 [1930], 154). One key aspect of this disciplinary order, for Weber, was the "rational organization of our social environment" (2000 [1930], 109). Weber's idealism is often contrasted with Karl Marx's historical materialism. Marx and his collaborator Friedrich Engels, for instance, insisted that "life is not determined by consciousness, but consciousness by life. ... . [The materialist view of history] does not explain practice from the idea but explains the formation of ideas from material practice" (1970 [1932], 47 and 58). At first glance De Witt's use of Cartesian perspective as an instrument to promote a religious ethic of disciplinary self-conduct may seem to support Weber's thesis. However, it must surely be acknowledged that both Morris's and De Witt's religious ideals did not emerge in an ethereal world disconnected from the material conditions in which they were immersed. One should therefore be cautious about placing too much weight on the religious "origins" of the modern grid plan, which we find in the work of J.B. Jackson or Richard Sennett (see, for example, Jackson 1979; Sennett 1990a). This being said, if the game of interpreting founding intentions is to be played—and I am suggesting here that this quest has serious interpretative limits—then one cannot fully understand the utilitarian rationale that underpinned the Commissioners' Plan of 1811 without taking into account how it was informed by a religious discourse on the methodical conduct of "civil affairs."

De Witt's obsession with the disciplinary conduct of the self is evident in many of his writings, and he insisted that the cultivation of the faculty of "reason" was essential to the production of self-disciplining individuals. He contended that, if such conditions were attained, leisure would be left "to the mind to wander through the mysterious, unfathomable repositories of possible things; to the boundless field of improvement before us" (De Witt 1813, ix; italics in the original). De Witt therefore turned to Cartesian perspective as a means of rendering the unfathomable realm of "possible things" into the calculable order of a "well disciplined reason" (Fig. 12.4). What better way was there to achieve such a goal than to devise a plan to remake the urban environment according to the principles of Cartesian calculation?

Genealogical Excavations of the Grid and the Perils of Historical Mythology

Over the past two centuries a historical mythology has emerged that narrates the story of the origins of New York's grid plan by revealing the utilitarian motivations and intentions that gave rise to the streets and avenues of modern Manhattan. In the preceding section, I sought to problematize this orthodox account of the grid's origins through a critical reading of several marginalized archival sources in addition to the foundational text that most scholars employ as historical evidence. Such a

Fig 12.4 Manhattan's landscape as Cartesian space (photograph by the author, 2001)

methodological technique has the effect of temporarily short-circuiting the mythologies of the grid by rendering complex what had previously been considered a relatively simple matter that is beyond dispute.

If the official storyline has suggested that the utilitarian logic of economic calculation motivated the grid's designers, I have not disputed this claim per se but have demonstrated how this utilitarian ethos was part of a broader vision of empire and disciplinary self-conduct informed by a metaphysics of divine revelation. If the prevailing narrative has constructed a binary opposition between utility and aesthetics, suggesting that the commissioners chose the former over the latter, I have challenged this historical explanation by showing how the symmetry of the grid satisfied the commissioners' desire to unite practical utility with the harmonies of proportion. Of course, this counternarrative is not meant to provide a definitive verdict on the essential meaning of the 1811 grid plan. Rather, it is to suggest that the historical mythology of the grid has narrowly constricted our understanding of urban form by reducing it to a singular explanation formulaically extracted from a foundational text.

As a general rule, historical mythology has the effect of constraining the past in the straightjacket of a repetitive narration. The messy contradictions of history emerge from such a reading as self-evident, coherent, intelligible, and unproblematic due in large part to the repeated recitation of a canonical narrative. If I perhaps overextended my argument somewhat in the preceding section, I did so precisely to convince the reader that the act of historical narration should be opened up to multiple interpretive readings rather than enclosed in a hermetically sealed envelope of historical explanation. One of the primary goals of a critical genealogy is to shake up the self-evidence of conventional explanations through what Foucault called the "pluralization of causes" (1991b, 76). By employing the technique of "causal multiplication," genealogical investigations seek to excavate the plurality of discourses and practices that constitute the events of the past. The aim, in other words, is not to replace one causal explanation with another; for instance, simply inverting the dominant narrative by arguing that the logic behind the grid was aesthetic or religious rather than utilitarian, which would be equally problematic. This would, no doubt, have the effect of challenging particular myths of history without problematizing the basic structure of historical mythology more generally.

In order to disrupt the recurring mythology of the grid, it was first necessary to strategically challenge individual myths on their own terms by turning the search for origins against itself, thereby expanding the realm of intentionality beyond the confines of official explanations found in canonical texts. If the analysis were to end there, however, the result would simply be a more nuanced form of morphological essentialism that remains in search of first causes which can allegedly be uncovered in the motivations and intentions of urban designers. Yet Gouverneur Morris himself warned against privileging "intentions" over the "effects" of social practices (1821, 29), and Simeon De Witt also confessed that he was "aware of the false estimate we are prone to make of our own productions" (1813, iv). Why, then, should we continue to place so much weight on the explicit intentions set out for us in the "Commissioners' Remarks"?

It was precisely against such an idealist quest for historical origins that Foucault was reacting when he developed his analytics of discourse. "I do not question discourses about their silently intended meanings," he insisted, "but about the fact and the conditions of their manifest appearance; not about the contents which they may conceal, but about the transformations which they have effected; not about the sense preserved within them like a perpetual origin, but about the field where they coexist, reside and disappear" (1991a, 60). How might a shift in focus from founding intentions to the performative world of effects reshape the narratives we tell ourselves about the grid?

First, such an interpretative realignment would reject the essentialist claim that there is a singular "cause" or "meaning" that definitively explains the origins of urban form. This anti-essentialist stance questions the desire to extract the "essence" of the 1811 grid plan from the authorial intentions expressed within a foundational text, whether this be the "Commissioners' Remarks" or De Witt's *The Elements of Perspective*. Any such founding intentions are necessarily enmeshed in an entire constellation of discourses and practices that have shaped the morphologies of landscape. If the grid has come to symbolize the primacy of a "ruthless utilitarianism," this arguably has more to do with the effect that the 1811 Plan had on the subsequent development of Manhattan's real estate economy than it does with the conscious intentions laid out by the plan's original designers.

Second, this focus on effects rather than first causes leads to a recognition that it is not enough to be content with tracing the origin of New York's grid plan back to earlier urban precedents, to the Land Ordinance of 1785, or to the Roman camp as part of an infinite regress, even if it is conceded that all of these were unquestionably precursors to the Plan of 1811. A widespread tendency exists in the literature on the grid plan to explain a specific use of the grid by citing a series of precedents as part of a broadly diffusionist theory of urban form (for a classic illustration of this approach, see Stanislawski 1946, 1947; for a critique, see Rose-Redwood 2008). A diffusionist explanation of the Manhattan grid plan, for instance, might cite Philadelphia, Pennsylvania, Savannah, Georgia, or other previous grid-plan cities in North America, the U.S. Township and Range Survey System, or the Law of the Indies in Spain's American colonies, all of which might then be traced back to prior grid plans in Europe, the Roman Empire, Greece, and the Indus Valley. Such a historical exercise may help situate a particular city plan within a broader lineage of urban forms, but it also reinforces the essentialist belief that an urban form can be explained by simply tracing its historical origins into a distant past.

Third, instead of viewing the grid as an ideal form that is emblematic of the rational design of cities throughout the ages, it may be more productive to see the grid as a "mythic creature" teeming with social contradictions (Higgins 2009, 11). These contradictions may go undetected if one is concerned only with the utilitarian logic of the plan itself rather than with the conflicting social uses that have unfolded as part of the ongoing process of producing gridded spaces. As Hannah Higgins argues, "whatever the origin of each grid in establishing a social standard, the recurrent transformations of grids, the ways in which they break down, shatter, bend, and adapt to unanticipated purposes, suggest that the homogenizing dimension of the grid-myth begs for reversal" (2009, 9–10). Such a reversal, however, does not come easily, nor is it based solely on a meticulous reevaluation of archival sources alone. Yet, if Higgins is right to suggest that "it is use that brings each grid to life," then the most effective means of problematizing the "grid-myth" of modernity may not be to demonstrate its empirical invalidity but rather to draw attention to the proliferation of countermyths that performatively redefine "the grid's constant making and unmaking" (2009, 11; italics in the original). At the very least, we might do well to question the ritualized obsession with reenacting the original planners' motivations in a perpetual search for historical origins and instead remain open to the possibility that the inhabitants of gridded space have always engaged in the act of making and unmaking the grid in the image of their own dreams and desires.

References

Adler, P., Howells, T., & McCorquodale, D. (Eds.). (2009). *Mapping New York*. London: Black Dog.

Barthes, R. (1982). Myth today. In S. Sontag (Ed.), *A Barthes reader* (pp. 93–149). New York: Hill and Wang.

Bridges, W. (1811). Commissioners' remarks. In W. Bridges (Ed.), *Map of the city of New-York and island of Manhattan; With explanatory remarks and references*. New York: T. & J. Swords.

Burrows, E., & Wallace, M. (1999). *Gotham: A history of New York City to 1898*. New York: Oxford University Press.

Callon, M. (1986). Some elements of a sociology of translation: Domestication of the scallops and the fishermen of St. Brieuc Bay. In J. Law (Ed.), *Power, action and belief: A new sociology of knowledge?* (pp. 196–233). London: Routledge and Kegan Paul.

Cook, A. (2004). The use and abuse of historical reenactment: Thoughts on recent trends in public history. *Criticism, 46*(3), 487–496.

De Witt, S. (1813). *The elements of perspective*. Albany: H. C. Southwick.

De Witt, S. (1819). *Considerations on the necessity of establishing an agricultural college, and having more of the children of wealthy citizens educated for the profession of farming*. Albany: Websters and Skinners.

Flage, D., & Bonnen, C. (1999). *Descartes and method: A search for a method in meditations*. London: Routledge.

Flagg, E. (1904). *The plan of New York and how to improve it* (pp. 253–256). August: Scribner's Magazine.

Foucault, M. (1991a). Politics and the study of discourse. In G. Burchell, C. Gordon, & P. Miller (Eds.), *The Foucault effect: Studies in governmentality* (pp. 73–86). Chicago: University of Chicago Press.

Foucault, M. (1991b). Questions of method. In G. Burchell, C. Gordon, & P. Miller (Eds.), *The Foucault effect: Studies in governmentality* (pp. 53–72). Chicago: University of Chicago Press.

Foucault, M. (2003). *Society must be defended: Lectures at the Collège de France* (trans: D. Macey). New York: Picador.

Gapps, S. (2009). Mobile monuments: A view of historical re-enactment and authenticity from inside the costume cupboard of history. *Rethinking History, 13*(3), 395–409.

Higgins, H. (2009). *The grid book*. Cambridge, MA: MIT Press.

Hubbard, B., Jr. (2009). *American boundaries: The nation, the states, the rectangular survey*. Chicago: University of Chicago Press.

Huxley, M. (2010). Problematizing planning: Critical and effective genealogies. In J. Hillier & P. Healey (Eds.), *The Ashgate research companion to planning theory: Conceptual challenges for spatial planning* (pp. 135–158). Farnham: Ashgate.

Jackson, J. B. (1979). The order of a landscape: Reason and religion in Newtonian America. In D. Meinig (Ed.), *The interpretation of ordinary landscapes: Geographical essays* (pp. 153–163). New York: Oxford University Press.

Marcuse, P. (1987). The grid as city plan: New York City and laissez-faire planning in the nineteenth century. *Planning Perspectives, 2*(3), 287–310.

Marx, K., & Engels, F. (1970 [1932]). *The German ideology. Part one, with selections from parts two and three, together with Marx's "Introduction to a critique of political economy"* (C. Arthur, Ed.). New York: International Publishers.

Morris, G. (1814). A discourse delivered before the New-York Historical Society, at their anniversary meeting, 6th December, 1812. New York: Collections of the New-York Historical Society, for the year 1814, 2: 117–148.

Morris, G. (1821). An inaugural discourse, delivered before the New-York Historical Society, by the Honourable Gouverneur Morris, President, 4th September, 1816. Collections of the New-York Historical Society, for the year 1821, 3: 25–40.

Mumford, L. (1961). *The city in history: Its origins, its transformations, and its prospects*. New York: Harcourt, Brace & World.

Olmsted, F., & Croes, J. (1971). The misfortunes of New York. In S. Sutton (Ed.), *Civilizing American cities: Writings on city landscapes* (pp. 43–51). Cambridge, MA: MIT Press. Reprint of "Preliminary report of the landscape architect and the civil and topographical engineer, upon the laying out of the twenty-third and twenty-fourth wards". City of New York, Document No. 72 of the Board of the Department of Public Parks, 1877.

Reps, J. (1965). *The making of urban America: A history of city planning in the United States.* Princeton: Princeton University Press.

Rose-Redwood, R. (2002). Rationalizing the landscape: Superimposing the grid upon the island of Manhattan. M.S. thesis, Pennsylvania State University.

Rose-Redwood, R. (2008). Genealogies of the grid: Revisiting Stanislawski's search for the origin of the grid-pattern town. *Geographical Review, 98*(1), 42–58.

Scobey, D. (2002). *Empire City: The making and meaning of the New York City landscape.* Philadelphia: Temple University Press.

Sennett, R. (1990a). American cities: The grid plan and the Protestant ethic. *International Social Science Journal, 42*(3), 269–285.

Sennett, R. (1990b). *The conscience of the eye: The design and social life of cities.* New York: Alfred A. Knopf.

Sennett, R. (1994). *Flesh and stone: The body and the city in Western civilization.* New York: W.W. Norton.

Spann, E. (1988). The greatest grid: The New York plan of 1811. In D. Schaffer (Ed.), *Two centuries of American planning* (pp. 11–39). Baltimore: Johns Hopkins University Press.

Stanislawski, D. (1946). The origin and spread of the grid-pattern town. *Geographical Review, 36*(1), 105–120.

Stanislawski, D. (1947). Early Spanish town planning in the New World. *Geographical Review, 37*(1), 94–105.

Trachtenberg, A. (1964). The rainbow and the grid. *American Quarterly, 16*(1), 3–19.

Weber, M. (2000 [1930]). *The Protestant ethic and the spirit of capitalism.* (trans: T. Parsons). New York: Routledge.

Chapter 13
Gridded Lives: Why Kazakhstan and Montana are Nearly the Same Place

Kate Brown

Abstract While the United States and the Soviet Union are normally conceptualized as polar opposites, by comparing Karaganda (Kazakhstan) and Billings (Montana), this chapter draws significant parallels between the use of the grid in these contrasting political contexts. Using a comparative approach, the author addresses the following questions: Is it possible to write the history of gridded spaces? If so, do the gridded spaces of Kazakhstan and Montana constitute the endpoint of larger processes that the United States and the Soviet Union shared? The present chapter explores these questions through comparative urban history to illustrate how the grid evolved just as the territories of the U.S. and Soviet Union were being swept into larger industrial and agricultural economies. The author concludes that, in both cases, political powers produced gridded spaces, often violently, to serve economic and political goals.

Keywords Grid plan · United States · Soviet Union · Mining cities · Railroad cities · Communism · Capitalism · Modernization · Propaganda · Colonization

From the map of Karaganda, it appears that its city plan was based on the model of the old Roman military camp—set up along a grid, the old Stalin Prospect ran north-south, the former Lenin Prospect bisecting it from east to west. The grid makes sense for a prison city because it creates wide open spaces and straight lines, an architecture designed not to be seen but to see, to survey the city's inhabitants so as to regulate and contain their conduct. Karaganda, located on the arid steppe of

This chapter is an abridged version of Brown, K. (2001). "Gridded Lives: Why Kazakhstan and Montana are Nearly the Same Place." *American Historical Review*, 106(1): 17–48. Copyright © 2001 by Oxford University Press. Reproduced with permission of Oxford University Press.

K. Brown (✉)
University of Maryland, Baltimore, MD, USA
e-mail: kbrown@umbc.edu

© Springer International Publishing AG, part of Springer Nature 2018
R. Rose-Redwood, L. Bigon (eds.), *Gridded Worlds: An Urban Anthology*,
https://doi.org/10.1007/978-3-319-76490-0_13

northern Kazakhstan, was founded in the early 1930s alongside KarLag,[1] one of the largest labor camps in the Soviet Union. Karaganda constitutes a prison city because it was built largely by convicts, and it was fed on crops grown in the labor camp's farms, while prisoners and deportees worked in the mines and factories of the city's blossoming industries. In 1930, Karaganda was not even a point on the map. By 1939, the city had 100,000 inhabitants, half of them wards (prisoners or deportees) of the Ministry of Interior's Gulag division (NKVD-Gulag) (Poliakov 1991, 180).

I had expected Karaganda to have that smoke-belching, wrecked look of industrial cities of Soviet Russia to the north. But I was surprised. After Joseph Stalin died in 1953, the prisoners were gradually given amnesty, the prison barracks were dismantled, the barbed wire was lifted, and, curiously, what remains is a neatly ordered city of broad avenues and shady sidewalks, monumental squares and symmetrically plotted parks, ample and verdant. There is plenty of parking, convenient shopping, and no cramped corners. No sign of the gulag's secrecy or human suffering is written into the urban landscape. Instead, Karaganda is an open-armed embrace that says it has nothing to hide. There are no old shops to dig out of back alleys, no tenements or crowded nineteenth-century courtyards of the kind Dostoyevsky haunted. In fact, Karaganda is so well-ordered, there is no great need to explore it on foot. Rather, it can be read easily from the upholstered comfort of a car at cruising speed.

The car slides by long columns of housing blocks, which replaced the prisoners' barracks in the 1950s. The residential tracts, built with assembly-line efficiency, are the Soviet equivalent of the American suburban development. The same three blueprints echo in row after row, the same efficient economy of occupancy and technology behind the lace curtains, the same segregation of space based on the daily repetition of meals, commuting, and recreation around which American homes are also designed. Built rapidly, rapidly looking obsolete, the buildings radiate that temporal quality of much of American architecture, as if designed not for generations of a family but for generations of a professional career, a familiar architecture responding to the unmatched social mobility of the twentieth century.[2]

One evening, I stood on the balcony of the Karaganda hotel room, looking at the neon signs glistening along the rain-soaked streets. The October wind breathed the first frost of winter and sent skyward small wrappers of candy imported from North America. In the distance, the comforting lights of thousands of living rooms lit up the expanse, revealing the soothing grid as it marched up and down, partitioning the electrified urban spaces from the black void of the steppe beyond. Here, far from home, in the midst of a former gulag on the Kazakh steppe, I had the uncanny feeling that I had seen this city before. Karaganda, with its gridded composure, easy repetition of residential units, carefully swept walks and afterschool dance classes,

---

[1] KarLag stands for Karagandinskaia lager, the Karaganda Labor Camp.

[2] It is curious to note that the same commentators who frequently comment on the repetition and monotony of Soviet urban spaces and who attribute these qualities to socialist authoritarian state control and uninspired top-down planning overlook, or momentarily forget, the monotony and repetition of the American subdivision located in thriving centers of capitalism.

seemed oddly familiar, as if I had landed not in Central Asia but in the American middle west, in Wichita, Topeka, Bismarck, or Billings.

***

Billings, Montana. Like most railroad cities, Billings can be navigated without a map. Broad arteries cut north and south, avenues east and west. The streets are platted out in numbered convenience beginning at one and can multiply to infinity in keeping with the grand aspirations of the founding fathers. The Yellowstone River flows unnoted on the outskirts of town, beyond the grain elevators, the railroad switching yards and oil refineries. Looking at Billings from the height of the cliffs above it, the mind drifts off to high-school geometry, trying to take in the ever-divisible asphalt grid of smaller and smaller blocks that break down to rectangular spaces etched with yellow paint on the parking lots. Fly over Billings, and this chessboard divisibility of space expands to cover the whole land: squared-off fields contained within square-mile sections fit into angular counties in the washboard abdomen of the country, where the states break up into rectangles and trapezoids.

Standing on the bluff overlooking Billings, I was better able to decipher what it was that made it feel like Karaganda: the divisibility and hierarchy of space, the abrupt, fortress-like partition of urban from agricultural territory, the lonely feeling of a city adrift like a ship on a sea of land that is inhospitable and unpredictable. Yet Karaganda is a city erected in the midst of a vast labor camp, a city where children planting trees in the schoolyard still come across human bones. Meanwhile, Billings was founded by railroad entrepreneurs, farmers, miners, and businessmen on the American frontier. One city is the product of an authoritarian state that employed and ruled everyone who toiled there; the other, a conglomerate of competing business interests and individual farmers. Two countries, worlds apart, two different histories, yet cities in the American West share the same modern, expansive, modular feel as Karaganda because Karaganda, like every western American railroad city, is built along a grid.

The fact of the grid may seem like no fact at all. For the grid is no novelty; it has been used as an architectural model for centuries, and it does not necessarily follow that all gridded cities are born of the same motivations. Kazakhstan and the Great Plains fall in the same topographical zone of vast, arid, high plateaus. One could argue that the flat, endless landscapes lend themselves easily to geometric dissection.[3] Yet it seems logical that two such contrasting societies—the communist Soviet Union and democratic United States—would naturally develop cities in distinct patterns expressing the vast differences between the two countries in ideas, politics, and economic structure. For, if one believes that form relates to content—that cities contain their histories, as Italo Calvino writes, "like the lines of a hand, written in

---

[3] The grid, however, on high, flat ground is not inevitable. Old Central Asian cities along the silk route, such as Tashkent, Samarkand, and Kashgar, center on the mosque and market, from which streets wind around without any specific pattern. In the American Southwest, Mesa Verde is an intricate labyrinth built into the cliffs of a mesa, and Pueblo Bonito circles around like a contemporary soccer stadium.

the corners of the streets and the gratings of the windows" (1974, 11)—then can it
be purely coincidental that Karaganda, a prison city, and Billings, a railroad town,
look alike?[4]

To attempt any kind of analogy between Karaganda and Billings, however, is to
ignore the polarities between the two places. For, at least in terms of imagery, one
can conceive of few regions more dissimilar. The American West represents the last,
inexhaustible frontier of American individualism, the place where people went to be
free. Northern Kazakhstan, conversely, conjures an image similar to that of Siberia;
it is a place of unfreedom, exile, and imprisonment, a place where masses of undif-
ferentiated people were sent against their will to serve a monolithic state. Placed in
the larger context of the United States and the Soviet Union, the contrasts between
the two cities intensify: the free market versus the planned economy, the democracy
of the people versus the dictatorship of the proletariat, the pioneer against the exile,
the self-made man and free labor versus the machinated relationship of prison guard
and convict. To liken Billings to Karaganda is to blur the domains, as we have
defined them, of freedom and bondage, of liberty and oppression. People were
deported to Karaganda against their will. They were either sentenced to hard labor
in camps or exiled to special settlements, and they starved, froze, and worked until
they dropped from exhaustion. Of course, it is true that on the Great Plains people
also starved, froze, and worked until they dropped from exhaustion, but in the
American Plains they did it of their own free will; they bought their own train tick-
ets. Is that difference of free will essential?

Just by posing the question, I threaten to relativize the oppression of the Soviet
penal system and the suffering of millions of people sent into exile or to the gulag.
Certainly, there is a difference between Billings and Karaganda, a difference calculable both in magnitude and outcome. As Soviet archives have been opened, documentary evidence has confirmed survivor accounts that narrate how Soviet security
forces, the OGPU, NKVD, MVD,[5] uprooted millions of peaceful citizens and subjected them to physical and psychological abuse, starvation, and conditions ripe for
disease, from which hundreds of thousands of people died.[6] The years of arrest and

---

[4] Henri Lefebvre argues that the passage from one mode of production to another must entail the
production of a new space. He calls for a study of history that looks at the "interconnections, dis-
tortions, displacements, mutual interactions and their links with the spacial practice of the particular society or mode of production" (1994, 42–6). As well, Marshall Berman notes the necessity for
revolutions to produce new spatial patterns. See Berman's discussion of Chernyshevsky's Crystal
Palace (1988 [1982], 241–4).

[5] The title and jurisdictions of Soviet federal and republic security branches changed frequently. In
1934, the Unified State Political Administration (OGPU) was subsumed into the National
Commissariat of Internal Affairs (NKVD), which was responsible for the gulag network and special settlements. In 1946, the bureau in charge of state security was renamed the NKVD-MVD, the
Ministry of Internal Affairs. To reduce confusion, in this chapter I will refer to the Soviet security
organs generally as the NKVD.

[6] Soviet security forces maintained broad and variegated categories of incarceration, arrest, and
exile. Those arrested were assigned to prisons or labor camps. Those deported were restricted to
living within a limited area called a "special settlement" or "labor settlement." For literature on the
Soviet penal system, see Jakobson (1993), Bacon (1994), Danilov and Krusil'nikov (1994), and
Ivanova (1997). For statistics, see Zemskov (1990) and Pohl (1997).

deportation tore apart families, destroyed communities, and changed permanently both social relations and the landscape.

Yet, setting aside for a moment the well-documented differences between the penal Kazakh steppe and free-market American frontier, I wonder if there is a significance to the spatial similarities of the grid in Montana and Kazakhstan—if a comparison would not be fruitful. Comparisons, after all, can be misleading or overtly political. Anything can be compared to anything. It is a trick of historians to place historic eras or regimes in juxtaposition to point out similarities or differences and thus win an argument. For example, since the onset of the Cold War, Stalin's Soviet Union has often been likened to Hitler's Nazi regime. The extremes of left and right are seen to fuse at one common point of total communist/fascist social control, illustrating the apex of state terror.[7] Contrasts, too, can be used for polemical effect. Since the Cold War, historians, journalists, and politicians in the United States have focused on Soviet transgressions such as the purge trials, collectivization, and the suppression of dissidents as a way to spell out what democratic America is not or should never become.[8] In the same way, Soviet historians and journalists for decades fixated on American ghettos, racial strife, social unrest, and rising crime rates as a sign that Soviet socialism was on the right track (Becker 1999).

Now, however, with the threat of the Cold War faded, there is more room to question whether knowledge itself has not been gridded into neat polarities, communist and democratic. Histories tend to prioritize texts, written matter, and ideological categorizations. And certainly, in the heated debates of the Cold War, words, rhetoric, and ideologies have been highly evaluated, perhaps over-evaluated, at the cost of ignoring and diminishing the history of the production of spaces and the lives that have been forged by and for those spaces. This is no new idea. Several decades ago, Henri Lefebvre asserted there is no communism, just two myths: "that of anti-communism, on the one hand, and the myth that communism had been carried out somewhere on the other." Lefebvre doubted the existence of communism because it had led to no new architectural innovation, no creation of specifically socialist spaces (1994, 55, 62). In other words, in the history of space, communism and capitalism have produced no qualities that distinguish one from the other.

---

[7] For an interesting review of the comparison of Nazi Germany and Stalinist Soviet Union as similar "totalitarian" states, see Kershaw and Lewin (1997). For a discussion on the changing concept of totalitarian states, see Gleason (1995).

[8] Before the Cold War, in the 1930s and during World War II, historians, political scientists, and journalists looked for and found similarities between the Soviet Union and United States. Not just left-leaning activists but right-minded businessmen and politicians saw affinities with the Soviet Union and made trips there to exchange information. For example, Rufus Woods, an influential Washington State newspaperman and one of the chief promoters of the Grand Coulee Dam, made several trips to the Soviet Union in the early 1930s. Though a conservative, Woods admired the Soviet industrialization drive and thought the same pattern of building big could revitalize the West (see Ficken 1995). For studies comparing, favorably, the United States and Soviet Union, see Wilson (1936), Tracy (1938), Startsev (1942), and Fox (1944). For an illuminating comparative history of slavery and serfdom in czarist Russia and the United States, see Kolchin (1987).

What would happen, then, if we discarded all that we know about the polarities of communism and capitalism and, just for the sake of argument, explored the spatial affinities? With this approach, it may turn out that historians and politicians in both countries have focused to the point of obfuscation on the differences between Soviet communism and American capitalism and ignored the parallels produced by the industrial-capital expansions of the twentieth century.[9] After all, a mirror image, the Soviet Union and United States, is just the same form reflected backward. We may even recognize how the two countries followed similar paths of development and destruction that differ more in scale than form. If that is so, then the decades of focusing on political systems and ideology appear in retrospect as a prolonged exercise in self-definition. Neither country could have existed without the other, because each country used its communist/capitalist nemesis as the self-justifying point of departure; each country projected a mirror image of the other in order to define and produce itself so as to rule. Without the specter of the counter-revolutionary capitalist or the subversive communist, each country would have had a much harder time defining the abnormal and the dangerous; it would have been more difficult to appropriate the power to condemn and exclude, to coax and coerce into conformity.[10] In short, by straining away the mountains of verbiage encircling the Cold War, we may find the Soviet Union and the United States share a great deal in common.

Or perhaps we are still too close to the twentieth century to see how greater forces of the last hundred years have put disparate lives in sync in strange ways. In order to do so, we have to ask a different set of questions than the Cold War theoreticians have posed. Rather than trying to determine where is freedom and where is bondage, who has choices and who does not, who wields power and who is powerless, we might ask, more simply, *how* is power produced (Foucault 1995 [1977])? And once that question flutters down to eye level, the gaze is drawn to spaces that once seemed innocent of manipulation—urban architecture, transportation routes, lines of communication, patterns of production—all of which represent a particular political and economic logic that has inhabited our societies, both Soviet and American, for the bulk of the century—inhabited them with an encompassing opacity.[11]

My question, then, is—is it possible to write the history of gridded spaces? If so, do the gridded spaces of Kazakhstan and Montana constitute the end-point of larger processes that the United States and Soviet Union shared? Lefebvre sees the grid as an abstraction, "a superstructure foreign to the original space," which serves as a

---

[9] As Iain Chambers writes, "The falling away of earlier dualities—the real and artificial, the original and false—leads to casting previous epistemological certainties into an instructive confusion" (1994, 58).

[10] See Foucault (1995 [1977]) on the art of coercive assignment. In the Soviet Union, the enemy and citizen-traitor was most often identified as someone sympathetic to capitalism or "bourgeois-nationalist" states. Meanwhile, in the United States, from the World War I-era Palmer Raids to the House Un-American Activities Committee hearings, socialists, communists, and "fellow travelers" constituted a threatening category of disloyal citizens (see Navasky 1980; Ball 1987).

[11] As David Rollison (1999) phrases it: "the organization (and imagination) of space is deeply implicated in the maintenance of existing power structures."

foothold to establish the basis of rule.[12] James C. Scott (1998) understands the grid as a way to simplify the opaque and complex quality of indigenous social practices so as to enhance centralized power at the cost of local rule. In short, the grid can serve as an apparatus for conquest, as a way to dominate space. In this chapter, I will compare Karaganda in Kazakhstan and Billings and Butte in Montana to illustrate how the grid evolved just as the territories were being swept into the larger industrial and agricultural economies of the two expanding states in eras of superlative industrial and bureaucratic expansion. During North America's second industrial revolution, which preceded World War I, the railroad, our first national bureaucracy, put Billings, Butte, and all cities of Montana on the map. The Communist Party and specifically the NKVD charted out Karaganda and many cities of northern Kazakhstan during the industrialization drive of the 1930s, which foreshadowed World War II at a time when the Soviet state first became an industrialized and bureaucratized power. In both places, I will argue, political powers produced gridded space, often violently, to serve economic and political goals.

But that is getting ahead of the story. To start from the beginning—there were no cities in northern Kazakhstan or the Great Plains before the steam engine and railroad. Pre-industrial cities in Central Asia and the American plains contained populations that were largely supported by surrounding agricultural communities, and grew only so large as the limits of the land, the reach of the walled fortifications, the scarcities of food, water, and cultivable soil allowed them. Without technology, the short grasslands of the steppe and range, the dry, continental climates, could not support more than small communities of sedentary peoples tilling the soil and were best suited for nomads living off the migratory grazing of range animals adapted to the extreme cold, heat, and aridity of the climate.

Innovations of the industrial age, however, greatly altered the landscape and economies of the Great Plains and Central Asia. Cities in the industrial age did not need to follow the lay of the land or feed populations with foodstuffs produced locally. Montana and Kazakhstan could support urban populations by means of technologies such as railroad networks to move people and goods, steam-powered engines, irrigation systems, the telegraph, and telephone, all of which required a concentration of capital investment so large that in both regions it fell to a small group of managers to try to direct from afar the means of production and labor that kept everything going. The managers in both places oversaw these vast networks with the help of time schedules, statistics, and production plans, and with the regimentation and subjection of labor.[13] In both Montana and Karaganda, the rush for land, water, minerals, and cash crops displaced the indigenous peoples who had

---

[12] Lefebvre (1994) points out how the Spanish-American town was laid down on the basis of the grid, which reflected the political and administrative authority of the new urban power. The grid enabled the Spanish colonizers to arrange space in terms of a hierarchy and segregate space into discrete units designated for different functions.

[13] For a study of how territory west of Chicago was charted and commodified in this way, see Cronon (1991).

formerly inhabited the territories, while the European populations who replaced them were sorted according to contrived understandings of race, class, and loyalty.

These patterns of production created corresponding patterns of subjection, which determined that people settled the American high plains and Central Asian steppe in similar ways by carving land into economic units for efficient exploitation. New towns were located for commerce and the quick extraction of resources at railheads and responded not to ecological limits but to the surveyor's rational grid (van der Ryn and Calthorpe 1986).[14] The grid made space modular and repetitious. The urban grid was a concentration of the expanding rural grid, which linked the hinterland economically and spatially with cities. As a consequence, there were no topographical limits to urban space, and the cities grew and multiplied, supplanting the nomadic cultures that came before. In fact, the cities born during this century gave new meaning to nomadism by ambling across the flat plains wherever transportation routes wandered, with nothing to stop them but sheer loneliness.

In both countries, as a result, conquest meant consumption; the newcomers ate—in coal, copper, wheat, sugar beets, ore—the territories they desired. In short, the histories of cities in Montana and Kazakhstan complement one another; taken in tandem, they tell not two stories but one—the history of gridded space.

***

The sun reaches low for the horizon, the exhaust rises up from the valley, and gazing down on Billings the mind wanders to those childhood stories about the frontier—about "hardy pioneers," "bringing civilization," "displacing savagery." These brave and arrogant aphorisms lay on the hardened sand like the rusted carcasses of the tin cans that followed European settlers wherever they went. American historians have discarded most of the myths of winning the West, and indeed it is hard to see that legend in the small corporate city of Billings.[15] In fact, Billings seems to have no history at all written into its carefully measured right angles. Or, rather, its history might be sought in the wake of the bulldozer and the moving van—in the vacated lots and disowned possessions of the long row of thrift stores—which makes sense, because Billings was not founded on precedent or history. Its story, instead, like that of many western cities, is located in a vaporously elusive understanding of the future. An early settler of Kansas instructed his readers: "The American of today must find his enjoyment in anticipating the future. He must look beyond the unsightly beginnings of civilization and prefigure the state of things a century hence" (quoted in Reps 1981, 454). The trick in the Great Plains involved overlooking the present to gaze at the future, but a future that never arrived, whether it be steers, coal, or grain.

Yet this myopia for the present tense helped to give Billings its start. In 1881, the land on which Billings stands today was considered worthless. It was a barren,

---

[14] Scott contrasts gridded industrial cities with the *medina* of an old Middle Eastern city, where each neighborhood and quarter are unique, "the sum of millions of designs and activities," without an overall plan or map (1998, 184).

[15] For a discussion of the changing stories about the American West, see Cronon (1992).

waterless alkali flat with only an oasis here and there of sage brush. The settlers and traders who first came to the region settled upstream at Clark's Fork Bottom, where the confluence of two rivers made a good trading post and where the land was fertile and the water supply more plentiful. The residents of Clark's Fork assumed that, when the railroad came through, it would logically create a terminal in their little settlement, as there were a few traders and farmers already waiting for trains to bring in goods and ship their produce off to market. But the railroad executives in St. Paul and New York had a different set of priorities for locating the new town. The federal government had deeded the Northern Pacific line alternating townships of 40 miles on either side of the tracks to help offset the cost of building a transcontinental railroad. Frederick Billings, the president of the Northern Pacific, and his engineers studied the U.S. surveyor-general maps and determined that, at a certain point on the map, the odd-numbered townships lay next to each other across the line of the railroad, instead of connecting at the corners as they did elsewhere (West 1993, 120). Sensibly, Mr. Billings decided to locate the new city at that point where the railroad owned twice as much land as usual.

Then Frederick Billings did something even more sensible. He and a few associates formed a real estate development company and bought from the railroad 29,394 acres in the newly proposed township for less than $4 an acre. It made no difference to Mr. Billings that the site for the new city planned for 20,000 residents would be established on barren flats, somewhat removed from the swampy edges of river, without drinking water, 2 miles north of the closest human habitation. Within the four walls of real estate speculation, the siting of Billings made sense; the fact that the site was barely habitable mattered little to Mr. Billings. After all, Frederick Billings never dreamed of living in Billings.

After the Minnesota and Montana Land and Improvement Company chose the site for Billings, the company designed the city plan, allocated building lots, and proposed future industrial development before any actual building took place, before the "city" was anything but a thicket of squatters' tents (West 1993). Nonetheless, the founding of the new city was trumpeted for hundreds of miles, and the profits to be made were fabulous. Once it was announced that Billings was going to be the next "Magic City," Frederick Billings's land development company was selling off the alkali flats at $250 for a quarter-acre lot. Whole blocks were sold in New York and Chicago, and a few months later the prices had risen to $1200 (Kliewer 1938). By the summer of 1882, most of the city property was purchased, yet two-thirds of the owners were absentee; people who bought lots never planned to live in the hot, dry, treeless flats but to sell them later at a profit (West 1993).

The cosmology that ordained the grid in Billings pivoted around economics and administration. Billings's real estate company subdivided land into parcels, uniform, and, from the perspective of a map, interchangeable because it made for efficient marketing and sales, especially from remote offices in St. Paul and Chicago. In this way, towns identical to Billings were established throughout the West— Laramie, Reno, Bismarck, Cheyenne. Engineers, land agents, and railroad executives established, planned, and promoted these cities following a uniform gridiron that placed the railroad in the center of the burgeoning city. The pioneering homesteader, the cowboy, and lonesome miner are essential parts of American mythology and self-identity, but historians of the American West have argued that the vanguard of settlement in the West were these corporate-owned towns, run by businessmen who operated on the profits of real estate speculation fueled by federal land grants and the promise of future growth and industrial development (Reps 1981; Cronon 1991; White 1995).

Karaganda, like Billings, was an unmarked void on the map before its founding as a city in 1930. It consisted of a ramble of shacks, a few abandoned buildings from a czarist-era coal mine, and a small and occasional market where Kazakhs would come to trade in sheep pelts and mutton steaks for salt, flour, and other necessities. In the late 1920s, Soviet geologists rediscovered the Karaganda coal basin, after which the Moscow-based Department of Mines set up the Karaganda Coal Trust and determined that the site would be home to a major new industrial city. Without visiting the region, architects in Moscow drew up plans for a city of 40,000 workers who would dig out a projected twelve new mines. Within the year, several thousand miners, most of them Kazakhs, began working underground in Karaganda. But the Coal Trust found that it could not keep its stores stocked with enough food to feed the miners, and despite the city plan calling for seven square meters of sanitary housing per person, housing conditions stumbled into proletarian disgrace, with most of the miners living in yurts or tents scattered near the mine shafts. In search of food, the Kazakh miners drifted to and from their native *auls* (villages), which made for a sporadic and ill-disciplined labor force, and coal production sagged below pre-revolutionary figures.[16]

In February 1931, however, the railroad arrived in Karaganda and with it a whole new form of discipline. The railroad brought supplies, geologists, and experienced miners from the Donbass in Ukraine, and it also brought NKVD officers who quickly realized the limitless possibilities of establishing a labor camp next to the Karaganda mines. Sounding as optimistic as a Billings railroad associate, an NKVD officer wrote that the combination of virgin land, mineral resources, and a rail connection meant that "Kazakhstan offers remarkable potential for the creation of a powerful agricultural base. Only a labor reserve is needed due to the sparsely populated territory."[17] A labor camp, NKVD officials proposed, would funnel a plentiful supply of workers to Karaganda to till the virgin soil and produce food for the miners. In 1931, the Gulag division of the NKVD set up KarLag on 281,000 acres of land around the growing settlement of Karaganda and began to import labor.[18]

---

[16] In 1930, the Karaganda mines produced all of 3000 tons of coal, a drop from the 1913 pre-revolutionary figure of 7200 tons (see Malybaev 1961).

[17] "Politburo resolutions," Secret Sector of the All-Union Resettlement Committee of the SNK SSSR, Rossiiskii Gosudarstvennyi Arkhiv Ekonomiki [Russian State Economics Archive] (hereafter, RGAE), 1/5675/48a.

[18] The administrative center of KarLag formed its own town, located outside the city of Karaganda. KarLag had divisions that stretched throughout Karaganda Province. By the beginning of 1936, there were 37,958 prisoners and 806 staff persons in KarLag (Dil'manov and Kuznetsova 1997).

The labor camp KarLag helped solve Karaganda's problem of workers and food. City leaders made use of prison labor to grow crops on the outskirts of the city and to work on construction sites in the city to build housing for the miners. To supervise the prisoner-laborers, NKVD guards walled districts into "zones" separated with barbed wire, each about the size of a city block. The guards required avenues straight and broad enough to march prisoners in columns to work sites and needed enough visibility to shoot in case anyone made a run for it. Although it is tempting to postulate that Karaganda's grid grew out of the demands of prison architecture, most modern Soviet cities are platted out in a grid—cities never intended for prisoners. In fact, Soviet planners designed and created many new industrial cities in the 1930s that are nearly interchangeable with Karaganda.[19] In the early 1930s, Soviet planners dreamed of building an entirely new kind of "socialist city," which would express the principles of socialism in every line of every building. A socialist city, they postulated, would be founded on the antithesis of the confusion and grime of a capitalist city. Soviet architects dreamed of "modernization without urbanism" and preferred to build cities on virgin soil from the ground up. They sought to design urban landscapes rationally where people would live safely, equitably, with plenty of light, space, and visibility. Architects submitted plans from as far away as Germany with blueprints for cities that did not look like cities at all but more like parks, spaceships, or modern art. But the strange thing is, once built, the new socialist cities looked alike, heedless of climate and topography; they were all plotted symmetrically along a grid, Lenin Prospect running east-west. What motivated the grid in the Soviet context?

Although private property was outlawed in Soviet socialism, the concepts of ownership and management determined the shape of Karaganda, much as it did Billings. Individuals in the Soviet Union could not own land, but after the Soviet government nationalized all property, it allocated land in vast proportions to state enterprises. The NKVD became a major recipient of huge tracts of land in northern Kazakhstan and one of the major exploiters of natural resources. By 1936, the NKVD controlled 795,600 acres of land appropriated from Kazakh pastureland. By 1941, the NKVD was responsible for 12 percent of all Soviet lumber, 54 percent of all nickel, 75 percent of all molybdenum, and 37 percent of all tungsten production. The total value of all gulag industrial production between 1941 and 1944 reached 3.6 billion rubles. Land that to Kazakh nomads had been a flowing body of winter and summer pastures marked with ancestral burial grounds became to the Europeans who conquered it a series of parcels, surveyed and assigned value in square meters and millions of rubles.

***

In order to make the transformation from ancestral land to commodified space, European settlers first envisioned indigenous land as empty space, waiting to be

---

[19] Gridded cities built during the industrial drive include Magnitogorsk, Nizhnii Tagil, Orsk, Novokuznetsk, Makeevka, Komsomol'sk, Bratsk, Magadan, and Noril'sk. For a discussion of Soviet urban planning and the creation of Magnitogorsk *ex nihilo*, see Kotkin (1995).

populated. Billings and Karaganda were conceived in the minds of people who first saw the territories for the proposed cities as representations on a map. The land for both cities was granted by federal governments to growing bureaucracies charged with settling the territories for the production of raw materials. In both cases, the cities were platted into being by planners from remote locations who drew a series of lines on paper and finalized century-long processes of transferring territory from indigenous to European hands. The first blueprints drafted Billings into a city for 20,000 residents; Karaganda fifty years later was to have 40,000. Once the transactions were complete, the cities came into being, contemporaries in Billings noted, like "magic": "the thoroughfares of Billings present a scene of business activity such as is not witnessed in any other town of Montana. The change seems almost as wonderful as some of those related in the old time tales of Eastern magic" (*The Billings Herald*, June 1, 1882, as quoted in West 1993, 133). In Karaganda, historians also marveled at how the city sprang into being. "Great changes have taken place under Soviet rule on the Kazakh steppe. Where there used to be a few felt yurts and adobe huts, now a beautiful city has arisen ... We see wide, tree-lined streets, avenues, parks and squares" (Mukhanov 1954).

One can read into this narrative on progress the classic subtext of the Soviet command economy at work: the city, planned from afar—but far from planned in actuality, significantly funded by the central coffers of the ominously expanding Soviet bureaucracy whose task it was to Industrialize-At-All-Cost—but primarily built by cheap or unpaid manual labor. The years of hard work and spent lives that went into making Karaganda are summed up in a brief origination thesis describing one seemingly effortless leap from empty steppe to modern city.

Both Soviet and American proselytizers emphasize origins. What was empty had been filled in, what was barren was made green, the primitive had found sophistication. Europeans arrived, found places empty of history, and gave them a beginning and thus meaning. And they did it, the writers stress, quickly. In these new places, in the dawning age of fossil-fuel technology, civilization did not need centuries to ripen, as it had in Europe. There was no time for that. The promoters of Soviet and American insta-cities were drunk on speed, efficiency, the "magic" of machines. They threw up hospitals, schools, courthouses, and libraries so the new cities would look like "a city," built not in decades, years, or even months, but weeks. Labor crews in Karaganda competed with builders in Leningrad in a construction race and won. In the American West, the English scholar James Bryce wrote critically of the pace at which it expanded: "Why sacrifice the present to the future? ... Why seek to complete in a few decades what the other nations of the world took thousands of years over in the older continents? Why do things rudely and ill which need to be done well, seeing that the welfare of your descendants may turn upon them? ... the unrestfulness, the passion for speculation, the feverish eagerness for quick and showy results, may so soak into the texture of the popular mind as to color it for centuries to come" (quoted in Reps 1981, 693).

Leaders in both countries set out to colonize vast new territories immediately, conquering by consuming land, crops, and minerals in assembly-line fashion. But the problem was that, although Soviet and American planners could imagine these insta-cities, they could not orchestrate their big designs with enough bricks, labor-ers, and lumber to build them. In this sense, the American booster press and Soviet propaganda read like science fiction. The words described a possible, even plausi-ble, future but one that did not yet exist.

T. C. Armitage discovered this fictional quality of the new urban spaces the hard way. He was an insurance man who worked in the Northern Pacific engineering office in St. Paul. He worked for the railroad and should have known better than to believe the booster press campaigns coming from Billings. Armitage put cash down on a few lots, sight-unseen, choosing a prime location by the Yellowstone River. Soon after, Armitage boarded the Northern Pacific to Billings. When he arrived, he was dismayed to find no depot, no real city, no town, not even an outpost, just a "dreary expanse, white with alkali flats." When Armitage inspected his lots, he found a good deal of his real estate was flooded, and he needed a boat to locate the corners of his property (Kliewer 1938, 22).

Fifty years later, a Soviet journalist, Semyon Nariniani, had a similar experience. He was sent on assignment to central Siberia, a few hundred miles north of Karaganda, to report on the newly built industrial city, the world-famous steel town of Magnitogorsk. As historian Stephen Kotkin tells the story, Nariniani rode the train for eight days, making five changes and waiting through many delays. One day, the train slowed in the midst of the empty steppe. Nariniani thought it was another breakdown, but the conductor called out, "Magnitogorsk!" Nariniani dis-embarked, looked around at the empty landscape, turned to the stationmaster and asked, "Is it far to the city?" "Two years," the man answered (Kotkin 1995, 106).

In memoir after memoir, what seemed to bother European settlers of the plains and steppe the most was the emptiness: "the stillness with nothing behind it" (White 1991, 216). Soviet deportees refer automatically to the land they first encountered as "the naked steppe"; they found it stripped of all things: water, trees, streams, houses, people—geography itself—empty of everything but space (Sierociuk 1994; Samborski 1995; Ciesielski and Kuczynski 1996; Skultans 1998). But what most people failed to mention was that the land was not empty but *emptied*. They came to territory that had recently been cleared of the nomadic pastoralists and hunters who once populated it, people who lived off the arid grasslands by moving through them, following herds that grazed on a carpet of grasses and plants. Since humans cannot digest grass, exploiting animals that do is a rational way to use the dry range and steppe not suited for agriculture or intensive husbandry. As the first settlers appeared in Kazakhstan and Montana and took up homesteads in fertile land along rivers, Kazakhs and Indians adjusted their economies accordingly, trading fur and meat with the newcomers for tools and commodities. It wasn't harmony and it wasn't an idyll of pastoral unity with nature, but it was life—a social system and economy that adapted adequately to the conditions of the plains and steppe.

But that is not the way Kazakhs and Indians were seen by the Europeans who came to colonize them. Nomadic pastoralists were understood as part of the land-scape. They came to symbolize the savage and precarious past, which still loomed over the present on the frontier with terrifying force. For instance, when high winds blew and unsettled the tent cities of Billings or Karaganda or when winter blizzards stranded people and livestock in blinding white confusion, it became clear how flimsy was the edifice white settlers occupied, an edifice linked only by a thin lifeline of steel rails to the distant sources of food and energy that kept their economies going. To Europeans, the unsettled nomad came to embody this cruel and undiscriminating nature. And so European colonizers constructed an ideological and principled crusade, casting themselves in the role of civilized man against primitive nature.

***

Now, tourists speeding along Interstate 90 in Montana can stop in Butte for a few minutes and stroll out to the platform extending over the Berkeley Pit, the cavity that was once the "richest hill on Earth," now a mile wide and mile deep, filled with flooded toxins left over from a century of mining. On the platform, it doesn't take long to hear the recorded message that describes the history of the pit and the wealth that was dug from the skin-colored cliffs, and when the message dies out, tourists can hear the eerie whizzing signals that warn off birds from landing in the pit, which is acidic enough to liquify steel. While tourists stare into the country's largest Superfund clean-up site, what they can no longer see are the neighborhoods that used to ramble over the hill that is now negative space.

Although nearly half the city has been voided, residents of Butte still chart the town by a mental geography established during the mining days. On the east side, they say, the Irish lived up the hill in Dublin Gulch, above the Finns in Finntown, which gave the Irish gangs the advantage bombarding the Finnish gangs in their regular brawls. Italians and Slavs lived in Meaderville, now an imaginary space over the pit, and on the precipice of the pit in the Cabbage Patch lived Mexicans, Indians, and African Americans, who had houses so transitory that today only empty gridded lots have endured. On the west side of town stand the Victorian mansions of the Copper Kings. The mansions have castle-like turrets from which one can survey the miners' homes huddled next to the mines' black headframes. As in Karaganda, Butte had the zone system, too, charting the population into distinctly divided sectors.

In Karaganda, as in Butte, residents were sorted by class, ethnicity, and race. By 1941, 41,000 prisoners worked in KarLag, and thousands of deportees arrived every month, swelling the city's population. Soldiers patrolled the streets, while prisoners marched from walled barrack zones to fenced-off labor sites. The fenced zones were important because the NKVD needed to segregate a complex hierarchy of prisoners incarcerated along a sliding scale of unfreedom—political prisoners, German POWs, Soviet citizens of German and Polish descent interned for the war, and regular prisoners convicted for criminal charges. Soviet-German Labor Army conscripts lived in one zone. German POWs lived in another, next to but separate from Japanese POWs. As the war continued, more and more suspect ethnic groups streamed into the region under guard: Ukrainians, Poles, Kalmyks, Bashkirs, Chechens. Each group was assigned a village or zone and told they could not venture from their homes. The zone system meant that most people generally remained where they were deposited, which strengthened ethnic ties and minority allegiances, ironically, the very traits for which these people were deported. But even when given a choice, the free populations of Russians and Kazakhs sought to live segregated from each other. At most factories, Russians and Kazakhs lived in separate dorms, but in one factory, Russian and Kazakh workers had to share a bunkhouse, and so the workers constructed a wall down the middle to divide the space (Martin 1996).

What, however, does the NKVD's enforced, zoned, and policed segregation of prisoners and exiles have to do with immigrant ethnic groups in Butte who chose to live together in their own neighborhoods? After all, it makes sense that immigrants would seek to live in a cushion of language and culture to help soften the blow of migration and assimilation. What is strange, however, is that in 1905 a Pole from Silesia, which was located in the south in the Habsburg Empire, had little in common with a Pole from Mazuria, who was a citizen of czarist Russia. These two Poles arrived from different political states; they practiced different customs and spoke different dialects of Polish, if not mutually incomprehensible languages. What compelled Mazurians and Silesians, who would have little in common in the old world, to join into one Polish community in the new world?

The forces that hammered Poles and other immigrant groups into discrete ethnic enclaves belonged to the industrial age. Between 1880 and 1920 in the United States, the way people worked and produced goods altered significantly, which in turn influenced how people lived and where. Corporate bureaucracies organized production from the top down. As production decisions moved up a lengthening hierarchy, skilled laborers were replaced by foremen supervising unskilled workers. Relations between foremen and workers slid into mutual aggression as the foremen were pressed to continually increase production, and in so doing threatened workers with dismissal and pay cuts (Schreuder 1989). Workers responded by organizing in unions. In order to fight the unions, firms altered their hiring practices, tending to employ immigrant laborers, who, because of their primitive knowledge of English, were less likely to unionize. On the shop floor, immigrant workers were grouped together because of language to allow work to progress more smoothly, and gradually the workplace became segregated. In turn, native-born workers began to resent the strike-breaking, wage-lowering immigrants and excluded them from their social and residential circles outside the workplace. Immigrants were relegated to the lowest-tiered labor and were promoted far more slowly than native-born workers. This and the experience of being labeled "foreign," "alien," and "inferior" brought members of ethnic groups together in a defensive posture. And so, immigrant neighborhoods, ethnic church, school, and fraternal orders formed around a circle-the-wagon-mentality. Each group tried to carve out its own space along hazy and porous borders defined as "nationality," which gangs of young men patrolled to inhibit others from crossing the invisible lines of race and class.

In other words, the ethnic segmentation of Butte and Karaganda had less to do with race than with discipline. As hierarchies and values were used to segregate and standardize stages of production along an assembly line, they also worked to both normalize and segregate workers inside and outside the factory. The gridded spaces that first organized on a huge scale the settling of Central Asia and the Great Plains made a lasting stamp on the nature of the lives that took up residence on the plains and steppe, because at some point the abstract survey lines turned into boundaries.

Boundaries fix labels in space, defining who is inside and who is outside. But boundaries can be porous, and so gradually boundary lines in Montana and Kazakhstan transformed into walls, laws, and social custom, which worked to define who was alien and who was native, who was a prisoner and who a guard, who lived in the migrant camp and who on the affluent east side. Perhaps for this reason, the same grid stretches across the American West and Soviet Central Asia—not only because of topography and efficiency but because the edifice of modernist dichotomies constructed urban spaces that employed the grid as the most effective means to control space by blocking it off into discrete and ever-divisible units. Each unit could be marked for exclusion or reward; each could be arranged in a hierarchy, supervised and observed in a constant division between the normal and the abnormal.

The grid worked to segregate lives and social relations, so that while new cities continually moved across the landscape multiplying and growing, the gridded nature of the cities eventually helped to fix social relations in place. Thus, despite the fact that both the United States and Soviet Union were founded on revolution and grew through rapid urbanization, leaders in both countries distrusted the revolutionary and spontaneous quality of urban space and worked to destroy it. With straight lines and the force of the grid, Soviet and American leaders planned new "garden cities" cut through with wide, rebellion-proof avenues, which negated the unpredictability and anarchy of nineteenth-century cities. As a result, both expanding American corporate power and expanding Soviet party-state power etched an anti-revolutionary conservatism onto twentieth-century urban scapes. Perhaps for this reason, Karaganda and Billings do not radiate the energy of New York or Moscow but instead emanate a feeling of listless suspension, of containers waiting to be filled, of the utopia of what Foucault calls the "perfectly-governed city." It is this utopian wish for gridded order and discipline that links the railroad city of Billings with the prison city of Karaganda.

References

Bacon, E. (1994). *The gulag at war: Stalin's forced labour system in the light of the archives.* New York: New York University Press.

Ball, A. (1987). *Russia's last capitalists: The Nepmen, 1921–1929.* Berkeley: University of California Press.

Becker, J. (1999). *Soviet and Russian press coverage of the United States: Press, politics, and identity in transition.* New York: Palgrave Macmillan.

Berman, M. (1988 [1982]). *All that is solid melts into air: The experience of modernity.* New York, Penguin Books; New York: Simon and Schuster.

Calvino, I. (1974). *Invisible cities* (trans: W. Weaver). San Diego: Harcourt Brace.

Chambers, I. (1994). *Migrancy, culture, identity.* London: Routledge.

Ciesielski, S., & Kuczynski, A. (Eds.). (1996). *Polacy w Kazachstanie: Historia i Wspolczesnosc.* Wroclaw: Wydawnistwo uniwersytetu Wroclawskiego.

Cronon, W. (1991). *Nature's metropolis: Chicago and the great west.* New York: Norton and Co..

Cronon, W. (1992). A place for stories: Nature, history and narrative. *Journal of American History, 78,* 1347–1376.

Danilov, V., & Krusil'nikov, S. (Eds.). (1994). *Spetspereselentsy v Zapadnoi Sibiri, 1933–1938*. Novosibirsk: Ekor.

Dil'manov, S., & Kuznetsova, E. (1997). *Karlag*. Alma-Aty: Vek.

Ficken, R. (1995). *Rufus woods, the Columbia river and the building of modern Washington*. Pullman: Washington State University Press.

Foucault, M. (1995 [1977]). *Discipline and punish: The birth of the prison* (trans: A. Sheridan). New York: Vintage Books.

Fox, W. (1944). *The super-powers: The United States, Britain, and the Soviet Union: Their responsibility for peace*. New York: Harcourt, Brace and Co.

Gleason, A. (1995). *Totalitarianism: The inner history of the cold war*. New York: Abbott.

Ivanova, G. (1997). *Gulag v sisteme totalitamnogo gosudarstva*. Moscow: Moskovskii obshchestvennyi nauchnyi fond.

Jakobson, M. (1993). *The origins of the GULAG: The Soviet prison-camp system, 1917–1934*. Lexington, KY: Kentucky University Press.

Kershaw, I., & Lewin, M. (1997). *Stalinism and Nazism: Dictatorships in comparison*. Cambridge: Cambridge University Press.

Kliewer, W. (1938). *The foundations of billings*. Montana. MA thesis, University of Washington.

Kolchin, P. (1987). *Unfree labor: American slavery and Russian serfdom*. Cambridge, MA: Belknap Press of Harvard University Press.

Kotkin, S. (1995). *Magnetic mountain: Stalinism as a civilization*. Berkeley: University of California Press.

Lefebvre, H. (1994). *The production of space* (trans: D. Nicholson-Smith). Oxford: Blackwell.

Malybaev, O. (1961). *Bor'ba KPSS za sozdanie i razvitie tret'ei ugol'noi bazy SSSR*. Alma-Ata: Kazakhskoe gosudarstvennoe izdatel'stvo.

Martin, T. (1996). *An affirmative action empire*. Ph.D. diss., University of Chicago.

Mukanov, S. (1954). *Karaganda*. Moscow: Foreign Languages Publishing House.

Navasky, V. (1980). *Naming names*. New York: Viking Press.

Pohl, O. (1997). *The Stalinist penal system: A statistical history of Soviet repression and terror, 1930–1953*. Jefferson: McFarland.

Poliakov, A. (Ed.). (1991). *Vsesoiuznaia perepis' naseleniia 1937 g*. Moscow: Kratkie itogi.

Reps, J. (1981). *The forgotten frontier: Urban planning in the American west before 1890*. Columbia: University of Missouri Press.

Rollison, D. (1999). Exploding England: The dialectics of mobility and settlement in early modern England. *Social History, 24*, 1–16.

Samborski, K. (1995). Zyczliwosci zadnoi. *Dziennik Polski*, July 6.

Schreuder, Y. (1989). Labor segmentation, ethnic division of labor, and residential segregation in American cities in the early twentieth century. *Professional Geographer, 41*, 131–143.

Scott, J. (1998). *Seeing like a state: How certain schemes to improve the human condition have failed*. New Haven: Yale University Press.

Sierociuk, J. (1994). Archipelag Kokczetaw. *Przeglad Akademnicki*, 13–14: n.p.

Skultans, V. (1998). *The testimony of lives: Narrative and memory in post-Soviet Latvia*. London: Routledge.

Startsev, I. (1942). *Amerika i rutsskoe obshchestvo*. Moscow: Izdatel'stvo Akademii nauk SSSR.

Tracy, M. E. (1938). *Our country, our people, and theirs*. New York: Macmillan.

Van der Ryn, S., & Calthorpe, P. (1986). *Sustainable communities: A new design synthesis for cities, suburbs, and towns*. San Francisco: Sierra Club Books.

West, C. (1993). *Capitalism on the frontier: Billings and the Yellowstone Valley in the nineteenth century*. Lincoln: University of Nebraska Press.

White, R. (1991). *It's your misfortune and none of my own: A history of the American west*. Norman: University of Oklahoma Press.

White, R. (1995). *The organic machine: The remaking of the Columbia River*. New York: Hill and Wang.

Wilson, E. (1936). *Travels in two democracies*. New York: Harcourt, Brace and Co.

Zemskov, V. (1990). Spetsposelentsi. *Sotsiologicheskie issledovaniia, 11*, 3–17.

Chapter 14
Urban Grids and Urban Imaginary: City to Cyberspace, Cyberspace to City

Paula Geyh

Abstract The question that stands at the heart of this chapter is how the postmodern city is changing under the impact of globalization and new information and communication technologies. More specifically, the author asks how the postmodern city changes our ways of knowing and experiencing the world and ourselves as postmodern urban subjects and citizens of postmodernity. The chapter provides a discussion of the grid as both a central aspect of modern urban imaginaries and material urban spaces as well as considers the role of the grid at the interface between the city and cyberspace. In doing so, the author explores the grid as part of twentieth-century literary and artistic modernism and its replacement by the postmodern imaginary, with a particular focus on the relation between cityscapes and cyberspace.

Keywords Grid · Postmodern city · Urban imaginaries · Information technology · Cyberspace · Virtual reality

Coordinations, Modern and Postmodern

With the rise of modernity, grids and their transpositions from one domain to another—for example, from mathematics to city planning—became a common logic and technology of culture. The beginnings of this process can be traced to Descartes, the thinker whose thought philosophically inaugurated modernity, and his most famous invention, the coordinate "grid," known as the Cartesian coordinate system ever since. Although part of human civilization throughout its history, the

This chapter is an abridged version of Geyh, P. (2009). "Urban Grids and Urban Imaginary: City to Cyberspace, Cyberspace to City." In P. Geyh, *Cities, Citizens, and Technologies: Urban Life and Postmodernity* (pp. 63–91). New York: Routledge. Copyright © 2009 by Taylor & Francis. Reproduced with permission of Taylor & Francis.

P. Geyh (✉)
Yeshiva University, New York, NY, USA
e-mail: geyh@yu.edu

grid in this deeper and broader conceptual and, ultimately, ideological sense of coordination of spaces, events, configurations, and so forth is one of the hallmarks of modernity. The logic and technology of the grid in this broader sense were especially crucial to the mechanisms of social discipline of the eighteenth and nineteenth centuries, powerfully examined by Foucault, in his late works in terms of "technologies of power." Many of these mechanisms continue into the present, in part producing the complexity of the relationships—the continuities and discontinuities—between modernity and postmodernity. The continuities are defined by the persisting role of these mechanisms, and the discontinuities by the transformations of these mechanisms and the rise of new ones, in particular those that, according to Deleuze, lead to a gradual shift from the "disciplinary societies" (and their institutions) to the "societies of control." This shift, Deleuze (1997) argues, is in part brought about and enforced through the digitalization of our information. This shift may thus be seen as part of a broader transformation, as defined by Lyotard (1984), from modernity, defined by the industrial revolution, to postmodernity, defined by the revolution in information technology. As Lyotard writes, "Along with the hegemony of computers comes a certain logic, and therefore a certain set of prescriptions determining which statements are accepted as 'knowledge' statements." Accordingly, "knowledge in the form of an information commodity indispensable to productive power is already, and will continue to be, a major—perhaps the major—stake in the worldwide competition for power" (1984, 4–5).

The conjunctions and interactions of the material and cyber spaces in which mechanisms of power are embedded and through which they operate are, I argue, among the significant forces of this cognitive and cultural transformation. As the transformation of urban spaces, this transformation is thus also a shift from modern to postmodern city grids or, in the postmodern city, sometimes the near dissolution of these grids, yielding to what Deleuze and Guattari (1983) call "smooth"—decoordinated and de-striated—spaces. This dissolution is never absolute, and it retains both some of the older (modern) grids and striations, and creates new (postmodern) ones, leading to a great complexity of the interactions between the smooth and the striated in postmodern urban spaces.

These spaces are, thus, comprised of multiple local spaces, smooth and striated, which may be related (via transitions between them, for example) but are in general heterogeneous, and thus resist and ultimately defeat any complete, global coordination of individual subjects, groups, or events in a particular postmodern landscape. Given, however, the role of striation in the local spaces involved, it is not surprising that, while now localized as well, the grid, as a common part of most actual striated spaces, retains its significance as one of the foundations of urban architecture, both material and conceptual. It is, inevitably, the character of urban architecture that enables the transfer or translation of the grid and particularly the urban grid into cyberspace, making it a cybercity. (The transfer is accomplished in part through the phenomenal and specifically visual imagery shaping urban architecture.) In general, this kind of transfer need not be that of the postmodern conceptual space defined by the multiple local interactions of the smooth and the striated, and thus by different local grids, and possible connections or disjunctures of local subspaces. The rise of cyberspace, however, coincides with the rise of postmodern urban spaces, conceptual and material. Hence the relationships between postmodern urban spaces and urban-like cyberspaces are equally defined by the postmodern spatiality of the smooth and the striated, as just explained. It is, moreover, not only a question of parallels or isomophisms between both types of spaces. In the postmodern city, both types of spaces, and thus the grids that support them and are supported by them, are interconnected and indeed are no longer always unequivocally dissociable in their form or functioning.

In order to understand these relationships and the forms of social discipline and control or freedom they entail, it may be helpful, first, to look more closely at how these forms of spatial organization relate to knowledge and, in particular, at the changes that computer technologies have led to in the forms and uses of information in the postmodern world. To do this requires a brief excursion into the practices of mapping (broadly understood as the technology that links space and knowledge) and, specifically, the coordinate grid, the conceptual structure that undergirds so many of our modern and postmodern cities, and our "real" and imaginary cyberspaces. As just explained, even though the postmodern city and cyberspace finally move beyond the grid towards smooth urban spaces, they do not and perhaps cannot leave the grid behind altogether, in either its negative or positive aspects. It is important that the grid can also play a positive, shaping role in the postmodern city, as shown by Lynch (1960) in his analysis of the grid's "legibility," to which I shall return in the next section.

Descartes's idea of the coordinate system extended the Euclidean vision of mathematics and the world, and gave this vision a more powerful encoding and mapping technology. This technology enabled the progress of multiple material technologies that were often based on mathematics, along with physics, which Descartes and, following him, Galileo and Newton also brought together, in part by using coordinate systems to map and analyze the physical world. Descartes's system allows one to locate particular events relative to the orthogonal (and hence easily measurable) lines of coordinates. It also, and conceptually more crucially, allows one to coordinate different events with one another within the same spatial and temporal frame of reference. In physics, this "coordinate dream" was fully realized, or was believed to have been fully realized, in Newton's mechanics, grounded in Newton's vision of absolute space and absolute time, which coupled this coordination of physical events to a strict causality. It may be noted that, as was quickly realized by mathematicians, a coordinate system can be curvilinear, as is the one we use on the surface of the globe in geography. This fact eventually helped in the discovery of non-Euclidean geometry. This discovery was one of the key steps in the process that eventually (it took a while) brought about the end of Newton's dream of classical physics and of the universe governed by its laws or, as William Blake would have it, "Newton's sleep."[1] The coordinate dream, sometimes becoming the coordinate nightmare, has persisted for much longer, in mathematics and science or, in its

---

[1] The phrase "Newton's sleep" occurs in Blake's "Letter to Thomas Butts, 22 November 1802" (1982, 693).

broader form, elsewhere in our culture. In philosophy, Descartes's and Newton's dreams were questioned from the outset, specifically by Leibniz, who astutely understood the philosophical problems involved in Newton's vision of space (as absolute space). Leibniz did not believe that it is possible to rigorously define the concept of absolute space or, to begin with, empty space, coordinated or not, which would then serve as an ambient space for material bodies. According to Leibniz, space and whatever coordinate systems could be introduced there could only be defined by a given configuration of material bodies. This view, as Einstein was to eventually discover through his relativity, ultimately implies the impossibility of, correlatively, both Newton's absolute space and a unique coordination of all physical events.

Such philosophical problems notwithstanding, the role and impact of Cartesian coordination was momentous and extended far beyond mathematics and physics, or geography (where the idea was of course especially helpful) and other scientific and technological applications, to the modern understanding of human thought and culture, and to modernity's self-understanding and even self-definition. Inevitably, in this broader domain the concept also took on more complex, including metaphorical, dimensions, and was coupled to a series of broader philosophical conceptualities, beginning with that of Descartes himself, now as a philosopher (especially a philosopher of conscious thinking, the cogito), and his contemporaries, such as John Locke. Extending to the key figures of the Enlightenment, such as Jean-Jacques Rousseau, Kant, Hegel, and beyond, this philosophical grounding of Cartesianism gave it a greater conceptual power and amplified its impact. With the help of philosophical thinking, the concept of the coordinate system led to both actual models of organization, such as that of particular cities built or rebuilt according to a coordinated and often rectangular grid, and a general model of defining human subjects and their behavior, and hence society, in relation to a proper system of coordinates. The coordinates could be economic, cultural, political, religious, or other, and they could be variously adjusted or subdivided within each of these categories. New coordinates could be and have been continually added as well, and different coordinate systems and transitions between them could be possible, just as they were in Newtonian physics. What was crucial, however, was that, as in Newtonian physics, everything would be seen, at least in principle and (hopefully) potentially in practice, as subject to overall global coordination. These coordinate systems were connected to or built around actual grids, those of material structures, such as those in cities, or institutions such as churches, schools, prisons, hospitals, and clinics, which were located on the city grid and thus partly defined this grid itself, culturally or even physically. The grid was also reproduced within many of these institutions, including hospitals, prisons, schools, and offices, again, as analyzed by Foucault (1979, 1997). By the nineteenth century, the power and impact of this thinking permeated the fabric of modernity and provided some of its strongest and most pronounced threads. Then, and sometimes even now, it appeared unassailable, even though (as Foucault's analysis also demonstrates) it was only a dream or a "sleep," albeit one with powerful and sometimes devastating real effects.[2]

It is not surprising that, even while reconfigured and often redeployed differently in postmodern urban spaces, the coordinate grid persists in and is one of the primary modern conceptual structures found in the postmodern city. Euclidean geometry and Newtonian physics largely remain our conceptual and practical models for "human-scale" urban spaces or cyberspace, in part and perhaps primarily because our phenomenal spatiality appears to be Euclidean and Newtonian, and shapes our phenomenal image of the world and, as a result, our visualization of cyberspace accordingly. (The "spaces" of modern physics, especially those of quantum theory, are non-visualizable phenomenally, and ultimately even the very denomination of space may no longer apply to them.)

Besides, the ideology of and the desire (for example, Oedipal and/as capitalist desire) for global grids or striations continue to persist. As a result, powerful ideological apparatuses and desiring-machines that aim at such global grids and striations threaten our desire for and our attempts to create new spaces defined by the complex interplay of local smooth spaces and striations or grids. As indicated above, the idea of this type of space or of smooth space, to begin with, has been given a mathematical conception by Riemann and his followers, which provided a mathematical model for both Einstein's general relativity (his theory of gravitation) and for Deleuze and Guattari's (1983) philosophical vision. The idea of smooth space has also grounded Deleuze and Guattari's anti-Oedipal conception of desire and their critique of the complicity between Oedipal desire and capitalism in *Anti-Oedipus*. Whether in the field of desire or elsewhere in human practice, it does not appear to be possible, however, to ever fully realize a completely smooth space. Only mathematical spaces and certain mathematically idealized physical models can be seen as rigorously enacting smooth spaces; but for better or worse, we do not live in purely mathematical spaces. Our practices defined by the idea of the smooth-space movement of desire do make it possible for us, however, to create spatial architectures in which striations are always local and are subordinated to smooth spaces and smooth motions, to the degree, hopefully the maximal degree to which these smooth spaces and motions are realizable. Our postmodern conceptions and realities of the city and of cyberspace inevitably reflect these complexities of the relationships between the smooth and the striated, from the persistence of the desiring-machines pursuing global striation to the shifts between the smooth and the striated within the alternative machines of (smooth) desire. These complexities are amplified by the fact that our postmodern urban spaces and, I would argue, in subtler ways (for example, given the digital codes on which they depend), our cyberspaces emerge amidst modern or still earlier spaces, striations, grids, ideologies, and desiring-machines, and cannot avoid co-existing and interacting with them. Indeed, as a base for urban design, the grid is ancient, and some of the pre-modern

---

[2] It is not possible to trace here the rich and complex history of Cartesian thinking (in the broad sense it acquired as modernity developed), but the territory has already been well explored in the scholarly literature, including that on postmodernity and its history.

aspects of it still have their effects even in the postmodern city. To some degree, the "fortress" part of the postmodern control logic involves some of these effects, as the term "fortress" indicates. My main concern for the moment, however, is Cartesianism and its impact on modernity, and with modernity itself, on postmodernity and its urban spatialities, actual and phenomenal, or virtual, such as those of cyberspace.

In *The Radiant City: Elements of a Doctrine of Urbanism to Be Used as the Basis of Our Machine-Age Civilization* (1967 [1935]), the great modernist architect and urban planner Le Corbusier lays out his philosophy, principles, and plans for the city of the future, a "Cartesian city" of cruciform "Cartesian skyscrapers" arranged in ranks and files amid vast green lawns overlaid with a grid of elevated highways.[3] His treatise is a model of high-modernist architectural thought and design, conceptually and materially founded upon the concept of the Cartesian grid. In the midst of his chapter entitled "Is Descartes American?" (the answer to this would be no, since Le Corbusier repeatedly contrasts the Cartesian order of his Radiant City to the chaotic disorder of Lower Manhattan), he interrupts his discourse on the history of architecture with a meditation on mathematical calculation, measurement, and the formula, in order to ground his new vision. His meditation essentially reveals the Newtonian conception of the world considered above, arguably in its most triumphant form reached in the nineteenth century, perhaps especially in France. "A formula," he asserts, "can ... be used in place of a reality that is itself too cumbersome to deal with ... Such formulas ... contain the laws of the cosmos, and they will not finally solidify until the mixture reaches a perfect conformity with all the universal laws involved" (Le Corbusier 1967 [1935], 130–1). These formulas link "the mathematician, the inventor, and the artist (the true artist!). Everything comes to the same thing in their mediating hands: a reabsorbence of chaos into harmony ... This accomplished, man ... is a demiurge. He has the power of decision over future events. Once his calculations are finished he is in a position to say—and he does say: 'It shall be thus!'" (Le Corbusier 1967 [1935], 131).[4] In other words, as in Newtonian mechanics, the future is determined and is determined in the right way once one sets the initial conditions properly (in this case, doing so is the affair of humans, as against Newtonian physics, where these conditions are set by nature), has the right laws, and performs one's calculations correctly. It should be noted, however, that Le Corbusier is well aware of the fact that this seemingly divine power of calculation is "only the mirror of our *human* divinity" and should not be worshiped in a religious manner (1967 [1935], 131; emphasis added). It can, he believed, and should be deployed not only to understand the world but also to change it, as Marx would have it in famously juxtaposing philosophy and revolutionary practice in his final thesis on Feuerbach.[5]

---

[3] For more detailed studies of Le Corbusier, see Curtis (1986), Frampton (2002), Blake (1996), and Ward (2002).

[4] The authoritative and authoritarian tenor of Le Corbusier's rhetoric and thought are neither accidental nor incidental. At the top of the title page of *The Radiant City* (1967 [1935]), above both Le Corbusier's name and the book's title, is the inscription: "This work is dedicated to AUTHORITY."

[5] "The philosophers have only interpreted the world, in various ways; the point is to change it" (Marx 1986, 23).

For Le Corbusier, as for the urban planners who preceded and followed him, the grid constitutes a Cartesian "rationalization" of the space of the city, the creation or, in cases of an already-existing urban fabric, imposition of order. The grid carries with it, above all, the advantages and disadvantages of particular forms and functions of *visibility* or *legibility*. Both simple and replicable to any scale, the grid facilitates the imaging, mapping (both literal and conceptual), and navigation of the city; the commodification of urban space by dividing land into abstract units that can be easily bought and sold; and certain municipal operations, including governance by precinct or borough, zoning, taxation, and security. Thus, the grid simultaneously serves the interests of individuals (sometimes), capital, and the state.

For individual inhabitants of the city, one of the primary advantages of the grid is its navigability. "Way-finding," Lynch writes in *The Image of the City*, "is the original function of the environmental image" (1960, 125), and the "legibility" of the cityscape can be measured by "the ease with which its parts can be recognized and can be organized into a coherent pattern" (1960, 2–3). The image of the city, however, "is valuable not only in this immediate sense in which it acts as a map for the direction of movement; in a broader sense it can serve as a general frame of reference within which the individual can act, or to which he can attach his knowledge. In this way it is like a body of belief, or a set of customs: it is an organizer of facts and possibilities" (Lynch 1960, 125–6).

What the form of the grid itself can tell us about a particular city or society is, however, not necessarily clear or uniform. As discussed above, as an urban form, the grid predates Descartes by at least eight thousand years, and throughout history, it has appeared in cities ruled by every economic and governmental system known to man. Its role has been shifting and often ambiguous in the past, and it remains complex and ambiguous in postmodern cities as well. In particular, despite the claims of recent advocates of the grid "as traditional, non-hierarchical and, perhaps, even democratic," it may well be that, as Jill Grant argues, "the grid and other patterns of urban form that derive from geometric principles and surveying technology [are] more frequently associated with the concentration of military power and wealth rather than with egalitarian traditions" (2001, 220).

Since the early modern period (which saw the "enclosure" and privatization of the public commons across England and other parts of Europe), capital has found in the "grid" a useful mechanism for commodifying land and "opening up" new areas for commercial exploitation. This was particularly true in the United States, where, in the nineteenth century, the grid was extended westward across the country as an aid to expansion and speculation. When the first grid was created in Manhattan by the Commissioners' Plan of 1811, the commissioners rejected the "supposed improvements ... [of] circles, ovals and stars" that graced L'Enfant's 1791 plan for the nation's capital and instead opted for a pure grid on economic and practical grounds. "A city is composed of the habitations of men, and that strait sided," they pointed out, "and right angled houses are the most cheap to build, and the most convenient to live in." For the commissioners, the glaring lack of public and recreational spaces in the plan was justified by "the price of land [which] is so uncommonly great, it seemed proper to admit the principles of economy to greater influence than might, under circumstances of a different kind, have consisted with the dictates of prudence and the sense of duty" (quoted in Marcuse 1987, 298). Even though the Plan extended only over the undeveloped land north of Washington Square to 155th Street, the commissioners found themselves juggling the conflicting demands of multiple present and future stakeholders, a situation that recurred when the grid was extended further north in 1870.[6]

Few cities are planned by one isolated individual or a single group of individuals from the ground up, so that it is doubtless generally true that, as Peter Marcuse argues, "City form is a residual. It results from clashes of diverse interests and reflects the compromises and accommodations worked out as a result of those clashes" (1987, 289). Nonetheless, Grant asserts that "the historical record refutes Marcuse's suggestion that 'there is a "democratic" aspect to the grid, in which all parcels are created equal and alike. Thus cities where the display of power to the local population is of importance are least likely to be laid out in a grid plan'" (2001, 221). Grant instead argues that "evidence shows that some of the most tyrannical regimes in history, committed to monopolizing power, have used the grid to establish their mark on the landscape" (2001, 221).

As an instrument of imperialism and colonization, the grid has a long history. As Mumford notes in *The City in History*, "the standard gridiron plan in fact was an essential part of the kit of tools a colonist brought with him for immediate use" (1961, 25). By instituting spatial separations and various types of *cordons sanitaires*, city grids striate urban spaces and facilitate both the visual surveillance and supervision of populations. In their colonial cities, the ancient Greeks "imposed the grid even on quite rough terrain, as the rationality of math and science triumphed over topography" (Grant 2001, 230). The occupying powers of ancient Rome used the grid, which was "based on the model of the military camp and reflect[ed] its discipline," in its colonial towns across the Empire: "Subjugated peoples in the colonies were often moved into towns, both for control and for assimilation ... [and] the grid plan, rigorously executed from Africa to Britain, made the global authority of Rome physically manifest" (Grant 2001, 231). Surveillance, control, and assimilation of subject populations were equally, and explicitly, part of numerous modernist proposals for newly colonized cities, among them Le Corbusier's unbuilt Obus project for Algiers, which was intended to "rationalize" the tangled, imbricated alleyways of the ancient Casbah that served as both a source of and refuge for resistance to the French colonial powers.[7]

---

[6] See Marcuse 1987, including for some of the critiques of the 1811 Plan, among them that of Frederick Law Olmsted (who subsequently designed a competing, more suburban plan for the 1870 extension which was rejected), and for accounts of the competing interests involved in both plans.

[7] See Smith (1998) and Çelik (1998) for more on this and other features of modernist colonial city design.

With modernity, from at least the eighteenth century on, the urban grid became part of the state's bureaucratic apparatus of social control within what Foucault has termed "disciplinary societies." Inscribed upon the urban landscape, the grid is related to the "cells," "places," and "ranks" through which, as Foucault observes in *Discipline and Punish*, "the disciplines create complex spaces that are at once architectural, functional and hierarchical" (1979, 148). Like the drawing up of tables, this ordering of the space of the city is "both a technique of power and a procedure of knowledge" (Foucault 1979, 148). It remains "a question of organizing the multiple, of providing oneself with an instrument to cover it and to master it ... a question of imposing upon it an 'order'" (Foucault 1979, 148). This order is, in its essence, *totalizing*: it governs not only physical space but also conceptual and social space. Like the disciplines themselves, the grid creates what Foucault refers to as "mixed spaces: real because [it] govern[s] the disposition of buildings, rooms, furniture, but also ideas, because [it is] projected over this arrangement of characterizations, assessments, hierarchies" (Foucault 1979, 148). It can constitute, therefore, a total and totalizing regime of power/knowledge.

This regime also involves, as Michel de Certeau points out, processes of purification and repression, standardization and homogenization, synchronization and assimilation. "The 'city' founded by utopian and urbanistic discourse," he writes, "is defined by the possibility of a threefold operation":

> 1. The production of its *own* space (*un espace propre*): rational organization must thus repress all the physical, mental and political pollutions that would compromise it;
> 2. the substitution of a nowhen, or of a synchronic system, for the interminable and stubborn resistances offered by traditions; univocal scientific strategies ... must replace the tactics of users who take advantage of "opportunities" and who, through these trap-events, these lapses in visibility, reproduce the opacities of history everywhere;
> 3. finally, the creation of a *universal* and anonymous *subject* which is the city itself: it gradually becomes possible to attribute to it ... all the functions and predicates that were previously scattered and assigned to many different real subjects—groups, associations, or individuals. "The city," like a proper name, thus provides a way of conceiving and constructing space on the basis of a finite number of stable, isolatable, and interconnected properties. (de Certeau 1984, 94)

This coordinate dream of the ordered and orderly city is a fantasy of life, as Le Corbusier expressed it, "brought to perfection, not something botched. It is mastery, not an abortive chaos. It is fecundity (the total splendor of a lucid conception) and not sterility (the dungheap into which we have been plunged by all those thoughtless admirers of the miseries now existing in our great cities)" (1967 [1935], 134). But it is not life as it is lived and experienced by real people in real places. Nor is it life as it is actually lived in the places into which projects of the kind Le Corbusier and his followers envisioned are, it appears, unavoidably converted once they are built (Chicago's infamous Cabrini-Green housing project, for example). Despite Le Corbusier's claims, there is such a thing as too much order, or at least too much Cartesian order, such as that envisioned by Le Corbusier, and too much of this order appears to be inimical to city life.

The history of urban spaces from modernity into postmodernity is also that of the transition from modern to postmodern forces and structures of control. Yet, as we

move from the "disciplinary society" to the "societies of control," the older disciplinary structures still persist, even in our newest spaces: the virtual spaces and cities of cyberspace. There are striking resemblances between the Cartesian grid upon
which so much modernist and now postmodernist urban design depends and the
grids of cyberspace. Indeed, these representations might equally be seen to resemble nothing so much as the great modernist "Futuramas" and "Cities of Tomorrow,"
including the designs of Le Corbusier and Oscar Niemeyer and their many imita-
tors. In *Neuromancer*'s cyberspace (Gibson 1984), the chessboard grids between
the corporate and governmental data holds are as empty and devoid of street life as
the unhappy green voids separating the massive edifices of Le Corbusier's Cartesian
cities and, not incidentally, as the windswept glacis that surround the governmental
and corporate citadels of present-day cities. It is as if many of the "architects" of
both fictional and actual cyberspace were driven by the same utopian imagination,
which, having failed in so many of its real-world incarnations, now sought "realization" in the ethereal realm of virtual reality.

The cyberspace of the film, *Tron* (1982), is rendered (through then-revolutionary,
computer-generated special effects) as a grid composed of intersecting, gleaming
lines of light laid out across a black void suspended in space. Arranged on this grid
are various geometrical structures that function as barriers, obstacles, and traps,
with the "Master Control" (in the form of a high-modernist edifice) at its center.
Similarly, the field on which *Neuromancer*'s cyberspace data holds are arrayed is
decidedly Cartesian—geometrical, abstract, transcendent: the realm of pure information is composed of "bright lattices of logic unfolding across that colorless void"
(Gibson 1984, 4), forming a "transparent 3-D chessboard extending to infinity"
(52), "lines of light ranged in the nonspace of the mind" (51). The Cartesian (street)
grid is equally ubiquitous in actual plans or achieved designs for cyberspaces,
including Silicon Graphic's 3-D Fusion Information Landscape Prototype
(Wexelblat 1993), Michael Benedikt's (1991) cybercity, Apple's e-World, and the
cyberspace renderings of Daniel Wise and Stan George (Benedikt 1991).

It is perhaps unsurprising that this new realm of information—of knowledge and
power—should have first and subsequently, with such frequency, been imagined on
the model of this Cartesian "data map" (the coordinate grid), this Foucauldian system of ranks and files, of discipline and order. And yet, as already noted and as will
be seen in more detail in the next section, it is, ironically, cyberspace that more than
any other technological or conceptual development appears to be taking us beyond
the grid, from the Foucauldian "disciplinary society," to the cyber-tech "society of
control" envisioned by Deleuze and Guattari (1983), which is based on a new cyber-
tech model of knowledge and power.

This new model is much more than an "electrification" or digitalization of the
grid. It is (and will perhaps remain) a hybrid of sorts. It incorporates the earlier
disciplinary model (which still continues to operate in many of the same spaces
Foucault described—from the prison to schools, hospitals, barracks, factories, and
offices), but, at the same time, synergistically intensifies it and yet is supplemented
(or perhaps is in the process of being replaced) by something quite new. Thus, what
makes the various technologies of surveillance depicted in the opening of Tony

Scott's 1998 film *Enemy of the State* (satellites, CCTV, etc.) most frightening is the demonstration of how effective they become when they are interlinked, when the networks become one, and when they are joined by what one might call "the tyranny of the (electronic) archive," the seemingly eternal nature of "data" and, for powerful forces like the state, its seemingly unlimited accessibility and manipulability. Now, as Pynchon's Oedipa feared in *The Crying of Lot 49*, "the tower is everywhere" and largely invisible (1966, 11). Deleuze speaks of "control [as] continuous and without limit" in our culture, as it moves beyond the culture of discipline and its institutions. In the Foucauldian model, the web of power was uneven, far tighter in some places than in others, and it had blind spots. There were still places where one might escape the gaze of power, places to hide, places in which and from which one might resist. Now, however, such zones seem fewer and largely limited to spaces "off the grid"—a position that is nearly impossible for the population of the First World to assume or maintain.

De-Coordinations, Modernist and Postmodernist

To counteract these new forces and structures of "power," alternative tactics and technologies of resistance must be developed from within these networks and from within other networks of forces, conceptual and cultural, that have, in fact, long subsisted alongside them. For, as indicated above, some doubts concerning the Cartesian way of thinking about nature or culture emerged immediately in its wake and persisted throughout its history, and even took the form of a radical critique of it, as in Nietzsche (1989), for example. These doubts and critiques, however, were at best only able to exist on the margins of modernity and the Enlightenment. Their general impact and specific effects were, we might say with Derrida, deferred— mostly into postmodernity. By early in the twentieth century, however, the Cartesian way of thinking was not merely in doubt; it was in fact under siege from where the attack might have been least expected, from inside the greatest Cartesian bastions of all, mathematics and science. The discovery of non-Euclidean geometry and other radical developments in nineteenth-century mathematics, the rise of thermodynamics in physics (which complicated the idea of causality), and the introduction of the theory of evolution by Darwin were earlier signs of trouble, but they, at least, appeared to allow space for the hope that they could eventually be brought into the Cartesian fold. The great twentieth-century physical assault on Cartesianism in physics came with Einstein's relativity and quantum theory. Einstein's special theory of relativity (1905) and then, more radically, general theory of relativity (1916), a non-Newtonian theory of gravity based mathematically on Riemannian spaces, which, as discussed earlier, are defined by the multiplicity of potentially Cartesian local neighborhoods and hence by local grids, but disallow any overall coordination. As also noted earlier, Einstein's ideas have a Leibnizian genealogy as well, and thus become part of the longer history during which non-Cartesian thought gradually developed alongside Cartesian thought and eventually came into the forefront of

science and culture. Einstein's general relativity also has major cosmological implications, whose significance only became apparent gradually, from the discovery of
the fact that the universe is expanding to the fact that this expansion originated in the
catastrophic singularity of the explosion known as the Big Bang to the most recent
cosmological theories. Most crucial in the present context are the new forms of
spatiality defined by Riemann and then Einstein, and given their postmodern philosophical conceptualization, via the relationships between the smooth and the striated by Deleuze and Guattari (1983).

Quantum mechanics (sometimes seen as the first truly "postmodern" theory, at
least in science) has since brought this impossibility to its ultimate limit by denying,
in view of Heisenberg's uncertainty relations, a classical-like mapping even to any
single event, which now could only be partially mapped—that is, if one sees this
mapping on the classical model.[8] The ultimate implication of quantum mechanics
was that this Cartesian or even Riemannian mapping was no longer applicable to the
ultimate constitution of nature, but was only applicable, now strictly partially, to our
observations concerning nature: we can, as it were, only see half of the classical
Cartesian picture. By the same token, at the subatomic level causality was no longer
possible and all our predictions could at best amount to estimating the probabilities
of the experiments we could stage. As a result, the epistemological architecture of
quantum mechanics entailed a number of features that brought it close to postmodern epistemology.[9] This proximity was later amplified by higher-level quantum
theories dealing with high-energy processes, which added even more radical aspects
to quantum physics, especially those aspects related to the multiplicities that these
theories entailed. For, as against the original form of quantum mechanics, it was no
longer possible to maintain the identity of elementary particles in physical processes: a given particle, such as an electron, could transform itself into another
particle, say, a photon, or even into several particles.

The collapse of Newtonian physics on the "small" or "extra-small" scale of the
atom and on the "large" or "extra-large" scale of the universe had a major impact on
postmodern knowledge and culture, including on our conceptions of postmodern
spatiality, particularly in considerations of postmodern cities and virtual spaces,
such as cyberspace. So had other radical, "postmodern" developments in modern
mathematics and science, such as Gödel's incompleteness theorems in mathematical
logic (which deprive us of our capacity to demonstrate the logically consistent
nature of mathematics itself); several major advances in genetics, molecular biology,
and neuroscience; and of course the advent of computer technologies, including

---

[8] Heisenberg's uncertainty principle states that we can measure or precisely predict either the position or the momentum of a quantum object, such as an electron, but never both simultaneously, as
we can in classical physics, which, by the same token, allows us to ascribe both reality and causality to classical physical objects. The uncertainty relations make such an assignment impossible in
quantum physics.

[9] For a detailed analysis of these connections, see Plotnitsky (2002).

those leading to the creation of cyberspace.[10] As Lyotard argues in *The Postmodern Condition* (1984), mathematics and science themselves became part of postmodern knowledge and culture, part, to use the subtitle of his book, of the postmodern condition and of postmodern practice, sometimes with science being ahead of philosophy or culture. Accordingly, if we want to accept the first axiom of the Enlightenment, which tells us to be guided by how nature or mathematics work in our models of humanity and culture, then nature and mathematics, as they appear now, seem to direct us away from other Enlightenment axioms, such as those of Cartesianism. This new, non-Cartesian thinking about our cultural, including urban, spaces is possible by virtue of alternative mathematical and physical conceptions of space available to us, in particular those of the Riemannian-Deleuzean type, defined by the heterogeneous yet interactive multiplicity of the smooth and the striated.

One can also link these postmodern spaces of multiple and multiply interactive forms of smoothness and striation to Lyotard's (1984) view of the postmodern heterogeneity and plurality of narratives, as against the "grand" and meta narratives of the Enlightenment, since each striation or grid carries a narrative with it, and vice versa. There are also smooth-space narratives, such as those of "minor" or "nomadic" types, as against those of "major" or "state" types (which are always linked to global, Cartesian grids and Euclidean spaces), as considered by Deleuze and Guattari in *A Thousand Plateaus* (1987). These are narratives of becoming, of multiple becoming, such as those of Virginia Woolf in *The Waves*, invoked by Deleuze and Guattari: "all kinds of becomings between ages, sexes, elements, and kingdoms," in which any "individuality ... designates a multiplicity," a wave-like moving front of multiplicities, overflowing grids (1987, 252).

Indeed, although the undermining of Cartesianism within mathematics and science has a special significance and while alternative philosophical thinking helps in our articulation of non-Cartesian conceptualities, the earliest and the most radical critique of Cartesianism and its scientific, philosophical, and ideological avatars has been undertaken in literature and art. One can think of earlier examples, such as Cervantes, a great literary nomadologist, or, between literature and philosophy, Montaigne. His essays fragment philosophical grids and create smooth literary and philosophical movements; and as such these essays are already quite "postmodern," according to Lyotard (1984, 81). By the time Cartesianism reaches its dominance in the Enlightenment, a powerful critique undertaken by literature is underway, especially as part of the Romantic movement that emerged in the end of the eighteenth century. Kleist, one of the most intriguing and most radical Romantic authors, is a crucial literary figure in *A Thousand Plateaus*, which juxtaposes him to both Goethe and Hegel, who are seen as "State thinkers" (Deleuze and Guattari 1987, 356). Kleist is a thinker and poet of nomadic becoming(s), and "*the most uncanny modernity* lies with him" (356; emphasis added). A brilliant choice of phrase, "uncanny modernity": this is the modernity that has always existed alongside the modernity

---

[10] Gödel's incompleteness theorems prevent us from ever rigorously, mathematically guaranteeing the truth or falsity of all mathematical propositions and the non-contradictory nature of mathematics itself, provided that the mathematical field considered is sufficiently rich to include arithmetic.

that aimed at the coordinated "residential development" for humanity and promised us a safe home in this abode of the rational.

The literary and artistic modernism of the twentieth century may be seen as an extension of this uncanny modernity as well, and it arguably pursues a critique of Cartesian modernity more persistently than its affirmation, to some degree even in modernist architecture, dominated as it might have been by Le Corbusier's and related visions and ideologies. Some of Le Corbusier's own projects, usually his separate buildings (such as the Villa Savoye, his most famous building, or Notre-Dame-du-Haut at Ronchamp), are marked by a kind of deconstruction in practice of his Cartesianism.[11] Similar, although more radical, deconstructions and self-deconstructions of the grid are deployed in Mondrian's paintings, sometimes associated (for example, by the Situationists) with Cartesianism and the celebration of the grid. This view is, as I would argue (the argument has of course been made before), quite mistaken.[12] Just about all of Mondrian's "grid" paintings enact subtle and yet radical deconstructions of Cartesianism, a strategy that appears especially impossible to miss (although it has been missed) in his last painting, "Broadway Boogie Woogie" (1942–43). Fittingly using New York City (to which Le Corbusier especially juxtaposed his Cartesian city), New York City portrayed in smooth motion, the painting made the grid dissolve to reveal the staccato or smooth-staccato space beneath it. One can speak here, somewhat paradoxically, of a "smooth-staccato" space because of the uninhibited movement this jazzy staccato rhythm creates, an idea in fact found in Deleuze and Guattari (1987) as well, and associated by them with Kleist.

Arguably, however, it is modernist literature, as "minor literature" in Deleuze and Guattari's sense (the subtitle of their book on Kafka), where modernism's fight against Cartesian modernity or Cartesian modernism is waged most passionately and most successfully. Apart from giving him a central role in *A Thousand Plateaus* (1987), Deleuze and Guattari devote to Kafka their important *Kafka: Toward a Minor Literature* (1986), which presents his work as a literary enactment of the program of nomadic, minoritarian resistance to the state apparatuses of capitalism. Lyotard similarly sees key modernist literature, most especially that of Joyce, as a literary enactment of the epistemology and, concomitantly, narrative strategies of postmodernity: "Joyce allows the unrepresentable to become perceptible in his writing itself, in the signifier. The whole range of available narrative and even stylistic operators is put into play without concern for the unity of the whole, and new operators are tried" (1984, 80).

It is, accordingly, not surprising that the urban spaces—the cities—created by modernist literary works (at least of this "postmodernist" kind) give us, and our urban imaginary, some of the best means of conceiving of a different, non-Cartesian city. Dos Passos's New York and Woolf's London, Joyce's Dublin, and Musil's

---

[11] The Villa Savoye is also perhaps the greatest realization of Le Corbusier's concept of the "machine à habiter" [the machine for living (in)].

[12] Rosalind Krauss's *The Originality of the Avant-Garde and Other Modernist Myths* (1985) similarly misreads Mondrian, in my view.

Vienna (in *The Man Without Qualities*, 1996) are among the greatest examples of such alternative cities in literary modernism. The postmodernist urban imaginary is not only a break from some, especially Cartesian, forms of modernist or modern urban imaginary, it is also a continuation of non-Cartesian modernism and modernity. It is a continuation of artistic, philosophical, scientific, and cultural, including political, urban thinking that was at work throughout the history of modernity.

More generally, as Deleuze and Guattari argue, minor or nomadic forces of resistance have always existed alongside major or state forces of the Cartesian logic and culture of modernity, and indeed alongside preceding dominant formations of power, perhaps inevitably defined by some form of globalizing or totalizing coordinated striations and grids. Both types of forces (minor and major, nomadic and state) and the respective types of desiring-machines that arise from them use as their resource the same field of energy, which Deleuze and Guattari define as "the body without organs" (a concept that is correlative although not identical to Foucault's concept of "power"). The same reservoir of energy, the same body without organs, which was reshaped by the history of modernity extending into postmodernity, can also provide resources for the postmodern resistance to the forces and global Cartesian striations aimed at by the *State* apparatuses (in both Althusser's [1971] and Deleuze and Guattari's [1987] sense) developed throughout modernity and now extending into postmodernity.

In "Postscript on the Societies of Control," Deleuze (1997) suggests as forms of resistance jamming, piracy, viruses—variations on "hacking." It is true that such tactics might sometimes, at least temporarily, be effective (as was, for example, the digg.com publication of the Sony copy-protection software code that, after Sony forced them to remove it from the Website, was independently posted and re-posted thousands of times across the Web, and even inscribed in the lyrics of a song posted on YouTube). In Nadia El Fani's 2003 film *Bedwin Hacker*, a Tunisian hacker interrupts French satellite television transmissions with messages that make visible the existence of France's former colonial subjects in Tunisia and Algeria and insist that they "are not a mirage."[13] At the same time, Bedwin's reminder that, "in the third millennium, there are other epochs, other places, other lives," does not really constitute a very effective critique. For the problem is precisely that, for the French, their former colonial subjects are indeed "the other," inhabiting the "other" epoch of "the primitive past," in places that no longer seem of much concern (except as potential export sources of terrorism). Effective resistance to the forces and structures of control, those of the fortress and those of the scanscape, clearly require a more complex and sophisticated array of strategies and tactics, as Deleuze and Guattari's own deeper philosophical reflections, such as those on smooth and striated spaces and their relationships, suggest. The grid, which, as I argue here, is part of both economies, that of control and that of resistance, may and even must still be used in this resistance, but, it also follows, it is not sufficient. What we need, what we seek, is an open-ended order. Perhaps in order to move to smooth urban (or other) spaces, actual and virtual, or interactively both, we need to start by creating a smooth space,

---

[13] "Bedwin" is a re-spelling of "Bedouine," the feminine form of Bedouin.

in the manner of parkour, which also involves and makes possible the creation of more resistant and (which is the ultimate aim of the process) more productive striations and grids.

References

Althusser, L. (1971). Ideology and ideological state apparatuses (notes towards an investigation) (trans: B. Brewster) *Lenin and philosophy and other essays* (pp. 127–186). New York: Monthly Review Press.

Benedikt, M. (Ed.). (1991). *Cyberspace: First steps*. Cambridge: MIT Press.

Blake, W. (1982). *The complete poetry and prose of William Blake* (H. Bloom & D. Erdman, Eds.). Berkeley: University of California Press.

Blake, P. (1996). *The master builders: Le Corbusier, Mies van der Rohe, and Frank Lloyd Wright*. New York: Norton.

Çelik, Z. (1998). Cultural intersections: Re-visioning architecture and the city in the twentieth century. In R. Ferguson (Ed.), *At the end of the century: One hundred years of architecture* (pp. 190–228). Los Angeles: The Museum of Contemporary Art.

Le Corbusier. (1967 [1935]). *The radiant city: Elements of a doctrine of urbanism to be used as the basis of our machine-age civilization*. New York: Orion.

Curtis, W. (1986). *Le Corbusier: Ideas and forms*. New York: Rizzoli.

de Certeau, M. (1984). *The practice of everyday life* (trans: S. Rendall). Berkeley: University of California Press.

Deleuze, G. (1997). Postscript on the societies of control. In N. Leach (Ed.), *Rethinking architecture: A reader in cultural theory* (pp. 309–313). London/New York: Routledge.

Deleuze, G., and Guattari, F. (1983). *Anti-Oedipus: Capitalism and schizophrenia* (trans: R. Hurley, M. Seem, and H. Lane). Minneapolis: University of Minnesota Press.

Deleuze, G., and Guattari, F. (1986). *Kafka: Toward a minor literature* (trans: D. Polan). Minneapolis: University of Minnesota Press.

Deleuze, G., and Guattari, F. (1987). *A thousand plateaus: Capitalism and schizophrenia* (trans: B. Massumi). Minneapolis: University of Minnesota Press.

Foucault, M. (1979). *Discipline and punish: The birth of the prison* (trans: A. Sheridan). New York: Vintage.

Foucault, M. (1997). Of other spaces: Utopias and heterotopias. In N. Leach (Ed.), *Rethinking architecture: A reader in cultural theory* (pp. 348–356). London: Routledge.

Frampton, K. (2002). *Le Corbusier: Architect of the twentieth century*. New York: Harry N. Abrams.

Gibson, W. (1984). *Neuromancer*. New York: Ace Books.

Grant, J. (2001). The dark side of the grid: Power and urban design. *Planning Perspectives, 16*(3), 219–241.

Krauss, R. (1985). *The originality of the avant-garde and other modernist myths*. Cambridge: MIT Press.

Lynch, K. (1960). *The image of the city*. Cambridge: MIT Press.

Lyotard, J.F. (1984). *The postmodern condition: A report on knowledge* (trans: G. Bennington and B. Massumi). Minneapolis: University of Minnesota Press.

Marcuse, P. (1987). The grid as city plan: New York City and laissez-faire planning in the nineteenth century. *Planning Perspectives, 2*, 287–310.

Marx, K. (1986). Theses on Feuerbach. In J. Elster (Ed.), *Karl Marx: A reader* (pp. 20–23). New York: Cambridge University Press.

Mumford, L. (1961). *The city in history: Its origins, its transformations, and its prospects*. New York: Harcourt.

Musil, R. (1996). *The man without qualities* (trans: S. Wilkins). New York: Vintage.

Nietzsche, F. (1989). *On the genealogy of morals and ecce homo* (trans: W. Kaufmann and R.J. Hollingdale). New York: Vintage.

Plotnitsky, A. (2002). *The knowable and the unknowable: Modern science, nonclassical thought, and the "two cultures."* Ann Arbor: University of Michigan Press.

Pynchon, T. (1966). *The crying of lot 49*. New York: Bantam.

Smith, E. (1998). Re-examining architecture and its history at the end of the century. In R. Ferguson (Ed.), *At the end of the century: One hundred years of architecture* (pp. 22–99). Los Angeles: The Museum of Contemporary Art.

Tron. (1982). *Dir*. Lisberger/Kushner and Walt Disney Productions: S. Lisberger.

Ward, S. (2002). *Planning the twentieth-century city: The advanced capitalist world*. Chichester: Wiley.

Wexelblat, A. (Ed.). (1993). *Virtual reality: Applications and explorations*. Cambridge: Academic Press Professional.

Index

A
Absolutism, 131, 138
Absolutist, 5, 58, 59
Adelaide, 83
Aesthetic, 7, 58, 111–116, 118, 155, 229, 230, 235–237, 240, 241
Africa, 10, 14, 16, 27, 42, 80, 81, 178, 179, 181, 183, 186, 190–193, 195, 198, 270
Agriculture, 8, 125, 146, 257
Alexander, 26, 27, 30, 42, 85, 86
Alexandria, 79, 85–86
Alfonse of Poitiers, 32
Al-Fustât/Al-Qāhirah, 9
Algiers, 191, 270
Algonquin, 145, 218
Alleyways, 109, 270
Alonga, 183
Americas, 5, 10, 14, 16, 39, 42, 44, 45, 141
Amsterdam, 69, 142
Ancient Chinese cities, 9
Anti-essentialist, 4–6, 241
Antiquity, 2, 4, 14, 25, 37, 41, 63, 102, 104, 123, 127, 128
Antwerp, 216
Arbitrary, 11, 213
Archaeology/archaeological, 10, 41, 42, 48, 76, 77, 93, 97, 155, 156, 158, 159, 162–166, 170–172, 179
Architecture, 2, 14, 26, 43, 48, 71, 148, 155–172, 181, 213, 214, 245, 246, 250, 255, 264, 267, 268, 274, 276
Aristocracy, 5, 58
Aristotle, 6, 7, 28, 55, 101–119
Armitage, T.C., 257

Art, 2, 26, 47–49, 90, 102, 104, 107, 114, 118, 195, 218, 229, 234, 235, 250, 255, 275
Asceticism, 220, 238
Asia Minor, 28, 29, 85
Assemblages, 8, 48
Assimilation, 80, 85, 188, 191, 193, 259, 270, 271
Athens, 28, 80, 89
Athens Charter, 71
Australia, 61, 82–84, 190
Authoritarian, 2, 46, 115, 118, 137, 178, 246, 247, 268
Authority, 6, 7, 13, 28, 31, 33, 40, 46, 69, 76–80, 83, 84, 87–91, 93, 94, 96, 114, 122, 132, 137, 138, 149, 157, 179, 228, 234, 251, 268, 270
Axis, 40, 68, 122, 123, 125, 128, 137, 182, 208
Aztecs, 44, 87

B
Babylon, 25, 79, 84–85, 105, 208
Babylonians, 208
Badao, 135–138
Bakanda, 188
Barbarism, 4
Barcelona, 55, 62, 166
Barceloneta, 55
Baroque, 5, 58, 59, 61, 72, 144, 147
Barricades, 95
Barrio, 55
Barthes, Roland, 229
Basra, 9

Printed by Printforce, the Netherlands